The Grand Deception

Churchill And The Dardanelles
Tom Curran
Edited By Andrew G. Bonnell

16

EasyRead Large

RHYW

Copyright Page from the Original Book

Big Sky Publishing Pty Ltd
PO Box 303, Newport, NSW 2106, Australia
Phone: 1300 364 611
Fax: (61 2) 9918 2396
Email: info@bigskypublishing.com.au
Web: www.bigskypublishing.com.au

Cover design and typesetting: Think Productions
Printed in China by Asia Pacific Offset Ltd.

See National Library of Australia for Cataloguing-in-Publication entry

ISBN: 978-1-925275-00-1

TABLE OF CONTENTS

THE AUSTRALIAN ARMY HISTORY COLLECTION

Winning with Intelligence
Judy Thomas
Duntroon
Darren Moore
The Warrior Poets
Robert Morrison
*The History of the Royal Australian Corps of Transport
1973–2000*
Albert Palazzo
Defenders of Australia
Albert Palazzo
The Fight Leaders
D. Butler, A. Argent and J. Shelton
Operation Orders
Pat Beale
Little by Little
Michael Tyquin
Red Coats to Cams
Ian Kuring
Bowler of Gallipoli
Frank Glen
Vets at War
Ian M. Parsonson
Only One River to Cross
A.M. Harris
The Fragile Forts

Peter Oppenheim
Hassett: Australian Leader
John Essex-Clark
Persian Expedition
Alan Stewart
The Chiefs of the Australian Army
James Wood
Never Late
Gordon Dickens
To Villers-Bretonneux
Peter Edgar
Madness and the Military
Michael Tyquin
The Battle of Anzac Ridge
25 April 1915
Peter D. Williams
Doves Over the Pacific
Reuben R.E. Bowd
The Lionheart
David Coombes
Battlefield Korea
Maurie Pears
Chemical Warfare in Australia
Geoff Plunkett
A Most Unusual Regiment
M.J. Ryan
Between Victor and Vanquished
Arthur Page
Country Victoria's Own
Neil Leckie
Surgeon and General

Ian Howie-Willis
Willingly into the Fray
Catherine McCullagh
Beyond Adversity
William Park
Crumps and Camouflets
Damien Finlayson
More than Bombs and Bandages
Kirsty Harris
The Last Knight
Robert Lowry
Forgotten Men
Michael Tyquin
Battle Scarred
Craig Deayton
Crossing the Wire
David Coombes
Do Unto Others
Alan H Smith
Fallen Sentinel
Peter Beale
Sir William Glasgow
Peter Edger
Training The Bodes
Terry Smith
Bully Beef and Balderdash
Graham Wilson
Fire Support Bases Vietnam
Bruce Picken
Toowoomba to Torokina
Bob Doneley

A Medical Emergency
Ian Howie-Willis
Dust, Donkeys and Delusions
Graham Wilson
The Backroom Boys
Graeme Sligo
Captains of the Soul
Michael Gladwin

LIST OF ILLUSTRATIONS

HMS *Queen Elizabeth* under Turkish fire off Cape Helles.

Churchill's and Asquith's performances before the Dardanelles Commission, *Punch,* 28 March 1917.

MAPS

The Balkans, August 1913 (Chapter 3).

Anglo-French naval attack on the Dardanelles, 18 March 1915 (Chapter 3).

From the Curran family:
T.C.
Husband, Dad, Pa Tom, Wordsmith,
Brother, Son & Friend.

You were a man of words. Throughout your lifetime, writing gave you the greatest pleasure and was also a necessity akin to breathing. What a rollercoaster ride this has been in your quest for a hidden truth to be shared. We are so very proud and miss you every single day.

Always in our hearts,
Your family (the Currans).

EDITOR'S PREFACE

A reader might justifiably wonder whether there can be anything new to say about either the history of the Dardanelles campaign or Winston Churchill. A subject search for 'Gallipoli' in the catalogue of the National Library of Australia brings up 859 entries (last time I looked—the number will no doubt continue to grow as the centenary inexorably approaches). As for Churchill, there are entire libraries devoted to him.1 The online British Library catalogue lists 555 titles on Churchill alone. The 'official biography', commenced by Randolph S. Churchill and continued from Volume 3 to 8 by Martin Gilbert, with its documentary companion volumes, constitutes an apparently definitive monument to the statesman, and a rich quarry for subsequent researchers.

Naturally, therefore, I was also sceptical when Tom Curran approached Professor Paul Crook and me at the University of Queensland's Department of History in 2001 with the proposal to write a PhD on the full story of Churchill and the Dardanelles campaign. I initially reckoned without Tom's dogged tenacity as a researcher and the enthusiasm and energy with which he pursued his project.

Tom Curran was a remarkable man. He came from the region near Newcastle on Tyne (born 1938), from a modest working-class background—his father was a shipyard painter. His earliest memory as a toddler was of having to put on a gas mask during the 'Blitz', when the German *Luftwaffe* bombed the Newcastle dockyards. Tom never lost his Geordie accent, despite decades in Australia. He found his way to Australia after qualifying as a pharmacist in Edinburgh in 1961. In 1966 he enlisted in the Royal Australian Army Medical Corps which took him to Vietnam where he commanded a field medical supply unit in 1969. He was promoted captain in the field after the previous commander of the unit became a casualty. Like many veterans of that conflict, Tom suffered severe health problems after his return from Vietnam, through which he was sustained by a strong and loving family, his wife Maureen, and his daughters Chris, Joc and Ky.

When Tom returned from Vietnam, but while he was still serving in the Army (posted to Townsville), he became acquainted with the story of John Simpson Kirkpatrick, and was struck by the fact that there was no modern biography of the 'man with the donkey' from Gallipoli. Tom felt considerable empathy with Simpson, another migrant to Australia from the Tyneside who served in the Army medical service, and he set out on a long quest to document and write Simpson's life. He began studying for a Bachelor of Arts in the mid-1980s, but was forced to interrupt his studies. In 1994 his biography of Simpson appeared (*Across the Bar,* Ogmios Publications, Brisbane). The book was clearly a labour of love and a product of thorough research, including travel to Gallipoli to traverse and photograph the terrain Simpson once walked. In the years that followed the publication of *Across the Bar,* Tom campaigned actively for the posthumous award to Simpson of the Victoria Cross. After the book's publication, Tom returned to his studies at the University of Queensland to take his honours degree in history in 1998. A few years later he commenced the PhD on Churchill and the Dardanelles campaign, which was submitted and awarded successfully in 2007. He was in the process of revising this book for publication when he passed away suddenly and unexpectedly on 23 May 2011.

Tom was indefatigable as a researcher as he followed up the various trails of evidence, published and unpublished, that led to the clarification of Churchill's role in the conception and execution of the Dardanelles campaign, and of the ways in which Churchill successfully obfuscated this history to minimise his responsibility. Indeed, I have rarely met anyone more passionate in, and excited by, his research. He presents this story in a more detailed and compelling fashion than any other previous account. In some parts he builds on and reinforces arguments made by Robin Prior in his 1983 critical analysis of Churchill's *The World Crisis* as history. However, while the Dardanelles campaign constituted a large and central part of Prior's study, it is the sole focus of the present work and Tom benefitted from more recently available evidence and literature.

Tom Curran shows how Churchill, in his capacity as First Lord of the Admiralty, effectively civilian Minister for the Navy, exceeded the normal boundaries of civilian political direction of the service in wartime to indulge in hands-on operational admiralship in the first few months of the First World War. Curran's close reading of available documentation exposes the way in which Churchill misled the Naval service chiefs on the views of the civilian political leaders and vice versa in order to win approval for his project of an assault on the Dardanelles in early 1915. In a crucial instance, Curran demonstrates that the authority Churchill claimed from a War Council meeting of 5 January 1915 to commence planning for a naval attack was bogus, as no such meeting took place. This is a significant finding as the 5 January War Council meeting continues to lead a phantom existence in such authoritative works as Martin Gilbert's Churchill biography and Gilbert's more recent essay on Churchill and Gallipoli in Jenny MacLeod's 2004 collection of essays.[2] Curran is not the first writer to note the security implications of Churchill's press release on the opening of the naval bombardment which saw Allied intentions advertised on the front page of *The Times* on 20 February 1915, but the matter has almost entirely faded from view in recent literature, and Curran integrates the episode into his overall account of Churchill's conduct of the campaign. Other writers have discussed the problems presented by the minefields in the Narrows and the difficulties experienced by naval gunnery in engaging land-based artillery, but Curran again presents the most thoroughly documented account of Churchill's own role in these matters, illustrating the way in which Churchill rode roughshod over expert advice in the pursuit of his strategy. Supplementing and broadening Prior's analysis of *The World Crisis,* Curran provides a detailed account of the way Churchill sought to rewrite the full story of his role in the campaign, through the Dardanelles Commission, through his own memoir (which profited from his appropriation of a mass of archival material for his own use) and in subsequent publications.

Curran's book contributes to several developing bodies of historical literature. On one level, parts of the book contribute to the body of work on the history of the historiography of the Great War, the study of how the history of the conflict has been handed down to us by writers and historians.[3] It may also be worth noting that our knowledge of the historiography of the Second World War has recently been enriched by David Reynolds' account of Churchill's memoirs of that war, which notes that Churchill was constantly influenced in his writing of that history by his experiences of the First World War and of Gallipoli in particular.4 It will also be of interest to scholars of civil-military relations, presenting an almost textbook case of how these can go wrong. Contemporary readers may like to reflect on modern examples of dysfunctional grand strategy as documented, for example, by Thomas Ricks' account of the invasion and occupation of Iraq, *Fiasco* (2006) or Bob

Woodward's volumes describing the George W. Bush administration at war.

Curran's book is not a comprehensive account of the Gallipoli campaign. Its focus is the role of Winston Churchill as First Lord of the Admiralty, front and centre. For recent accounts which provide a more rounded picture of the campaign, the reader may be referred to Tim Travers, *Gallipoli 1915* (2001) and Robin Prior, *Gallipoli. The End of the Myth* (2009). Inevitably, none of these books on Gallipoli, for all their strengths, is likely to remain the last word on the subject for long, especially with the imminence of the centenary of the campaign. The great merit of Tom Curran's work, however, is that it provides the most detailed, most thoroughly documented and most vigorously argued critical analysis of the role of Winston Churchill in the campaign and the later attempted cover-up of that role. In its contribution to our understanding of this aspect of the history of the Dardanelles (and of the history of Churchill's political career), Curran's work is unlikely to be superseded soon. The book is also testimony to one man's passion for setting the historical record straight, particularly where that historical record concerns the suffering and death of thousands as a result of politicians' decisions.

In editing this manuscript I have sought to intervene only where necessary to avoid repetition and to make copy-editing improvements; I have not altered the content, and have sought to preserve Tom's authorial voice (I am only sorry that Tom's Geordie accent, seemingly undiluted by decades of living in Queensland, does not translate to the printed page). Interested researchers may, if they choose, compare this book with the original PhD dissertation in the University of Queensland library. Prior to his death, Tom was also able to complete an article for the *Australian Journal of Politics and History* which summarises his findings.[5] He provided full acknowledgements to all who assisted his research in his thesis, and these are reproduced here as Author's Acknowledgements. I would like to express my own thanks to the Curran family for the privilege of assisting Tom's book into print.

Andrew G. Bonnell
13 January 2015

AUTHOR'S ACKNOWLEDGEMENTS

I would like to thank the staff of the Document Delivery Service at the Social Sciences and Humanities Library, University of Queensland, particularly Kev and Alison, for their brilliance in obtaining so many obscure and invaluable publications from libraries both in Australia and overseas.

I wish to send special thanks to the archivists at all the archives where I researched in Britain. Their friendliness in rendering assistance and sharing their expertise came as a very welcome surprise and made this research project a most enjoyable experience. In particular I would like to thank Ian Hopkins and Liz at the Churchill College Archives Centre; Daphne Knott at the National Maritime Museum, Greenwich; Dr Geoff Browell and Alan Kucia at the Liddell Hart Archives Centre, Kings College; Terry Charrnan and Nigel Steel at the Imperial War Museum; David Prior at the House of Lords Record Office; and Tim Padfield and William Spencer at the National Archives.

I would like to thank my supervisors, Dr Andrew Bonnell and Professor Paul Crook, not only for their academic expertise, but more especially for their constant encouragement, without which I doubt that this thesis would have been brought fully to fruition.

Finally, I would like to thank my wife Maureen and all my family for their forbearance and support throughout this prolonged, obsessive period.

Tom Curran

EDITOR'S ACKNOWLEDGEMENTS

I am indebted to the Curran family for entrusting me with the editing of this book, which has been a privilege. It is also a pleasure to thank Margaret Higgs for her very generous assistance in getting the manuscript into the right format and her usual expert production work. I would like to thank Guy Webster for assistance with Tom's computer files. I am also very grateful, as was Tom, for Professor David Horner's support for the project of transforming the thesis into a book, and I gratefully acknowledge the assistance of Dr Andrew Richardson of the Australian Army History Unit and Denny Neave of Big Sky Publishing in this process. Thanks also to Cathy McCullagh for her professional editing work within remarkably rapid turn-around times.

Andrew G. Bonnell

INTRODUCTION

Charles Bean, Australia's official military historian of the First World War, was the first historian to accuse Winston Churchill of being responsible for the Dardanelles/Gallipoli disaster, writing in 1921: 'So, through Churchill's excess of imagination, a layman's ignorance of artillery, and the fatal power of a young enthusiasm to convince older and slower brains, the tragedy of Gallipoli was born.'[1]

Churchill replied in *The World Crisis* in 1923: 'It is my hope that the Australian people, towards whom I have always felt a solemn responsibility, will not rest content with so crude, so inaccurate, so incomplete and so prejudiced a judgment, but will study the facts for themselves.'[2] Bean's accusations were dismissed at the time as hyperbole on the part of a disgruntled colonial. This polarisation of opinion over Churchill's responsibility for the failed Dardanelles campaign has persisted ever since.

While researching the biography of Simpson, the man with the donkey at Anzac (published in 1994 as *Across the Bar),* I became acquainted with Churchill's role in the Dardanelles campaign through *The World Crisis* and works sympathetic to Churchill by the likes of Alan Moorehead, John North and Basil Rhodes James, Lord Hankey, Captain Stephen Roskill and Dr Robin Prior on the other.[3]I had intended Rhodes James, Lord Hankey, Captain Stephen Roskill and Dr Robin

Prior on the other.[3] I had intended including a chapter in Simpson's biography as explanatory background to the Gallipoli campaign but it soon became apparent that a much more comprehensive exposition of this subject was indicated. Indeed, if all of the associated evidence was to be fully analysed, then a doctoral thesis would be required. In effect, the subsequent thesis, on which this book is based, became a response to Churchill's injunction that Australians should study the facts for themselves.

This topic is of particular relevance to the people of Australia. Gallipoli was pivotal in helping to lay the foundations for their cultural identity and, within the framework of that legend, they have been provided with a variety of explanations for the campaign's inception as well as for its failure.[4] They have been told that the concept was fundamentally sound, even brilliant, in the prospects it offered. That it failed was due to many factors: the reluctance of the Army and Navy to cooperate in a combined operation; the incompetence of a fledgling War Council in organising such an enterprise; the incompetence of the military commanders; the intransigence of the Russian government in vetoing the assistance of a Greek army at a time when its participation could have proved decisive and more. But essentially, failure was due to Lords Fisher and Kitchener, heads of the Royal Navy and British Army respectively—Fisher for his fainthearted unwillingness to order a renewal of the naval attack on 18 March with the Turks resigned to defeat, and Kitchener for his intransigent refusal to provide the large-scale troop support which everyone knew was essential (and available throughout) until it was too late. In this scenario, Churchill, the architect of the campaign, was robbed of a victory which could well have changed history. On the other hand, a minority of prominent naval and military experts maintained that a purely naval attack against the Dardanelles defences was an inherently flawed concept from the outset, with no realistic hope of success, and should never have been attempted.[5] That it was undertaken was due essentially to Churchill's deception of the Cabinet War Council. It would be of considerable interest to the people of Australia if the truth of this matter could be resolved.

Between 1915 and 1923, Winston Churchill was overwhelmingly held by the British public to have been responsible for the Dardanelles disaster, being regularly shouted down at political meetings with taunts of 'What about the Dardanelles!' It was only after the publication of his memoir-history, *The World Crisis,* that he began answering, then silencing, that criticism. Churchill flouted Section 2 of the *Official Secrets Act* in 1923 to include a wealth of official documents in *The World Crisis*—mostly his own Cabinet and Admiralty memoranda, letters, reports and telegram instructions. As his presentation and interpretation of this material could not be challenged for accuracy or veracity until the mid-1960s, this lent his version of events considerable authority, which was reflected in the book's great popularity. During the 1930s a fortuitous, sympathetic shift occurred, with the growing romance of the Gallipoli/Dardanelles campaign (along with a more tolerant attitude towards its instigator, Churchill), contrasting markedly with the demonisation of the Western Front and the incompetent butchers deemed responsible for that bloodbath. In addition, the British official history of the Gallipoli campaign, published between 1929 and 1932, endorsed Churchill's explanation that the campaign had been 'one of the few great strategical conceptions of the World War'.[6] This judgement by the British official historian is scarcely surprising given that Brigadier Aspinall-Oglander was one of the staff officers at Gallipoli responsible for the planning of that campaign.

Partly due to the nimbus which Churchill acquired after 1945 by virtue of his personification of Britain's defiance of the Nazi threat in the country's 'Finest Hour', his account of the events at the Dardanelles increasingly became largely accepted as the authentic explanation. As a consequence, two conflicting accounts of those events continue to co-exist. In the popular Churchill version, supported by eminent social historians such as Geoffrey Best, brilliant journalists like Alan Moorehead and Churchill biographers of the calibre of William Manchester, his heroic status during the Second World War was accorded retrospectivity, and it is claimed that he was denied the spectacular victory his visionary strategy merited only by the weakness and irresolution of others, notably Lords

Fisher and Kitchener.[7] In the minority expert appreciation on the other hand, Churchill was deemed to have been almost entirely responsible for the Dardanelles naval fiasco himself, through his interference in naval affairs and his usurping of control from the hands of the Admiralty experts in order to direct the naval operation himself. By the 1970s, following his death in 1965, a complete reversal of opinion had taken place, with the majority opinion holding Churchill to have been blameless in the matter of the Dardanelles.

Some very fine books have been written on the Dardanelles/Gallipoli campaign in recent years, notably by Jenny Macleod, Nigel Steel and Peter Hart, Tim Travers, Geoffrey Miller, and others.[8] I have made little reference to these publications in the text, however, as my work addresses a very specific aspect of the Dardanelles campaign (the extent of Churchill's culpability for the failed campaign and how this has been withheld from public knowledge over the succeeding decades) which is addressed only minimally, if at all, by other writers on the subject, and with which Macleod, Steel and Hart, Travers and Miller are not concerned. My particular interest, in fact, lay in primary sources hitherto largely ignored by other scholars.

The primary source evidence necessary for a resolution of this matter is contained within the official documents of the British Cabinet, Admiralty, War Office and Foreign Office (at The National Archives, Kew), within the private papers of the individuals concerned and within the evidence presented to the Dardanelles Royal Commission. All of this material has been freely available for public scrutiny since the late 1960s with the expiration of the Fifty Year Rule on official secrecy. Further evidence in the form of confidential letters written with no expectation of their being published (or even revealed to a third party) from Prime Minister Asquith to his confidante Venetia Stanley detailing the events in question, often twice a day, and similarly confidential revelations recorded in her diary by Lloyd George's secretary and future wife, Frances Stevenson, became available during the 1970s and 80s, together with other invaluable diary evidence from Charles Hobhouse, Lord Hankey and a great many more.[9] Yet, for some inexplicable reason, this evidence has never been subjected to an exhaustive examination by Britain's scholars to determine the exact role played by Churchill in that unfortunate campaign and the extent of his, Lord Fisher's and Lord Kitchener's culpability. It is the purpose of this book, therefore, with the evidence now available, to reconstruct the events at the Dardanelles and within the British Cabinet and Admiralty between January and May 1915 in order to redress that deficiency.

With reference to the primary sources, special mention needs to be made of the Dardanelles Commission's first report. Evidence was presented in 1916 to this Royal Commission enquiry into the circumstances surrounding the failure of the naval attack at the

Dardanelles on 18 March 1915—while the war was still in progress. It would have been irresponsible in the extreme to have presented the enemy with evidence of governmental incompetence, at the highest level, in war planning and operations at this time. Scapegoats were clearly needed, and these were readily to hand in the persons of Lord Kitchener, former head of the British Army, and recently drowned in June 1916 when his ship, the *Hampshire,* struck a German mine; and 75-year-old Lord Fisher, conveniently retired as head of the Royal Navy. That the findings of the Commission's first report, delivered in March 1917, were seriously flawed can scarcely be denied (the conduct of the subsequent military invasion of Gallipoli was the subject of a final report, delivered in 1919). Three members of the ten-man Commission (former Prime Ministers of Australia and New Zealand, Andrew Fisher and Sir Thomas Mackenzie, and Welsh lawyer and Liberal MP, Walter Roch) rejected the findings in the strongest terms. Roch disagreed so strongly that he refused to sign the report altogether and presented his own Minority Memorandum instead. A comparison of the evidence presented (at The National Archives, Kew) with the findings and conclusions arrived at, purportedly based on that evidence, reveals considerable discrepancies. Much evidence presented by eminent and expert witnesses attesting to the non-culpability of Fisher and Kitchener in the fiasco was simply ignored in the official findings, as is described in Chapter 6 of this book. Instead, many of Churchill's unsubstantiated accusations against

Kitchener and Fisher were endorsed by the Commission, diverting attention from Churchill himself and to be repeated by the latter in *The World Crisis* six years later.

Special mention also needs to be made of the enormous contribution of Sir Maurice, later Lord Hankey, to Cabinet records and procedures, notably through his CAB 63 or 'Magnum Opus' file, which includes the documentation he prepared for the Dardanelles Commission (CAB 63/17-18). As is described in Chapter 7, Cabinet kept no official minutes of its meetings in 1915. Hankey's unofficial longhand record of all War Council proceedings (Secretary's Notes of War Council Meetings) would, therefore, prove especially invaluable for later historians of this episode—as would his personal diary record of the events in question, located at the Churchill College Archives Centre, Cambridge.

The neglected and rarely mentioned compilation by Commander Thomas Crease, Lord Fisher's Naval Secretary and Personal Assistant, is also worthy of mention. Crease kept a record of all Fisher's correspondence, in copies of letters to and from Churchill, Asquith, Hankey, Balfour, Lloyd George, Jellicoe, Esher, Bonar Law and others, from the time of Fisher's recall as First Sea Lord in November 1914 to his resignation in May 1915. Captain Crease, as he then was, maintained a correspondence with Churchill following the publication of *The World Crisis* in 1923, in which he pointed out to the former First Lord the many factual errors in his book. One drawback of the Crease Compilation is that it is not paginated. The correspondence is, nevertheless, presented in chronological order and the information is thus readily accessible. Both Crease and his compilation proved invaluable to Admiral Sir Reginald Bacon in his official biography of Lord Fisher which was completed in 1929.

In determining the format of this book I have decided to follow Churchill's lead. The remarkable success he enjoyed in winning over his readers to his viewpoint with *The World Crisis* has been reflected here, with that book representing his evidence source, together with his resignation speech to Parliament in November 1915 and his evidence to the Dardanelles Commission in 1916. The evidence for the minority expert explanation will be drawn from the official documents, together with the papers of Fisher, Hankey, de Robeck, Richmond and others.

Winston Churchill's role in the Dardanelles naval operation of 1915 brings into sharp focus an enduring problem confronting democracies—the relationship between a nation's leading politicians and their military advisers, and who should determine the direction of the country's armed forces in time of war. Churchill made no secret of his belief in the superiority of his strategic judgement over that of his naval (and military) colleagues[10]—a belief shared by Presidents Lincoln 50 years earlier and George W. Bush 88 years later. French statesman Georges Clemenceau summarised this belief neatly, commenting that: 'War is too important a matter to be left to the generals.' In the case of the former cavalry officer Winston Churchill, the line between political oversight and interference in operational matters seems to have been unusually blurred, to the point of being non-existent.

The wealth of (hitherto neglected) evidence brought to light in the process of this investigation might well suggest that a re-evaluation of the Dardanelles/Gallipoli campaign may be opportune, particularly the reasons for its inception and for its ultimate failure.

CHAPTER 1

First Lord

To understand how and why Winston Churchill was able to exercise unprecedented control over the naval operations which culminated in the failed Dardanelles campaign, we need to look back into European history, just prior to the outbreak of the First World War. In 1911 a crisis at a Moroccan port resulted in the determination by Britain's leaders that Winston Churchill's autocratic temperament would be ideally suited to the task of bringing the Royal Navy into line with government thinking on war policy, should hostilities break out (as seemed likely) within a very few years. Churchill was installed as First Lord of the Admiralty in October 1911 with absolute authority over the admirals. Over the next three years, in the process of preparing the Royal Navy for the coming Armageddon, Churchill's attitude towards the senior Admiralty staff hardened into one of complete disdain, with the new First Lord adamant that his grasp of naval affairs was superior to that of the naval 'experts'. The authority of First Sea Lord, hitherto paramount in the conduct of naval operations at sea, gradually became subsumed by the First Lord into his own office as he assumed responsibility for 'all business of the Admiralty'.

War was Winston Churchill's passion. He loved it, as he freely admitted to Prime Minister Asquith, Lloyd George, Margot Asquith and others. It comes as no surprise, therefore, to find him embarking on his own naval and military 'adventures' with the outbreak of hostilities. The extent to which Churchill was prepared to indulge this passion would be witnessed by the people of Britain over the following months, to their growing apprehension.

The Agadir Crisis

Germany's deliberately provocative act in sending the gunboat *Panther* to the Moroccan port of Agadir on 1 July 1911 was an unmistakable test of France's resolve to defend her colonial interests and of Britain's determination to stand by her Entente partner (as of 1904) in the face of German aggression. Admiral Lord 'Jacky' Fisher, former First Sea Lord, had accurately predicted that German hostilities in Europe would commence in the autumn of 1914, following the deepening of the Kiel Canal to allow the passage of Germany's new dreadnought battleships.[1]David Lloyd George, Britain's most prominent pacifist during the Boer War, provided his nation's answer to Germany in an historic speech on 21 July:

> If [he said], a situation were to be forced upon us in which peace can only be preserved by the surrender of the great and beneficent position Britain has won by centuries of heroism and

achievement, by allowing Britain to be treated where her interests were vitally affected as if she were of no account in the cabinet of nations; then I say emphatically that peace at that price would be a humiliation intolerable for a great country like ours to endure.[2]

On 23 August 1911, Prime Minister Herbert Asquith called a special meeting of the Committee of Imperial Defence (CID) to consider the crisis and determine Britain's state of readiness in the event of war, which now appeared inevitable. Brigadier General Henry Wilson, Director of Military Operations (DMO), explained the General Staff's war plan: 'that we should mobilise and dispatch the whole of our available regular army of six divisions and a cavalry division immediately upon the outbreak of war', to be committed on the extreme left of the French Army in the vicinity of Maubeuge, in support of the French. Field Marshal Sir William Nicholson, Chief of the Imperial General Staff (CIGS), then asked for Admiralty confirmation that the requisite transport and protection for this force would be provided by the Navy. To the chagrin of Asquith, Wilson and Nicholson, First Lord of the Admiralty Reginald McKenna and First Sea Lord Sir Arthur Wilson, VC, declined to offer any such assurances.[3] McKenna stated unequivocally that: 'assistance could not be given [to the Army] during the first week of the war. The whole efforts of the Admiralty would be absorbed in mobilising the Navy' and this 'inability to guarantee the transport of troops at the outbreak of war ... had actually [been] recorded in a CID Paper.'[4]

Sir Arthur Wilson explained to the assembly that the Navy's war plan involved the destruction of the German Navy at the outbreak of war. This could be achieved, the Admiralty believed, by attacking the German North Atlantic coast, thus forcing the German Navy into a major confrontation on the Royal Navy's terms.[5] In 1916, Grand Admiral von Tirpitz, the German Navy Minister, confessed his surprise that these tactics had not been adopted by Britain, writing that:

> The English only needed to conduct a feint attack on our coast. An attack, for example, on Borkum or Sylt might easily force a battle on us ... we should then be fighting near our own ports, but against an overwhelming superiority of forces and at a point which could be rendered most unsafe and so unfavourable by mines and submarines ... The English did not even seek battle under these favourable circumstances.[6]

Sir Gerald Ellison, Captain Basil Liddell Hart, naval historian Sir Julian Corbett, Captain E.J. Slade, former Director of the War College, Captain G.A. Ballard, former Director of Naval Operations, CID Assistant Secretary, Captain Maurice Hankey and, curiously, Henry Wilson, all expressed a belief in the Navy's strategy.[7] As Lieutenant General Ellison, military adviser to the government in the implementation of the army reforms recommended by the Esher Report of 1904, subsequently wrote:

[Admiral] Fisher was no dreamer. Time and again he had been proved in practice to be right ... He himself had no doubts as to the ultimate success of the North Sea-Baltic scheme and [Arthur] Wilson shared his views ... The fear that the Germans had of a vigorous initiative on our part in the North Sea is, in itself, the most complete justification of the Fisher-Wilson strategy.[8]

Basil Liddell Hart, Britain's most highly regarded military historian during the interwar period, further explained the Navy's war plan in 1930:

> ... the close relations established between the British and French General Staffs since the Entente ... induced a "continental" habit of thought among the [British] General Staff, and predisposed them to the role, for which their slender strength was unsuited, of fighting alongside an Allied Army. This obscured the British Army's traditional employment in amphibious operations through which mobility given by command of the sea could be exploited. A small but highly trained force striking "out of the blue" at a vital spot can produce a strategic effect out of all proportion to its slight numbers.[9]

Brigadier Henry Wilson had expressed a similar opinion only a month prior to the CID meeting, observing in conversation that the Royal Navy (freed from its defensive duties) could have given the British Army power far beyond its numerical strength. Had the British Expeditionary Force (BEF), together with the Belgian Army, been 'promptly applied to the German flank [somewhere along the Belgian or German Atlantic coast, this] might mean the subtraction of as much as 10 or 12 [German] divisions from the decisive battle front.'[1]0

Unfortunately Admiral Wilson, unsurpassed as a tactician at sea, was prone (like Fisher) to keeping his ideas locked in his head. His failure to have the Navy plan prepared with sufficient care and set down in writing by the Admiralty staff for prior discussion with the War Office—together with his natural inability to articulate—fatally compromised the Admiralty's case. His answers to the probing questions of the Army's silver-tongued intellectual Henry Wilson (who had by this time returned to the 'continental' fold) were vague and unconvincing. Arthur Wilson plunged himself deeper into a morass when attempting to explain in detail exactly where, when and how the fleet was to launch its amphibious assaults.[11] Sir William Nicholson finally observed with contempt that: '[T]his class of operation possibly had some value a century ago, when land communications were indifferent, but now, when [railway communications] were excellent, they were doomed to failure. Wherever we threatened to land the Germans could concentrate superior forces...' He added that, in his 'considered opinion the military [amphibious] operations ... proposed ... were madness.'[12]

As a consequence of this meeting, Asquith decided that a change of attitude as well as personnel was indicated at the Admiralty, to bring it into line with the war plans of the government and War Office. Lord Haldane, who during his six years as Secretary of State for War had put into effect the army reforms recommended by the Esher Committee (which included the creation of a General Staff), offered to perform a similar task with the Royal Navy. After talking the matter over with the King, Asquith decided that the forceful personality of Home Secretary Winston Churchill was better suited to introducing the reforms needed to bring the Royal Navy into the twentieth century. The new First Lord of the Admiralty (installed on 25 October 1911) was given the specific commission of putting the fleet 'into a state of instant and constant readiness for war in case we are attacked by Germany.'[13] He was also required to create a Naval War Staff along similar lines to its army counterpart. But above all, his was the task of 'educating' the Navy out of its amphibious aspirations and accepting its role as transporter of Britain's troops to the Western Front (ironically, it would be Churchill himself who would reverse this policy, within six months of the outbreak of war).[14]

The New Broom

In October 1911 Winston Churchill was 36 years old. The son of a Lord (Randolph), grandson of a Duke (of Marlborough) and born in a palace (Blenheim), he entered Parliament in 1900 as a Conservative, almost as a patrician birthright. From the outset, Churchill was a young man in a hurry. Believing that, like his father, he was destined for an early death, he was perfectly happy to cut corners to achieve his ends. Unwilling to serve the normal 'apprenticeship' to advancement, Churchill sought to make an instant name for himself (like his father before him) by attacking his own Conservative leadership (which he had been elected to support), in particular Secretary of State for War St John Brodrick, on the question of army finances.[15]

In 1904 Churchill aroused the enduring wrath of the Tories by deserting to the Opposition, taking his seat provocatively next to the Liberal champion Lloyd George. If he could not attain rapid promotion with one party he would gain it with the other. Blessed with boundless energy, imagination and outstanding oratory and literary skills (he would be awarded the Nobel Prize for Literature in 1953), high office seemed to be his for the asking. Churchill made no secret of his vaunting ambition. This, together with his 'egotistical, bumptious personality' and seeming 'lack of moral [scruple]' (again, like his father before him), made him almost universally unpopular. As one of his colleagues wrote: 'Churchill made no attempt to dispel the suspicion and dislike with which he was regarded by the majority of the House of Commons. He seemed to enjoy causing resentment.'[16] On 7 March 1915, Asquith described Churchill to his wife, despairingly, as 'by far the most disliked man in my Cabinet'. And on the 25th of this same month, Asquith wrote to his female confidante Venetia Stanley: 'He [Winston] will never get to the top in English politics, with all his wonderful gifts; to speak with the tongue of men and angels ... is no good, if a man does not inspire trust.'[17]

Winston Churchill as a Member of Parliament, 1904 (IWM Q_042037).

Charles Hobhouse, Postmaster General in 1915, kept the only (unofficial) record of Cabinet meetings, from July 1908 until his early retirement through ill health in October 1915. On 27 July 1908 he recorded in his diary: 'Winston Churchill's introduction to the Cabinet has been followed by the disappearance of that harmony which its members all tell me has been its marked feature ... personal discourtesy is C[hurchill]'s chief weapon.'[18] On 7 March 1909 Hobhouse added: 'The whole Cabinet atmosphere has been upset by Churchill, before whose advent there had been no electricity.' In character sketches Hobhouse compiled of the other 21 Cabinet members (with the exception of Asquith) in March 1915, he wrote that Sir Edward Grey, whom 'we all like, admire and respect, for his transparent sincerity and honesty as well as for his courage, skill and steadfastness', contrasts significantly with Churchill, who was 'always in a hurry to be conspicuous ... voluble, intolerably bumptious and conceited, he squanders our time and his own in increasing orations.' On another occasion Hobhouse recorded: 'Churchill is ill mannered, boastful, unprincipled, without any redeeming qualities except his amazing ability and industry ... He is really a spoilt child endowed by some chance with the brain of a genius.'[19]

The office of First Lord of the Admiralty was created in 1709, replacing that of Lord High Admiral (created in 1627), which in its turn had superseded the original office of High Admiral, or Lord Admiral, of Henry VIII's reign. In 1513 the Tudor Lord Admiral was expected to personally lead the King's navy into battle, a practice which ended officially in 1672. Following Lord

Barham in 1805, and officially ratified in 1832, First Lords have invariably been civilians, although two retired admirals have since served in this role (from 1852 to 1853 and from 1931 to 1936).[20]

From the earliest days, the Lord Admiral had been supported by a civil 'Navy Board', responsible for the administration of the Navy and for the procurement and fitting out of ships etc. The Board of Admiralty in 1911, or to give it its full title, 'The Lords Commissioners for Executing the Office of Lord High Admiral', combined this dual (naval and civil) role under the auspices of a First Lord who, through the Royal Letters Patent, was 'responsible to Crown and Parliament for all the business of the Admiralty'.[21]

The Board comprised the First Lord, four Sea Lords and two Civil Lords, assisted by a Naval and a Parliamentary Secretary, together with a Financial Secretary. Each had his own sphere of responsibility: the Second Sea Lord for manning and training the fleet; the Third Sea Lord for the design of ships etc. The exact role of the First Sea Lord was formally defined by Sir John Fisher when holder of that office in October 1904, as being responsible for the 'fighting and sea-going efficiency of the Fleet' as well as being the chief professional adviser to the First Lord.[22] As Professor Marder points out, the First Lord's authority 'for all business of the Admiralty' was absolute. By tradition his decisions may well have been guided largely by his professional advisers, but he was under no statutory obligation to comply with that advice. His alone was the ultimate responsibility to Parliament for the Board's actions.[23] Hugh Childers demonstrated the extent to which autocracy could be taken during his tenure as First Lord in Gladstone's reforming government of 1868–74.

Installed, as was Churchill, with the task of bringing the Admiralty into line with government policy (in his case, to reducing naval expenditure), Childers subjected the Sea Lords to a period of sustained contumely. Childers rendered the Board virtually an irrelevance during his term of office, reducing their meetings to very infrequent half-hour sessions to approve decisions he had already made. The Sea Lords 'were in and out of his private room all day long', and often important decisions were made without the First Sea Lord (Sir Sydney Dacres) even seeing the relevant papers. When he demanded to see them, Dacres often disagreed violently with their contents, but to no avail.[24]

Churchill appears to have taken his lead from Childers in his condescension towards the Admiralty chiefs and his assertion of absolute authority over all matters pertaining to the Admiralty. No civilian First Lord, however, had ever assumed absolute control of the conduct and direction of naval operations in time of war as Churchill would do. As Professor Lewis (late of the Royal Naval College, Greenwich) reveals:

> The advisory function [of the Board, but especially of the First Sea Lord] was a most important

one—indeed, indispensible when the [civilian] First Lord himself possessed little or no professional experience, as has always been the case since 1832 ... The First Sea Lord ... has for more than two centuries, though under various names, been the principal naval adviser to the First Lord, when the latter was not a naval officer ... on "operations".[25]

The public reaction to Churchill's appointment was one of apprehension, with the *Spectator* noting: 'He has not the loyalty, the dignity, the steadfastness and the good sense which makes an efficient head of a great office. He must always be living in the limelight, and there is no fault more damning in an administrator.' The *National Review* went further, describing Churchill as 'a windbag ... a political gambler of the worst type', and 'a self-advertising mountebank'.[26]

Churchill's whirlwind energy galvanised naval preparations for the coming war, in which he was assisted considerably (from his retirement in 1910) by former First Sea Lord Admiral 'Jacky' Fisher. Churchill described the 71 year old as 'a veritable volcano of knowledge and inspiration'.[27] In an unpublished note written in 1916, Churchill wrote that, when he assumed office in 1911, 'many of the most important early decisions I took ... were the result of discussions with [Lord Fisher].'[28] Churchill later disowned this admission, claiming credit for most of these innovations himself. There is no doubt, however, that it was Fisher who designed the 'dreadnought' class battleships with their 15-inch guns (for which Churchill claimed credit only four days after his appointment as First Lord), together with the revolutionary battlecruiser and the pioneering conversion from coal-fired to oil-fired ships powered by turbine engines.

Between 1906 and Churchill's assumption of power at the Admiralty, Fisher, as First Sea Lord, had supervised the construction (and design) of 20 dreadnought battleships and nine battlecruisers, along with scores of ancillary cruisers and destroyers—as well as the introduction and improvement of the submarine. Churchill certainly forced on Cabinet the hastened construction of an armada with which he could respond to his critics on his dismissal in May 1915 that '[at least], the Fleet was ready'—which it was, but thanks in large measure to 'Jacky' Fisher.[29]

There was an obverse side to the Admiralty's new First Lord, however. Within just a few months of his appointment Churchill had aroused the ire of the entire naval hierarchy by arguing with the admirals on matters of strategy and tactics. As Admiral Jellicoe, then Second Sea Lord, recorded:

> It did not take me long to find out that Mr. Churchill ... was very apt to express strong opinions upon purely technical matters, moreover, not being satisfied with expressing opinions, he tried to force his views upon the [Admiralty]

Board. It is quite true Mr. Churchill proved himself to be a very clever and able First Lord in some directions, but his fatal error was his inability to realise his own limitations as a civilian.[30]

Admiral Sir Reginald Bacon, a Director of Naval Ordnance, gunnery expert and Lord Fisher's official biographer, assessed Churchill thus:

[Mr Churchill's] keen brain and fertile imagination served to strengthen his belief in his own infallibility. His indomitable energy caused him to meddle in innumerable details that were infinitely better left to the technical officers who had the practical experience to deal with them. His immense range of superficial knowledge beguiled him into believing that that knowledge was accurate and profound.[31]

Winston Churchill as First Lord of the Admiralty, May 1914, with the Naval Wing of the Royal Flying Corps (IWM CH_004778).

At the annual naval manoeuvres in 1912 Churchill 'lectured to the flag officers on how the manoeuvres should have been conducted, and this even before the umpire had concluded his report.'[32] Churchill's utter belief in the superiority of his judgement over that of the naval experts (with the exception of Fisher, initially) was unshakable. He had already written in 1899: 'Put all the elements of a problem before a civilian of first rate ability and enough imagination, and he would reach the right solution, and any soldier could afterwards put this solution into military terms.'[33] Maturity had, apparently, wrought no change to this conviction—quite the reverse, in fact. As he wrote in 1932:

> The astonishing fact is that the politicians were right, and that the Admiralty authorities were wrong. The politicians were right upon a technical, professional question ostensibly quite outside their sphere, and the Admiralty authorities were wrong upon what was, after all, the heart and centre of their own peculiar job ... But the British politicians—we apologize for their existence—were powerful people, feeling they owed their positions to no man's favour. They asked all kinds of questions. They did not always take "No" for an answer. They did not accept the facts and figures put before them by their experts as necessarily unshakable. They were not under moral awe of professional authority, if it did not seem reasonable to the lay mind. They were not above

obtaining secretly the opinions of the junior naval officers concerned with the problem, and using these views to cross-examine and confute the naval chiefs.[34]

The greatest bone of contention at the Admiralty would prove to be the office Churchill had been sent there to introduce, Chief of the Naval Staff, created on 8 January 1912. As Professor Marder points out (and Admiral Bacon concurred): 'The First Sea Lord should have been Chief of Staff. The divorce of the two offices [with an intermediary officer placed between First Sea Lord and the Naval Staff] was unworkable.'[35] In fact, had the two offices been combined, the First Sea Lord could well have become a genuine naval adviser to the government, as the CIGS proved to be, particularly after December 1915 and the appointment of Sir William Robertson.

Instead, as Churchill took on more and more of the role and responsibilities of First Sea Lord, the office of the Chief of Staff became a useful channel through which the First Lord's instructions could be issued directly to Naval Operations, thus bypassing the First Sea Lord who was, nevertheless, still required to initial said instructions as having sighted them, whether they had been already actioned or not.[36] In certain instances the First Sea Lord would not be consulted at all (as during the Hugh Childers regime).[37] The Chief of Staff would also prove useful to Churchill in the provision of a convenient scapegoat, to whom blame could be apportioned when the First Lord's instructions produced disastrous results, as in the escape of the *Goeben* and defeat in the Battle of Coronel.

Admiral Sir Arthur Wilson vehemently resisted the proposed introduction of a naval Chief of Staff in a memorandum of 30 October 1911. As a consequence, Churchill persuaded Prime Minister Asquith to replace him as First Sea Lord with Admiral Sir Francis Bridgeman. The change was effected on 28 November 1911.[38] Bridgeman's tenure lasted for almost one year. The Bridgeman-Churchill association was probably doomed from the outset, with the new First Sea Lord unable to tolerate 'the First Lord's interference in everything'.[39] As Penn notes: 'Without consulting naval members, he [Churchill] issued orders and sent telegrams to the fleet'—a practice which would have dire consequences with the outbreak of war. Within ten months of his appointment, Bridgeman and the Admiralty Board were in 'strident discord' with their First Lord, whose vehement dogmatism that his judgement was superior to theirs exasperated them.[40]

By 28 November 1912 Churchill had decided to get rid of his uncooperative First Sea Lord. This occasioned a sequence of events which would prove both ludicrous and demeaning to the noble institutions of Parliament and the Admiralty.[41] Churchill's initial approach was to ply Bridgeman with flattery: 'I am so grateful for the aid you have given me during what will certainly be regarded as a memorable year in naval administration'—and promises: 'I should consider it my duty to submit your name, on retirement from your present office, to the King, for promotion to the rank of Admiral of the Fleet.'[42] Both of these advances were expunged from Churchill's Cabinet paper in which his emphasis was solely on Bridgeman's supposed ill health, 'which causes me concern both as a colleague and a friend'.[43]

On 2 December 1912 Churchill advised Bridgeman that his resignation had been approved. 'I [have] consulted the Prime Minister and informed the King', Churchill wrote. 'The conclusion at which I have arrived must necessarily be final; and I am confident that it will command your assent.'[44] Bridgeman was astonished at this *fait accompli,* his reputed 'ill health' coming as a surprise to the hale and hearty admiral. The First Sea Lord did concede that he had been overworking and was slightly run down as a result, but this was a minor problem which a short holiday would cure. He replied to Churchill that:

> ... if my health was not good enough to allow me to continue the duties of my office, I should apply to resign. [But] I have carefully thought the matter over, and as it seems to be more a question for the doctors to give an opinion on, I have consulted [my doctor] Dr. Wexley-Smith [who affirmed that there was] nothing organically wrong [with me]. [Consequently] I don't think there is a necessity to resign.[45]

On 4 December, however, Bridgeman wrote to Churchill: 'I had no idea that my leaving the Admiralty had already been settled, and that you had discussed it with the King and Prime Minister ... I now understand that you expect me to resign and I am happy to be able to meet your wishes.'[46]

On 14 December Churchill wrote to Bridgeman concerning various accusations which had appeared in the *Morning Post* that day concerning his resignation, essentially that friction between himself and Churchill had been the cause and that the Sea Lords 'had threatened more than once to resign [*en masse*] during the last month' over differences with the First Lord. Churchill virtually demanded Bridgeman's support in refuting this charge, suggesting that he may have been the source of the article.[47]

Churchill insisted that Bridgeman make a written statement to the effect that no 'cause of difference or disagreement in policy or view existed between us which has led, or was about to lead, to your resignation.'[48] Bridgeman agreed, writing to Churchill the following day, telling him 'I don't know where "Morning Post" article came from.'[49] Churchill's actions had been the subject of concern not only to the *Morning Post,* however, as *The Times* headlines on 14 December announced:

MR CHURCHILL REFUTED—WHY SEA LORD RESIGNED—NO ILL-HEALTH—STATEMENT BY SIR

F. BRIDGEMAN—FLAT CONTRADICTION—QUITE WELL AND FIT FOR WORK.[50]

On the previous day, the *Standard's* special correspondent had reported:

I have just seen the healthiest invalid in England, Sir Francis Bridgeman ... Asked if his resignation was voluntary or on the grounds of ill-health, he replied smilingly—"The answer is in the negative."

Enjoying the best of health and all the robust pleasures of an English country gentleman, the [previous] First Sea Lord hunts three days a week, and is generally well up to the front.[51]

The Times naval correspondent added on 14 December under the headline 'SCANDALOUS PIECE OF TYRANNY–Methods of Mr. Churchill':

The resignation of Sir Francis Bridgeman is another instance of the dictatorial methods of Mr. Churchill's Admiralty regime ... It is well known in Admiralty circles that Mr. Churchill objects to the First Sea Lord having any views of his own, and a rupture with a strong man like Sir Francis Bridgeman, it was clear from the first, was sure to come ... The First Sea Lord's position is now untenable except by a man prepared to bow to Mr. Churchill and accept the new tyranny ... [Churchill's] continuance at the Admiralty is ... a real and dangerous menace to our life as a powerful nation.[52]

Bridgeman's resignation was made official and retrospective from 2 December 1912. He was replaced by Prince Louis of Battenberg, who would prove a much more pliant First Sea Lord for Churchill, offering him little opposition. Throughout the previous 100 years, no First Sea Lord had ever resigned his office because of differences with his First Lord (Hugh Childers notwithstanding). Between November 1911 and May 1915 three First Sea Lords (Wilson, Bridgeman and Fisher) would resign their office because of 'the total impossibility' of working with Winston Churchill.[53] In addition, Prince Louis would be asked to resign on political grounds shortly after the outbreak of war (because of his German ancestry).

Outbreak of War and the Escape of the Goeben

In August 1914, Churchill created an Admiralty War Staff Group to discuss the progress of the war at daily meetings and plan strategy accordingly. It comprised himself, as its head, together with the First Sea Lord (Battenberg), Chief of Staff (Admiral Sturdee), Permanent Secretary to the Admiralty (Sir William Graham Greene) and Churchill's Naval Secretary (Commodore de Bartolomé). Admirals Wilson and Sir Henry Jackson were also invited to attend on an unofficial basis. In November 1914 Lord Fisher replaced Battenberg and Admiral Oliver replaced Sturdee.[54]

As Admiral Bacon points out, the Admiralty War Staff Group 'should have been presided over by the First Sea Lord, and not by the First Lord.' The First Sea Lord alone was 'responsible for the movements of all ships and their actions.' Bacon adds: 'Technical matters were the business of experts, and not of an amateur.'[55] Churchill was well aware of normal procedure, advising his readers in *The World Crisis* that: 'only the First Sea Lord can order the ships to steam and the guns to fire'.[56] Nevertheless, the outbreak of war witnessed a continuation of the practice which had infuriated Bridgeman and the Sea Lords: that of the First Lord sending his own instructions and orders direct to naval commanders at sea. As will be described further in Chapter 2, Churchill conducted War Staff Group meetings in a dictatorial fashion, asserting his opinions over those of the other members, and afterwards drafting, in his own hand, 'the orders that were necessary to carry out what he *believed* to be the decisions reached at the meeting.'[57] Approval from the First Sea Lord was very often sought by Churchill in retrospect. Graham Greene, a participant at these meetings, told the Dardanelles Commission: 'While Mr. Churchill was First Lord of the Admiralty he would initiate orders to the Fleet, and consult the First Sea Lord afterwards.'[58] Churchill allowed no minutes to be recorded of these meetings.

During the final days of peace the Admiralty decided to take precautions against the German naval presence in the Mediterranean, recognising the threat posed by the battlecruiser *Goeben* and its consort *Breslau,* as well as guarding against other eventualities. On 30 July, by his own admission, Churchill sent the following telegram-instruction to Admiral Sir Berkely Milne, Commander-in-Chief of the Mediterranean Fleet, advising him:

Sh[oul]d war break out and England & France engage in it, it now seems probable that Italy will remain neutral & that Greece can be made our ally. Spain also will be friendly & possibly our ally. The attitude of Italy is however uncertain and it is especially important that your squadron should not be seriously engaged with Austrian ships before we know what Italy will do. Your first task should be to aid the French in the transportation of their African Army by covering, and if possible bringing to action individual fast German ships, particularly *Goeben,* who may interfere with that transportation. You will be notified by telegraph when you may consult with the French Admiral. Do not at this stage be brought to action against superior forces [later claimed by the Admiralty to be referring to the Austrian Navy, with its dreadnought battleships], except in combination with the French, as part of a general battle. The speed of your Squadron is sufficient to enable you to choose your moment. We shall hope later to reinforce the Mediterranean, and you must husband your forces at the outset.[59]

As Captain Penn points out, this message violates all the cardinal rules of naval signalling which required brevity, clarity and accuracy. It is verbose, unnecessarily detailed and packed with ambiguities and uncertainties. Most importantly, as Marder notes, the term 'superior forces' and the injunction to 'husband your forces' are left vaguely undefined. Exactly what is meant and required is unclear.[60] The official naval historian, Sir Julian Corbett, attributed to this telegram from Churchill 'very regrettable consequences'.[61]

Milne later claimed that these instructions left him in little doubt that his first priority was to protect the French troop transports, with the prospect of engaging the *Goeben* a secondary consideration. This belief dominated all his subsequent actions. Had Milne been allowed to communicate with the French admiral earlier, he would have been informed that the French troop movements were to take place in convoy, and only when an adequate force was available. Milne could then have focussed on proper surveillance of the *Goeben's* movements. In the event, from the 3rd to the 9th of August, Milne would receive a succession of conflicting telegrams from the Admiralty, sending his warships in one direction then the other, in a 'Keystone-cops' pursuit of the elusive German battlecruiser.[62] Marder attributes the confusion to

Churchill, claiming that the Admiralty should have clearly instructed the admiral on the spot of his objective—following then sinking the *Goeben*—then fed him all the information available and allowed, indeed encouraged him, to act on his own initiative according to circumstances. Instead, 'the ambiguous language of many of the Admiralty operational telegrams, which were drafted hurriedly, and often by the First Lord, confused Milne. He could never be sure he was getting his priorities straight or that he was correctly interpreting his instructions.'[63] Another significant factor which affected Milne's decisions was the need to respect neutral Italy's territorial waters where much of this drama was played out.

At 8.30pm on the 3rd of August, Milne received an Admiralty instruction to detach his two battlecruisers *Indomitable* and *Indefatigable* 'to proceed to the Straits of Gibraltar at high speed to prevent the *Goeben* leaving the Mediterranean [and attacking shipping in the Atlantic]'.[64] At 2.35am on 4 August, orders reached Admiral Souchon, commander of the *Goeben,* that an alliance had been concluded between Turkey and Germany, and that the two German warships were to proceed to Constantinople. Souchon then embarked on a cat-and-mouse chase with the British, to 'obtain as long a start as possible towards the Dardanelles before England's entry into the war' (at midnight, on the 4th).[65]

After a brief bombardment of the Algerian ports of Bona and Philippeville to give the impression that they intended quitting the Mediterranean, the *Goeben* and *Breslau* turned back eastward, making for the Straits of Messina, where they ran straight into the two British battlecruisers, heading west at full speed. However, with war not yet declared, no hostile action could be taken. Disdaining Italian neutrality, the *Goeben* and *Breslau* disappeared into the Straits to begin coaling at Messina.

Souchon's deception convinced Milne that the French troopships were the *Goeben*'s prime objective, and he made his dispositions accordingly, sending *Indomitable* to Bizerta (Tunisia) to coal (at 5.30pm on 5 August), and stationing his other two battlecruisers, *Inflexible* and *Indefatigable,* off Pantelleria Island, midway between Sicily and Tunisia, to protect the French transports. His 1st Armoured Cruiser Squadron, under Rear Admiral Troubridge, he positioned at the mouth of the Adriatic Sea, in accordance with Admiralty advice, to continue watching 'for double purpose of preventing the Austrians emerging unobserved and preventing Germans entering'—although, as Marder points out, just exactly what these cruisers were expected to do against Austrian battleships, if they did come out, was unclear.[66]

At 4.00am on 3 August, after learning of the proximity of the *Goeben,* the French admiral (de Lapeyère) decided to convoy his troop transports in three groups under the protection of 11 French battleships plus sundry cruisers and destroyers. Milne's assistance was, therefore, no longer necessary. But no-one at the

Admiralty (particularly at the highest level of executive command) thought fit to inform Milne of this significant development. He consequently saw no reason to alter his dispositions. Had Milne been so informed he could well have directed all his forces to the task of chasing and sinking the *Goeben.* [67]

At 5.00pm on 6 August, the *Goeben* and *Breslau* slipped out of Messina and, once out of the Straits, headed east. An hour later they suddenly altered course (a feint, as it transpired) north-easterly towards the Adriatic and towards Troubridge's armoured cruiser squadron, with the British light cruiser *Gloucester* shadowing. Troubridge had already told Milne that 'he regarded the *Goeben,* owing to her speed and the range of her guns, as in daylight a superior force to his own, with which his instructions were not to engage, but his intention was to neutralise the German advantage by engaging at night.'[68]

At 10.46pm the *Goeben* suddenly altered course again, this time southeasterly (heading for the Dardanelles). At this time, Troubridge's cruiser squadron was the only force close enough to intercept the German battlecruiser, the three British battlecruisers being positioned well to the west of Sicily (protecting the French transports). At 4.05am on the 7th, Troubridge, 67 miles astern of the *Goeben,* signalled Milne to advise him that:

> ... as he could only engage the *Goeben* [in broad daylight] outside the range of his guns, and inside

the range of hers, he had abandoned the chase ... Since only darkness or half light offered a chance of his being able to engage [the *Goeben]* successfully ... when he found it impossible [Troubridge] thought it his duty not to risk his squadron against an enemy who, by his superior speed and gunpower, could choose his distance and out-range him.[69]

At 12.30am on the 8th, now cognisant of the *Goeben's* position, Milne sent his three battlecruisers in fast pursuit. However, at 2.30pm, while making up ground on the German warships (*Goeben* had developed boiler problems), he received yet another gaffe from the Admiralty in the form of a telegram warning him to: 'Commence hostilities at once against Austria.' Marder writes that this horrible blunder was allegedly committed by an Admiralty clerk.[70]

Milne broke off the chase at once and steamed north to reinforce Troubridge at the mouth of the Adriatic, in accordance with 'long-standing and explicit orders as to what he should do if Austria entered the war.'[71] At 12.50pm on the 9th, Milne received another telegram from the Admiralty, telling him: 'Not at war with Austria. Continue chase of *Goeben.* ' The chase was resumed, but 24 vital hours had been lost. By the 9th of August the *Goeben* and *Breslau* were already in the Aegean. At 8.30pm on the 10th they entered the Dardanelles and proceeded to Constantinople.[72]

Scapegoats were essential to explain away this incredible display of ineptitude on the part of the Royal Navy. After all, three British battlecruisers had been in the near vicinity of the *Goeben* and should have been able to make short work of the German warship. Milne was accused of lacking initiative throughout this whole sorry affair, but was later exonerated. Predictably, his career then went into limbo. The Admiralty presented Troubridge as the real villain of the piece at a court martial, alleging that he: 'from negligence or through other default, [did] forbear to pursue the chase of His Imperial German Majesty's ship *Goeben,* being an enemy then flying' (a euphemism for cowardice in the face of the enemy).[73]

The prosecution's claim was that Troubridge's armoured cruisers should have engaged the *Goeben.* Despite the disparity of speed and firepower, his squadron could, at the cost of perhaps two of his cruisers, have inflicted sufficient damage to allow the British battlecruisers time to catch up with and sink the German warship. No support was forthcoming from the First Sea Lord, who contended that: '[Troubridge's four cruisers, between them, mounted] twenty-two 9.2-inch guns, fourteen 7.5-inch, and twenty 6-inch, [as against] the Goeben's ten 11-inch and twelve 5.9-inch guns.' Further, Battenberg claimed that: 'The German single target was much larger than each of the four separate British targets ... [and] superior speed ... in a single ship can be nullified by proper tactical dispositions of four units.'[74] In his signal to Milne, Troubridge had explained that:

> I had hoped to engage her [the *Goeben]* at 3.30 in the morning in dim light ... In view of the immense importance of victory or defeat at such an early stage of the war, I would consider it a great imprudence to place the squadron in such a position as to be picked off at leisure and sunk, while unable to effectively reply. The decision is not the easiest to make, I am well aware.[75]

The Court determined that: 'the accused was justified in considering the *Goeben* was a superior force to the First Cruiser Squadron at the time of day they would have met, viz., 6am on the 7th August, in full daylight in the open sea ... The Court therefore finds that the charge against the accused is not proved, and fully and honourably acquits him of the same.'[76] Although Troubridge was eventually promoted (to vice admiral in 1916 and admiral in 1919), he was never given another command at sea, a terrible punishment for this very proud man, a descendant of the Troubridge who served under Nelson.

As Marder points out, the arrival of the German warships *Goeben* and *Breslau* at Constantinople (where they were renamed and became part of the Turkish Navy) was probably the decisive factor in bringing Turkey into the war on Germany's side. This led to the costly and unsuccessful Dardanelles campaign which saw Russia isolated from her allies and knocked out of the war.[77]

Churchill remained completely unabashed in terms of his management of and responsibility for this fiasco, writing subsequently:

> I accepted full responsibility for bringing about successful results, and in that spirit I exercised a close general supervision over everything that was done or proposed. Further, I claimed and exercised an unlimited power of suggestion and initiative over the whole field [he then cynically added the caveat], *subject only to the approval and agreement of the First Sea Lord on all operative orders.* [78]

The degree of input and authority allowed to the First Sea Lord by Churchill in the initiation of these orders has already been illustrated, but will be demonstrated further in the course of this narrative.

The escape of the *Goeben* was a blow to British naval prestige and naval morale, the full extent of which would be tragically illustrated two months later at Coronel. Admiral Sir David Beatty, along with Jellicoe, Britain's most celebrated naval commander, summed up the mood of the Navy: 'To think that it is to the Navy to provide the first and only instance of failure. God, it makes me sick.'[79]

Antwerp

'Hardly one war was enough for him', Lord Birkenhead wrote of Winston Churchill in 1914, adding that neither, apparently, was the command of only 'one [Service] Department'.[80] Assistant Director of Naval Operations Captain Richmond agreed with Birkenhead's observation, confiding to his diary on 20 August 1914: 'I really believe Churchill is not sane.'[81]

On this occasion the source of Richmond's consternation was Churchill's brainchild, the newly created Royal Naval Division (RND). According to Churchill, this was to consist of the existing Royal Marine Brigade (3000 highly trained regulars), together with two further naval brigades of as-yet-untrained reservists, and volunteers drawn from the 'many thousands of men ... for whom there would be no room in any ship of war.' The role of these reluctant sailors-turned-soldiers would be 'to assist in home defence in the early stages of the war'.[82]

Churchill was described as 'Public Enemy No 1' at this time by many of these men who had enlisted 'primarily for service afloat' and had no wish to be soldiers. In other quarters it was suggested that 'Churchill, not content with the naval forces under his command, wanted to control land operations as well.'[83] Richmond wrote:

> The whole thing is so wicked that Churchill ought to be hanged before he should be allowed to do

such a thing. The Cabinet appears to have opposed it, but it is said (rumour of course, only) that he said he'd resign if his scheme wasn't approved ... But how the Board can permit him to indulge in such foolery, without a word of serious protest, I don't know. What this force is to do, Heaven only knows.[84]

An answer of sorts was provided, courtesy of CID Secretary Hankey, only a few days later. Asquith recorded the incident thus:

> When I came back from the House I had a long visit from Winston and Kitchener ... They were bitten with an idea of Hankey's to despatch a brigade of Marines, about 3,000, conveyed and escorted in battleships to Ostend, to land there and take possession of the town and scout about the neighbourhood. This would please the Belgians and annoy and harass the Germans, who would certainly take it to be the pioneer of a larger force, and it would further be a quite safe operation as the Marines could at any time re-embark ... Winston, I need not say, was full of ardour about his Marines, and takes the whole adventure, of which the Cabinet only heard an hour ago, very seriously.[85]

The Marines were duly despatched on 26 August and landed at Ostend on the 27th. The ruse was successful beyond everyone's expectations. The 'invasion' had been well advertised, even announced in Parliament (by Churchill, as a landing of a 'strong force of British Marines'). Indeed, it almost developed into a much larger exercise. The French offered 4000 troops with the promise of another 10,000 to follow. Most importantly, the Germans were deceived into diverting a number of divisions away from the main theatre to meet this perceived 'threat'. Their mission accomplished, the Royal Marines were reembarked on 31 August and brought home, having suffered virtually no casualties.[86]

The battle of the Marne, in early September 1914, effectively ended Germany's hopes of a swift victory over the French, British and Belgian forces. Now began the so-called 'race to the sea', with both armies attempting to outflank the other. By 2 October, a soon-to-be impregnable trench line extended from Switzerland to Arras, 60 miles from the English Channel. The key objective, however, for both the Germans and the Allies, was the Belgian fortress city of Antwerp, which guarded the Channel ports. While Antwerp stood, no German advance on Ostend, Dunkirk, Calais and Boulogne was possible.[87]

On the evening of 2 October, Churchill had left London for a weekend visit to France to discuss the deployment of the Royal Marine Brigade (located at Dunkirk) with the British Commander of the BEF, Sir John French, in view of the rapid German advance towards the coast. Outside Dover, Churchill's special train was suddenly reversed and returned to London.

The First Lord was rushed to Kitchener's house, where he was informed that the Belgian government intended to evacuate Antwerp, which had been under siege since 28 September, the next day. Kitchener, Sir Edward Grey, the First Sea Lord, and Churchill discussed the danger to the Channel ports and to Britain's cross-Channel communications for several hours before they decided to send the Royal Marine Brigade to help defend the city, in advance of greater reinforcements from the main army. A telegram was sent to the Belgian Prime Minister to this effect. Churchill then suggested that he should proceed to Antwerp to keep the government abreast of the situation and, hopefully, bolster the Belgians' resolve. This being agreed, he arrived at the beleaguered city the following afternoon to find Antwerp's outer forts falling to the fire of giant German 17-inch siege howitzers.[88]

Churchill persuaded the Belgian government to continue its resistance with the promise of immediate assistance in the form of his 2000 Royal Marines (who arrived in Antwerp on 4 October) together with a further 6000 men of the naval brigades which Churchill telegraphed the Admiralty to send at once—minus the recruits. This last instruction appears to have been ignored. In reply to another telegram request from Churchill, Kitchener promised reinforcements, comprising the 7th Division and part of a cavalry division (22,000 men in total), to disembark at Zeebrugge on 6–7 October. In an emergency session, the French government agreed to send two Territorial divisions to Antwerp 'with the shortest delay', to arrive between 6 and 9 October. Unfortunately, both of these relief forces were delayed and arrived too late to do more than cover the retreat of the Belgian Army to the coast. The only assistance given to the Belgians, therefore, was that provided by Churchill's RND.[89]

The Marine brigade went into action on the afternoon of the 5th and, by evening, had sustained 150 casualties, killed or wounded. The two naval brigades arrived during the early hours of the 6th, and were sent immediately into the line. Churchill assumed personal responsibility for the deployment of (as he described) 'the inexperienced, partially-equipped and partially-trained' naval brigades to a position where these nevertheless 'ardent, determined men would not easily be dislodged'.[90] Churchill seems to have been in his element, according to one of his men, who remembered how:

> Mr. Churchill dominated the proceedings ... He put forward his ideas forcefully, waving his stick and thumping the ground with it. After obviously pungent remarks, he would walk away a few steps and stare towards the enemy's direction. On other occasions he would stride away without another word, get into the car and wait impatiently to go off to the next area.[91]

News reaching the Cabinet from the battlefield (so Lloyd George recounted) portrayed a similar

Churchillian performance, with the First Lord behaving 'in rather a swaggering way ... standing for photographers & cinematographers with shells bursting near him, & actually promoting his pals on the field of action.'[92]

On the morning of 5 October Churchill telegraphed Asquith, offering to resign as First Lord, and requesting that he be given command of all the British forces in, and about to arrive at Antwerp (two divisions), together with the necessary rank and authority. The amazed Prime Minister related his response to Venetia Stanley:

> Of course, without consulting anybody, I at once telegraphed to him warm appreciation of his mission and his offer, with a *most decided* negative, saying that we could not spare him at the Admiralty etc. I had not meant to read it [Churchill's telegram] to the Cabinet, but as everyone, including K[itchener] began to ask how soon he was going to return, I was obliged to do so ... I regret to say that it was received with a Homeric laugh. W[inston] is an ex-lieutenant of Hussars, and would if his proposal had been accepted, have been in command of 2 distinguished Major Generals, not to mention Brigadiers, Colonels etc.[93]

Kitchener had, incidentally, agreed to provide the necessary rank, had Asquith decided on such an appointment, writing in the margin of Churchill's telegram to Asquith: 'I will make him a Lt-General if you give him the command.'[94] It should be noted, however, that this does not necessarily denote Kitchener's endorsement of Churchill in that role, as some historians have claimed. In fact, when a similar proposition was raised again, in November 1915, Asquith and Kitchener refused to grant Churchill even the rank of brigadier in the field. Following his resignation from Cabinet and decision to renew his army career (albeit briefly), Major Churchill spent a month gaining battlefield experience in France—at his own request—before accepting a command. His six-month tour of duty, in a quiet sector of the line (with a generous leave allowance in March to attend a Parliamentary debate, and rendered the more bearable by weekly hampers requested from his wife, of 'slabs of corned beef: stilton cheeses: cream: hams: tins of sardines—dried fruits [and] a big beef steak pie', together with his 'splendid bath (portable) & a tolerably hot water supply'), would be spent, not in command of a corps, a division or a brigade, but of a battalion, with the rank of lieutenant colonel.[95] But Asquith had already vetoed Churchill's request in the most decisive manner. Churchill's 'adventure' (as Asquith described it) came to an end on 7 October with his return to London. Soon after, he contacted the Prime Minister, requesting again that he be given a senior military appointment. Asquith recalled the incident to Venetia Stanley thus:

I have had a long call from Winston, who, after dilating in great detail on the actual situation, became suddenly very confidential and implored me not to take a conventional view of his future. Having, as he says, tasted blood these last few days, he is beginning, like a tiger, to raven for more, and begs that sooner or later—and the sooner the better—he may be relieved of his present office and put in some kind of military command. I told him that he could not be spared from the Admiralty, but he scoffs at that ... His mouth waters at the sight and thought of K[itchener]'s New Armies. Are these "glittering commands" to be entrusted to "dug-out trash", bred on the obsolete tactics of twenty-five years ago, "mediocrities who have led a sheltered life mouldering on military routine" etc. etc.

For about a quarter of an hour he poured out a ceaseless cataract of invective and appeal, and I much regretted that there was no shorthand writer within hearing, as some of his unpremeditated phrases were quite priceless. He was, however, three parts serious and declared that *a political career was nothing to him in comparison with military glory.* [96]

Asquith further recorded, this same day: 'The [Belgian] Court and Ministers have retreated to Ostend and the Belgian Army is completely worn out and demoralised.' On the 8th, he wrote: 'The news from Antwerp was distinctly bad. The Germans have been bombarding away all night.' Then followed talk of evacuating Winston's RND from the trenches.[97]

Antwerp fell to the Germans on the 9th. During the retreat, one of Churchill's naval brigades proved so inexperienced that the men marched in the wrong direction and ended up in Holland, where they were interned. The RND sustained 215 casualties, killed or wounded, with a further 936 men taken prisoner and 1500 interned.[98] At the Admiralty, Richmond was furious with Churchill, writing on 4 October:

> I don't mind his tuppeny untrained rabble going, but I do strongly object to 2000 invaluable [Royal] marines being sent to be locked up in the fortress and become prisoners of war. They are our only reserve ... It is a tragedy that the Navy should be in such lunatic hands at this time.[99]

Admiral Sir David Beatty was equally incensed, fuming that Churchill had made 'such a darned fool of himself over the Antwerp débâcle. The man must have been mad to have thought he could relieve [Antwerp] ... by putting 8000 half-trained troops into it.'[100]

The newspapers agreed. Criticism of Churchill was scathing, ascribing the failure to the 'vanity and mock-heroism of the First Lord'. In an article entitled 'The Antwerp Blunder' published on 13 October, the *Morning Post* asserted:

It is not right or proper that Mr. Churchill should use his position as Civil Lord to press his tactical and strategic fancies upon unwilling experts ... We suggest to Mr. Churchill's colleagues that they should, quite firmly and definitely, tell the First Lord that on no account are the military and naval operations [of the nation] to be conducted or directed by him.[101]

The Times commented the following day: 'When rumours first got about in this neighbourhood that these raw levies were going to the front, it was scoffed at as incredible. The opinions of many naval and military officers were unanimous that to send the Brigade in their present condition to any fighting line was nothing less than "deliberate murder".'[102] On the 19th the *Morning Post* announced:

What we desire chiefly to enforce upon Mr. Churchill is that this severe lesson ought to teach him that he is not, as a matter of fact, a Napoleon; but a Minister of the crown with no time either to organise or to lead armies in the field ... To be photographed and cinematographed under fire at Antwerp is an entirely unnecessary addition to the risks and horrors of war.[103]

Lloyd George told his secretary and future wife, Frances Stevenson, that he was 'rather disgusted with Winston ... about Antwerp, and thinks that the PM is too. Having taken untrained men over there, he left them in the lurch.'[104] Asquith was, in fact, totally disgusted with the whole affair, confiding afterwards to Venetia Stanley:

> Strictly between ourselves I can't tell you what I feel of the *wicked folly* of it all. The marines of course are splendid troops and can go anywhere and do anything; but nothing can excuse Winston (who knew all the facts) for sending in the other two brigades ... only about one quarter were reservists and the rest were a callow crowd of the rawest, most of whom had never fired off a rifle, while none of them had ever handled an entrenching tool.[105]

Asquith omitted to add that one of the naval brigade officers (his son Arthur) had been in the Army for just three days when he was sent to Antwerp.[106]

The lasting impression on the British consciousness from this episode was not whether Churchill had effected some singular military coup at Antwerp, but rather one of concern over the First Lord's behaviour and judgement. It is generally conceded by modern military historians that Churchill's intervention at Antwerp in October, by helping to delay the evacuation of the Belgian Army by five days, was instrumental in saving Calais, Dunkirk and Boulogne for the Allies. His means of achieving that end, however, remain contentious.

Professor Marder grudgingly concedes Churchill's claim that persuading the Belgians to resist for 'several crucial days [after their planned evacuation date of 3 October] ... had given the Allies time to secure Dunkirk and Calais.' However, Marder adds, 'it was Kitchener who had initiated [the idea]' which never envisaged sending untrained men into the firing line. Penn is similarly equivocal. Rhodes James, on the other hand, considered, in 1970, that 'the Antwerp episode can now be seen to have been substantially to Churchill's credit.'[107] In 1932, Churchill singled out Antwerp as something which, with hindsight, he would have done differently, or not done at all.[108] Many Britons were alarmed at Churchill's swaggering and theatrical behaviour. Rightly or wrongly, for years to come, the imagery evoked by Antwerp would be largely that of raw recruits abandoned and sacrificed to the enemy to satisfy the fantasies of a posturing military adventurer.

A.G. Gardiner, editor of the *Daily News,* had already penned a character portrait of Churchill in 1913 which, for many, was amply confirmed by the First Lord's behaviour in October 1914. As Gardiner had told his readers:

> He [Churchill] is always unconsciously playing a part—an heroic part. And he is himself his most astonished spectator. He sees himself moving through the smoke of battle—triumphant, terrible, his brow clothed with thunder, his legions looking to him for victory, and not looking in vain ... In

(*Monmouth* mounted only fourteen 6-inch guns). The German cruisers were more heavily armoured and manned by long-serving regulars, 'the pick of the German Navy, renowned for their gunnery'. By comparison, the British squadron was manned by reservists, the crew aboard *Good Hope* and *Monmouth,* Cradock's most powerful ships, having had no opportunity to fire their guns since their enlistment and hurried despatch to their station.[114]

Cradock replied on 8 October (received at the Admiralty on 11 October 1914 at 5.35pm), advising: 'Without alarming, respectfully suggest that, in event of enemy's heavy cruisers and others concentrating on West Coast of South America, it is necessary to have a British force on each coast strong enough to bring them to action.'[115] This was to guard against the possibility of the Germans slipping past him on the west coast and creating havoc with British trade and coaling stations on the east coast, in the South Atlantic. From his more reliable sources in the area, Cradock was able to advise the Admiralty that there were in fact three light cruisers in Spee's squadron, *Leipzig, Nürnberg* and *Dresden,* not one. As Corbett writes, he could not see how the problem was to be solved with a single squadron on the west coast. In view of Cradock's appreciation of the enemy's strength, he suggested that his force be increased by the addition of the modern cruisers *Cornwall* (from the North American station) and *Defence* (from the Mediterranean). Each mounted four 9.2-inch and ten

7.5-inch guns. Cradock sent a second telegram to the Admiralty the same day (which was received on 12 October) advising: 'Have ordered *Canopus* to Falkland Islands [off the south-east coast of South America] ... where I intend to concentrate and avoid division of forces.'[116]

Sending Cradock the pre-dreadnought *Canopus* as a reinforcement was, in Admiral Bacon's words, an act of which 'anything more futile can hardly be imagined'. This old battleship was due for scrapping in 1915. Her top speed at launching had been 17 knots, but boiler problems had reduced this to 12 knots (Churchill claimed 15). Churchill dismissed this disparity in speed between *Canopus* and the 23-knot enemy cruisers, stating that: 'The old battleship, with her heavy armour and artillery, was in fact a citadel around which all our cruisers in those waters could find absolute security. The *Scharnhorst* and *Gneisenau* would never have ventured ... within range of her four 12-inch guns.'[117]

Nor would they. But just how this old battleship was ever expected to get close enough to the enemy to fire those guns Churchill omitted to explain. Tied to a 12-knot encumbrance, Cradock would have been powerless to prevent the German cruisers sinking British merchant ships at will. Captain Richmond challenged Churchill's fundamental strategy, with which he strenuously disagreed from the outset. As Richmond recorded in his diary:

[At Naval Operations: Churchill] proceeded to argue that *Canopus* and *Good Hope* were good enough to stop [*Scharnhorst* and *Gneisenau*], a thing I ventured to differ about. He grew very angry and seeing that he was annoyed and in no humour for having his dispositions or opinions discussed, I left him ...

Seeing I could get nothing out of him [Churchill], I went over & talked to Hankey at the CID & pointed out the responsibility of doing things like this & he said he could do nothing ... It is sickening to see these people wrecking the Empire and feel oneself impotent to prevent it. [Richmond added] Churchill is absorbed in [his] Naval Brigades, the defence of Antwerp and the Flying Corps, & High Seas strategy is a thing he does not understand—nor any sea strategy for the matter of fact.[118]

Cradock received no reply for almost a week. As Corbett notes, this was a time of 'extreme pressure at the Admiralty, with the Naval Division in dire straits at Antwerp'. However, as Bacon points out, 'there was no excuse for the orders that were sent.'[119]

At a War Staff Group meeting, Sir Henry Jackson advocated a single force 'strong enough to fight [the Germans] concentrated at the Falklands', with additional fast, light ships to scout and report the German ships' whereabouts. Had Jackson's sensible suggestion been adopted, Bacon writes, 'there would have been no Coronel'. But, unfortunately, Jackson was present as an adviser only, in an unofficial capacity, 'so his advice was ignored'—as was Cradock's request for one strong squadron on each coast.[120] Instead, there would be one equally weak British squadron on either coast.

Churchill wrote a minute on Cradock's telegram of 12 October, specifying that the German warships, 'and not [protection of] trade, are our quarry for the moment, *we must not miss them'*.[121] First Sea Lord Battenberg concurred. A telegram was sent to Cradock on the 14th, informing him: 'Your concentration of *Canopus, Good Hope, Glasgow, Monmouth, Otranto* for combined operations concurred in.' Cradock was further told that a second squadron was to be formed on the east coast under Rear Admiral Stoddart. This was to comprise four cruisers, including *Defence,* and two merchant cruisers (comparable in overall strength to Cradock's squadron).[122]

That Cradock believed, from these instructions, that he was expected to seek out and engage the enemy as best he could, is apparent in his telegram reply to the Admiralty of 18 October 1914 which stated: 'I fear that strategically the speed of my squadron cannot exceed 12 knots owing to *Canopus,* but shall trust circumstances will enable me to force an action.'[123] On 27 October Cradock exercised his initiative, taking advantage of the vague wording of his telegram instructions with regard to a 'combined operation', and informed the Admiralty:

> With reference to orders contained in Admiralty telegram received 7th October, to search for enemy and our great desire for early success, consider it impractical on account of *Canopus'* slow speed to find and destroy enemy's squadron. Consequently, have therefore ordered *Defence* to join me ... *Canopus* will be employed on necessary work of convoying colliers.[124]

Cradock's decision to rid himself of his 12-knot encumbrance and attempt to provide his squadron with some sort of parity with the enemy, in company with *Defence,* received an immediate Admiralty response on 28 October. Cradock was informed: 'Your [telegram] 325. *Defence* is to remain on East Coast under orders of Stoddart. This will leave sufficient force on each side in case the hostile cruisers appear there on the trade routes.'[125] As Marder notes, this last Admiralty telegram, by once again describing his west-coast squadron as 'sufficient force' to meet the German squadron (albeit, as Churchill maintained, in company with the 'citadel' *Canopus),* and by denying him *Defence,* left Cradock with no option other than to search for and engage the enemy on his own. 'Tired of protesting his inferiority', Marder writes, 'the receipt of this telegram would be sufficient spur to [the proud and intrepid] Cradock to hoist his signal, "Spread twenty miles apart and look for the enemy".'

The enemy squadron was located in the late afternoon of 1 November off Coronel on the Chilean coast and, in the ensuing one-sided battle, Cradock's flagship, *Good Hope,* along with *Monmouth,* was sunk, with the loss of all hands (1600 men).[126]

The question inevitably asked throughout Britain was *why* a distinguished admiral such as Sir Christopher Cradock had deliberately engaged what he knew to be a superior enemy force with little or no chance of success. Lieutenant Commander P.B. Portman, on the *Glasgow,* and a witness to the battle, interpreted Cradock's behaviour thus:

> The *Defence* was refused him and he was as good as told he was skulking at [the Falklands]. What else was there for him to do except go and be sunk? He was a very brave man and they were practically calling him a coward. If we hadn't attacked that night, we might never have seen [the German cruisers] again, and then the Admiralty would have blamed him for not fighting.[127]

Marder added another interpretation, 'one which [he] believed to be closest to the truth'. When searching for the German squadron, Cradock wrote to a high-ranking officer, alluding to Troubridge's court martial for not having engaged the *Goeben.* 'I will take care I do not suffer the fate of poor Troubridge', Cradock had written.[128]

Two days before the battle at Coronel, Lord Fisher had been recalled as First Sea Lord. He immediately ordered *Defence* to be sent to join Cradock's squadron. But it was too late. The Admiralty was informed, from Valparaiso on 4 November, of the naval disaster. Churchill announced to the press that Cradock had 'let himself be caught or has engaged recklessly with only *Monmouth* and *Good Hope'*, and subsequently wrote: 'I cannot therefore accept for the Admiralty any share in the responsibility for what followed. The first rule of war is to concentrate superior strength for decisive action and to avoid division of forces.'[129]

This version of events was accepted by Cabinet, as Asquith reported to the King, after a Cabinet meeting on 4 November: 'The mishap is the more regrettable as it would seem that the Admiral was acting in disobedience to his instructions, which were expressly to the effect that he must concentrate his whole squadron, including the *Canopus* and *Defence,* and run no risk of being caught in a condition of inferiority.'[130]

Cabinet was thus completely deceived. Asquith confided to Venetia Stanley the same day: 'If the admiral had followed his instructions, he would never have met [the German ships] with an inferior force but would have been by now the other side of South America with the *Canopus* and *Defence* in overwhelming superiority. I am afraid the poor man has gone to the bottom; otherwise he richly deserved to be court-martialled.'[131] The admirals were not duped, however. As Sir David Beatty wrote to his wife:

> Poor old Kit Cradock has gone poor chap. He has had a glorious death, but if only it had been in victory instead of defeat ... his death and the loss of the ships and the gallant lives in them can be laid to [the] door of the incompetency of the Admiralty. They have as much idea of strategy as the Board School boy, and have broken over and over again the first principles ... No one trusts the Admiralty. They have made so many mistakes that should never have been made.[132]

Others, outside the Royal Navy, were similarly unimpressed by the official explanation. As Lloyd George told Frances Stevenson:

> Churchill is too busy trying to get a flashy success to attend to the real business of the Admiralty. Churchill blames Admiral Cradock for the defeat in South America—the Admiral presumably having gone down with his ship & so unable to clear himself. This is characteristic of Churchill. When he returned from Antwerp after his failure he said to the Cabinet, "Now that the administration of such serious & important affairs lies entirely in the hands of a few of us—since Parliament is not sitting—it behoves us to be quite frank with each other." Everyone agreed, thinking that he was about to confess his mistake. Instead, he went on to shift the whole of the responsibility for the

disaster on to Kitchener, who happened to be absent from Cabinet that day.[133]

Admiral Sturdee, as Chief of Staff, would subsequently be burdened with responsibility for the Coronel disaster along with Cradock but, as Richmond has made clear, this was Churchill's personal project from the outset, and one in which any dissenting opinion (to his own) was unwelcome. As the Admiralty telegrams leave no doubt, the escape of the *Goeben* and the Coronel tragedy can be attributed directly to Churchill's interference and mishandling of those operations.

By the end of October Churchill's reputation throughout the country was in tatters. Most newspapers were calling for his sacking, holding him responsible for the litany of unrelieved disasters which had dogged the Royal Navy since the beginning of the war. On 22 September, three cruisers, the *Hogue, Cressy* and *Aboukir,* patrolling in the North Sea, were torpedoed and sunk by the same German submarine in an hour, with the loss of 1400 lives. Commodore Keyes had spoken, in Churchill's presence, of this 'live-bait' squadron. When asked what he meant, Keyes explained the vulnerability of cruisers patrolling this particular area. Churchill wrote a memo to Battenberg to have this practice stopped. It was, but all too late. Keyes wrote that 'the sinking of the *Pathfinder, Aboukir, Hogue, Cressy* and *Hawke* ... was about as simple an operation for a submarine captain as the stalking of tame elephants, chained to trees.' Then,

56

on 27 October, one of Britain's newest dreadnought battleships, *Audacious,* was sunk by a German mine off the north coast of Ireland, deep within what should have been safe home waters.[134] On 21 October, the *Morning Post* informed its readers that:

> In the Admiralty ... there is a First Lord who is a civilian and cannot be expected to have a grasp of the principles and practice of naval warfare. This position would not be dangerous if the First Lord recognised that his proper function was to represent the Government in the Admiralty and the Admiralty in the Government, and to be guided in matters of warfare by his expert advisers. But we have now sufficient evidence to demonstrate that the First Lord seeks to guide operations of war.[135]

On the following day, the *Morning Post* predicted that 'there would be further mistakes and further disasters' if Churchill remained in charge of the Admiralty.[136] It was in an attempt to restore his blighted reputation that Churchill brought back the nation's most revered admiral in his former role of First Sea Lord. Fisher immediately demonstrated to Churchill exactly how a naval operation should be conducted. It may have been too late to save Cradock, but von Spee's squadron still posed the same threat to vital British trade. Fisher ordered two battlecruisers (*Invincible* and *Inflexible)* to be detached from Jellicoe's Grand Fleet and sent, with the minimum of delay, to the Falklands.

He was immediately confronted with a bureaucratic delay. Fisher wanted his ships to sail from Devonport within three days, on 11 November. He was informed by the dockyard that the *Invincible's* boilers needed repairs and could not be ready before the 13th. Fisher responded in typical fashion, instructing the Admiral Superintendent by telegram that the ships *would* sail on time, that: 'They are needed for war service and dockyard arrangements must be made to conform; if necessary dockyard men should be sent away in the ships to return as opportunity may offer.'[137] The difference of two days, Fisher well knew, might (and did) prove crucial. The battlecruisers sailed on the 11th with workmen still on board to finish the electrical firing circuits.

In *The World Crisis* Churchill presented a facsimile reproduction of this telegram to the Admiral Superintendent, which Fisher dictated to him. There is no question of the authorship. However, as Bacon notes, this instruction 'being in [Churchill's] handwriting convey[s] the impression [which Churchill was happy not to contradict] ... that the indomitable urgency insisted on was due to him and not to Lord Fisher.'[138]

Fisher issued clear and precise instructions to the squadron commander, Admiral Sturdee (relieved of his position as Chief of Staff), who was told simply to: 'proceed to South American waters. Your most important duty is to search for the *Scharnhorst* and *Gneisenau* and bring them to action.'[139] On learning that the *Canopus* had developed further boiler problems, Fisher ordered its captain to anchor the ponderous warship in Stanley Harbour:

> Moor the ship so that the entrance is commanded by your[12-inch] guns. Extemporise mines outside the entrance. Send down your topmasts [so that the ship could not be spotted from a distance] and be prepared for bombardment from outside the harbour.[140]

As Penn writes, Captain Grant had no means of knowing that Fisher had been recalled to the Admiralty. Yet he turned to his second-in-command and said, 'Fisher wrote that telegram.'[141] Admiral Sturdee's squadron, which comprised four cruisers including *Cornwall* and *Defence* in addition to his battlecruisers, arrived at the Falklands on 7 December to await the approach of the Germans. Von Spee arrived in the early hours of the next day. At 9.00am the captain of *Gneisenau* spotted the tripod masts of *Inflexible* and *Invincible,* but he refused to believe that any battlecruisers could be in the South Atlantic (they were all thought to be in the North Sea or the Mediterranean), and continued on towards Port Stanley, which he intended to shell. An hour later *Canopus* opened fire. Von Spee ordered his ships to break off and retreat. But escape was impossible from the 26-knot battlecruisers, each armed with eight 12-inch guns, which outranged the German guns by 3000 yards. The German squadron was annihilated.

Scharnhorst, Gneisenau, Leipzig and *Nürnberg* were sunk with the loss of 2200 German lives. Only the fast light cruiser *Dresden* escaped. On the British side, one man was killed and three wounded on board *Invincible.* [142]

Coronel was the first naval defeat suffered by the Royal Navy in over a hundred years. The Falklands was hailed as the greatest and most significant naval victory since Trafalgar. As Marder writes: 'The sweeping victory wiped out the defeat of Coronel [and] raised the morale of the nation.' Bacon adds: 'the Falklands ... removed a grave menace to our trade in three oceans ... and gave renewed confidence to our Fleet and the Fleets of the Allies.'[143] Fittingly, the Falklands battle had been won by the brainchild of Fisher, and one of which he was particularly proud—the battlecruiser, the only heavily armed warship fast enough to arrive at the Falklands in time. Churchill acknowledged Fisher's triumph, writing to him:

> My dear,
>
> This was your show and your luck. I should only have sent one greyhound [battlecruiser] and *Defence.* This would have done the trick. But it was a great coup. Your flair is quite true. Let us have some more victories together and confound all our foes abroad—and (don't forget) at home.[144]

Even here, Bacon notes, Churchill's judgement was faulty. One battlecruiser may not have been enough. 'One lucky salvo [from the Germans] ... might have reversed the difference in strength as shown on paper.' It was not *flair* on Fisher's part that decided the issue, but rather the benefit of six decades of experience.[145] On Christmas Day Churchill wanted to trumpet the Admiralty's Falklands victory throughout the land, but Fisher cut him short, warning him that 'the murder of Cradock is best left alone—and you will also have to go back and explain similar past criminal follies also which time has eaten up. *Hawke, Cressy, Aboukir, Hogue, Pegasus* ... the *Goeben,* all will be resuscitated. So let your facile pen have a Christmas rest.'[146]

As a postscript to the Coronel disaster, in 1916 a memorial was unveiled to Rear Admiral Sir Christopher Cradock in York Minster. In his eulogy, Arthur Balfour, then First Lord of the Admiralty, delivered an entirely different appreciation of the admiral's actions to that presented by Churchill and Asquith in 1914. Balfour concluded by asking:

> What, then, was his design in attacking a force obviously greatly superior to his own ... Was it that he refused to count the risks? Such deeds of uncalculating daring make our blood tingle within us. Yet there is a higher wisdom than such calculation, and a higher courage than such daring, and that higher courage I believe Admiral Cradock to have possessed.

I think a satisfactory explanation can be given ... Remember what the circumstances of the German squadron were ... The German admiral was far from any port where he could have refitted ... If, therefore he suffered damage, even though ... he apparently inflicted greater damage than he received, yet his power for evil ... might suddenly, be destroyed. Admiral Cradock could only judge ... that his squadron, that he himself and those under him, were well sacrificed if they destroyed the power of this hostile fleet.

If I am right ... there never was a nobler act, unsuccessful though it was, than that which he performed off the coast of South America ... He and his gallant comrades lie far from their pleasant homes of England. Yet they have their reward, and we ... are surely right in saying that theirs is an immortal place in the great roll of naval heroes.[147]

By the end of 1914, after five months of fighting on the Western Front, Britain had lost 96,000 men killed or wounded, France 995,000 and Germany 667,000. It was apparent by now that, under the existing conditions, both the German and Allied lines were impregnable, and Britain's leaders thus began to cast about for an alternative for their troops to 'chew[ing] barbed wire in Flanders' (in Churchill's telling phrase).[148]

In view of subsequent events it is important to understand exactly what measures were proposed by Hankey, Lloyd George and Fisher at the beginning of January 1915 to make the best use of Kitchener's 100,000-strong New Armies (the first four divisions of which were expected to begin taking the field in mid-April 1915) in order to break the stalemate on the Western Front.[149]

Lloyd George's memorandum, circulated to the War Council on 1 January 1915, envisaged thinning out the German lines on the Western Front by opening up new fronts elsewhere. His plan called for 600,000 men to mount an attack on Austria from Salonika or some other part of the Adriatic coast. An essential aspect of the plan was to secure the cooperation of Serbia, Romania and Greece and also, hopefully, Italy. A subsidiary plan involved a landing on the Syrian coast (of 100,000 British troops) with the object of severing Turkey's communications with Egypt. Lloyd George placed 'utmost emphasis' on the fact that months of very careful preparation would be required for 'an enterprise of this kind'. He ended his memorandum, prophetically, with the warning that 'expeditions decided upon and organised with insufficient care and preparation generally end disastrously.'[150]

Hankey believed that his plan, as outlined in a memorandum of 28 December, did not differ considerably from Lloyd George's, but he thought 'it would first be necessary to open the Dardanelles. This was to be accomplished not by an attack on the Gallipoli Peninsula (the success of which I had doubted since my visit in 1907), but by offering an army to co-operate with the Balkan States, which had defeated Turkey shortly before the war, in an attack on their old enemy.'[151] Hankey pointed out that, in a few months' time, without endangering the position in France, Britain could devote three army corps (100,000 troops) which, in conjunction with the armies of 'Greece[200,000] and Bulgaria[300,000], ought to be sufficient to capture Constantinople. Once the Dardanelles was opened, my plan was almost identical with Lloyd George's, namely an attack on Austria in conjunction with Russia, Roumania and Serbia.'[152]

Lord Fisher, having read Hankey's and Lloyd George's memoranda, wrote a letter to Churchill on 3 January in which he said: 'I CONSIDER THE ATTACK ON TURKEY HOLDS THE FIELD! But ONLY if it's IMMEDIATE [Fisher's emphasis].' He then outlined a plan which called for the withdrawal of all the Indian troops (one army corps) together with 75,000 seasoned troops from Sir John French's command in France, replacing them with Territorials, and landing them at Besika Bay, to the south of the Dardanelles. This would follow closely on previous feints at Haifa and Alexandretta by troops drawn from Egypt. Simultaneously, a Greek army was to be induced to attack the Gallipoli Peninsula, a Bulgarian army to attack Constantinople, while the Russians, Serbians and Romanians were to concentrate on Austria-Hungary.

The Royal Navy, at the same time, was to force the Dardanelles using older battleships. Fisher concluded: 'But as the great Napoleon said "Celerity; without it Failure."' The following day Fisher wrote to Churchill: 'The naval advantages of the possession of Constantinople and the getting of wheat from the Black Sea are so overwhelming that I consider Hankey's plan for Turkish operations vital and imperative and very pressing.'[153]

It should be noted that an essential element of Hankey's, Lloyd George's and Fisher's plans was a *massive* military component, to be supplied largely by the Balkan States and assisted by at least 100,000 men of Kitchener's New Armies. The other essential was meticulous preparation and planning (on the naval, military and political fronts).

CHAPTER 2

The Original Deception(s), 3–28 January 1915

The means by which Winston Churchill was able to persuade Lord Kitchener, the Cabinet War Council, then Lord Fisher to pledge their support to a purely naval attack against the Dardanelles defences are of particular interest to this narrative.

Kitchener and Fisher, as the government's senior military and naval advisers, were convinced at the outset that an operation of this sort, by its very nature, could not succeed. In the final analysis, Kitchener was persuaded otherwise. Fisher remained obdurate throughout in his belief that Churchill's venture to the Dardanelles was doomed to failure. Yet he too could be persuaded to pledge his support.

The civilian War Councillors were simply the victims of a very clever deception.

The Russian Request for a Demonstration

On 2 January 1915 a telegram reached the Foreign Office in London containing an urgent appeal from the commander of the Russian Army, Grand Duke Nicholas, asking Lord Kitchener to mount a naval or military demonstration to draw Turkish forces away from the Caucasus, where his troops were under serious pressure.[1] It was vital that Britain's leaders respond favourably to such a direct request from the Russians at this time. By the end of December 1914 the Russian Army had lost some 1.8 million soldiers killed, wounded or taken prisoner.[2] From mid-November, British diplomats had begun receiving intelligence reports of German peace overtures to Russia, France and Belgium, designed to divide the Allies.[3] With the failure of the Schlieffen Plan, the Germans knew they could never hope to win a war on two fronts. In December 1914, German Chancellor Bethmann-Hollweg wrote that 'for us everything depends on shattering the [enemy] coalition, i.e. on [concluding] a separate peace with one of our enemies.'[4] If Russia could be persuaded to abandon the war, then the German army in the west, reinforced by around 26 divisions of their comrades (from the *Eighth* and *Ninth German armies)* released from the Eastern Front, would in all likelihood have completely overwhelmed the British, French and Belgian forces (as they very nearly did in the spring of 1918, just before the arrival of the Americans).[5]

Kitchener discussed the situation with Churchill at the Admiralty later in the day, stressing the point that a military demonstration was impossible as there was only one spare division available, the 29th. Any such demonstration would have to be naval. Kitchener then discussed the matter with his advisers at the War Office and wrote to Churchill, advising him that: 'We have no troops to land anywhere ... the only place that a demonstration might have some effect in stopping [Turkish] reinforcements going East would be at the Dardanelles—particularly if as the Grand Duke says reports could be spread at the same time that Constantinople was threatened ... We shall not be ready for anything big for some months.'[6] The following day Kitchener sent a telegram to Petrograd (St Petersburg) which stated: 'Please assure the Grand Duke that steps will be taken to make a demonstration against the Turks. It is, however, feared that any action we can devise and carry out will be unlikely to seriously affect numbers of enemy in the Caucasus, or cause their withdrawal.'[7] As Churchill subsequently wrote in *The World Crisis,* '[t]his telegram committed us to a demonstration against the Turks of some kind, but it did not commit us in respect of its direction, character or scope.'[8]

In January 1915 Winston Churchill was in desperate need of a spectacular naval victory (for which he alone could claim the credit) in order to restore his battered reputation with the British press and public. As Hankey recorded two months later: 'In my own belief, Churchill wanted to bring off the coup [at the Dardanelles] by Navy alone to rehabilitate his reputation.'[9] Churchill's deception began on 3 January when he extracted part of Fisher's ambitious plan for an attack against Turkey (namely, the use of older battleships to force the Dardanelles) and sent the following telegram to Vice Admiral Carden, Commander-in-Chief of the Mediterranean Fleet:

> Do you consider the forcing of the Dardanelles by ships alone a practicable operation? It is assumed that older battleships fitted with mine bumpers would be used preceded by colliers or other merchant craft as bumpers and sweepers. Importance of the results would justify severe loss. Let me know your views.[10]

Churchill admitted to the Dardanelles Commission in 1916 that this telegram was deliberately phrased so as to elicit a positive response, 'that action, if possible, would be very desirable [and] ... that we should have been very glad if he had a good plan.'[11] Dr Prior suggests that a certain measure of coercion may have been applied by Churchill. After all, 'if severe losses are justified what commander would admit that the operation should not be attempted?'[12] Even so, there was little enthusiasm in Carden's cautious reply, which was about as non-committal as honour decently permitted. His reply telegram on the 5th stated: 'I do not think that the Dardanelles can be rushed, but they might be forced by extended operations with a large number of ships.'[13] It could be argued that, given sufficient time and matériel, anything might be possible. Nevertheless, Churchill later wrote that '[This reply] was *remarkable.* '[14] On the afternoon of 5

January, according to Churchill in *The World Crisis,* a meeting of the War Council took place, at which: ...

> ... the question of an attack on Turkey and a diversion in the Near East was one of the principal subjects discussed. Everyone seemed alive to all its advantages, and Admiral Carden's telegram, which I read out, was heard with extreme interest. Its significance lay in the fact that it offered a prospect of influencing the Eastern situation in a decisive manner without opening a new military commitment on a large scale; and further it afforded an effective means of helping the Grand Duke without wasting the Dardanelles possibilities upon nothing more than a demonstration.[15]

This is pure fabrication. There was no meeting of the War Council on 5 January 1915. The next meeting, after that held on 16 December 1914 (convened to discuss home defence), was held on 7 January 1915, at which no mention was made of an attack on Turkey, nor of Carden's telegram. Churchill's official biographer, Martin Gilbert, takes this fiction even further, writing:

> When Carden's reply arrived early on the afternoon of January 5 it surprised everyone at the Admiralty, including Churchill and Fisher; for Carden declared that he might be able to force the Dardanelles by ships alone ...

> The War Council met late that afternoon ... Kitchener pressed his colleagues for action at the Dardanelles. Churchill was able to give some support to Kitchener's appeal by reading out to the War Council the telegram which he had received from Carden an hour before ... On the following afternoon, January 6, supported by the specific enthusiasm of Oliver and Jackson, sustained by the desire of Kitchener and the War Council to follow this slim opportunity ... Churchill telegraphed Carden.[16]

But no such War Council meeting had ever taken place. Consequently, Churchill had never been given any authorisation from the War Council, nor any specific encouragement from Kitchener, Oliver and Jackson to contact Carden and proceed with his scheme the following day. This was entirely his own idea.

I find it curious that Churchill's fabrication has never been discussed by any military or naval historian to date, despite the printed War Council 'Secretary's Notes of all Meetings' (CAB 22/1), and Minutes of the same on microfilm (CAB 42/1) having been on open access for public scrutiny at The National Archives, Kew, since 1966. Political historian Lynn Curtright alerted me to this fiction in her book *Muddle, Indecision and Setback.* [17] Like some other instances of deception on Churchill's part, it has been largely overlooked in recent historical literature.

Churchill replied to Carden the following day, 6 January, in a telegram which read: 'First Lord to Admiral Carden. Secret and Personal. Your view is agreed by high authorities here. Please telegraph in detail what you think could be done by extended operations, what force would be needed, and how you consider it should be used.'[18] It should be noted that Carden's true assessment of the situation, which he would share with his successor, Vice Admiral de Robeck, two months later, was that large-scale military support was essential for any chance of a successful forcing of the Dardanelles.[19]

Carden explained to the Dardanelles Commission that, when he was informed (by Churchill) that 'high authorities' at the Admiralty favoured this radical, purely naval operation, he naturally assumed this referred to First Sea Lord Fisher and/or Chief Planning Officer Sir Henry Jackson.[20] In fact, both Fisher and Jackson were vehemently opposed to any such concept. When asked by the Dardanelles Commissioners, 'Did you think [an attempt to force the Dardanelles by the Fleet alone] a feasible operation?' Jackson replied, 'No, I never did; I wrote that quite plainly.' When questioned further on why then he had recommended a naval bombardment of the outer forts, Jackson replied: 'Because we wanted to be able to watch the exit and entrance of the Dardanelles, as we were blockading Turkey.'[21]

Lord Fisher told the Commissioners that he never saw Churchill's reply telegram (of 6 January) to Carden, and if he had, he 'should have objected ... [and] asked him (Mr. Churchill) to word it in some other way. Naturally, Carden would think I was in it, would he not?'[22] By 'high authorities', Churchill advised the Commissioners, he meant Sir Henry Jackson and Admiral Oliver, Chief of the Naval Staff.[23] On 3 January, the day he sent the first telegram to Carden, Churchill had asked Jackson to write a feasibility study on the forcing of the Dardanelles by ships alone. Jackson, in fact, wrote two appraisals. In a brief note which Churchill may well have seen the same day, Jackson explained that any benefits the ships may have won by forcing the Straits alone 'would be small & of a very temporary nature in the absence of large [Allied] land forces to confirm the success, & at present no troops are available for the enterprise.'[24] In a more detailed five-page memorandum which he gave to Churchill on 5 January, Jackson left the First Lord in no doubt of the necessity for large-scale military assistance to silence the enemy shore batteries in the proposed naval operation:

> [An Allied fleet] might dominate [Constantinople] and inflict enormous damage, [but] their position would not be an enviable one, unless there were a large [Allied] military force to occupy the town ... To arrive off Constantinople with depleted magazines and ships almost out of action from gun fire, and with shore batteries still intact both in front and rear, would be a *fatal error,* and tend to annul the effect of the appearance of the

squadron, as soon as its real state was known [italics added].[25]

Jackson told the Dardanelles Commission in 1916 that 'he had "always stuck" to this memorandum [of 5 January]: "that it would be a very mad thing to try and get into the Sea of Marmora without having the Gallipoli Peninsula held by our own troops or every [enemy] gun on both sides of the Straits destroyed." He had never changed that opinion and he had never given any one any reason to think he had.' The Dardanelles Commissioners noted that Churchill had neglected to circulate Jackson's 5 January memorandum to the members of the War Council.[26] Alone of all the major figures at the Admiralty, Oliver seems to have offered some kind of support to Churchill's plan, lukewarm though that may have been. Oliver had been most impressed by the effects of the 17-inch siege howitzers employed by the Germans against the Belgian forts at Liège and Namur in September 1914. He also shared Jackson's interest in the destruction of the outer forts at the Dardanelles. Oliver told the Dardanelles Commission that 'his opinion was always that we might go a certain length by naval attack but it would depend on [enemy resistance] how far we would go ... He would have preferred [waiting, however], to make a big attempt with Army and Navy.'[27]

Churchill's 6 January 'Secret and Personal from First Lord' telegram to Carden was his first use of a device which he would subsequently employ to devastating effect in order to circumvent and usurp Admiralty authority, substituting his own—to the growing frustration and fury of Lord Fisher.[28] As naval historian Captain Geoffrey Penn points out: 'Such messages should have been from "Admiralty", implying Board approval. But Churchill's wording was authoritative and compelling; an admiral would regard it as a directive, to be disobeyed at his peril.' Admiral Bacon adds that the Commander-in-Chief of the Grand Fleet, Admiral Sir John Jellicoe, became suspicious of Churchill's messages to him at sea, and arranged a code with Fisher whereby he could telegraph the First Sea Lord personally for his confirmation of Churchill's 'directives' before acting on them.[29]

Between 3 and 13 January Fisher had little to do with the Dardanelles enterprise. As he told the Commissioners: 'He "was instinctively against it" and … more or less left it alone.' What had been promised the Grand Duke was simply a demonstration so there was no need for Fisher to become personally involved. 'Sir Henry Jackson was a very able man and so was Admiral Oliver, and he [Fisher] more or less stood aside [although] he backed it up in every possible way as far as executive work was concerned.'[30]

Expert Opinion on the Naval Attack

On 11 January Carden's plan for the forcing of the Dardanelles by ships alone arrived at the Admiralty.

Churchill claimed in *The World Crisis* that 'this plan produced a great impression upon everyone who saw it. It was to me in its details an entirely novel proposition ... We all felt ourselves in the presence of a new fact.'[31] Dr Robin Prior, on the other hand, asserts that 'Carden's plan is seen to be hardly a plan at all but merely a statement of the order in which the Dardanelles defences were to be reduced', with sketchy details as to how this was to be achieved. 'The problems of the Turkish field guns and the minefields were scarcely mentioned.' Naval historian Professor Arthur Marder was even more scathing in his criticism, stating that Carden's proposals were 'unworthy to be dignified as a "plan" ... they might have been applied to any enterprise anywhere from an attack on a Norman keep to a landing in Timbuctoo.'[32]

Throughout most of January, according to Churchill in *The World Crisis,* opinion at the Admiralty was universally in favour of the Dardanelles venture:

> Both the First Sea Lord and the Chief of Staff seemed favourable to it. No one, at any time threw the slightest doubt upon its technical soundness. No one, for instance, of the four or five great naval authorities each with his technical staff, who were privy, said, "This is absurd. Ships cannot fight forts", or criticised its details. On the contrary, they all treated it as an extremely interesting and hopeful proposal, and there grew

up in the secret circles of the Admiralty a perfectly clear opinion favourable to the operation.[33]

In reality, this was precisely what all the experts did say—that the idea *was* absurd, and that ships, unaided by a large military force, *cannot* fight forts—but to no avail. Churchill seems to have studiously avoided all the negative expert opinion (naval and military) of his scheme at this time—particularly with regard to perhaps its most important aspect. Asked by the Dardanelles Commissioners '[w]as any gunnery expert at the Admiralty consulted about the effect of [naval] gunfire on the forts?' Churchill replied: 'Oh, yes I am sure it was so. The Chief of Staff [Oliver] who produced the plan is responsible that all these gunnery aspects have been investigated.'[34]

In fact, none of the Admiralty's gunnery experts was consulted. Rear Admiral Morgan Singer, DNO, when asked: 'Were you consulted about the naval expedition to the Dardanelles...?' answered: 'No.' When further asked: 'If you had been asked would you have opposed it?' he replied, 'Certainly!'[35] Former DNO, Vice Admiral Bacon, who held a similar viewpoint, was similarly not consulted. Neither was former DNO, Third Sea Lord, Rear Admiral Tudor. Tudor told the Commissioners that sometime in early January he was in the First Lord's room and had told him: 'I have heard some rumours about [the naval operation to the Dardanelles]', adding, 'Well you won't do it with ships alone.' Churchill had replied: '"Oh yes we will."

I shrugged my shoulders and said, "Well if you are going to do it with ships it will be a very long and difficult business."'[36] The Navy's top gunnery expert, Admiral Sir Percy Scott, *was* consulted by Churchill, on 13 January. Admiral Jellicoe's expertise was not sought (even though Churchill regularly corresponded with the Commander-in-Chief, Grand Fleet). As Jellicoe wrote to Second Sea Lord, Admiral Hamilton, on 29 November 1915:

> My opinion on this [Dardanelles] scheme was never invited [by Churchill, because] ... I certainly expressed a strong opinion that as a purely naval operation it was most unsound. The idea that naval guns could so silence the Dardanelles forts as to admit the passage of a Fleet through minefields ... was inconceivable to me, and I did not hesitate to say so. There was a further problem ... unless the Gallipoli Peninsula was occupied and strongly held by [our] troops, it was obvious that the passage of those necessary vessels [colliers and unarmoured supply ships] could be prevented by even field guns firing from the mainland.[37]

Churchill was already familiar with the attitude of the military towards his plan. On 31 August 1914 he had asked the General Staff, in conjunction with two officers from the Admiralty, to examine 'a plan for the seizure of the Gallipoli Peninsula, by means of a Greek army of adequate strength, with a view to admitting a British fleet to the Sea of Marmara.' Director of Military Operations, Major General Sir Charles Callwell, submitted his report on 1 September (his prior knowledge of this subject making this 'a simple task for me'). Callwell found that, 'Considering the strength of the Turkish Garrison & large force already mobilised in European Turkey [around 200,000 troops], he did not regard it as a feasible operation.'[38]

Callwell was asked by Churchill to return to the Admiralty on 2 September for further talks, when 'the matter was thrashed out again'. Callwell subsequently submitted a second report the following day which conceded that, on the basis that the peninsula was garrisoned by about 27,000 Turks, with further reinforcements at hand, a force of no fewer than 60,000 would be required to effect its capture. Nevertheless, Callwell stressed, such an attack 'is likely to prove an extremely difficult operation of war'.[39]

Martin Gilbert posed the inevitable question of 'how far Churchill had prevailed upon Callwell to reverse his opinion, by the weight of evidence, [and] how far by an assertion of his authority.' Gilbert also points out that, in *The World Crisis,* Churchill cited Callwell's report of 3 September, but 'made no reference to their meeting on the previous day, nor of Callwell's abrupt change of mind.'[40] However, neither Churchill nor Gilbert made any reference to Churchill's third meeting with Callwell. One morning in late October 1914 (a few days before the resignation of Prince

Louis as First Sea Lord on the 28th), Churchill sent a message to Callwell asking him 'to come over to his room and discuss possibilities in connection with the Dardanelles.' Callwell later recalled:

> I found the First Sea Lord and Fourth Sea Lord waiting, as was Mr. Churchill, and we sat round a table with all the maps and charts necessary for our purpose spread on it. The problem of mastering the straits was examined entirely from the point of view of a military operation based upon, and supported by, naval power. If the question of a fleet attack upon the defences ... was mentioned at all, it was only referred to quite incidentally ... By far the best plan of gaining possession of [the Kilid Bahr Plateau] would, I considered be to land, by surprise if possible, the biggest military force that could be very rapidly put ashore ... about the locality that has since been immortalized as Anzac Cove.
>
> I pointed out the difficulties and dangers involved, i.e. the virtual impossibility of effecting a real surprise ... and the fact that, at the moment we had no troops to carry such a scheme out ... My exposition was intended to be dissuasive, and I think that Mr. Churchill was disappointed ... The story of this informal pow-wow has been recorded thus at length, because it was really the only occasion on which the General Staff was afforded anything like a proper opportunity of expressing

an opinion as to operations against the Dardanelles, until after the country had been engulfed up to the neck in the morass ...

[Callwell added:] Had the three eminent naval experts who dealt with the project and who ... were by no means enthusiastic about it [Admirals Lord Fisher, Sir Henry Jackson and Sir Arthur Wilson] met three representatives of the General Staff, Sir J. Wolfe-Murray, General Kiggell and myself, let us say, sitting around a table with no Cabinet Ministers present, I am certain that the report that we should have drawn up would have been dead against the whole thing.[41]

But Churchill was well aware of this situation. As Home Secretary, in 1911 he had informed the Cabinet, 'that it is no longer possible to force the Dardanelles, and nobody would expose a modern fleet to such peril'.[42] And as recently as 25 November 1914, he had told a War Council meeting that 'the ideal method of defending Egypt was by an attack on the Gallipoli Peninsula. This, if successful, would give us control of the Dardanelles, and we could dictate terms at Constantinople. This, however, was a very difficult operation requiring a large [military] force.'[43]

The Dardanelles Commissioners found that Fisher's attitude towards the proposed Dardanelles operation was common knowledge. 'Lord Fisher', they noted, 'in fact, like all other experts, both naval and military, was in favour of a combined attack, but not of action by the Fleet alone. It is certain that, from the very first, he disliked the purely naval operation.'[44] War Council Secretary Hankey wrote to Arthur Balfour on 10 February stressing (underlining in red pencil) the fact: 'From Lord Fisher downwards every naval officer in the Admiralty believes that the Navy cannot take the Dardanelles position without troops. The First Lord still professes to believe that they can do it with ships, but I have warned the Prime Minister that we cannot trust to this.'[45]

In December 1906 the First Sea Lord, Admiral Fisher, had represented the Royal Navy in a General Staff-Admiralty investigation into the possibility of forcing the Dardanelles in any conflict between Britain and Turkey. Major General Callwell was the General Staff's representative. The conclusions of this enquiry, which were endorsed by the CID in February 1907, found that a purely naval attempt should not be undertaken under any circumstances, as 'military cooperation was essential for success'. The General Staff 'was then [in fact], opposed to any naval or military action at the Dardanelles'. Admiral Fisher concurred, adding that 'even with military cooperation the operation was mightily hazardous.'[46]

At a meeting of the War Council on 8 January 1915, Lloyd George asked: 'Was there no alternative theatre [to the Western Front] in which we might employ our surplus armies [when they became available from May onwards]?' Kitchener anticipated Churchill's subsequent proposal by stating:

> The Dardanelles appeared the most suitable objective, as an attack there could be made in cooperation with the Fleet. If successful, it would re-establish communications with Russia; settle the Near East question, draw in Greece and, perhaps Bulgaria and Roumania; and release wheat and shipping now locked up in the Black Sea.

Kitchener estimated that 150,000 troops might be sufficient for the capture of the Gallipoli Peninsula, but he reserved his final opinion until a closer study had been made. Lloyd George 'expressed surprise at the lowness of the figure'.[47] Kitchener thus indicated that he was fully aware of the possible benefits of a successful Dardanelles operation, which had been placed on the agenda for future consideration. He also indicated that he was well aware of the need for thorough planning and preparation before any such venture was undertaken.

On the eve of the 13 January War Council meeting, Kitchener was called to a conference with Churchill (presumably in Churchill's room). Kitchener's Private Secretary, Sir George Arthur, was unsure of the date, but the surrounding circumstances dictate that this could only have been on 12 January 1915 (Kitchener was unable to provide a later account, having been drowned when the *Hampshire* struck a mine on 5 June 1916). Sir George Arthur related the details of this meeting to the Dardanelles Commission on 1 December 1916, preceding his evidence with the statement: 'Lord Kitchener told me, and told me very distinctly':

> ... that at the conference to which he was invited by the First Lord of the Admiralty, when the passage of the Dardanelles was the subject of discussion [Kitchener] protested vigorously against any such undertaking by the Navy without very strong and carefully prepared support from and cooperation with the Army. [Churchill] replied that, although this protest was well founded on experience and military knowledge, it was no longer admissible by reason of the marvellous potentialities of the "Queen Elizabeth", [which] rendered a task hitherto impossible now comparatively easy, or at any rate, wholly practicable.[48]

Queen Elizabeth, which was about to be sent to the Dardanelles, carried eight 15-inch guns, the largest naval guns in the world at that time. Churchill had rejected Kitchener's 'protest' and 'inevitable uneasiness' by asserting that the Secretary of State for War neither 'understood or appreciated at anything like their full value the destructive powers of this new vessel ... which the First Lord had alleged would revolutionise all previous estimates of naval warfare.'[49]

Sir George's statement was independently corroborated by Major General Callwell in 1920:

The chief [Kitchener] always claimed to have been led astray by Mr. Churchill concerning the potentialities of the *Queen Elizabeth* ... Lord Kitchener sent for me one morning ... "They've rammed that ship down my throat", said he in effect. "Churchill told me in the first place that she would knock all the Dardanelles batteries into smithereens, firing from goodness knows where. He afterwards told me she would make everything all right for the troops as they landed and after they landed." [Callwell continued:] Now there was no question of the *Queen Elizabeth* being a most powerful ship of war, but the fact is ... Mr. Churchill had somehow persuaded himself, and what is worse, he had managed to persuade Lord Kitchener as well as Mr. Asquith and others, that she would just about settle the Dardanelles business off her own bat.[50]

Sir George's statement was further corroborated by Major General Sir Stanley von Donop, Master-General of the Ordnance, and H.J. Creedy, Kitchener's Departmental Secretary (in their evidence to the Dardanelles Commission), to whom Kitchener had confided similar concerns regarding Churchill's claims in February 1915.[51] Kitchener confirmed Sir George's statement himself (from the grave) in an angry tirade to the War Council on 14 May 1915 when he complained bitterly of having been misled as to the *Queen Elizabeth's* firepower and the role she was to perform at the Dardanelles.[52]

The 13 January War Council Meeting

From 3 to 12 January 1915, it was a *demonstration* only (that is, a show of force with no intention of follow-up action) that was promised to the Grand Duke. By its very nature this could not result in a disaster of any kind. Indeed, by this time even the need for a demonstration had passed. On 6 January Reuters published news of a massive Russian victory over the Turks in the Caucasus.[53] Nevertheless, a promise had been made by the British government to a sorely needed ally and this could not be ignored. Lord Fisher was thus committed to supporting the government on a matter of 'high policy'. In that context, on 12 January Fisher gave orders for Britain's newly commissioned battleship, *Queen Elizabeth,* to conduct her gunnery trials at the Dardanelles, 'firing all her ammunition at the Dardanelles forts instead of uselessly into the sea at Gibraltar'.[54]

Between 13 and 28 January the concept of a demonstration at the Dardanelles was transformed by Winston Churchill into a far more ambitious undertaking. The means by which this was accomplished was subsequently described by Lord Fisher in his own inimitable style:

> A MIASMA brought about the Dardanelles Adventure ... A Miasma like the scentless, poisonous—deadly poisonous—gas, imperceptibly to each of them in the War Council, floated down

on them with rare subtle dialectical skill, and proved so incontestably to them that cutting off the enemy's big toe in the East was better than stabbing him to the heart in the West.[55]

The eighth meeting of the War Council was held on 13 January. This Cabinet War Committee was a most unsatisfactory arrangement and would be replaced in June 1915 by the Dardanelles Committee, but with scarcely any demonstrable improvement. Britain's peacetime defence requirements had been under the supervision of the CID since its inception in 1904. With the appointment of Captain Maurice Hankey as Secretary in 1912 this organisation had been brought to a peak of efficiency. The agenda of meetings, which were held on a regular basis, was sent out to all Ministers and Departmental Heads concerned beforehand as well as to invited experts, with researched memoranda on the various topics provided. Detailed minutes of these meetings were recorded by assistant secretaries. After being actioned by the appropriate department, all papers were filed as officially secret documents, 'The Property of His Britannic Majesty's Government'.[56]

With the outbreak of war, a Cabinet Committee—the War Council—took over responsibility for the direction of Britain's war effort from the CID, which remained in existence providing sub-committees to examine various topics. There were a number of significant differences between the CID and the War Council.

First, the CID was merely an advisory body to the 22-man Cabinet, possessing no executive powers. In addition, invited experts were encouraged to speak out on their particular areas of expertise. When Lord Fisher attended CID meetings 'he had joined in all the discussions', freely, as was expected of all expert advisers.[57]

More significantly, whereas CID meetings were held within the precincts of the Defence Department at 2 Westminster Gardens, War Council meetings were held at 10 Downing Street along normal Cabinet lines and, following a centuries-old tradition, Cabinet proceedings did not adhere to any set agenda.[58] No-one, consequently, had any precise idea of what was to be discussed. But perhaps the War Council's greatest failing, as Hankey noted, was that matters were seldom investigated in any great depth. Rather, ministers aired their views at length, discoursing on all manner of related topics until conversation was exhausted, at which point the chairman/Prime Minister wound up the meeting.[59] Again, following tradition, the only records kept of these proceedings were the conclusions decided on by the chairman, which may or may not have been read out at the close, plus a brief note the Prime Minister wrote afterwards for the advice of the King. As a consequence, very often members left these meetings with 'a very indistinct idea' of what had been decided, or indeed, whether 'any decisions [had] been arrived at all'.[60]

The War Council, which met at irregular intervals, sometimes weeks apart, initially consisted of seven members. A triumvirate of Prime Minister Asquith, Secretary of State for War Kitchener and First Lord of the Admiralty Churchill came to dominate proceedings, assisted by Lloyd George (Chancellor of the Exchequer), Sir Edward Grey (Foreign Secretary), Lord Crewe (Secretary for India) and Viscount Haldane (Lord Chancellor). By January 1915, the War Council had grown to 11 members with the addition of Arthur Balfour (former Conservative Prime Minister), Lord Fisher, Admiral Sir Arthur Wilson, VC, and Lieutenant General Sir James Wolfe Murray (CIGS).[61] Other interested parties, for example, Lord French, also sometimes attended. As the Dardanelles Commissioners noted, the War Council assumed executive authority, making decisions which were subsequently passed on to the full Cabinet for belated approval.[62]

Significantly, however, as the War Council was a Cabinet body, the Army and Navy experts (Wolfe Murray, Fisher and Wilson), were not expected to speak out unless their viewpoint was specifically requested by a minister.[63] As Lord Crewe observed: 'The political members did too much of the talking and the expert advisers too little.'[64] One fortunate bonus was the appointment of Lieutenant Colonel Hankey (as he now was) as War Council Secretary. Hankey, on his own initiative, kept an unofficial record of all proceedings in longhand notes which would prove invaluable to the Dardanelles Commission.[65] This, then, was the setting for one of Churchill's most memorable performances. His presentation of Carden's plan to the War Council (which, incidentally, in *The World Crisis* he claimed to have already delivered on 5 January) was masterly in its timing and delivery.[66] Hankey recorded the scene:

> The meeting now seemed to be drawing to an end. The War Council had been sitting all day. The blinds had been drawn to shut out the winter evening. The air was heavy and the table presented that rather dishevelled appearance that results from a long session. I was looking forward to release from the strain of following and noting the prolonged and intense discussion. I suppose the councillors were as weary as I was. At this point events took a dramatic turn, for Churchill suddenly revealed his well-kept secret of a naval attack on the Dardanelles! The idea caught on at once. The whole atmosphere changed. Fatigue was forgotten. The War Council turned eagerly from the dreary vista of a "slogging match" on the Western Front to brighter prospects, as they seemed, in the Mediterranean. The Navy, in whom everyone had implicit confidence and whose opportunities had so far been few and far between, was to come into the front line ...
>
> Churchill unfolded his plans with the skill that might be expected of him, lucidly but quietly and without exaggerated optimism. He told the

councillors how: "He had been interchanging telegrams with Carden", who had proposed a scheme for the destruction of the old Turkish forts at the Dardanelles by battleships and battle-cruisers of the Royal Navy. The First Lord had added that: "The Admiralty were studying the question, and believed that a plan could be made for systematically reducing the forts within a few weeks. Once the forts were reduced the minefields would be cleared, and the fleet would proceed up to Constantinople and destroy the *Goeben.* They would have nothing to fear from field guns and rifles, which would be merely an inconvenience."[67]

Kitchener, with Churchill's vision of an all-destroying *Queen Elizabeth* vivid in his mind, thought it 'worth trying' adding, 'We could leave off the bombardment if it did not prove effective.' Kitchener had earlier told the War Council that no spare troops 'were then available for action against Turkey; [that] every man who could be mustered was needed on the Western Front.'[68] No-one had challenged him on this statement. Throughout Churchill's peroration, and afterwards, Lord Fisher and Admiral Wilson sat silent. Neither had been asked for his opinion, so they had little choice. The Councillors naturally assumed that the First Lord was presenting the expert viewpoint of the Admiralty staff—which was most decidedly not the case. In fact, as Dr Prior observes, with Jackson's memorandum of only eight days earlier (which laid primacy on large-scale troop support) still clear in his mind, 'Churchill *must* have been aware of this need, and it seems possible that he *deliberately* concealed this fact from his [War

Council] colleagues in order to get his operation accepted.'[69] (Indeed, Churchill would rely on essentially this same Jackson memorandum on 16 February to demand large-scale military assistance from Kitchener.) Churchill would subsequently claim that Kitchener was entirely responsible for the resultant disaster through his refusal to supply the necessary troops until it was too late. He would further claim that everyone would have preferred a joint military and naval attack at the outset, but had to settle for this inferior naval attack through Kitchener's intransigence. This explanation would be accepted by the Dardanelles Commission.[70] Sir Edward Grey was Foreign Secretary and a War Council member on 13 January. His unblemished reputation, unlike that of Churchill and Asquith, was not placed at risk by the Dardanelles fiasco, and he consequently had no reason to withhold or distort any of the facts surrounding this fateful meeting. As he recalled in his memoirs:

> My recollection is very clear that the attack on the Dardanelles was agreed to on the express condition that it should be a naval operation only; it was under no circumstances to involve the use of troops. The British and French armies were at death's grip with the Germans on the Western Front, the situation was critical for the Allies, and

it was important that there should be no diversion of force to other parts of the world, except under the pressure of absolute necessity. If the attack on the Dardanelles did not succeed, it was to be treated as a naval demonstration and abandoned. It was on this condition only that Kitchener agreed to it. Grey then added a footnote:

It is said that the operation on the Dardanelles should have been planned from the first as a joint military and naval operation. It will be apparent from what has been said here, that if this had been proposed the operation would never have been agreed to.[71]

The major attraction of Churchill's plan to the War Councillors and to Kitchener lay in his insistence that troops were neither needed nor wanted—the fleet would do the job alone. Any misgivings Kitchener may have had were thus assuaged within the illusion of *Queen Elizabeth*'s awesome destructive powers, and the knowledge that the naval attack *would* be abandoned, should any serious difficulties be encountered, reverting merely to the demonstration requested by the Grand Duke. Indeed, as Sir Edward Grey noted, Kitchener was instrumental in ensuring that this precondition was included.

Arthur Balfour wrote in September 1915 that 'Churchill would not have tolerated for a moment the independent examination of the First Sea Lord by a member of the War Council.'[72] This may explain in part the disinclination of the War Councillors to question the naval experts on any aspect of the proposed naval operation, leaving them with only the First Lord's sanguine (and fallacious) appraisal. Incidentally, the Turkish field guns, which Churchill assured the War Councillors would be 'merely an inconvenience', would prove responsible for the crippling of three battleships (*Gaulois, Suffren* and *Agamemnon)* as well as severe damage to the battlecruiser *Inflexible* (see Chapter 3).

After some desultory conversation Asquith wound up the proceedings, reading aloud four conclusions. Among these it had been decided:

> ... that the Admiralty should also prepare for a naval expedition in February to bombard and take the Gallipoli Peninsula, with Constantinople as its objective. Also, that if the position in the Western theatre becomes in the spring one of stalemate, British troops should be despatched to another theatre and objective, and that adequate investigation and preparation should be undertaken with that purpose, and that a Sub-Committee of the [CID] be appointed to deal with this ... situation.[73]

Closure of the meeting was attended by a certain measure of customary confusion—and not only in the quaint wording of the conclusion. It has never been satisfactorily explained just how any fleet could be expected to capture a peninsula, and then subdue a city the size of Constantinople. Most of the Councillors had different perceptions as to what had actually been decided. Chairman Asquith believed that the decision had been 'merely provisional, to prepare, but nothing more'. Lord Crewe and other Councillors understood that the operation 'was approved subject to the occurrence of any unforeseen events which might have made it ... unnecessary.' Commodore de Bartolomé subsequently said that 'my impression was always that the naval members ... only agreed to a purely naval operation on the understanding that we could always draw back—that there should be no question of what is known as forcing the Dardanelles.' Admirals Jackson and Oliver believed the War Council had only sanctioned a 'probing action'.[74]

'Lord Fisher and Admiral Wilson', as the official military historian recorded, 'left the meeting before the conclusions were read out, and were unaware that anything definite had been settled.'[75] But as far as Winston Churchill was concerned, his naval operation had been officially sanctioned. *Immediately* after the War Council meeting he issued a minute to the Chief of Staff, Oliver (which, incidentally, was not seen and initialled by Fisher until two days later). This reads:

Secretary.

First Sea Lord. (initd) "F", [for Fisher] 15.1.15 (received and sent on same date).

January 13. 1915.

Chief of Staff.

In future, the Mediterranean plan discussed today will always be referred to as "Pola" [the name of the Austrian naval base in the Adriatic]

[Then follows nine more paragraphs of detailed orders, which include the following instructions:]

4. The orders for concentrating the Fleet required cannot be delayed. *It is not necessary to delay the preliminary bombardment* of the entrance until all the ships have arrived; but the ships should start for the Mediterranean ports *at once...*

9. Admiral Carden's proposals should be carefully analysed by an officer of the War Staff in order to show exactly what guns the ships will have to face at each point and stage of these operations, the character of the guns, and their range; *but this officer is to assume that the principle is settled, and all that is necessary is to estimate the force required.*

10. *This enterprise is regarded by the Government as of the highest urgency and importance* [italics added].[76]

It scarcely needs pointing out that Churchill was overstepping the accepted practice of First Lord and usurping the role of First Sea Lord, as well as that of the Admiralty War Staff and Naval Operations. He possessed neither the training nor the expertise to assume responsibility for the planning of a naval operation of this magnitude. His role, as First Lord of the Admiralty, required him to lay down matters of naval policy, as decided by Cabinet, to be translated into action by the Admiralty staff. As Captain Penn observes, Churchill's behaviour 'was comparable to a modern Health Minister telling surgeons how to perform an operation.'[77]

Of this minute, Churchill wrote in *The World Crisis*: 'In full harmony with the Chief of Staff and with the steady and *written concurrence* of Lord Fisher, I issued the following minutes.' These include the previously mentioned 13 January minute, plus another, detailing a list of instructions issued to the DNO on 15 January concerning the ammunition requirements for the Dardanelles operation.[78] It should be borne in mind that, as Penn points out, in naval practice 'the mere initialling of a document did not equate to concurrence' as Churchill implies. Concurrence demanded a positive statement to that effect. Fisher's initialling of a particular document signified only that he had sighted it—not that he agreed with its contents. Sir Henry Jackson clarified this point in his comments on Carden's 'plan'.[79]

It should also be remembered that Fisher had no knowledge of any decision made by the War Council, having left the meeting before the end. Also, as no official record was kept of those proceedings at this time, he had to accept Churchill's word that such a decision, 'regarded by the Government as of the highest urgency and importance', had been made. Shortly after completing his minute to Oliver, Churchill summoned the Royal Navy's top gunnery expert, Admiral Sir Percy Scott, to his room. Scott recalled that meeting four years later:

> On the 13th January, 1915, I was sent for by the First Lord (Mr. Winston Churchill) and he told me that H.M.S *Queen Elizabeth* was going out to the Dardanelles, that the Navy was going to smash all the forts and go through to Constantinople, and that I could go in command. I could not accept the offer as I knew it was an impossible task for the inefficient ships then in the Mediterranean to perform.[80]

No mention of this incident appears in *The World Crisis.* Two entirely distinct and disparate versions of the events between 13 and 28 January have been passed down to the reading public: the Churchill version, and that revealed by the primary source evidence now available. According to the Churchill version:

> Up to January 20th there seemed to be *unanimous agreement in favour of the naval enterprise against the Dardanelles* ... The War Council had taken its decision.

It is true it was not a final or irrevocable decision. It authorised and encouraged the Admiralty to survey their resources and develop their plans. If these plans broke down in preparation, it would be quite easy for us to report the fact to the War Council and go no farther. But staff work continued to progress smoothly, and *all the Admirals concerned appeared in complete accord. It was not until the end of January,* when negotiations with the French and Russian Governments were far advanced ... that Lord Fisher *began* to manifest an increasing dislike and opposition to the scheme.[81]

Sir Julian Corbett, the official naval historian of the Dardanelles campaign, had a somewhat different appreciation of the situation, writing:

So long as it was a mere question of a demonstration to relieve pressure on the Russian Caucasus Front, the First Sea Lord had not a word to say against the fleet trying to do its best alone. He even ... proposed that the *Queen Elizabeth,* which was under orders to do her gunnery at Gibraltar, might as well spend the ammunition on the Dardanelles forts. But when the enterprise began to take on the aspect of a serious attempt to force the Straits, and reduce Constantinople, without military co-operation, he began to contemplate it each day with graver apprehension.[82]

Hankey, Asquith and Balfour were well aware that Fisher's dilemma began much earlier than Churchill claims—immediately after the 13 January War Council meeting, in fact. As Hankey recorded on 28 January:

> I was perfectly aware of Fisher's attitude. During the previous fortnight [that is, from 14 January onwards], he had paid me several visits, usually early, just after my arrival at the office and had poured out all his grievances. All my efforts had been directed towards inducing him to speak out his mind at the War Council. Asquith in his diary describes my report to him on January 20th of one of these interviews as follows:
>
> "Hankey came to see me today to say that Fisher, who is an old friend of his, had come to him in a very unhappy frame of mind. He likes Winston personally, but complains that on purely technical naval matters he is frequently over-ruled ('he out-argues me'), and he is not by any means at ease about either the present disposition of the fleets or their future movements."[83]

Hankey continues: 'Day after day Fisher would call on me to tell me of his woes and difficulties, until I came to dread his visits. I never failed to urge and beg him to speak his mind openly at the War Council. The reason why he would not do so was his loyalty to and friendship for Churchill.'[84] Balfour was advised of the Fisher problem by Hankey, who wrote to him on 21 January: 'Fisher, I find, frequently disagrees with statements made by the First Lord at our War Councils. I wish he would speak up.' Hankey, as War Council Secretary, was Fisher's proper avenue for recourse to the Prime Minister. He and Balfour referred the matter to Asquith, who, true to character, did nothing.[85] Fisher was constrained by protocol from speaking out at War Council meetings and contradicting his political head in front of his Cabinet colleagues. As he told the Dardanelles Commission:

> Mr. Churchill knew my opinion ... I was dead against the Naval operation alone, because I knew it must be a failure ... [But] I did not think it would tend towards good relations between the First Lord and myself nor to the smooth running of the Board of Admiralty to raise objections in the War Council's discussions.[86]

Fisher added: 'I determined I would not depart from my rule of not going against Winston in the War Council ... He was the head of the department ... We were not to quarrel there. We had to wash our dirty clothes at home.'[87] By 12 March the War Councillors would all be aware of Churchill's deception. But by then, of course, it was too late. Hankey recalled, at that time, how Balfour was '[v]ery angry ... because he knows Churchill decided to make attempt contrary to opinions of his Naval Advisers, though Churchill never told War Council this & never allowed Naval members to express their view at War Council.'[88]

Hankey would further record on 19 March that, 'on the first day [the Dardanelles] proposal was made I warned PM, Lord K, Chief of Staff, Lloyd George & Balfour that fleet could not effect passage without troops & that *all naval officers thought so.* I also begged Churchill to have troops to cooperate but he would not listen insisting navy could do it alone.'[89]

With regard to the daily War Staff Group meetings over which Churchill presided (attended by Fisher, Oliver, Jackson, Wilson, de Bartolomé and Graham Greene), and at which 'unanimous agreement in favour of [his Dardanelles] enterprise' had purportedly been expressed, it has already been described how no minutes or record of these proceedings was kept, and how Churchill alone determined what had been decided and, in his own hand, drafted orders accordingly. Permanent Secretary to the Admiralty, Sir William Graham Greene, who was present at these meetings, explained (seemingly condoning) Churchill's behaviour to the Dardanelles Commission, thus: 'Mr. Churchill combined such a power of mastering detail as well as general policy, that he was able to sum up more quickly and easily the result of long discussions than would be possible with any ordinary man, and his enormous energy and industry all contributed to establish this practice.'[90]

The Dardanelles Commissioners were singularly unimpressed with this explanation, commenting adversely on the 'objectionable change of practice made ... while Mr. Churchill was First Lord.'[91]

Fisher's official biographer was similarly critical, adding: 'After meetings of the [War Staff Group], Mr. Churchill drafted the orders that were necessary to carry out what *he believed* to be the decisions reached at the meeting. Undoubtedly he was often carried away by the optimism and enthusiasm of his ardent nature.'[92] Captain Penn agreed, pointing out that Churchill's 'misunderstanding of professional views, [his] ignorance of naval language and signalling terminology [and of gunnery, and minesweeping, it could be added], led to misunderstandings and ambiguities [and worse].'[93] Nevertheless, at these *in camera* meetings it was always the Churchillian viewpoint which prevailed. Churchill made no secret of, or apologies for his conduct, freely admitting in *The World Crisis* to having 'exercised an unlimited power of suggestion and initiative over the whole field, subject only to the approval and agreement of the First Sea Lord on all operative orders.' Churchill added:

> Moreover, it happened in a large number of cases that, seeing what ought to be done and confident of the agreement of the First Sea Lord, I myself drafted the telegrams and decisions in accordance with our policy, and the Chief of Staff took them personally to the First Sea Lord for his concurrence before despatch.[94]

On 15 January Churchill sent another 'Secret and Personal from First Lord' telegram to Carden, advising him, disingenuously, that: 'Your scheme was laid by the First Sea Lord and myself before the Cabinet War Council yesterday and was approved in principle [Lord Fisher's input in this respect has been described]. We see no difficulty in providing the forces you require.' Carden was then informed: 'We propose to entrust this operation to you ... the sooner we can begin the better.'[95]

On 19 January Churchill sent a telegram to Petrograd informing the Grand Duke that the British government had 'determined to force the passage of the Dardanelles [and] ... to press the matter to a conclusion.' The First Lord then requested assistance from the Russian government, 'by having troops ready to seize any advantage that may be gained for the allied cause.' The reply, on 25 January, regretted that Russia could provide no military assistance, 'great as was her desire to do so', due to pressure on the Eastern Front. The Grand Duke concluded that any action against Turkey 'of the kind contemplated would have important results for the allied cause.'[96] On 19 January Fisher sent a confidential letter to the Commander-in-Chief, Grand Fleet, Jellicoe, telling him:

> ... and now the Cabinet have decided on taking the Dardanelles solely with the Navy, using 15 battleships and 32 other vessels, and keeping out there three battle cruisers and a flotilla of destroyers—*all urgently required in the decisive theatre at home!* There is only one way out and that is to resign! But you say "no", which means I am a consenting party to what I absolutely

disapprove. *I don't agree with one single step taken,* so it is fearfully against the grain that I remain on in deference to your wishes. The *way this War is conducted both ashore and afloat is chaotic!* [97]

Two days later, Fisher confided in Jellicoe again, advising him more closely of his quandary: ... I've fought against it [the Dardanelles operation] tooth and nail [doubtless at War Staff Group meetings]. But of course, if the Government of the Country decide on a project as a subject of high policy, one cannot put oneself up to govern the diplomatic attitude of the nation in its relation to foreign powers, and *apparently the Grand Duke Nicholas has demanded this step, or—I suppose he would make peace with Germany. The making of peace with Germany behind our backs by France and Russia is really quite a possible event, I hear.* I just abominate the Dardanelles operation, unless a great change is made and it is settled to be a military operation with 200,000 men in conjunction with the Fleet. I believe Kitchener is coming now to this sane view of the matter ...[98]

And herein lay the crux of Fisher's dilemma. Being obliged to accept Churchill's duplicitous appraisal of the situation he was torn between two courses of action: to give his support to a government matter of 'high policy' which he and the entire naval staff knew to be impossible to implement—or resignation.

But, as he told the Dardanelles Commission, the only justification for resignation would have been to prevent a disaster. And as matters stood there was no way a disaster could occur. Fisher subsequently told the Dardanelles Commission:

> It is not the business of chief technical advisers of the Government to resign because their advice is not accepted, unless they are of the opinion that the operation proposed must lead to disastrous results. The attempt to force the Dardanelles, as a purely naval operation, though a failure, would not have been disastrous so long as the ships employed could be withdrawn at any moment.[99]

And that is precisely what the 13 January War Council had agreed. On 20 January Churchill advanced his naval operation even further, issuing the following minute to the Chief of Staff:

> The attack on the Dardanelles should be begun as soon as the *Queen Elizabeth* can get there. Every effort will be made to accelerate her departure, so that fire can be opened on February 15. It is not desirable to concentrate the whole fleet of battleships required for the operation at the Dardanelles at the outset. This would only accentuate failure, if the forts proved too strong for us. *Indefatigable, Queen Elizabeth,* and three or four other battleships, with the mine-sweepers and the *Ark Royal,* will be sufficient at the outset,

having regard for the French battleships available. The rest of the fleet should be distributed between Malta, Alexandria and Alexandretta, from which points they can readily concentrate as soon as progress begins to be made. [Provision for breaking off and attacking Alexandretta followed, with more instructions, then:]

All preparations for the attack on the Dardanelles are to proceed in general accordance with my minutes of January 12 and 13. The Chief of Staff has already given the necessary orders, and the ships are moving. [100]

Concerning this minute, Churchill writes in *The World Crisis*: '*At the same time, while giving decided orders and allowing no doubt or uncertainty to appear in the Admiralty attitude,* I was careful to preserve the means of breaking off the operation, if it began to miscarry.'[101]

Perhaps nowhere else is Fisher's dilemma better illustrated than here, with Churchill's hubristic demonstration of the extent to which he had usurped control from the hands of the Naval Staff. He then had the temerity to add: 'The First Sea Lord concurs', which denoted only that Fisher had dutifully initialled the minute, as having sighted it. Unfortunately, the War Councillors could have no knowledge of the situation prevailing at the Admiralty. In the meantime, planning of the Dardanelles operation progressed in strict accordance with the 'orders' (in his own words) of the First Lord. Churchill continues:

> It will be seen that the genesis of this plan and its elaboration were purely naval and professional in their character. It was Admiral Carden and his staff gunnery officers who proposed the gradual method of piecemeal reduction by long-range bombardment. It was Sir Henry Jackson and the Admiralty staff who *embraced this idea and approved its detail.* Right or wrong it was a Service plan. Similarly, the Admiralty orders were prepared exclusively by the Chief of Staff and his assistants ... At no point did civilian interference mingle with or mar the integrity of a professional conception.
>
> I write this not in the slightest degree to minimize or shift my own responsibility. But this was not where it lay. I did not and could not make the plan. But when it had been made by the naval authorities, and fashioned and endorsed by high technical authorities and approved by the First Sea Lord, I seized upon it and set it upon the path of action; and thereafter espoused it with all my resources. *When others weakened or changed their opinion* without adducing new reasons, *I held them strongly to their previous decisions;* and so in view of the general interest of the Allies, *thrust the business steadily forward into actual experiment.* [102]

In such manner, and through the resource of such 'rare subtle dialectical skill', did the miasma descend on the entire Dardanelles proceedings. Within the space of only two pages, Churchill described the manner in which he ordered the Admiralty staff to prepare plans 'for the attack on the Dardanelles' in strict accordance with his minutes/instructions and then, a page later, he disavowed, completely, any part in, or responsibility for those very plans.

The 28 January War Council Meeting

As Fisher explained to the Dardanelles Commission, between 14 and 28 January 'he had taken every step—short of resignation—to show his dislike of the proposed operations [in the Dardanelles].'[103] The inevitable outcome of fighting 'tooth and nail' at War Staff Group meetings was that he was invariably 'out-argued' by Churchill and his concerns ignored. Protocol denied him the facility of informing the War Councillors directly of his opposition to Churchill's plan, so Fisher opted for a more indirect route. As the next War Council meeting approached, Fisher enlisted Hankey's assistance to prepare a lengthy memorandum setting out his major objections to the Dardanelles venture, which he then expected to be circulated to the War Councillors.[104] In this memorandum Fisher made little mention of the technical problems associated with Churchill's plan. Instead he pointed to an even greater danger to Britain, as he saw it, from the proposed operation. The essence of the Royal Navy's 'Steady Pressure Policy', Fisher explained thus:

> We play into Germany's hands if we risk fighting ships in any subsidiary operations such as coastal bombardments or the attack on fortified places without military cooperation, for we thereby increase the possibility that the Germans may be able to engage our fleet with some approach of equality of strength. The sole justification of ... attacks by the fleet on fortified places, such as the contemplated prolonged bombardment of the Dardanelles Forts, by our fleet, is to force a decision at sea, and so far and no farther can they be justified. So long as the German High Sea Fleet preserves its present great strength and splendid gunnery efficiency, so long is it imperative and indeed vital that no operation whatever should be undertaken by the British Fleet calculated *to impair its present superiority* [in numbers] ... *Even the older ships should not be risked, for they cannot be lost without losing* [irreplaceable] *men* as they form our only reserves behind the Grand Fleet [italics added]. Ours is the supreme necessity and difficulty of remaining passive except in so far as we can force the enemy to abandon his defensive [stance] and expose his fleet to a general action.[105]

As Fisher would repeatedly enjoin Churchill: 'We can recover from an indecisive or even unsuccessful result of these operations in the Dardanelles ... but we could never recover from a reverse to our Main Fleets in the decisive theatre at home. *It would be ruin.* Our existence depends on our unchallengeable *Naval supremacy.* '[106]

Indeed, it was Churchill himself who made the celebrated observation that 'Jellicoe was the only man on either side who could lose the war in an afternoon.'[107] Admiral Bacon provided the bald statistics of the situation. Although by April 1915 the Grand Fleet comprised 22 dreadnought and eight pre-dreadnought battleships, plus four battlecruisers against the German High Sea Fleet of 16 dreadnought and 16 pre-dreadnought battleships and five battlecruisers, in January 1915 refitting and repairs had temporarily reduced the number of dreadnoughts in the Home Fleet to 18. It was Fisher's concern that, in a major confrontation, the German superiority in pre-dreadnoughts might shift the balance in their favour (after the dreadnoughts had accounted for one another). In such a scenario the pre-dreadnoughts and battlecruisers targeted for the Dardanelles could prove decisive.[108]

Admiral Sir John 'Jacky' Fisher (Library of Congress
LC-DIG-ggbain-18059).

Asked at an unspecified War Council meeting: 'How
many battleships would be lost [if the naval attack at
the Dardanelles was pressed to a conclusion]?' Lord
Fisher had replied, 'twelve'.[109] In Marder's analysis,
Churchill failed to appreciate the true role of the Grand
Fleet in protecting home waters: 'that it might go

through the entire war without fighting a battle and yet have been the dominating factor all along'. Battle would not be refused. It was, in fact, welcomed—but it would be on Jellicoe's terms, not the enemy's. He would not, for instance, risk his battleships being lured on to the torpedoes or mines of the enemy.[110]

This mode of thought, however, was totally alien to Churchill who, in Admiral Bacon's words, suffered from 'a disease common amongst those not accustomed to war ... the itch to be always doing something.'[111] Defeat of the Grand Fleet would have signalled the end for Britain, either through blockade and starvation, or through invasion. Doubtless it was Fisher's intention that, in explaining Britain's 'Steady Pressure Policy' to the War Councillors, he would have the opportunity to present and expand on his objections to Churchill's scheme at the Dardanelles. Fisher presented his memorandum to Churchill on 25 January. He attached a brief covering note which stated his position unequivocally, and which read: 'First Lord, I have no desire to continue a useless resistance in the War Council to plans I cannot concur in, but would ask that the enclosed may be printed and circulated to its members before the next meeting.'[112] Churchill confirmed Bacon's diagnosis, writing subsequently in *The World Crisis* that Fisher's memorandum was 'absolutely counter to all my convictions ... [it] would have condemned us to complete inactivity.'[113] Nevertheless, he replied to Fisher the same day stating that 'there was no difference in principle between [us]

... But when your special claims are met, you must let the surplus [ships] be used for the general cause.' He then suggested that he show both Fisher's memorandum and his reply to Asquith 'instead of printing and circulating the documents [Crease].'[114]

Fisher unwisely agreed. Two days later Churchill sent Fisher's paper to Asquith, accompanied by a memorandum of his own which in essence stated: 'The main principle of the First Sea Lord's paper is indisputable. The foundation of our naval policy is the maintenance in a secure position of a Battle Fleet ... capable at any time of defeating the German High Sea Fleet in battle.'[115] Churchill then proceeded—within a very lengthy and verbose discursion—to impress on Asquith the superiority of British over German naval guns; likewise the superiority in numbers of British as against German dreadnoughts; and how the advances in technology had rendered battleships over 12 years old redundant to the point of obsolescence.

In short, he concluded, it was only these naval dinosaurs—'not needed and not suited to fight in the line of battle' which were intended for the Dardanelles. 'And, if a certain proportion of loss of life among officers and men of the Royal Navy serving on these ships can achieve important objects of the war and save a very much greater loss of life among our comrades and allies on shore', he continued, 'we ought certainly not to shrink from it.'[116] Asquith agreed and declined to have Fisher's memorandum circulated to the War Councillors.[117] Fisher, now aware of the futility of his position at the War Council, sent a letter of resignation to the Prime Minister on 28 January, which read:

My dear Prime Minister,

I am giving this note to Colonel Hankey to hand to you to explain my absence from the War Council. I am not in accord with the First Lord and do not think it would be seemly to say so before the Council. His reply to my memorandum does not meet my case. I say that the Zeebrugge and Dardanelles bombardments can only be justified on naval grounds by military cooperation ... As purely naval operations they are unjustifiable ... I am very reluctant to leave the First Lord. I have great personal affection and admiration for him, but I see no possibility of a union of ideas, and unity is essential in war, so I refrain from any desire of remaining as a stumbling block. The British Empire ceases if our Grand Fleet ceases. No risks can be taken.[118]

Churchill hastened across to 10 Downing Street where a furious Asquith immediately sent out the following summons, via Churchill:

My dear Fisher,

The Prime Minister considers your presence at the War Council indispensable, and so do I. He will receive us both at 11.10, so that we can talk beforehand.

You have assented to both operations in question, and so far as I am concerned there can be no withdrawal, without good reason, from measures which are necessary, and for which preparations are far advanced. I would infinitely sooner work with you than with [the less-than-efficient] Sturdee, who will undoubtedly be forced upon me [as First Sea Lord] in the eventuality of which you write so lightheartedly.[119]

The outcome of the 20-minute talk between Churchill, Fisher and Asquith prior to the War Council meeting was that it was agreed to shelve the Zeebrugge operation—thus (to Churchill's mind) releasing the surplus ships needed at the Dardanelles.[120] There were three meetings of the War Council on 28 January. The first began at 11.30am, with Kitchener telling his colleagues of a Turkish force which, having crossed the Sinai desert, was threatening the Suez Canal. There could be no question of transferring troops from Egypt at this time.[121]

Churchill opened the discussion on the Dardanelles by presenting the Russian and French reactions to it in glowing terms. 'The Grand Duke had replied with enthusiasm', Churchill stated, 'and believed that this [operation] might assist him. The French Admiralty had also sent a favourable reply, and had promised co-operation.'[122] With the prospect of acquiring Turkish territory in Syria, France would contribute four battleships: *Bouvet, Suffren, Gaulois* and *Charlemagne,* and a division of 18,000 troops. Churchill neglected to add, however, that the Russian Foreign Minister and the Russian military both regarded the seizure of the Straits as 'difficult, almost impossible to achieve', and that French Naval Intelligence believed that 'an attempt to force the Dardanelles without military support would achieve nothing.'[123]

At this point Fisher interjected to say that 'he understood that this question would not be raised today [and that] the Prime Minister was well aware of his own views in regard to it.' Asquith replied that, in view of the steps already taken, 'the question could not well be left in abeyance'.[124] Fisher himself recorded what then took place:

> The Prime Minister gave the decision that the Dardanelles project must proceed; and as I rose from the Council table Kitchener followed me, and was so earnest and even emotional that I should return that I said to myself after some delay: "Well, we can withdraw the ships at any moment, so long as the Military don't land," and I succumbed. [Fisher added the following footnote, in the third person]:
>
> The dramatic scene which followed may one day furnish material for the greatest historical picture of the war. Lord Fisher sat and listened to the

men who knew nothing about it, and heard one after another pass opinion in favour of a venture to which he was opposed. He rose abruptly from the table and made as if to leave the room [to tender his resignation to Mr Bonham-Carter, Asquith's Private Secretary[125].

The tall figure of Lord Kitchener rose and followed him. The two stood by the window for some time in conversation [with Kitchener appealing to Fisher's sense of duty towards his country in her hour of peril], and then both took their seats again ... Mr. Asquith saw that drama enacted, and Mr. Asquith knew that it arose out of Lord Fisher's opposition to the scheme under discussion. But he allowed his colleagues on the Council to reach their conclusions without drawing from the expert his opinion for their guidance. The monstrous decision was therefore taken without it. But they all knew it—such a scene could not occur without everyone knowing the cause.[126]

The Councillors continued their discussion, seemingly oblivious to Fisher's objection. Balfour declared himself keen on the project. 'A successful attack on the Dardanelles', he claimed, 'would cut the Turkish Army in two ... put Constantinople under our control [and] ... enable Russia to resume exports ... it was difficult to imagine a more helpful operation.' Kitchener was similarly enthusiastic. 'If successful', he said, 'its effect would be equivalent to a successful campaign fought

118

with the New Armies.' He added: 'One merit of the scheme was that, if satisfactory progress was not made, the attack could be broken off [reverting to the demonstration only, requested by the Grand Duke].'

Churchill told the Councillors he did not anticipate 'that we should sustain much loss in the actual bombardment, but in sweeping for mines, some losses must be expected. The real difficulties would begin after the outer forts had been silenced, and it became necessary to attack the Narrows. He explained the plan of attack on a map.'[127]

Under the spell of Churchill's deceptive imagery, of *Queen Elizabeth* and the other battleships emulating the destruction wrought by the German 17-inch siege howitzers in Belgium, Sir Edward Grey articulated the general, euphoric opinion that: '[T]he Turks would be paralysed with fear when they heard that the forts were being destroyed one by one.'[128] Unfortunately, the two naval experts were constrained from explaining to the civilians the essential difference between artillery and naval gunfire.[129]

The War Council adjourned in the early afternoon and Churchill summoned Fisher to his room. There, as he later admitted in *The World Crisis,* he put 'great and continuous pressure ... upon the old admiral ... not to turn back from the Dardanelles operation.'[130] Fisher interpreted these events somewhat differently to Jellicoe in a letter to him the next day, in which there is no trace of despondency on Fisher's part: *'Don't worry about anything at all'*, Fisher wrote, *'for everything is quiet and going nicely!* I had fierce rows with Winston and the Prime Minister, and it was a near thing! I was six hours with them and War Council sat till 8pm! They are a *flabby lot!* However a calm has resulted and I go on pegging away.'[131] At 6.00pm Churchill announced, on behalf of the Admiralty Board, that the Dardanelles operation would go ahead.

Winston Churchill deceived Lord Kitchener into supporting his naval operation through the exaggerated claims he made for *Queen Elizabeth's* firepower, claims the Army chief lacked the expertise to refute. *Queen Elizabeth,* incidentally, would perform a minor role against the Turkish forts through the absence of adequate spotting facilities to report the battleship's fall of shot. Churchill deceived the War Councillors into sanctioning his naval venture by withholding from them the opposing opinion of the naval experts and presenting them instead with his own sanguine viewpoint. Without large-scale troop support, Lord Fisher knew that Churchill's plan must fail, but he was persuaded by Churchill and Asquith to withhold his resignation at the 28 January War Council meeting through the inclusion of a significant precondition. As Asquith explained to the Dardanelles Commission, the decisive factor, 'which appealed to Lord Kitchener and everybody [else] was that if it was merely a naval attack, it could have been abandoned at any moment without any serious loss of prestige.'[132] Churchill similarly acknowledged, in *The World Crisis,* that an essential precondition of the operation was that it *would* be abandoned 'if the difficulties and the Turkish resistance proved too great'.[133] Within such a safeguard no kind of disaster was possible, and Fisher had little choice but to pledge his support for the scheme as the chief naval adviser to the government.

'When I went in', Fisher later stated, 'I went in *totus porcus*—the whole hog', to give the operation every chance of success.[134] But his inner conviction remained unaltered. As he told the Dardanelles Commissioners: 'To forbid, before it had been tried, an experiment on which rested so many sanguine hopes, would have been an impracticable step. The experiment had to be made, and I did accept in that connection responsibility, though reluctant responsibility.'[135]

CHAPTER 3

The Anglo-French Naval Attack

A variety of factors contributed to the failure of the Allied naval attack at the Dardanelles on 18 March 1915. In retrospect, responsibility has been attributed largely to indecisive planning and a lack of resolve in the execution of a concept which was, allegedly, not only sound, but brilliant in its potential. Additional contributory factors, such as the role of the minesweepers and Churchill's press release, have featured minimally, if at all, in this explanation.

Revised Plans and Priorities for the Naval Attack

During the week following 28 January, the Admiralty prepared detailed instructions for Carden. On 2 February Churchill sent a draft copy to Sir Edward Grey, who hoped, presciently: 'that these detailed plans will be communicated to as few persons as possible here outside the Admiralty.'[1] Admiral Oliver's instructions placed restrictions on the firing of *Queen Elizabeth's* guns and limited the other battleships' expenditure of ammunition. Carden's plan had stipulated that a large amount of ammunition would be needed to silence the forts. Yet he was instructed to use ammunition sparingly, lest 'wasteful expenditure resulted in the operations having to be abandoned'. Already, one of the key elements in his plan had been discarded. Carden was also told not to hurry operations, 'to the extent of taking large risks and courting heavy losses', thus overturning the second major premise of his plan. Churchill concurred, writing 'Excellent' on the orders. Further, Carden was sent none of the fast fleet sweepers he had requested.[2]

On 6 February, Churchill sent another 'Secret and Personal from First Lord' telegram to Carden, encouraging the admiral to deal directly with him concerning any problems which might arise:

> I wish you to keep me closely informed of the daily progress of these operations. Do not hesitate to send me full reports by telegraph and let me know all your difficulties.
>
> Are you getting all you want, and is everything progressing satisfactorily? I attach great importance to fire being opened punctually on the 15th, by which time *Queen Elizabeth* should have arrived.[3]

Churchill had earlier telegraphed Carden: 'This is a great opportunity, and you must concentrate absolutely upon it ... I am expecting you to formulate all your requests for mine-sweepers, mine-bumpers and all special appliances in the greatest possible detail ... All your wants that cannot be supplied locally should be fully reported by telegram.'[4] On 9 February Carden took advantage of Churchill's personal interest to inform him of a need which would become progressively more urgent (but to which the First Lord would pay scant attention), advising him that: 'We shall not be prepared to begin before 19th as mine-sweepers cannot be ready sooner.'[5] The delay was caused by the French provision of 13 trawler-minesweepers from Toulon and Bizerta.[6]

At a War Council meeting on 9 February Kitchener volunteered 'that if the Navy required the assistance of land forces at a later stage, that assistance would be forthcoming.'[7] The tacit understanding was that these troops would be employed in a garrison role, to clear and occupy the forts once their guns had been silenced by the Navy. As Admiral Sir Arthur Wilson told the Dardanelles Commission, '[Churchill] kept on saying he could do it without the army; he only wanted the army to come in and reap the fruits [of victory], I think was his expression.'[8] Churchill wrote in *The World Crisis,* in response to Kitchener's 9 February offer, 'once it began to be realized that troops in considerable numbers were becoming available, Sir Henry Jackson and Lord Fisher *began* to press for their employment in the Dardanelles operation.'[9]

The Dardanelles forts: view across The Narrows to Chanak from above Kilid Bahr, December 1918 (AWM A00338).

On 14 February, in collaboration with Hankey and the naval historian Sir Julian Corbett, Assistant Director of Naval Operations, Richmond, presented a memorandum which concluded that: 'The naval bombardment of the Dardanelles, even if all the forts were destroyed, can be nothing but a local success which without an army to carry it on can have no further effect.' Richmond recommended that an adequate land force be prepared at once, otherwise the Turks would soon discover 'the real limitations of sea power divorced from military power'.[10]This memo was shown to Fisher who, since 28 January, had been bombarding Lloyd George with similar imprecations, advising him of the futility of attacking the Dardanelles 'without soldiers'.[11]

Hankey had already delivered this self-same warning in the strongest terms to Churchill and Asquith as early as 2 February in a memorandum entitled 'The

War: Attack on the Dardanelles'—but to no avail.[12] Fisher wrote to Richmond, congratulating him on his paper: 'Dear Richmond, your paper is excellent! Give your original to I.F. Phillips (he is opposite Sir A.K. Wilson's room) and he will make another copy tell him not on Admiralty paper.'[13]

The significance of Fisher's instructions to Richmond to have a copy of his memorandum made will become apparent in chapters 7 and 8 (with particular regard to Churchill's massive archive of official documents). As Hankey pointed out in 1916 in his Memorandum for the Dardanelles Commissioners, during the war:

> Owing to the fact that a great part of the proceedings [of the War Council and subsequent War Committees] dealt with matters of extreme secrecy, such as forthcoming naval and military operations, it was not considered advisable to reproduce them, and *only a single manuscript copy was kept* ... Only the conclusions have been communicated to those concerned in their execution, and latterly to the Cabinet [Hankey's underlined emphasis].[14]

The following day Sir Henry Jackson completed an Admiralty War Staff Memorandum on the same subject which he sent to Carden, as advice only, essentially reiterating the objections set down in his earlier memoranda, but this time spelling them out in clear, unequivocal language. In his 'General Remarks' Jackson stressed that:

Every [Turkish field] gun must be silenced ... To complete their destruction strong military landing parties with strong covering forces will be necessary. [Jackson recommended] the occupation of the Peninsula by a military force acting in conjunction with the naval operation [as the presence of a strong Turkish field army, together with its artillery], would render the passage of the Straits impracticable by [unarmoured supply ships carrying coal stores and ammunition] ... even though all the [forts'] guns had been silenced. [Jackson concluded]:

The naval bombardment is not recommended as a sound military operation, unless a strong military force is ready to assist in the operation, or at least, follow it up immediately the forts are silenced.[15]

Churchill claimed that Jackson's assessment—while the product of 'much mixed thinking'—did force him finally to acknowledge the Naval Staff's concerns and to question the viability of Carden's plan.[16] According to Churchill's biographer, 'for a month he had based his plans on Carden's belief that ships alone might be sufficient.' Now, 'the criticisms of Richmond and Jackson caused him to wonder whether he had been right to accept Carden's assessment—over, it should be pointed out, the expert opinion of Fisher, Jackson, Jellicoe, Scott, Morgan Singer and the Admiralty gunnery experts, Callwell, the CID and the General

Staff.'[17] Who, then, was this authority, on whom Churchill had placed such reliance?

It was Churchill himself, in fact, who had promoted Rear Admiral Sackville Carden to the position of Commander-in-Chief, Mediterranean Fleet, on 21 September 1914, replacing the discredited Sir Berkeley Milne.[18] Prior to his surprising elevation, Carden had filled the role of Superintendent, Malta Dockyard, put there, according to Fisher, 'to shelve him'. Carden had no experience of battle command whatsoever, not even of a cruiser squadron.[19] Lieutenant General Birdwood, who would command the Australian and New Zealand Army Corps (ANZAC) at Gallipoli, sent a character report to Kitchener in February 1915 describing Carden as 'very second-rate—no go in him, or ideas, or initiative.'[20] Nevertheless, this was the 'expert' to whose authority Churchill had deferred.

A meeting of the War Council was held on the 16th, at which Jackson's memorandum was read out. With a relaxation of German pressure in France, and possibly under the influence of Jackson's memorandum, Kitchener decided to honour his pledge and send the experienced 29th Division to Lemnos 'at the earliest possible date, hopefully, within nine or ten days'. It was also decided that 'a force [ANZAC] be despatched from Egypt, if required', together with the RND, already despatched, 'to be available in case of necessity'.[21] Churchill asserted in *The World Crisis* that: 'The decision of February 16th was the foundation of the military attack upon the

128

Dardanelles.'[22] On the evening of this same day Churchill recorded that he received a demanding letter from Fisher: 'I hope you were successful with Kitchener in getting divisions sent to Lemnos *tomorrow!* Not a grain of wheat will come from the Black Sea unless there is a military occupation of the Dardanelles.' Fisher's position, at this stage, Churchill asserts, was perfectly clear. 'He wanted the Gallipoli Peninsula stormed and held by the Army. This idea neither Lord Kitchener nor the War Council would at this time have entertained.'[23]

Churchill claimed to have been bemused by this sudden turnaround, courtesy of Jackson and Richmond, then Kitchener, and now Fisher. 'The resolve to concentrate an army undoubtedly carried with it acceptance of the possibility of using it in certain eventualities', Churchill continued. 'But these were not as yet defined.'[24] The miasma was settling.

On 18 February the French government, experiencing similar qualms to those of Fisher and Jackson et al., urged the British government to suspend naval operations at the Dardanelles until the arrival of troops. Churchill immediately telegraphed back: 'The naval operations having begun cannot be interrupted but must proceed continuously to their conclusion, every day adding to the dangers of the arrival of German or Austrian submarines.'[25] In *The World Crisis* Churchill was somewhat reticent on the proceedings of the War Council which met on 19 February, apart from recording the vigorous protestation he made over Kitchener's withdrawal of his offer of the 29th Division. As he wrote: 'When we met in Council again on the 19th, it became clear that Lord Kitchener had changed his mind. He gave as his reason the dangerous weakness of Russia and his fear lest large masses of German troops be brought back from the Russian Front to attack our troops in France.'[26] In fact, Kitchener was quite prepared to send the 39,000-strong Australian and New Zealand force in lieu of the 29th Division which he wanted to hold in reserve. The Anzacs were stationed in Egypt and 'would arrive at Lemnos sooner'.[27] Churchill's response was that:

> It would be a great disappointment to the Admiralty if the 29th Division was not sent out. The attack on the Dardanelles was a very heavy naval undertaking. It was difficult to over-rate the military advantages which success would bring ... He had hoped that we should have 50,000 men within reach of the Dardanelles, which could be concentrated there in three days.[28]

Churchill failed to acknowledge in *The World Crisis* that, together with the 10,000 troops of the RND already despatched, he would have had his requested force. But the First Lord was not satisfied, demanding the experienced 29th Division as well, and telling the War Council: 'On the Western Front, among the vast forces engaged, they [the 29th Division] could not make any difference. At the Dardanelles, on the other hand, they might well make all the difference ... We should never forgive ourselves if this promising operation failed owing to insufficient military support at the critical moment.'[29]

A counter-argument could equally have been presented by Kitchener concerning what possible difference *any* single British division of 18,000 men could have made against an estimated 250,000 Turkish troops located near the Straits, in and around Constantinople, and near at hand on the Thracian border, should a full-scale military campaign have been contemplated. British diplomat C. Heathcote-Smith had telegraphed the British Foreign Office from Dedeagatch on 17 January that: 'Turkish troops in "Dardanelles area" were a quarter of a million'.[30]

Churchill now quoted from Jackson's memorandum, seeking 'to lay stress upon the fact that the navy could only open the Straits for armoured ships, and could not guarantee an unmolested passage for merchant ships unless the shores of the Dardanelles were cleared of the enemy's riflemen and field guns.'[31] Churchill 'did not ask for troops actually to be sent to the Dardanelles, but only that they should be within hail.' He was still claiming that the Navy would do the job alone, but his ambivalent quest for military cooperation had now gained the support of Lloyd George, Asquith and Balfour. Lloyd George suggested 'that we ought to send more than three divisions[50,000 troops] ... It was worthwhile to take some risks in order to achieve a decisive operation, which might win the war.' Balfour 'suggested that if the Gallipoli Peninsula was occupied, and our passage through the Dardanelles secured, we should obtain all we required... [He] then asked when the New Armies would be ready [to which Kitchener replied] that the 10th April was the present date for the first army.'[32]

At this juncture Asquith belatedly read aloud from the CID Paper of 1906 which concluded that 'military co-operation was essential to success [at the Dardanelles].' However, the Councillors decided, after 'some ... desultory discussion' that the circumstances obtaining in 1906 no longer applied, particularly given the increased power of modern artillery and the decline of Turkey's military reputation since the Balkan Wars of 1912–13.[33] Still ostensibly committed to an all-naval attack, as Professor Higgins points out, Churchill, by his own later admission, had already surmised that without a '[very] public naval commitment', Kitchener would never have been persuaded to lend his full support to 'what remained for him a most unwanted military enterprise'.[34] Churchill now addressed this provision, subsequently writing:

> I have asked myself in later years, [w]hat would have happened if I had taken Lord Fisher's advice and refused point blank to take any action at the Dardanelles unless or until the War Office produced on their own responsibility an adequate army to storm the Gallipoli Peninsula? ... I think myself that nothing less than the ocular

demonstration and practical proof of the strategic meaning of the Dardanelles, and the effects of attacking it ... would have enabled Lord Kitchener to wrest an army from France and Flanders. In cold blood it could never have been done.[35]

Churchill's 20 February Press Release

At 9.51 on the morning of [Friday] 19 February, the Anglo-French Fleet at the Dardanelles opened fire on the outer forts of Orkanie, Helles, Sedd-el-Bahr and Kum Kale.[36]

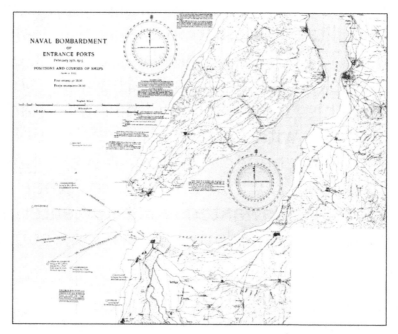

The naval bombardment of the Dardanelles entrance forts, 19 February 1915 (AWM G7432G1S65XXVI5).

The sound of those guns reverberated around the world the following day in a press release issued by the Admiralty and authorised by the First Lord. A prominent two-column, full-front-page article appeared in *The Times* on Monday 22 February, which gave an exhaustively detailed account of the naval attack, along with the planned objectives, stressing that 'having begun, it must be successfully carried through at all costs'.[37]

DARDANELLES ATTACKED.

OPERATIONS BY SEA AND AIR.

FORTS VERSUS SHIPS.

By Our Military Correspondent.

The attack on the Dardanelles by the Allied Fleets has at last begun, and, having begun, it must be successfully carried through at all costs.

It is scarcely necessary to point out the great political and military consequences which will follow if the attack is successful. The whole situation in the Balkans will be immediately altered to our profit ; Constantinople must either surrender or be reduced to ashes ; the trade with the Black Sea will be reopened ; and while the enemy will be struck at a very sensitive spot, the decisions of wavering neutrals will be immediately affected. The reasons in favour of this operation are overwhelming, provided that the risks and necessary preparations have been coolly calculated in advance, and that such naval and military force as may be allotted to the object in view can be spared from the decisive theatre of war.

'Dardanelles Attacked', The Times, 22 February 1915, p. 6.'

The Allied Attack On The Dardanelles', The Times, 22 February 1915, p. 7.

Lloyd George was furious with Churchill, as he later (on 15 May 1915) told Frances Stevenson: [W]hen the Cabinet gave their consent to a bombardment of the Dardanelles forts (very unwillingly) it was on the strict understanding that the operations should not be announced in the first place, so as not to commit the Government, & to enable them, if the thing should turn out to be impossible or a more lengthy proceeding than was anticipated, to withdraw from the campaign without any discredit to themselves. This did not suit Churchill, however. On the very first day that the bombardment commenced, he broke faith with his colleagues & caused the announcement to be made in the Press with great eclat that we had begun the bombardment of the Dardanelles forts, & intended to force the Straits. Thenceforth it was, of course, impossible for the Government to withdraw.[38]

James Masterton-Smith, Churchill's Parliamentary Secretary, confirmed his chief's 'indiscretion' to Lord Riddell in July 1916 during a long conversation at the Admiralty. Masterton-Smith explained that:

> The War Council intended that the Fleet should endeavour to force the Dardanelles, but that very little should be said publicly, and that if the operation proved unsuccessful, it should be treated as a feint and the real objective described as Alexandretta. Winston's *communiques* to the Press wittingly or unwittingly obscured this programme. The attack came to be regarded as the sole operation.[39]

Hankey recorded that:

> The [press] announcement had a remarkable effect on the attitude of the War Council. When the decision had been reached to undertake the naval bombardment it had been generally assumed that the attack would be broken off in the event of failure. But when the War Council met on February 24th, notwithstanding that the Outer Forts had not been finally reduced, it was felt that we were now committed to seeing the business through.
>
> Speaker after speaker reflected this view, "*Moreover, we were absolutely committed to seeing through the attack on the Dardanelles*" (Churchill), [Kitchener] "felt that, if the fleet could not get through the Straits unaided, the Army

ought to see the business through. The effect of a defeat in the Orient would be very serious. There could be no going back. *The publicity of the announcement had committed us"*. [40]

It was unthinkable that Great Britain might suffer any kind of setback, let alone a military or naval defeat at the hands of a 'third-rate power' like Turkey. As a former Sirdar of Egypt, Kitchener was acutely sensitive to the fact that Britain's military and imperial reputations (over her Eastern subjects in particular) were intimately interlinked. Whether Churchill's motivation was, as Higgins suggests, to coerce Kitchener into supplying the army he had known all along was essential or whether it was simply one of hubris and the desire to parade his master plan before the world, the result was the same. By announcing Britain's Dardanelles operation to the enemy, Churchill gave the Turks (and their German commanders) two months' grace in which to prepare the most formidable defences, thus seriously compromising any chances of success the operation may have had.

Curiously, with the exception of Hankey, Sir Gerald Ellison, Higgins and George Cassar, there has been scarcely any mention of Churchill's press announcement in accounts of the Dardanelles operation. Kitchener's statement that 'the publicity of the announcement had committed us', where quoted, is seldom, if ever, explained further. Alone among modern historians, George Cassar describes the full implication of Churchill's press release:

Without any authorization from the cabinet or the Prime Minister, Churchill gave the press a detailed account of the first day's bombardment ... Churchill's indiscretion set in motion a tragic sequence of events that was to destroy Kitchener's effectiveness in the cabinet and War Council, bring down the Liberal government, set back Allied diplomacy in the Balkans and lead to the vain expenditure of thousands of lives. The operation had attracted such world-wide attention that, for the sake of British prestige, Kitchener was anxious to avert defeat, even if the cost was high.[41]

Churchill's account made no mention of his 20 February Admiralty press release. Gilbert cites Hankey's letter to Esher complaining that '[t]here ought to have been no blatant press announcement at the outset', but provides no further details.[42]

The proceedings of the War Council meetings held on 24 and 26 February, as described by Winston Churchill in *The World Crisis* and as recorded in the Secretary's Notes of War Council Meetings, differ to such an extent as to merit a detailed comparison. It should be noted at the outset that Churchill's account of these two vital meetings is sketchy in the extreme, occupying less than two pages in his 552-page volume, and with rhetoric taking the place of factual analysis.[43] For example, in *The World Crisis* Churchill writes: 'If [February] the 16th had been a day of Resolve ... the 24th and 26th were days of Compromise and Half-Measures.' He had earlier told his readers that: 'The decision of February 16 is the foundation of the military attack upon the Dardanelles.' That decision was compromised, Churchill claimed, by Kitchener telling the War Council on the 24th that: 'If the Fleet could not get through the Straits unaided the Army ought to see the business through. The effect of a defeat in the Orient would be very serious. There could be no going back.' But Churchill declined to finish the quotation—that 'the publicity of [his own press] announcement had committed us'. Instead, Churchill continued: 'Thus, at a stroke, the idea of discarding the naval attack, if it proved too difficult ... was abandoned and the possibility of a great military enterprise seemed to be accepted.'[44] The escalation to a military invasion was thus presented to readers of *The World Crisis* as a unilateral decision taken out of the hands of the War Councillors by Kitchener, who nevertheless refused to supply the vital 29th Division. Or, as Churchill wrote:

> ... After the Council [on the 26th] I waited behind. I knew the Prime Minister agreed with me, and indeed the whole Council, with the exception of Lord Kitchener were of one mind. I urged the Prime Minister to make his authority effective and insist upon the despatch of the 29th Division to Lemnos or Alexandria. I felt at that moment in

an intense way a foreboding of disaster ... The Prime Minister did not feel that anything more could be done. He had done his best to persuade Lord Kitchener. He could not overrule him or face his resignation upon a question like this ... Lord Kitchener notwithstanding his pronouncement [of the 24th] adhered to his refusal [to send the 29th Division thus, in Churchill's belief, sealing the fate of the operation].[45]

Churchill's thesis then, as expounded in *The World Crisis,* embraced two propositions: that Kitchener had usurped War Council authority on 24 February to convert the naval attack to a combined operation; yet at that War Council meeting, and again at the 26 February meeting, he had refused to release the vital component essential for success at the Dardanelles, namely the 29th Division.

The War Council Secretary's Notes reveal a somewhat different situation. At the 24 February War Council meeting Churchill had, in fact, demanded that 115,000 soldiers be sent to the Dardanelles comprising the 29th Division, a British Territorial division, the Naval Division, the ANZAC Corps, the French Division and a Russian brigade.[46] Kitchener, not surprisingly, was somewhat taken aback, reminding Churchill that the attack on the Dardanelles had been planned as a naval one; did 'Mr. Churchill now contemplate a land attack' as well, Kitchener asked:[47]

Mr. Churchill said he did not, but it was quite conceivable that the naval attack might be temporarily held up by mines, and some local military operation required. He asked how 2 divisions could make the difference between success and failure in the Western theatre of war, especially as by the middle of April, 4 divisions of the New Army would be available.

Kitchener replied that, although 'he would risk a good deal in order to open up the Dardanelles, he was, however, unable to understand the purpose for which so many troops were to be used.'[48] Kitchener again reminded Churchill of his claims to the War Councils of 13 and 28 January, that victory would be achieved by naval guns alone:

In [Kitchener's] opinion, once the British Fleet had forced its way through the Dardanelles, in fact, as soon as the forts were clearly being silenced one by one, the Gallipoli garrison would evacuate the peninsula; the garrison of Constantinople, the Sultan, and not improbably the Turkish Army in Thrace, would also decamp to the Asian shore ... [or] run the risk of being cut off and starved out [Kitchener was still clearly in thrall to the illusion of *Queen Elizabeth*'s awesome destructive powers]. How then could the large forces contemplated by Mr. Churchill be employed?[49]

At this War Council, in response to Churchill's press announcement, Lloyd George 'strongly rejected' the proposition that the Army should have to see the business through if the Navy suffered a setback. Instead, he hoped that:

> ... the Army would not be required or expected to pull the chestnuts out of the fire for the Navy. If we failed at the Dardanelles [he insisted], we ought to be immediately ready to try something else. In [Lloyd George's] opinion, we were committed by this operation to some action in the Near East, but not necessarily to a siege of the Dardanelles.[50]

At the 26 February War Council, Churchill answered Kitchener's question from the previous meeting (of the purpose of such large numbers of troops), asserting that: 'They were required to occupy Constantinople and to compel a surrender of all Turkish forces remaining in Europe after the fleet had obtained command of the Sea of Marmara.'[51] As Prior observes, the number of troops recommended by Churchill (around 100,000) 'would not be sufficient to "compel" any Turkish surrender ... unless the Turks felt disposed to capitulate.'[52] Balfour had presented a War Office memorandum on 24 February stating that there were at least 400,000 Turkish troops 'in the area of the fleet's operations, including 150,000 in nearby Asiatic Turkey.'[53] Finally, after all his appeals to Kitchener had failed, Churchill made the following dramatic statement, which War Council Secretary Hankey recorded:

> Mr. Churchill said that the 29th Division would not make the difference between success and failure in France, but it might well make the difference in the East. He wished it to be placed on record that he dissented altogether from the retention of the 29th Division in this country. If a disaster occurred in Turkey owing to the insufficiency of troops, he must disclaim all responsibility.[54]

By this time Churchill had placed himself in an almost impossible position. As Prior notes, '[He] first gained the War Council's agreement to the naval attack [by] deliberate deception ... before pointing out the need for follow-up or occupation troops.' The 'day of Resolve' (16 February), in Churchill parlance, had opened the door in this respect. Now he was faced with the dilemma of holding two diametrically opposing positions at the same time; of arguing for the massive army he knew 'was essential to the Dardanelles operation', while at the same time 'disguising his real attitude' and publicly supporting the purely naval attack.[55]

It should be remembered that no change had been authorised at this stage, nor had the suggestion been put to the War Council that any such change *should* be made to the original plan concerning large-scale troop support. It might also be remembered that

Kitchener had agreed to the despatch to the Dardanelles of the ANZAC Corps (39,000 men) plus the RND (10,000 men), together with a French division (18,000 men) committed by this time. This force numbered well in excess of the 50,000 troops requested by Churchill to be on hand three days away for garrison duty or for 'some local military operation[s]'.

Only the 29th Division was missing. But such was Churchill's oratorical and literary skill that, in his statements to Parliament, to the Dardanelles Commission and subsequently in his writings, he could persuade his audiences that it was the absence of this single division which was the cause of the entire disaster.

Seasonal stormy weather in the Aegean brought a temporary halt to the naval bombardment. Over the next week, two days of fine weather were all the battleships would need to subdue the outer forts, plastering them with gunfire while lying well outside the range of their guns. Somewhat disturbingly, on 27 February, landing parties of marines discovered that most of the guns in the vacated forts of Sedd-el-Bahr, Kum Kale and Orkanie and the adjacent batteries, were still intact. Twenty guns were destroyed with guncotton before the marines were re-embarked, with the loss of one man killed and one wounded. For the next ten days similar landings were conducted in the face of increasing Turkish resistance and 30 more guns destroyed. On 4 March, however, a company of the Plymouth Battalion was driven from Seddel-Bahr with the loss of 22 men killed and a similar number wounded. No subsequent attempt was made to land marines for this purpose.[56]

A Turkish 9.4-inch Krupp gun wrecked in its emplacement at Fort No. 1 on the cliffs of Cape Helles. This was believed to be one of the guns destroyed on 26 February 1915 by British Marine landing parties (AWM H16496).

Nevertheless, the fall of the outer forts created a major sensation throughout Britain, Europe and America. Speculation was rife that the remaining Dardanelles forts were doomed, as was Constantinople. On 27 February *The Times* reported: 'The news that the forts at the entrance to the Dardanelles have been successfully reduced is good ... Further news of the operations will be awaited with intense interest.' From a neutral standpoint the *New York Times* was far less restrained, with front page headlines proclaiming: 'Ships Ready to Engage Last Turkish Defences before reaching Sea of Marmora', 'A Third of Straits Passed', and 'Fleet Nears Big Dardanelles Forts'.[57]

The following day the *New York Times* reported: 'Forty Warships of Allied Fleet Penetrate the Straits for Fourteen Miles', 'Four Forts Demolished', and 'Landing Parties Complete the Destruction Wrought by Two Days' Bombardment'; while the *Observer* proudly proclaimed that 'one of the memorable efforts of all history will be steadily carried to success'.[58] In fact, the fleet penetrated six miles into the Straits ('to the limits of the Kephez minefield').[59] On 1 March the *London Daily Chronicle*'s headlines read: 'Allies Likely to Seize Isthmus [Gallipoli Peninsula]'. This newspaper also pointed out, erroneously, that: 'The guns of the squadron of the Dardanelles are more powerful than the heaviest howitzers that Germany used against Liège', adding that 'the Allies will seize isthmus on the European side of the Dardanelles above Bulair, thus cutting off the forts on that side from all succour'. On this same day the *New York Times* speculated similarly, under the banner headlines: 'Plan a Land Attack on the Dardanelles', and 'Allies believed to Be Preparing to Take Forts in the Rear'.[60]

On 2 March the *New York Times* reported: 'Fort Dardanos, twelve miles up the Dardanelles, on the Asiatic side, has been silenced by the Allied Fleet', adding that 'The more optimistic minds expect Constantinople to fall [but warned] that the ships face no easy task'. The *New York Times* published a special cable from Athens which reported that: 'The Turkish forces are hurriedly concentrating on the Asiatic side of the Dardanelles', and that serious rioting in

Constantinople 'had been suppressed after many arrests had been made'. The *New York Times* headline on 3 March read: 'More Dardanelles Forts Destroyed', with the claim that 'the fire from the Allied Fleet had destroyed the batteries [forts] of Kilid Bahr and Chanak Kalesi', which was quite misleading. The two principal forts at the Narrows, the most massive structures in the Dardanelles, would remain intact throughout the campaign.[61] *The Times* published a minor corrective on 3 March which stated that 'some of the news which is coming through about the Dardanelles is obviously premature and incorrect ... [and cautioning that] The most difficult part of the business is yet to be tackled, the destruction of the forts in the Narrows [i.e. Kilid Bahr and Chanak].'[62]

The Political Situation in the Balkans, March 1915

At a meeting of the War Council held on 3 March, Winston Churchill stated that: 'In consequence of the success of the bombardment of the outer Forts Russia was preparing to embark an army corps [of 40,000 men] at Batoum [for an anticipated assault against Constantinople] ... With a Russian army corps, three divisions from Greece, a French division, and our own troops from Egypt, we should dispose of from 120,000 to 140,000 men.'[63]

A euphoric, celebratory atmosphere pervaded the 3 March War Council, with Churchill echoing the

148

newspaper reports and announcing at the start of the meeting 'that forts 8 and 9 [in the Straits] were in the process of being destroyed, and that the forts at the entrance had been practically demolished.' Success seems to have been taken for granted by the Councillors, whose attention was focussed on 'questions likely to arise after the fall of Constantinople'.[64] Broaching this thorny question, Foreign Secretary Grey informed his colleagues of Russia's request for control over the Straits (and Constantinople), warning that 'in dealing with this question it had to be remembered that Germany was very desirous of concluding a separate peace with Russia and France.' Grey doubted 'whether the question could be left in abeyance much longer. Russia wanted an immediate decision.' Haldane concurred, pointing out that 'unless Britain made a definite offer Germany would seize the opportunity to conclude a separate peace with Russia.'[65]

On 5 September 1914, Britain, France and Russia had signed the Pact of London. This loose alliance (which would be ratified in April 1915 by the Treaty of London) ensured that each of these nations would continue to fight on in support of the other two.[66] As stated earlier, from November 1914, with the failure of the Schlieffen Plan, the British began receiving intelligence reports through diplomatic channels of German peace-feelers to Belgium, France and Russia, in an attempt to break the alliance.[67] Bearing in mind Russia's horrendous losses during the first five months of the war (by December 1914, 1.8

million soldiers, or half the trained army had been killed, wounded or taken prisoner), it was always a possibility that the Russians might find an accommodation with Germany more comfortable than the Entente with Britain.[68] Consequently, on 12 November 1914, Grey had given Russian Foreign Minister Sazonov an assurance 'that the Russians could do as they pleased with Constantinople at the end of the war'.[69] Grey now defended that decision to the 3 March War Council, stating: 'It was very important to avoid anything in the nature of a breach with Russia, or any action which would incite Russia to make a separate peace.'[70] He subsequently added, at a Cabinet meeting on 9 March, that he 'would prefer to have all the Balkan states in opposition rather than alienate Russia at this crisis.'[71]

Grey would write in retrospect in 1916 that 'Russia would never have stood for five months of reverses, in 1915, but for the hope of Constantinople.'[72] At the end of January 1915, Russia was tying down 26 German divisions (446,000 troops) on the Eastern Front. By the end of April 1915, some 1,767,000 Russian troops were opposing 639,000 Germans and 664,000 Austro-Hungarians in the east.[73] A Russian accommodation with Germany, releasing these German troops for the Western Front, would have been fatal to France and Britain. Russia's claim to Constantinople was ratified by the War Council of 10 March 1915, with Grey proposing 'that we should agree to the Russian claims', Balfour and Bonar Law concurring, and Asquith concluding that: 'A reply be sent to Russia ... that we should agree to the proposals put forward.' Grey informed Ambassador Buchanan at Petrograd the following day.[74]

In Churchill's opinion, the fall of Constantinople was significant primarily for the fact that it would bring the Balkan states into the war against Austria-Hungary. As he wrote to Jellicoe on 9 March: 'Constantinople is only a means to an end, and that is the marching against Austria of the five re-united Balkan States.'[75] The prospect of a resurrected Balkan League with a united army of over a million men launched against the 'soft underbelly' of Austria-Hungary and thus bringing the war to a successful, early conclusion, was a chimera dear to Churchill's heart. Even with months of preparatory diplomacy (which was never conducted), it would have been difficult to imagine these most bitter of enemies resolving their differences and mutual mistrust to the extent of joining together in such an enterprise.

***

In 1912, Balkan nationalism had inspired Serbia, Greece, Bulgaria and Montenegro to unite and form the Balkan League to oppose Turkish oppression. In October, Montenegro declared war on Turkey and, by the end of the month, the League had defeated every Turkish army in Europe. The Treaty of London in May 1913 brought the war to an end and established Albania as an independent state. The Balkan League immediately broke up because Serbia had occupied and kept most of Macedonia; Bulgaria had captured Adrianople, and the Greeks had seized Salonika and much of the Aegean hinterland. The Bulgarians were aggrieved because they had done most of the fighting against Turkey, with little reward. Believing they could defeat Greece and Serbia together, Bulgaria attacked them on 29 June without warning. However, Greece and Serbia more than held their own. Romania, which had hitherto remained neutral, entered the war against Bulgaria in order to acquire the Dobrudja, and Turkey followed suit so as to regain Adrianople.

When the Second Balkan War was brought to an end with the Treaty of Bucharest in August 1913, Bulgaria was forced to pay out its opponents. Romania gained the Dobrudja, with Adrianople going to Turkey. Serbia took the bulk of Macedonia, with Greece acquiring the rest, along with Salonika, Kavalla and Western Thrace (see Map 1). Henceforth, as Professor French points out, few of the Balkan armies were in any shape to face another war, and Bulgaria was left seething with resentment, bent on revenge, and mistrusted by all the other Balkan powers.[76]

Map 1: The Balkans.

On 1 March 1915 Greek Prime Minister Venizelos had offered Britain three Greek divisions to assist in the capture of the Gallipoli Peninsula. Hankey recorded an 'Extra-ordinary telegram from Greece [on 1 March]' in which 'They [the Greeks] say they want to march into Constantinople, to be the first to take communion at St. Sophia, but their interest is purely sentimental, they did not want to stay there & would not accept the city if offered them.'[77] Asquith and Kitchener accepted the offer with alacrity. Churchill believed the Greek troops would more than compensate for the missing 29th Division. The Russian reaction was predictable. On 3 March Sazonov informed Britain's ambassador, Sir George Buchanan, that: 'The Russian Government could not consent to Greece participating in operations at the Dardanelles.' The French were told even more emphatically the following day that: 'The Russian Government would not, at any price accept the cooperation of Greece in a Constantinople expedition.'[78] As the Russians well knew, once Constantinople was occupied by a large Greek army, 'with all the authority of an Allied and victorious power, no amount of Russian diplomacy could dislodge them.'[79]

On 3 March Buchanan telegraphed Grey that the Russians had informed him that 'on no account would they allow Greek soldiers to aid the British'.[80] In fact, as Britain's Minister at Athens, Sir Francis Elliot, informed Grey the same day, the Greek General Staff was 'absolutely opposed to sending any force to the Dardanelles', fearing that the Bulgarians would 'stab Greece in the back' if it attacked Turkey.[81] The Greek offer was withdrawn on 6 March. Having acted unilaterally without consulting the army chiefs, Venizelos was forced to resign.

Much has been made, subsequently, of this Russian veto, with Churchill assigning Russia responsibility for the loss of the Greek divisions at a critical time when their employment might well have ensured the capture of the Gallipoli Peninsula and the success of the operation.[82] It features prominently in Churchill's 'terrible ifs' which accumulated and conspired to rob him of victory. But the reality is that it was Bulgaria, not Russia, which effectively vetoed Greek military assistance in March 1915, regardless of who was to have Constantinople. King Constantine (of Greece) had been in complete agreement with his generals' position *before* the Russian veto was made public.[83] Hence the Greek offer had been illusory from the outset.

On 7 November 1914, in an effort to win over Bulgaria to the Allied cause, the British, French and Russians had offered King Ferdinand all the territory his country had lost to Turkey in the Second Balkan War. The Bulgarian monarch demanded a large part of Serbian Macedonia as well, which the Serbs (who loathed the Bulgarians) refused to concede. Lloyd George and Churchill sought to offer Bulgaria the whole of Macedonia, to which Grey remarked: 'Bulgaria would not be bought by the size of the promise, but would consider which group would most be in a position to redeem its promises.'[84] In August 1914 Ferdinand had refused to join any Balkan confederation against the Central Powers unless the Greeks first surrendered Kavalla to Bulgaria which, as far as the Greeks were concerned, was never an option.[85] In February 1915

Ferdinand gave the Allies a strong indication of where his sympathies lay when he accepted a large loan from Germany.[86] Indeed, once the rumour of the British and French pledge to Russia began to spread, intense hostility was generated among the Balkan powers, who had no wish to see Constantinople and the Straits controlled by the Russian bear. Bulgaria made a counter proposal to Greece and Romania that they should join her in opposing Russian ambitions in the area.[87]

It thus becomes apparent that any attempt to induce the Balkan states into an alliance on the same side as Russia (to help achieve Russian aims in the region) was fraught with difficulty. It becomes equally apparent that Churchill's confidence in a coalition of Balkan forces performing the role of a massive, missing Allied army was somewhat misplaced. Only *after* the Dardanelles had been forced was there any possibility of Bulgaria joining the Entente (to scavenge on the Turkish carcass). And by 10 March, despite all the newspaper ballyhoo, the pro-German Bulgarian Cabinet remained singularly unimpressed by the fleet's progress. London was notified that the Bulgarian Prime Minister 'was convinced that the fleet would not get through'.[88] Similar doubts were voiced by the King of Romania.[89] By 10 March, in fact, Carden's progress at the Dardanelles had come to a grinding halt.

∗∗∗

156

Carden had been ill-served from the start. His battle orders limited the number of shells available to his battleships. In addition, during the preliminary bombardment of the outer forts, the ominous discovery was made that the ships produced their most accurate fire while riding at anchor. Once inside the Straits this had become a serious problem, with the 14-inch and 11-inch guns of the forts at the Narrows forcing the warships to keep moving, considerably reducing the accuracy of their fire.[90] In formulating his battle plan, Carden's gunnery officers had calculated that, from long range, 'only two shells in a hundred could be expected to hit [individual] gun[s in the forts]'.[91] Mobile field guns, which could not even be located, let alone put out of action, further added to the conundrum. On 10 March Carden advised the Admiralty that: 'The methodical reduction of the forts is not feasible without expenditure of ammunition out of all proportion to that available.'[92] A supplementary appreciation of the situation was sent the same day via Admiral Limpus at Malta, which stated that:

> Ships inside Straits are constantly exposed to fire from concealed guns with which it has been found impossible to deal effectively [,] their plunging fire is very destructive but up to the present its accuracy has been poor though that is improving ... We are for the present checked by ... necessity of clearing mine fields and presence of large number of movable howitzers on both sides of Straits whose position up to the present we have

not been able to locate. Our experience shows [naval] gun fire alone will not render forts innocuous[,] most of the guns must be destroyed individually by demolition.[93]

Vice Admiral Arthur Limpus had been the logical choice for Commander-in-Chief Mediterranean Fleet, having headed the British Naval Mission to Turkey between 1912 and 1914. In 1913 he had supervised the laying of the Dardanelles minefield. The Naval Mission was withdrawn in September 1914. Not wishing to offend Turkey, which was still neutral at that time, in an act of '[schoolboy] chivalry which surely outstripped common sense', and to appease the Foreign Office, Carden was given the Mediterranean command, with Limpus replacing him at the Malta Dockyard.[94] On 11 March, Jackson sent a memo to the Chief of Staff, pointing out:

[Re] Admiral Carden's report ...

His operations are now greatly retarded by concealed batteries of howitzers, and their effects are now as formidable as the heavy guns in the [forts]. He also states that demolition parties are essential to render guns useless. The enemy's military forces have prevented this work from being effectively completed at the entrance, and they will be in *an even better position to prevent it further up the straits* ... [T]here are now ample military forces ready at short notice for

158

cooperation with [Carden], if necessary; and I suggest the time has arrived to make use of them ... I suggest the Vice-Admiral be asked if he considers the time has now arrived to make use of military forces to occupy the Gallipoli Peninsula, and clear away the enemy artillery on that side.[95]

In *The World Crisis,* Churchill claimed that 'the Admiralty War Group all were agreed upon the [answering 'Secret and Personal from First Lord'] telegram [he sent] to Carden' (No.101) on the 11th, in which no mention was made of military support:[96]

Your original instructions laid stress on caution and deliberate methods, [Churchill advised] and we approve highly the skill and patience with which you have advanced hitherto without loss.

The results to be gained are however great enough to justify loss of ships and men if success cannot be obtained without. The turning of the corner at Chanak may decide the whole operation and produce consequences of a decisive character upon the war, and we suggest for your consideration that a point has now been reached when it is necessary, choosing favourable weather conditions to overwhelm the forts at the Narrows at decisive range by fire of the largest number of guns great and small that can be brought to bear upon them.

Under cover of this fire the guns at the forts might be destroyed by landing parties and as much as possible of the minefield swept up. The operation might have to be repeated until all the forts at the Narrows had been destroyed and the approaches.

We do not wish to hurry you or urge you beyond your judgment, but we recognize clearly that at a certain period in your operations you will have to press hard for a decision and we desire to know whether you consider that point has now been reached.[97]

Churchill had reassured the War Council the previous day that the forts in the Straits and at the Narrows were doomed and the naval operation was well on schedule. He made no mention of the fact that the outer forts' guns had been destroyed, not by naval gunfire, but by demolition parties of marines who could no longer be put ashore. Churchill told the Councillors at this meeting that:

Admiral Carden did not expect to get through the Straits for a week or two. The forts must be thoroughly broken up [but] there was no hurry. [With regard to the clearing of the minefield, Carden had reported]:

... that he could not undertake this until the [mobile howitzer] batteries [protecting the minefield] were smashed up. Once this was accomplished, the clearing of the minefields would, Admiral Carden said, only take a few hours.

[Churchill added, disingenuously, that]: The Admiralty still believed that they could effect the passage of the Straits by naval means alone, but were glad to know military support was available, if required.[98]

Notwithstanding the massive numbers of Turkish troops known to be in the area (*The Times* had speculated 200,000), and the absence of either a Balkan or Allied counter-force, the mood of the 10 March War Council remained surprisingly celebratory, as the order of business demonstrates. The Councillors were intent on apportioning out the Turkish Empire, in anticipation of its imminent demise, their growing optimism reflected in a tougher stance they were prepared to adopt with Russia, for example. Grey reminded the assembly that 'Russia had absolutely vetoed Greek co-operation', and Balfour pointed out that '[i]f the Russians obtained [Constantinople] now they might slacken their efforts in the main theatre of war. We ought to consider what we want [in return], for example in the Persian Gulf and elsewhere.'[99]

Lloyd George 'pressed that our desiderata be formulated at once' to obviate any 'friction in the division of the spoils'. Accordingly, while Syria was reluctantly apportioned to France, Britain would compensate itself by taking Alexandretta, with its 'special importance as an outlet for the [anticipated British] oil supplies from Mesopotamia and Persia'.[100] Sir Edward Grey had remarked at the 24 February War Council that: 'It was not impossible that we might have a *coup d'état* in Constantinople, if success was achieved at the Dardanelles.' Grey qualified this observation at the next War Council meeting by stating: '... what we really *relied on to open the Straits* was a *coup d'état* in Constantinople.'[101] By 10 March, in the absence of a massive Balkan or Allied army to assist, this belief had become Churchill's and the War Council's *only* strategy. But how realistic was the Councillors' conviction that Turkey would collapse 'of its own accord' once the Allied Fleet had forced the Straits?

General von Falkenhayn, former Minister of War, then (on 29 September 1914) Commander-in-Chief of all German military and naval forces, wrote of the rumour that Turkey would capitulate should the Dardanelles be forced: 'Upon one thing it was possible to depend absolutely, on the firm determination of the leading men in Turkey to defend every inch of Turkish soil and to continue the war even if Constantinople was to be lost. During the whole length of the war Enver Pasha [Turkey's Minister for War] never wavered for a moment in this heroic fidelity to the alliance.'[102] Grand Admiral von Tirpitz clarified Germany's position in August 1915 when he wrote: 'Should the Dardanelles fall, the world war has been decided against us.'[103] A reinvigorated, adequately armed Russia, with restored shipping access to the Mediterranean via the Straits, would have meant the certain eventual defeat of Germany. The German military and naval commanders at the Dardanelles, General von Sanders and Admiral von Usedom, had no intention of allowing that to happen.

Turkish and Allied Preparations

David French has provided a very plausible explanation of how the War Councillors could have persuaded themselves that victory was nevertheless possible against a clearly numerically superior enemy. He suggests that the Councillors may have been under the impression that they were conducting a campaign along the lines of one of 'Victoria's little wars'—that is, against a third-rate, backward Oriental power in which sheer numbers were not the decisive factor. Hence the normally meticulous planning and preparation which would have been *de rigueur* in a war against a modern, industrialised nation, was not considered necessary against the Turks.[104]

The Turkish Army had contributed significantly to its poor martial image in recent times, not the least through a farcical incident which took place on 18 December 1914 when the British cruiser *Doris* landed a party of sailors north of Alexandretta to cut the railway line. The Turks were extremely cooperative and assembled the locomotives for their destruction.

A British lieutenant agreed to a Turkish request to become a Turkish officer for the day, while the Turks assisted in blowing up the locomotives.[105]This comic-opera episode, allied with their poor showing when a Turkish force attacked the Suez Canal on 3 February 1915, together with their dismal form in the 1912–13 Balkan Wars, allowed Churchill later to tell the Dardanelles Commissioners that he believed 'Turkish resistance would not immediately be of the most efficient character.'[106] Nevertheless, this was the same Turkish Army described by Lord Fisher in 1911 from personal contact as 'the very best fighting army in the world'.[107]

The political situation in Constantinople in March 1915 has similarly been cited to justify the War Councillors' optimism. In January 1915 the Director of Naval Intelligence, Captain W.R. Hall, had sent three agents to Athens to open secret negotiations with members of the Turkish government. It was not until 16 February that Cabinet was told by Churchill: 'We are promised a military rising and ultimate revolution on the fall of the first forts.' 108 At the beginning of March, Hall's agents opened discussions with Talaat Pasha, Grand Vizier, Minister for the Interior and, along with Enver and Djemal, one of the three most powerful men in Turkey. Talaat was offered a bribe of £4 million to persuade his fellow 'Young Turk' leaders to 'withdraw from their alliance with Germany, end the war, and open the Dardanelles.'[109] Churchill had further raised Cabinet hopes on 2 March by informing the members of the existence of 'a friendly and bribable Pasha [in Constantinople]'.[110] Talaat, however, demanded assurances that Turkey would retain Constantinople as its capital in any post-war settlement; assurances which Britain could not give, having promised the city to Russia on 10 March. The talks were consequently broken off on 17 March, on the eve of the Allied naval attack. Believing Talaat to have been a traitor motivated by greed, Hall's agents discovered, too late, that they had been dealing with a patriot, interested only in negotiating an honourable peace for his country.[111]

Henry Morgenthau, American Ambassador to Constantinople from 1913 to 1916, provided another credible source of evidence concerning the possibility of a *coup d'état,* subsequently writing:

> In early March ... the exodus from the capital had begun; Turkish women and children were being moved into the interior; all the banks had been compelled to send their gold into Asia Minor; the archives of the Sublime Porte had already been carried to Eski Sher; and practically all the ambassadors and their suites, as well as most of the government officials, had made their preparations to leave.[112]

This 'evidence' was published in the international newspapers at the time. Far from being conclusive, however, it could equally indicate that resistance was planned to continue from the interior—as General von

Falkenhayn had asserted. And, as Prior notes, similar scenes would have been observed in Paris in August/September 1914, 'yet no one has suggested that the French were on the point of surrendering'. In addition, trenches were being dug in Constantinople, and the artillery defences of the city increased—all signs that the Turks had no intention of capitulating.[113] From his privileged position as witness to these events and confidant to the Turkish leaders, Morgenthau mounted a strong argument, claiming:

> Had the Allied fleets once passed the defences at the Straits, the administration of the Young Turks would have come to a bloody end ... As soon as the guns began to fire [against the outer forts] placards appeared on the hoardings denouncing Talaat and his associates as responsible for all the woes that had come to Turkey ... Every day the Turks expected the news that the Bulgarians had declared war and were marching on Constantinople, and they knew that such an attack would necessarily bring in Rumania and Greece.

> The domestic situation was deplorable; all over Turkey thousands of the populace were daily dying of starvation; practically all able-bodied men had been taken into the army, so that only a few were left to till the fields; the criminal requisitions had almost destroyed all business ... It was a

common report that ... this revolution was feared more than the British fleet.

And now ... this mighty armada of England and her allies was approaching, determined to destroy the defences and capture the city. At that time there was no force which the Turks feared as they feared the British fleet ... It seemed to them superhuman—the one overwhelming power which it was hopeless to contest.[114]

According to Morgenthau, every official in Constantinople, military and civil—with one exception—believed that the capital was doomed and expected the imminent arrival of the Allied fleet in the Bosphorus. Enver Pasha, the Minister for Defence (and thus, perhaps, the one person most aware of the true situation), was equally certain that the Allies would fail. Referring to the 'silly panic that had seized nearly all classes in the capital', he explained the reasons for his confidence to Morgenthau (as he took him on an inspection cruise of the Dardanelles defences on 15 March 1915):[115]

We shall defend Constantinople to the end [Enver had said.] We have plenty of guns, plenty of ammunition, and we have these on terra-firma, whereas the English and French batteries are floating ones [thus capable of being sunk]. And the natural advantages of the straits are so great that the warships can make little progress against them ... Indeed, I do not know just what these English and French are driving at. Suppose they rush the Dardanelles, get here into the Marmora, and reach Constantinople, what good will it do them? They can bombard and destroy the city, I admit; but they cannot capture it, as they have no troops to land. Unless they do bring a large army, they will be caught in a trap. They can perhaps stay here for two or three weeks, until their food and supplies are exhausted, and then they will have to go back—rush the straits again and again run the risk of annihilation.

In the meantime we should have repaired the forts, brought in troops, and made ourselves ready for them. It seems to me to be a very foolish enterprise.

Enver took Morgenthau on an inspection of the forts, beginning with fortress Hamidie at Chanak, where the Minister told him that 'all its officers and 85 per cent of the men on duty [were German], from the cruisers *Goeben* and *Breslau*.'[116] German efficiency and meticulous preparation were evident along both shores of the Straits; from the teams of buffalo Morgenthau was shown hauling mobile howitzers 'from one emplacement to another [once] the fleet had obtained their range', to lengths of sewer pipe discharging clouds of 'inky smoke' and attracting 'more than 500 shots, while the real artillery pieces [some distance away] remained intact and undetected.'[117] Enver's assessment would be totally vindicated by subsequent events.

British preparations for the naval attack provided a stark contrast to German efficiency, with Carden facing an apparently insoluble conundrum. In order to silence the guns of the Turkish forts and proceed to Constantinople, his battleships needed to approach close enough to the forts to overwhelm them with their superior firepower. But the minefield kept the battleships at a safe distance and the long-range guns of the forts kept the warships moving, reducing their accuracy of fire. A channel would have to be cleared through the minefield which was protected by batteries of mobile field guns which could neither be located nor destroyed. Until such time as a channel was swept, the battleships would make no progress against the forts. It was, in fact, the minefield, not the forts at the Narrows (as Churchill insisted), which constituted the heart of the Dardanelles defences as the Allies would soon come to realise (see Map 2).[118]

From 6 March the minesweeper trawlers had mounted numerous attempts to sweep a channel, but all had failed miserably. Manned by their fishermen crews, these defenceless wooden boats were so slow and underpowered they could barely make three knots against the strong, five-knot current flowing down the Dardanelles. The draught of a trawler (14 feet) was greater than the depth of the mines (12 feet) they were sweeping, so they stood a good chance of being blown up as they 'trawled' them to the surface. Two boats, steaming 500 yards apart, dragged a steel wire between them (at a depth set by a heavy wooden kite) and the mines thus snared were dragged into shallow water where they could be destroyed by gunfire—and where the Turkish gunners were presented with almost perfect targets.[119]

The answer to Carden's problem had always been at hand, but had not been adequately considered. Accompanying the fleet were eight Beagle class destroyers which were ideal for conversion to heavy minesweepers. Given a three-week fitting out and training period for the crews, these converted warships were capable of sweeping with a heavy 21/2 inch wire at 14 knots, at which speed the mine's mooring cable would be sliced through, bringing it to the surface where it could be destroyed. With a draught of only 101/2 feet, these ships sat higher in the water than the mines and were thus safe from contact explosion. Their armour plating also gave them a certain measure of protection from artillery fire. Unfortunately, no converted Beagle minesweepers were available on 10 March. Nor were the four fast fleet sweepers Carden had repeatedly requested from Churchill. Eight Beagles would be fully converted three weeks after the abortive naval attack, followed by another eight two weeks later, when they would fully prove their potential. But, by that time, it was too late.[120]

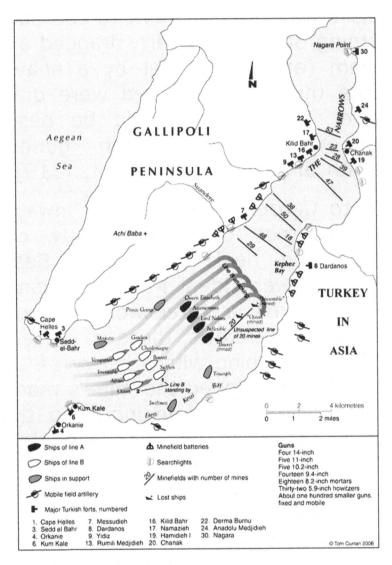

Map 2: Anglo-French naval attack on the Dardanelles, 18 March 1915.

On the night of 10 March seven trawlers, accompanied by four destroyer escorts, attempted to sweep the Kephez minefield, moving downstream with the current. The first pair of trawlers swept up two mines which exploded, sinking one of the trawlers. This explosion alerted the Turks, who switched on their searchlights, and the boats came under intense artillery fire, forcing them to retreat under cover of the destroyers, which had proven totally ineffectual against the mobile howitzer batteries. Three mines had been swept up. The next night the Turks were waiting and the trawlers were immediately subjected to a storm of fire. They fled down the Straits without even belaying their sweeps and with shells falling all around them.[121]

On the 13th, Carden informed Churchill: 'Sweeping operations last night not satisfactory owing to heavy fire, no casualties.'[122] Churchill was furious, telegraphing back to Carden: 'Your [telegram] 203 gives the impression of your being brought to a standstill both by night and day. I do not understand why minesweeping should be interfered with by fire which causes no casualties. Two or three hundred casualties would be a moderate price to pay for sweeping up as far as the Narrows.'[123] Carden's Chief of Staff, Commodore Keyes, was equally cavalier with his men's lives, writing: 'It did not matter if we lost all seven sweepers, there were 28 more, and the mines had to be swept up ... The Admiralty were prepared for losses, but we had chucked our hand in and started squealing before we had any.'[124]

That night Carden decided on an all-out attempt to sweep the Kephez minefield. The trawler crews were stiffened by volunteers from the Royal Navy and each boat was commanded by a commissioned officer. The seven trawlers were escorted by the battleship

Cornwallis, the cruiser *Amethyst* and a number of destroyers. The heavy firepower laid down by these warships made little impression on the Turkish searchlights or minefield batteries. The trawlers endured the same storm of shellfire as before, but the new crews were more determined and persistent. As a result, in two of the trawlers all the crew were either killed or wounded, and the others were so badly damaged that only two boats were able to belay their sweeps. Seventy casualties were sustained, with 22 killed and 28 wounded on board the *Amethyst,* where:

> A watch of stokers had been washing themselves in the bathroom [an officer reported,] A shell burst right among them, so that all the walls and roof were plastered with flesh and blood. The remains of the victims were put into sacks, but on mustering, it was discovered that instead of twelve men having been in the room (as thought), there had been nineteen.[125]

Churchill and Keyes had their casualties, but to no effect. Hardly any mines had been swept up. Carden telegraphed Churchill at noon on 14 March, conceding that he now 'fully concur[red]' with Churchill's telegram 101 of 11 March and adding: 'It is considered stage is reached when vigorous sustained action [has become] necessary for success. [However, Carden added:] In my opinion military operations on large scale should be commenced immediately.'[126] Carden sent Churchill another telegram at 4.55pm on the same day, advising him that: 'Fleet sweepers will be urgently required to precede the Fleet in Sea of Marmara. They were asked for in my [Telegram] 19, [of] January 10th.'[127] Carden would plan an all-out assault, utilising the combined firepower of his entire armada simultaneously to overwhelm the forts and silence the minefield batteries while leaving his minesweepers free to clear a passage for his battleships.

18 March 1915

At a War Staff Group meeting on 14 March, Fisher offered to go to the Dardanelles to take over command—not, as Churchill claimed in *The World Crisis,* because of his enthusiasm for the project—but rather because he had no confidence in Carden.[128] 'It was "touch and go" yesterday whether I did not go off to Dardanelles this morning', Fisher wrote to Jellicoe on 15 March, 'but it was decided otherwise' (by Churchill, who prevailed on him to allow Carden to remain in command).[129] In contrast to Churchill's sanguine appraisal of the situation (and his glowing, misleading reports to the War Council), Fisher told Jellicoe that: 'Things are going badly at the Dardanelles.'[130] Fisher wrote to Churchill the same day, setting out his concerns and requesting a War Council to decide on the action to be taken (with a naval attack looming): 'Everything points to instant action by a collective vote & decision of the War

Council with the Opposition joined in...', Fisher insisted.[131] Churchill replied at once:

Secret. My dear Fisher,

I don't think we want a War Council on this. It is after all only asking a lot of ignorant people to meddle in our business. I expect K[itchener] will do what we want about the troops being concentrated at Mudros ... meanwhile the naval operations are proceeding within safe and sure limits.[132]

In lieu of a War Council, Churchill sent Carden another bullying telegram which, under the guise of reiterating Carden's own plans, dictated to him, yet again, precise instructions as to how Churchill wanted his all-naval attack carried out. Churchill wrote:

Secret and Personal from First Lord [Telegram No 109]:

You must concert any military operations on a large scale which you consider necessary with General Hamilton when he arrives on Tuesday night [the 16th. In the event, Carden, would be allowed no time to liaise with Hamilton].

Secondly, we understand that it is your intention to sweep a good clear passage through the minefields to enable the forts at the Narrows eventually to be attacked at close range, and to cover this operation whether against the forts, or the light and movable armament, by whatever fire is necessary from the Battle Fleet, and this task will probably take several days.

After this is completed, we understand you intend to engage the forts at the Narrows at decisive range and put them effectually out of action.

You will then proceed again at your convenience with the attack on the forts beyond, and any further sweeping operations that may be necessary.

If this is your intention, we cordially approve it. We wish it to be pressed forward without hurry, but without loss of time.[133]

Carden once again concurred with Churchill's instructions, adding: 'Almost one third of the minesweepers are already sunk or out of action ... Fleet sweepers urgently required. Meantime I am fitting some destroyers for this purpose with light sweeps.'[134] Carden's fourth request to Churchill for fast fleet sweepers (steamers with a shallow draught and, like Beagles, ideal as minesweepers), had been ignored yet again, Churchill fobbing him off (in his last telegram) with: 'You will be informed later about ammunition, aeroplanes and minesweepers.'[135]

Belatedly, Carden had begun converting some of his destroyers for the most critical role at the Dardanelles, but it would prove too little, too late. Finally recognising the impossibility of his task of having to clear a passage through a minefield comprising 353 contact mines, laid in ten lines and stretching for five miles from the Narrows to Kephez Point—with only slow-moving, defenceless wooden trawlers in the face of point-blank artillery fire—Carden suffered a nervous collapse. He was replaced by his second-in-command, Rear Admiral John de Robeck. Carden sent a telegram to Churchill on the 16th, advising him: 'With regret obliged to go on sick list ... De Robeck continues operations on lines indicated in Admiralty telegram 109 ... I have fullest confidence in his judgment and determination.'[136]

Churchill sent a 'Secret and Personal from First Lord' telegram to de Robeck on the 17th, informing him:

> In entrusting to you with great confidence the command of the Mediterranean Fleet I presume you are in full accord with Admiralty telegram 101 and Admiralty telegram 109 and Vice-Admiral Carden's answers thereto, and that you consider, after separate and independent judgment, that the immediate operations proposed are wise and practicable. If not, do not hesitate to say so. If so, execute them *without delay and without further reference at the first favourable opportunity.* [137]

Once again a 'Secret and Personal from First Lord' telegram was employed to intimidate and deliver a thinly veiled ultimatum—and in this instance, to launch the naval attack. De Robeck was left in no doubt that his assumption of command was contingent on acceptance of 'Carden's' plan and its prompt execution. De Robeck could refuse neither the command nor its consequences. He replied to Churchill on the 18th:

> First Lord of Admiralty. Secret and Personal. Telegram No.747. Thank you for your telegram. I am in full agreement with telegrams mentioned. Operations will proceed [as specified] ... My view is that everything depends on our ability to clear the minefields for forcing the Narrows and this necessitates silencing the forts during the process of sweeping ...[138]

At 10.30 on the morning of 18 March, 'under a cloudless sky in all the jewelled serenity for which the Aegean is famous at its best', 16 Allied battleships, 12 cruisers and 22 destroyers 'swept majestically across the glittering waters' of the Dardanelles Straits. It was, as all who saw it later recalled, a magnificent spectacle, 'an unforgettable picture of aloof grandeur'.[139]

At 5.00pm, Admiral de Robeck recalled the fleet, bringing an end to a disastrous day. One third of his battle fleet had been lost: battleships *Bouvet, Ocean* and *Irresistible* sunk, with *Gaulois, Suffren* and *Inflexible* crippled and out of action for an indefinite period. At a cost of almost 700 Allied sailors (mostly French) killed, only four of the 78 heavy and medium guns had been put out of action. None of the 100 smaller howitzers and field guns had been touched. Turkish losses totalled 40 men killed and 70 wounded.[140] The Royal Navy had suffered one of the worst defeats in its long, proud history, and at the hands of a 'third-rate, Oriental power'.

Most of the damage had been caused by an undetected line of 20 mines laid by the Turkish steamer *Nousret* in the early hours of 8 March in Eren Kui Bay, parallel to the shore. *Bouvet* ran into one of these mines, almost simultaneously hit by a plunging shell from Fort Hamidie which smashed into her magazine.[141] The resultant explosion saw the ship sink in less than three minutes, taking almost all of her 640 crew to the bottom. *Irresistible, Inflexible* and *Ocean* ran into this same line of mines. Considerable damage was also inflicted (on *Suffren, Gaulois, Inflexible* and *Agamemnon*) by plunging artillery fire which crashed into their lightly armoured decks and unprotected superstructures (their heavy armour plating was designed to protect them essentially from low-trajectory, side-on naval gunfire).

The French battleship Bouvet sinks after hitting a mine, 18 March 1915 (IWM SP_000682A).

The forts at the Narrows and those of the intermediate defences may have taken a serious pounding, forcing the heavy guns into eventual silence, but the firepower of the entire fleet had been unable to subdue the Turkish mobile howitzers and curtail their dominance over the trawler-minesweepers. As a consequence, very few mines were swept before the trawlers were once again sent fleeing ignominiously back down the Straits, with shells splashing all around them.[142] With his battleships unable to make any progress through the unswept minefield, and ignorant of the cause of the devastating explosions (it was conjectured that they might have been the result of torpedoes fired across the Straits, or mines that had drifted down with the current), de Robeck had little choice other than to call a halt to proceedings.[143]

De Robeck fully expected to be replaced when he telegraphed details of the disastrous attack to the Admiralty the following day.[144] He concluded:

With the exception of the ships lost and damaged Squadron is ready for immediate action, but the plan of attack must be reconsidered and means found to deal with floating mines [which de Robeck erroneously believed had been the cause of the explosions] ...

Only a few saved from *Bouvet,* practically whole crew *Ocean* and *Irresistible* were taken off by destroyers under heavy fire: much gallantry and fine seamanship was displayed by all officers and men concerned.

Casualties not yet received. [In fact, 33 British sailors had been killed on *Inflexible,* 14 on *Irresistible* and one each on *Albion, Majestic* and *Ocean].*[145]

***

Winston Churchill's press release of 20 February, in providing the enemy with an advance warning of the Allies' intentions, might well have gravely compromised any chance of success by the naval attack. But it was his premature launching of that attack against a fortified minefield without a competent minesweeping force in attendance that ensured its defeat.

Churchill's press announcement also made it '[t]henceforth ... impossible for the [British]

Government to withdraw' from an all-out campaign against Turkey.

CHAPTER 4

The Case for Perseverance or Abandonment

Churchill's claim—that an immediate renewal of the naval attack within a few days of 18 March 1915 must be successful—has been echoed by his supporters ever since. The substance of that claim, together with an assessment of the strategy on which it was based, deserves to be tested. It would also be useful, if possible, to finally determine who was responsible for the escalation of the failed naval attack into a military invasion of Gallipoli.

Immediate Aftermath of the Naval Attack

In *The World Crisis,* Churchill took the official naval historian severely to task for his account of the 18 March naval attack (published in 1921), claiming that:

> ... the essential facts known at the present time ... are presented with so little order, with such confusion in chronology, and with such slight or erroneous discrimination between the relative importance of facts and events that no clear picture is afforded to the lay reader ... Torn

between a benevolent desire to avoid throwing blame upon the Admiralty for ordering the attack, or upon the Admiral for not succeeding in it ... the author almost seems to have sought refuge in obscure and inconclusive narration.[1]

Such criticism is unwarranted. Sir Julian Corbett's lucid description of those dramatic events provides the lay reader with a picture which is not only clear, but quite often harrowingly so, in its attention to essential detail.[2] Churchill's displeasure with Corbett derived essentially from the widely differing conclusions in their respective texts. The naval historian had written that: 'The great attempt to force the Narrows with the fleet had ended in what could only be regarded as a severe defeat ... [and at] such a rate of loss, with results apparently so meagre, it looked extremely doubtful whether the navy unaided [by the Army] could ever force a passage.' Corbett also described in detail the devastating effects of 6-inch howitzer shells on the battleships' lightly armoured decks and superstructures.[3]

Churchill's response to the naval reversal he recorded thus: 'I regarded this news only as the results of the first day's fighting. It never occurred to me for a moment that we should not go on within the limits of what we had decided to risk, until we had reached a decision one way or another.'[4]

A War Council met on 19 March and discussed the naval attack. For the first time Admiral Wilson was asked his opinion. 'Wilson said, so far as he gathered from [de Robeck's] telegrams, the forts had only been temporarily silenced.'[5] Churchill told the Council: 'We had information that the Turks were short of ammunition and mines.' The First Lord was authorised 'to inform the Admiral that he could continue operations at the Dardanelles if he thought fit.'[6]

That the Turkish forts were dangerously short of ammunition and could not have repulsed another determined attack by the fleet became, in later years, central to Churchill's argument—that victory was within the Allies' grasp, had de Robeck only persevered for one more attempt on or around 19 March. Churchill's contention was given powerful support by his official biographer, Martin Gilbert, in the following scene from *Winston S. Churchill* which, incidentally, Churchill made no mention of in *The World Crisis.* Gilbert writes:

During the afternoon of March 19 Churchill and Fisher received news which dispelled their gloom at the suspended action, for it pointed to the chance of certain victory as soon as de Robeck renewed the attack. Naval Intelligence had intercepted a message from the Kaiser to Admiral Souchon [Commander-in-Chief of the Turkish Navy], begging him at all costs to hold out at the Dardanelles and promising to send ammunition at the first opportunity. From the Kaiser's message it was clear that there must have been some panic among the German officers, and a grave shortage of ammunition in the forts of the Dardanelles. As soon as the message was decoded the Director of Naval Intelligence, Captain Hall, took it to Churchill's room, where he found the First Lord standing with Fisher by the fireplace. [Then, allegedly, follows Hall's account of what took place]:

"First Sea Lord", said I, "we've just received this."

Lord Fisher took the message, read it aloud, and waved it over his head. "By God", he shouted,

"I'll go through tomorrow!"

Mr. Churchill, equally excited, seized hold of the telegram and read it through again for his own satisfaction. "That means," he said, "they've come to the end of their ammunition."

> "Tomorrow!" repeated Lord Fisher, and at that moment I believe that he was as enthusiastic as ever Mr. Churchill had been about the whole Dardanelles campaign. "We shall probably lose six ships, but I'm going through."

> The First Lord nodded. "Then get the orders out."

> And there and then Lord Fisher sat down at Mr. Churchill's table to draft out the necessary orders.[7]

This ludicrous scene never, in fact, took place, as Professor Marder and Admiral James affirm. The message from the Kaiser was intercepted and decoded in Room 40 of Naval Intelligence on the 12th, not the

19th of March. Then it was taken *immediately* to Lord Fisher, *who was alone* in his room.[8] Hall's biographer, Admiral Sir William James, provided an account of this scene somewhat at variance with that related by Gilbert. To begin with, according to James, it took place on the 13th of March and it involved Lord Fisher only. Churchill was not present. The telegram from the Kaiser, via von Müller, reads:

> For Admiral Usedom. H.M. the Kaiser received the report and telegram relating to the Dardanelles. Everything conceivable is being done here to arrange the supply of ammunition. For political reasons it is necessary to maintain confident tone in Turkey. H.M. the Kaiser requests you to use your influence in this direction. The sending of a German or Austrian submarine is being seriously considered.[9]

Hall took this decoded message straight to Lord Fisher:

> He knew that Fisher was very lukewarm about ... the war effort at the Dardanelles ... This quite unexpected news that the Turks were short of ammunition had quite an immediate, if temporary, effect on Fisher's attitude to the operations. Indeed, he seemed as enthusiastic as the members of the Cabinet, whose views he had hitherto bitterly opposed.[10]

Just how temporary Fisher's new-found enthusiasm was can be gauged by the fact that, only one or two days later (according to the various accounts), he was offering, at the War Staff Group, to go out to take over command, and telling Jellicoe the next day (15 March) that: 'Things are going badly at the Dardanelles.' In James' account, Fisher's enthusiasm was accompanied by none of the histrionics described by Gilbert. There was no waving of the decoded message over his head, nor any exuberant cry that: 'We shall probably lose six ships, but [by God] I'm going through.'

The date of this decoded message was confirmed by Churchill himself in a telegram he sent to Carden on the 13th, but which was not received by the admiral until the 14th. This message, which does not appear in *The World Crisis,* reads: 'Telegram 105. We have information that the Turkish forts are short of ammunition, that the German officers have made despondent reports, and have appealed to Germany for more.'[11] On 22 March Churchill once again confirmed the date of the message, informing de Robeck of the status of 'Turkish ammunition—it is known that the forts *on the[12] instant* were short, and that steps were being taken to obtain replenishments from Germany. It is not considered that these steps have as yet been successful.' De Robeck was also advised of 'Reports from various sources as to alleged transit of German artillerymen, arms and ammunition through Roumania to strengthen the Dardanelles.'[12]

The orders drafted 'there and then' by Fisher scarcely bear any evidence of a new-found sense of confidence or urgency. The alleged Turkish ammunition shortage was not even mentioned in his reply telegram to de Robeck, which reads:

20 March 1915.

> We regret the losses you have suffered in your resolute attack. Convey to all ranks and ratings Their Lordships' approbation of their conduct in action and seamanlike skill and prudence with which His Majesty's ships were handled. Convey to the French squadron the Admiralty's appreciation of their loyal and effective support, and our sorrow for the losses they have sustained. [Replacement battleships] *Queen* and *Implacable* should join you very soon, and *London* and *Prince of Wales* sail tonight. Please telegraph any information as to damage done to forts, and also full casualties and ammunition expended. It appears important not to let the forts be repaired or to encourage enemy by apparent suspension of operations. Ample supplies of 15" ammunition are available for indirect fire of *Queen Elizabeth* across the Peninsula.[13]

But another, equally significant event had apparently taken place on the 19th. In a continuation of this same scene, according to Martin Gilbert, Captain Hall made an outrageous admission to Churchill, advising him of the £4 million bribe he had offered to Talaat

Pasha to persuade the Young Turks to break with the Germans and open the Dardanelles:

> [Churchill] was frowning. "Who authorized this?" he demanded.
>
> "I did, First Lord" [Hall confessed].
>
> "But—the Cabinet surely knows nothing about it?"
>
> "No, it does not. But if we were to get peace, or if we were to get a peaceful passage [of the Dardanelles] for that amount, I imagine they'll be glad enough to pay."
>
> It was one of those moments when dropped pins are supposed to be heard. Then Mr. Churchill turned to Lord Fisher who was still busily writing." D'you hear what this man has done? He's sent out people with four millions to buy a peaceful passage! On his own!"
>
> "What!" shouted Lord Fisher, starting up from his chair. "Four millions?
>
> No, no. I tell you I'm going through tomorrow."[14]

According to Gilbert, 'Fisher was determined to have a naval victory. Turning to Hall he said: "Cable at once to stop all negotiations. All. No. Offer [two million pounds] for the *Goeben,* and [one million pounds] for the *Breslau.* But nothing else. We're going through."'

Remaining in Churchill's room, Hall drafted the necessary telegrams. Churchill shared Fisher's enthusiasm at the prospect of an immediate and decisive naval victory, and Hall had to abandon his plan for a negotiated peace ... Churchill and Fisher were insistent that de Robeck renew the attack as soon as possible. Because of the Turkish shortage of ammunition and the inability of the Germans to make the shortage good *for at least a week,* victory seemed to them inevitable.[15]

What actually transpired, according to Admiral James was that, on learning of the £4 million bribe offered to the Turks, Fisher's attitude hardened. 'He told Hall to cable at once to stop negotiations, except to offer 200,000 pounds for the *Goeben* and 100,000 for the *Breslau.* '[16] This fabricated scene serves to establish a number of important fallacies: that the Turks had come to the end of their ammunition, and of the Allies' consequent proximity to victory; of Fisher's passionate commitment to a renewed naval attack, and his contribution to the operation's failure through his reckless and overbearing rejection of peace negotiations in his desire for a naval victory. In fact, by 19 March, the Turks' ammunition problems had largely been resolved.

The Case for Perseverance

In *The World Crisis* Churchill devoted a significant chapter, entitled 'The Case for Perseverance and Decision', to explaining how a renewed naval attack, within a few days of 18 March, would almost certainly have succeeded. In Churchill's analysis, the Dardanelles defences 'consisted of four factors—forts, mobile howitzers, minefield batteries and minefields—all well combined but mutually dependent.'

Their functions he elaborated as:

> The minefields blocked the passage of the Straits and kept the Fleet beyond their limits. The minefield batteries prevented the sweeping of the minefields. The forts protected the minefield batteries by keeping the battleships at a distance with their long guns. The mobile howitzers kept the battleships on the move and increased the difficulty of overcoming the forts. So long as all four factors stood together, the defences constituted a formidable obstruction. But not one could stand by itself [Churchill concluded], and if one were broken down, its fall entailed the collapse of the others.[17]

While Churchill's first four statements are irrefutable, his conclusion is a false one. The Dardanelles defences may well have been mutually dependent, but they were also, to an equal degree, mutually independent.

The silencing of the forts' guns, for example, would not have signalled the automatic demise of the minefield batteries or the mobile howitzers, as Churchill claims. In fact, by March 1915, the forts were no longer the dominant factor in the Straits as Liman von Sanders later attested: 'The mines were the primary defence of the Dardanelles', von Sanders affirmed, 'and the function of the guns in the forts was simply to protect the minefields from interference.'[18] As long as the minefield remained unswept, the fleet was powerless to make any progress towards Constantinople. And even had the minefield been cleared, the Turkish mobile artillery on both shores would still have prevented the passage of unarmoured supply ships along that waterway to the fleet.

In Churchill's estimation everything depended on taking advantage of a fortuitous and temporary shortage of ammunition in the Turkish forts, the vulnerability of which he explained as:

> The forts themselves could not withstand the Fleet ... They could be dominated and greatly injured by direct fire from inside the Straits below the minefields. [This was incorrect; the battleships had to be within close range of the forts to effect any real damage, and] ... they [the forts] could be forced to exhaust their ammunition in conflict with the Fleet [this assertion is equally fallacious, there being no valid reason for the forts to expend ammunition needlessly while the battleships were

kept at a safe distance from them by the minefield]. The amount of ammunition possessed by the Turks is therefore [in Churchill's scenario] cardinal.[19]

In terms of the actual ammunition levels in the forts on 19 March 1915, Churchill's figures[20] accord essentially with those revealed by the Mitchell Committee,[21] the official naval and military historians, and with Turkish General Headquarters. These specify that, on 19 March, available ammunition amounted to some 271 rounds of 14-inch ammunition, 868 rounds of 9.4-inch, 720 rounds of 8.2-inch mortar and 3706 rounds of 6-inch howitzer ammunition—more than enough to withstand at least two more determined attacks by the fleet on the scale of 18 March. The ammunition levels for the 100 smaller guns of 3.4-inch and 5.6-inch calibre, mobile field guns and howitzers were also considerable.[22]

One pertinent factor which Churchill conveniently ignored was that the alleged shortage of ammunition in the forts lasted only a few days. In fact, by 19 March, it was well on its way to being resolved as the Germans rushed replenishments through Bulgaria and Romania, both countries turning a blind eye to this breach of their neutrality. Admiral Fisher sent a copy of a *Morning Post* article to Churchill on 25 March which reported that:

During the last fortnight about 150 mines, any amount of ammunition, guns &c had been coming

> through Roumania from Germany. Six weeks ago ... 40 [German] officers brought with them cases and cases full of ammunition, all marked Red Cross; now, however, there is no attempt at concealment; the ammunition comes through quite openly, and there is nothing to prevent the Germans bringing in even bigger guns.[23]

Churchill was horrified to learn that Romania was permitting Germany to violate her neutrality in such fashion and, on 25 March, asked Grey to send an immediate protest to Bucharest. During the day a military intelligence report was received from Petrograd confirming that 'the Romanians were allowing their territory to be used for the transit of German weapons, and that Bulgaria was doing likewise'.[24] A report from Constantinople, through neutral sources, 'confirmed that the [ammunition] shortage was over by 18 March'.[25]

On 2 August 1914, Turkey and Germany had signed a secret alliance committing Turkey to support Germany in a war against Russia. In return Germany pledged to assist her ally with military and naval personnel, plus war matériel. On 18 August the 800 German naval officers and men requested by Admiral Souchon were despatched, to be followed by half a million artillery shells demanded by Enver Pasha (to be supplied by Krupp). From 22 August to 24 September 1914, war matériel, including howitzers and mines for the Dardanelles, reached Turkey via

Romania, but under severe restrictions—only eight freight cars per day were allowed to cross the Romanian border. This was reduced to seven from 24 September until 2 October, when all shipments of arms were officially banned by the Romanian government. The Turks had received around 300 freight cars of essential armaments, but some 200 'were standing idle on German and Hungarian sidings ... when the Ottoman Empire entered the war in the beginning of November 1914. The flow of German personnel and war *matériel* had been effectively blocked; the Turks were on their own for many months to come.'[26]

Notwithstanding this later German report, sufficient munitions had already passed to the Turks to provide not only formidable defences at the Dardanelles, but also to repulse the subsequent Allied military invasion. 'The alleged [munitions] shortage did not materialize during the Gallipoli campaign', Prior observes. And, as the official British and Russian sources at the time clarify, the Turks were being substantially resupplied with arms by mid-March 1915.[27]

Churchill would have been well aware of the true ammunition situation within the forts on 19 March when he wrote Volume II of *The World Crisis* in 1923.

***

On 20 March de Robeck replied to Fisher, explaining his priorities:

Plan for re-organising mine-sweeping progressing. Eight Beagle class [destroyers] being fitted as mine-sweepers. Six River class [destroyers] and four torpedo boats as mine-seekers with light sweeps, and a flotilla of picket boats with explosive creeps. Fifty British minesweepers manned entirely by volunteers, and twelve French sweepers will be available. [De Robeck stressed an inevitable delay before operations could commence] as new crews and destroyers will need some preliminary practice.[28]

According to Commodore Keyes, who was given a free hand by de Robeck to reorganise the minesweeping force, the first eight Beagles would not be ready until 4 April at the earliest.[29] On 21 March de Robeck advised Fisher further: 'From experience gained on the 18th I consider Forts at the Narrows and the batteries guarding minefields can be dominated after a few days engagement sufficient to enable [destroyer] minesweepers to clear minefields. [However,] howitzer and field gun fire must be faced [by other means], *as it is impossible for the ships to deal with it.'* [30] There is no mention of this telegram in *The World Crisis.* De Robeck had already arrived at this conclusion on 9 March in an appreciation he wrote of the situation.[31] He then stressed again what he saw as his most urgent priority: 'Our first consideration must be organizing strong military mine sweeping force with which to clear first the area in which squadron will manoeuvre to cover the minesweepers operating in the Kephez minefields. *Until preparations for this thoroughly completed I do not propose to engage the forts by direct attack.* '[32]

In 1919, the Mitchell Committee decided that the fleet would have stood a 50% chance of successfully sweeping a channel as far as the Narrows 'if attempted after 4 April'.[33] If attempted after 18 April, the new minesweeping force then available could have cleared a channel half a mile wide in one determined thrust forward of the fleet in line ahead. This capability was tested and confirmed on 18 April 'when two "Beagles" swept at 20 knots ahead of two battleships inside the Straits'. The 16 destroyer-minesweepers, plus eight fast fleet sweepers then available, would have been able to sweep successfully in the face of Turkish artillery fire. Turkish artillery spotting was found to be poorly coordinated and unable to target fast-moving ships. Marder established that destroyers sweeping at 14 knots would have been virtually immune from Turkish artillery fire.[34] It scarcely merits mentioning that any attempt to sweep the Kephez minefield before 4 April, employing the same ineffectual trawler-minesweepers against the same unsubdued mobile howitzers and minefield batteries could have offered no hope of success. Yet this is precisely what Churchill would demand on 23 March.

Admiral Wester Wemyss, later First Sea Lord and the Senior Naval Officer at Lemnos at the time of Carden's breakdown, had graciously permitted de Robeck (his

198

junior in rank) to retain command of the fleet. Wemyss visited de Robeck on the 19th, immediately following the naval fiasco, to offer some advice:

> The experience we had gone through [Wemyss suggested], pointed to the following argument: [that] the battleships could not force the Straits until the minefields had been cleared—the minefields could not be cleared until the concealed guns which defended them were destroyed—they could not be destroyed until the Peninsula was in our hands, hence we should have to seize it with the Army. Any main operations must therefore be postponed until such time as preparations for a combined attack could be made.[35]

On the 21st, de Robeck also advised Fisher of 'telegrams exchanged between himself and General Hamilton on 20th March' when he had sounded out the general over the prospects of limited military cooperation in the form of '[a] feint of landing [troops] on a large scale on several points of the coast of Gallipoli [which] might tend to draw off field guns from the general action [which de Robeck was contemplating] when they are likely to seriously hamper our sweeping operations.'[36] Such then was de Robeck's thinking on the 21st. Even now his mind seems to have been gravitating towards some form of troop assistance to help him cope with the Turkish howitzers. He ended this telegram to Fisher: 'I will confer with General Hamilton as soon as possible.'[37]

De Robeck conferred with generals Hamilton and Birdwood the next day aboard *Queen Elizabeth.* At this time the necessity for large-scale troop involvement was finally confirmed.

The battleship HMS Queen Elizabeth leaving the island of Lemnos in the Aegean (AWM A02719).

Churchill made great play, in *The World Crisis,* over who actually initiated this course of action. 'It will be seen that there is a distinct discrepancy between the statements of Admiral de Robeck and Sir Ian Hamilton', Churchill writes.[38] It matters little. Birdwood had recognised this need on 5 March (in a letter to Kitchener), and Hamilton had written similarly to Kitchener on the 19th after watching the naval attack: 'that if the Army is to participate, its operations will not assume the subsidiary form anticipated [by Churchill] ... [It] will not be a case of landing parties ... but rather a case of a deliberate and progressive military operation carried out in force in order to make good the passage of the Navy.'[39]

De Robeck's telegram to Hamilton on the 20th strongly suggests that he had made up his mind on the necessity for large-scale military cooperation even before Hamilton and Birdwood came aboard *Queen Elizabeth.* Both generals later agreed that this had been the case.[40] De Robeck telegraphed the Admiralty on 23 March:

> At meeting today with Generals Hamilton and Birdwood the former told me army will not be in a position to undertake any military operations before 14th April. In order to maintain our communications when the Fleet penetrates into the Sea of Marmora it is necessary to destroy all guns of positions guarding the Straits ... Only a small percentage can be destroyed by [naval] gunfire ... From our experience on the 4th March it seems in future destruction of guns will have to be carried out in face of strenuous and well prepared opposition. I do not think it a practicable operation to land a force adequate to undertake this service inside Dardanelles. General Hamilton concurs in this opinion. If the guns are not destroyed any success of Fleet may be nullified by Straits closing up after ships have passed through and, as loss of material will possibly be heavy, ships will not be available to keep Dardanelles open. The mine menace will continue

until the Sea of Marmora is reached being much greater than was anticipated. It must be carefully and thoroughly dealt with as regards mines and floating mines. This will take time to accomplish but our arrangements will be ready by time Army can act. It appears better to prepare a decisive effort about middle of April rather than risk a great deal for what may possibly be only a partial solution.[41]

The voice of reason had finally made itself heard. Churchill's response was predictable. He *demanded* that de Robeck continue the naval attack, convening 'an immediate meeting of the Admiralty War Group, and placing the following [his] telegram before them [for their concurrence, before sending]': 42

Admiralty to Vice-Admiral de Robeck [reproduced in full].

> Your [telegram no.] 818. In view of the dangers of delay through submarine attack and of heavy cost of army protection, and possibility that it will fail or be only partly effective in opening the Straits, and that danger of mines will not be relieved by it, we consider that you ought to persevere methodically but resolutely with the plan contained in your instructions and in Admiralty telegram 109, and that you should make all preparations to renew the attack begun on 18th at the first favourable opportunity. You should *dominate the forts at the Narrows and*

sweep the minefield and then batter the forts at close range, taking your time, using your aeroplanes, and all your improved methods of guarding against mines. The destruction of the forts at the Narrows may open the way for a further advance. The entry into the Marmora of a fleet strong enough to beat the Turkish Fleet would produce decisive results on the whole situation, and *you need not be anxious about your subsequent line of communications. We know the forts are short of ammunition and supply of mines is limited.* We do not think the time has yet come to give up the plan of forcing the Dardanelles by a purely naval operation. Commodore de Bartolome, who starts today, will give you our views on points of detail. Meanwhile all your preparations for renewing attack should go forward.[43]

This 'verbose message' (in Captain Penn's words) was simply calling for a repetition of what had clearly failed on the 18th, while contributing no meaningful advice on 'how the miracle was to be performed'.[44]There was no basis for Churchill to reassure de Robeck not to be anxious over his line of supply. The alleged shortage of ammunition in the forts did not apply to the mobile howitzers and minefield batteries and the threat they offered to unarmoured supply ships. As the Mitchell Committee and the Turkish General Staff made clear, there was an abundance of ammunition remaining for the Turkish field artillery. Churchill continues:

> But now immediately I encountered insuperable resistance. The Chief of Staff [Oliver] was quite ready to order the renewal of the attack; but the First Sea Lord would not agree to the proposed telegram, nor did Sir Arthur Wilson nor Sir Henry Jackson who was present.[45] Lord Fisher took the line that hitherto he had been willing to carry the enterprise forward because it was supported and recommended by the Commander on the spot. But now that Admiral de Robeck and Sir Ian Hamilton had decided on a joint operation, we were bound to accept their views.[46]

Churchill, however, was not prepared to accept such a 'revolt' by his subordinates. As he writes: 'For the first time since the war began, high words were used around the octagonal table.' But to no avail. 'Nothing that I could do could overcome the Admirals now they had definitely stuck their toes in... [Consequently,] I took the draft of my telegram to the Prime Minister.' But for once, Asquith gave his full support to the Admiralty chiefs, refusing to overrule them. 'I was therefore compelled', Churchill concludes, 'under extreme duress to abandon the intention *of sending direct orders to Admiral de Robeck to renew the attack'.*[47] He subsequently added: 'It was with grief that I announced to the Cabinet on the 23rd the refusal of the Admirals and the Admiralty to continue the naval attack, and that it must, at any rate for the time being, be abandoned.'[48]

This entire passage is highly illuminating, illustrating as it does the First Lord's *modus operandi* at the Admiralty. The 'we' constantly referred to in the proposed 'Admiralty' telegram order (and which de Robeck, and Carden before him, would have understood to have been Fisher and the War Staff Group), is revealed to be Churchill himself, using this body virtually as a rubber stamp. Hitherto, Fisher and the Admiralty chiefs had been obliged to accept this usurpation of their authority on higher political grounds, leaving Churchill free to conduct his own private operation of war in their name. Now, at last, Fisher and the Admiralty heads were able to assert their authority, albeit temporarily.

On 22 March Churchill had telegraphed Vice Admiral Limpus at Malta, somewhat belatedly asking: 'Have you communicated to Admiral Carden or to Admiral de Robeck the valuable information you must have acquired when in charge of the naval mission [to Turkey] ... by which the Dardanelles are defended ... If so, communicate with Admiralty and direct to Admiral de Robeck.'[49] Limpus replied to Churchill on the 23rd that he had already conveyed this information to Carden.[50] He sent another telegram to Churchill the same day advising him further: 'I now think it possible there may be minefields above the Narrows of which we know very little ... [and] Of course there will still be howitzers which are so difficult to locate from the sea.' He concluded: 'In my opinion Gallipoli Peninsula will have to be taken and held by land forces before Dardanelles can be passed with certainty by [warships] ... and by colliers and other vessels.'[51]

On 24 March Churchill sent a revised version of his foregoing telegram to de Robeck, approved by Fisher and the War Staff Group, and conceding that: 'It is clear that the army should at once prepare to attack [the Dardanelles] at the earliest opportunity ... the question now to be decided by the Admiralty, is whether the time has come to abandon the naval plan of forcing the Dardanelles without the aid of a large army.' Churchill could not resist adding, however:

> What has happened since the 21st to make you alter your intention of renewing the attack as soon as weather is favourable? We have never contemplated a reckless rush over minefields and past undamaged primary guns ... [The] original Admiralty instructions and telegram 109 prescribed a careful and deliberate method of advance, and I should like to know what are the reasons which in your opinion render this no longer possible. We know the forts are short of ammunition. It is probable they have not got many mines. You must of course understand that this telegram is not an executive order but is sent because it is most important that there be no misunderstandings at this juncture.[52]

In his 'Case for Perseverance and Decision' chapter, Churchill insisted that his confidence in the success of a renewed naval attack immediately after 19 March was shared by virtually all the Turkish and German leaders (political, naval and military) at the Dardanelles at that time. This claim deserves to be tested, particularly in the light of its subsequent acceptance by such eminent historians as Basil Liddell Hart, A.J.P. Taylor and William Manchester, and its continued acceptance by modern writers.

Churchill drew on the authority of Turkish War Minister, Enver Pasha, the aide-de-camp to the German Navy Minister in Berlin, Lieutenant Commander Balzer and other officers to validate his case. Enver is quoted as having said during the war: 'If the English had only the courage to rush more ships through the Dardanelles, they could have got to Constantinople; but their delay enabled us to thoroughly fortify the Peninsula, and in six weeks' time [following 18 March] we had taken down there over two hundred Austrian Skoda guns.'[53] Balzer is quoted as stating: 'Berlin was quite certain that the British Fleet could push through the Dardanelles after March 18, as the Turks had practically exhausted their ammunition.'[54]

The opinion of other officers present at the time would seem to confirm this assessment. Turkish artillery officer Captain Serri was fairly representative in stating: 'I was in Fort Hamidieh on March 18, 1915. I expected that the attack would be renewed and, owing to the shortage of ammunition, I personally thought that the Fleet would succeed in getting through the Straits.'[55] General Mertens, the chief German technical officer at the Dardanelles, virtually paraphrased Churchill's assessment of the situation, maintaining that the shortage of armour-piercing shells in the forts would have spelled their demise once the fleet renewed its attack:

> The troops at all the fortifications had their orders to man the guns until the last shell had been fired and then to abandon the forts [he later told Henry Morgenthau, adding]: Once these defences became helpless, the problem of the Allied fleet would have been a simple one. The only bar to their progress would have been the minefield. But the Allied fleet had plenty of minesweepers, which could have made a channel in a few hours [thus exposing the forts to the close-range fire of the battleships].[56]

In the interests of presenting a perceived balance, Churchill cites Djevad Pasha, the Turkish Military Commander-in-Chief at the Dardanelles who, while conceding the likelihood of the British forcing the Dardanelles, added the qualification (echoing Enver Pasha and Liman von Sanders in this respect) that: 'Unless the [naval] attack on March 18 [or immediately after] had been accompanied by a [military] landing and advance on land [to silence the Turkish artillery], I do not think any advantage would have been obtained.'[57] Henry Morgenthau recorded a uniform conviction among his fellow ambassadors at Constantinople (from Germany, Austria, Sweden, Italy, Persia and Bulgaria) that the British would be successful in forcing the Straits.[58] The overwhelming body of opinion then, among the Turks, their allies, and neutrals alike, civil and military, was that a renewed naval assault by the Allies, on or around 19 March, must inevitably have been crowned with success—thus, apparently vindicating Churchill in his stance against the Admiralty chiefs.

But this uniform consensus was predicated on a seriously flawed assumption. The possibility that the finest navy in the world would ever have launched a major attack against a fortified minefield without a competent minesweeping force would surely never have occurred to, let alone been seriously considered by any of those German or Turkish commanders (as General Mertens illustrates). There was simply no precedent for such incompetence throughout the long, proud history of the Royal Navy. Yet this is precisely what had happened, and would have been repeated, had Churchill prevailed. What should have been a routine task of clearing a channel through a minefield was entirely beyond the capability of the inept minesweepers assigned to the fleet. The forts were thus never at serious risk, on or around 19 March, regardless of how much ammunition remained, as long as the battleships were prevented (by the minefield) from closing to within effective range. Up until 4 April, at the earliest, when the first Beagles became available, the Allied naval threat against the Dardanelles was an empty one.

Churchill made an admission, of sorts, to this effect in *The World Crisis* when he effectively handed over responsibility for this *faux pas* to the Admiralty, claiming: 'Up until and including the action of March 18 the force of mine-sweepers provided by the Admiralty was—it must be freely admitted—inadequate both in numbers and efficiency.'[59] Commodore Roger Keyes, Churchill's most ardent supporter and the most vocal advocate for a renewed naval attack (although not before 4 April), was much more scathing in his condemnation of the trawler-minesweepers. 'The *Nousret* minefield [in Eren Kui Bay] ... and the inefficiency of our sweepers at that time, were the sole cause of the failure of the Fleet on 18th March', he angrily insisted two decades later.[60] In this chapter of *The World Crisis,* Churchill reveals that the situation concerning the trawler-minesweepers had been well known to him at the time. Prior to 18 March, he writes:

> ... there were only available twenty-one trawlers, whose speed was too slow for sweeping against the current. They were manned by fishermen, unsupported by trained and disciplined naval personnel ... By the middle of March it was realized that large numbers of [destroyer] sweepers, fast enough to sweep against the current, cutting up the mines as they advanced,

and manned by highly trained and disciplined crews, was needed. [This is a significant admission, even with the benefit of hindsight].[61]

Ironically, had Churchill been prepared to wait two weeks for his first eight Beagle minesweepers to participate in the naval attack, the fleet could well have succeeded in forcing a passage through the Straits. But, as Enver Pasha, Djevad Pasha, Fisher, Jackson, Callwell, Scott and every other expert had impressed upon Churchill, without a large army to occupy both shores of the Straits, no 'advantage would have been obtained' by the fleet. So where did responsibility rest for this lamentable state of incompetence concerning the minesweepers—within the Admiralty, as Churchill maintained, or elsewhere?

The Minesweeper Problem

In his plan of 11 January, Vice Admiral Carden had specified the need for four fast fleet-sweepers and 12 trawler-minesweepers to clear the Dardanelles minefield.[62] This requirement was duly actioned by the Admiralty staff who made the following request to French Marine on 19 January in Telegram 1103: 'It is considered indispensible to assemble in the Mediterranean a large number of minesweepers in about a fortnight's time. The Admiralty being able to send only about 20 would be much obliged if you could assist [with] steam trawlers, small tugs etc with the object of obtaining two dozen sweepers.'[63]

On 25 January Churchill had assured Carden that all his needs would be accorded special attention (especially those in the minesweeping department), telegraphing: 'I am expecting you to formulate all your requests for minesweepers, mine-bumpers, and all special appliances in the greatest possible detail. Malta will execute them if possible but we will supplement her resources from England.'[64] On 4 February the Admiralty informed the French Marine further, in Telegram 1204:

> Admiralty not having a large number of minesweepers to send to Mediterranean, have not on account of urgency, attached much importance to the draught of water in their choice. Those which have been sent are trawlers of from 14-15 feet draught ... It is advisable if you have the option, to choose those with least draught of water.[65]

On 6 February Churchill telegraphed Carden to deal directly with him: 'I wish you to keep me closely informed of the daily progress of these operations. Do not hesitate to send full reports by telegraph and let me know all your difficulties.'[66] By 6 March, when the first attempt was made to sweep inside the Straits, there were 35 trawlers available, but none of the fast fleet sweepers requested by Carden. There is no record of any telegram request having been made from the Admiralty, either to the Grand Fleet or to French Marine, for these craft at this time, so the fault would appear to lie with the Admiralty staff.

In mitigation, it should be noted that, up to 10 March, the incapacity of trawlers to sweep in confined waters in the face of close-range artillery fire had not been fully realised or taken into account. Trawlers were meant to sweep up mines in the open sea, where they were quite effective. A further problem lay in the fact that, during the early months of the war, all available minesweepers were desperately needed in the North Sea to combat the German mine threat against the Grand Fleet and against merchant shipping. On the very first day of the war (5 August), the Germans laid 180 mines off the Suffolk coast in a single day.[67] They continued in similar vein over the following months, laying mines 'from merchant vessels flying neutral or even, possibly, British colours, as well as from regular mine-laying ships', in defiance of the Hague Convention. On 22 March 1915, when he was obliged to send to the Dardanelles 'the six small steamers, specially fitted as mine-sweepers for the Grand Fleet', Jellicoe noted 'the increasing number of [German] mines in the North Sea and the paucity of [British] minesweepers' there, which led him to fit 16 destroyers as additional minesweepers.[68]

Nevertheless, the failure of daylight sweeping at the Dardanelles between 6 and 10 March and then of night sweeping between 10 and 13 March revealed a very serious 'difficulty' which Carden telegraphed to Churchill for his special attention as promised in his telegrams of 25 January and 6 February. But that special attention failed to materialise. In its place, the First Lord's furious response to Carden's plea precipitated the disastrous attempt at minesweeping on the night of 13 March.[69] It could be argued that the full extent of the trawlers' ineffectiveness only became apparent at this time. Carden's urgent request to Churchill the following day for genuine sweepers, however, was not even acknowledged by the First Lord. Not until Carden had sent a follow-up, urgent telegram on the 15th for fleet sweepers did he receive a reply from Churchill, albeit undoubtedly not the reply he was expecting, or hoping to receive.[70] In fact, Carden sent five requests for fleet sweepers to Churchill: on 11 January, 19 January, 4 February, 14 March and 15 March. He also described the inept performance of the trawlers from 10 March.[71]

If Churchill displayed little interest in Carden's predicament, the same could not be said for the Admiralty staff. On 15 March the French Marine was informed, via Telegram 1579, that the fleet was in need of 'faster mine sweepers than trawlers to go in front of the squadron. Admiralty considers that ships of at least 15 knots will be necessary ... Admiralty asks if you could manage to supply some.'[72] The action demanded, following the night of 13 March, indicated that at least the inadequacy of the trawlers must be acknowledged by Churchill, as described by Carden, Jackson, Limpus and the Admiralty staff, and remedial action taken in the form of competent minesweepers. These could have been provided, either as converted Beagle destroyers already with the fleet or as fast fleet sweepers from either the French Marine, as requested in Telegram 1579 on 15 March, or from the Grand Fleet. Clearly a short delay of around two weeks would have been involved.

But Churchill was not prepared to wait that long. In his estimation, and in his reply to Carden on 15 March (which echoed his similar response to Cradock at Coronel), the means at hand were deemed adequate to the task (of forcing the Dardanelles). In the opinion of the First Lord, the question of 'ammunition aeroplanes and minesweepers' could be left in abeyance.[73]

***

Had Churchill's demand for a renewed naval attack on or around 19 March been met, the result could only have been another 'severe' Allied defeat. If pursued with the same determination and heroism as on the night of 13 March, the result could well have been a disaster, with the loss of all the minesweepers plus a significant number of battleships. That was the opinion of Sir Julian Corbett, Sir Henry Jackson, Dr Prior and the Dardanelles Commission. With the inability of the trawlers to clear a channel, and/or being sunk in the process, the battleships would have been faced with the dilemma of rushing the forts at the Narrows. Sir Julian Corbett estimated that, in an advance over an unswept minefield comprising 353 mines in ten lines, only one battleship in every 15 could expect to survive intact.[74] Admiral Jackson was slightly more optimistic. He forecast that: 'Of 16 ships that attempted to rush the Straits ... four badly damaged ones might with luck return.'[75]

Churchill insisted to Lord Fisher on 25 March that the appearance of even 'four or five [battle]ships' off Constantinople (but it would almost certainly have been less), would have been sufficient to frighten the Turks into capitulation.[76] On the contrary, Dr Prior maintains that the appearance of such a badly depleted fleet off Constantinople would have boosted Turkish morale considerably.[77] It also needs to be remembered that the German battlecruiser *Goeben* remained in the Marmora—bearing in mind that the only two British warships fast enough and powerful enough to meet the *Goeben* on its own terms (*Queen Elizabeth* was not to be risked in the Marmora and *Inflexible* had been crippled by mines and gunfire) were not available.[78] *Goeben* could out-range and out-run all the older battleships.

The Dardanelles Commission arrived at a similar finding: 'Had the attack been renewed within a day or two [of 18 March] there is no reason to suppose that the proportion of casualties would have been less, and, if so, even had the second attack succeeded, a very weak force would have been left for subsequent naval operations'. This conclusion was expunged from page 40 of the published report. It does, however, appear in the 'Public Documents' section of the *Annual*

Register, 1917. [79] Nevertheless, Churchill's *cri de coeur* would ring out through the decades, that victory was there for the taking, shortly after 18 March. 'Not to persevere', he would famously insist, 'that was the crime.'[80]

***

In the penultimate chapter of his book, Churchill impresses upon his reader the authority and authenticity of his source material, deriving as it did from his privileged position at the very centre of those events. 'When the secrets of all the General Staffs are revealed', he writes, 'we shall know how profound were the anxieties with which a renewal of the naval attack of the 18th March was regarded by the Turkish and German commanders.'[81] Having established his case (to his own satisfaction at least), Churchill explains *why* he was denied the victory that was within his grasp. This was due, he writes, to Admiral de Robeck's sentimental attachment to his battleships:

> To statesmen or soldiers [Churchill explains], ships in time of war possess no sentimental value. They are engines of war to be used, risked, and if necessary expended in the common cause and for the general policy of the State ... an old battleship marked for the scrapheap was an instrument of war to be expended in a good cause as readily as artillery ammunition is fired to shelter and support a struggling infantry attack.

But to an Admiral of [de Robeck's] standing and upbringing, these old ships were sacred. They had been the finest ships afloat in the days when he as a young officer had first set foot on their decks. The discredit and even disgrace of casting away a ship was ingrained deeply by years of mental training and outlook ... Whereas a layman or soldier might have rejoiced that so important an action as that on March 18 could have been fought with a loss of less than thirty British lives and two or three worthless ships ... Admiral de Robeck was saddened and consternated to the foundations of his being. These emotions were also present around the Admiralty table in Whitehall. Full weight [Churchill concludes], must be attached to Admiral de Robeck's reasons for not renewing the attack.[82]

As Marder insists, this claim was quite absurd and somewhat insulting to de Robeck: 'The Admiral's decision was based on hard facts, not sentiment', Marder writes.[83] And leaving aside the fact that the death toll on 18 March was close to 700 sailors, most of whom were Frenchmen, and that six battleships had been lost or disabled, de Robeck's decision not to renew the disastrous attack and his concern (like Fisher's, Wilson's and Jackson's) was not so much for those 'worthless ships' as for the irreplaceable sailors on board (see Chapter 2 on the Royal Navy's 'Steady Pressure Policy').[84]

Admiral de Robeck, in fact, demonstrated considerable moral courage in his refusal to be intimidated by the First Lord. As he wrote to Admiral Limpus on 27 March: 'I will not be hurried [into a rash action] by W[inston] C[hurchill].'[85]

The Case for Abandonment

On 27 March de Robeck sent a lengthy reiteration of a situation well known to the Admiralty within Telegram 282, addressed to the First Lord. This stated that:

> The original approved plan for forcing the Dardanelles by ships was drawn up on the assumption that [naval] gunfire alone was capable of destroying forts. This assumption has been conclusively proved to be wrong when applied to the attacking of open forts with high-velocity guns ... shells burst uselessly within the forts ... to obtain direct hits on each [fort] gun has been found impracticable, even at ranges of 700 to 800 yards ... Conclusions drawn from the attack on the cupola forts at Antwerp by heavy[17-inch German] howitzers are quite misleading ... Further, wear of old guns [of the battleships] is causing me some anxiety, on the 18th there were several premature bursts of common shell, and the guns were out of action from time to time ... To destroy forts, therefore, it is necessary to land demolition parties. To cover these parties [against

enemy action] at the Narrows is a task General Hamilton is not prepared to undertake, and I fully concur in this view ... Success [of a naval action] depends largely on the effect that the appearance of the Fleet off Constantinople would produce on the Turkish army, which appears to control the situation in Turkey at present, *and which itself is dominated by the Germans,* but if the Turkish army is undismayed by the advent of the Fleet into the Sea of Marmora and the Straits are closed behind it [by the Turkish artillery], the length of time which ships can operate ... depends almost entirely on the number of colliers and ammunition which can accompany the Fleet ... The passage of supply ships for the Fleet through the Dardanelles with the forts still intact is a problem to which I can see no practical solution. In such a case it would be vital for the Army to occupy the Peninsula, which would open the Straits, as [Turkish] guns on Asiatic side can be dominated from the European shore sufficiently to permit ships to pass through. The landing of an army of the size contemplated in the face of strenuous opposition is, in my opinion, an operation requiring the assistance of all the naval forces available ... With Gallipoli Peninsula held by our Army and Squadron through the Dardanelles, our success would be assured. The delay possibly of a fortnight will allow cooperation, which would really prove a factor that will reduce length of time necessary to complete the campaign in the Sea of Marmora and occupy Constantinople.[86]

Churchill replied the same day, finally conceding to de Robeck that 'the reasons you give make it clear that a combined operation is now indispensible.'[87] But if ever the time had arrived for the entire operation to be abandoned and converted to a demonstration only, as requested by the Grand Duke, and made the essential precondition of the 13 and 28 January War Councils—with those unforeseen difficulties having been well and truly encountered—this was surely that time. Between 27 March and 25 April, Hankey, Fisher, Richmond and (to a lesser extent), Balfour would plead for the operation to be abandoned. They would be persistently overruled or ignored. Three days before the disastrous naval attack had taken place, Hankey had confided his anxieties about the entire operation to Lord Esher in a letter marked Secret, in which he insisted that:

> Troops ought to have been there [at the Dardanelles], or at any rate, within a day or two's reach when the initial bombardment [on 19 February] began. There ought to have been no blatant press announcement at the outset, and the bombardment ought to have been announced merely as a demonstration. While the bombardment was commencing the transports ought to have appeared at some entirely different point of the Turkish coast, such as Alexandretta,

Haifa or elsewhere. Then the troops ought to have come in as a bolt from the blue, immediately following the collapse of the outer forts ... I urged this at the outset, but my suggestions fell on deaf ears. Now we have given the Turks time [two months] to assemble a vast force, to pour in field guns and howitzers, to entrench every landing place, and the operation has become a most formidable one.[88]

Hankey submitted a memorandum to Asquith on 19 March, immediately following the naval attack: 'imploring him to appoint naval and military technical committee to plan out military attack on Dardanelles so as to avoid repetition of naval fiasco, which is largely due to inadequate Staff preparation.' Hankey pointed out a whole body of other considerations to Asquith, which included: the provision of landing piers, pontoons etc; hospital arrangements; the type of warfare to be conducted, e.g., surprise attack or siege operations and the consequent type and quantity of artillery and ammunition required; arrangements for the transport from the landing place of all ammunition, water, food etc. over rough country with very few roads to the army in the field—all problems which would be encountered in the months ahead.[89]

Hankey added: 'Up to the present time ... no attempt has been made to estimate what [size] Force is required to make sure of success. We have merely said that so many troops are available and that ought to be enough.' He suggested, finally, that Sir Ian Hamilton (appointed commander of the Dardanelles military force on 12 March) be brought home to examine the many factors involved, and: 'to submit a report showing exactly how it is contemplated to carry out the operation ... I feel sure that a fortnight lost at this end in careful diagnosis and examination of the problem may save many months in carrying out the operation.'[90] Hankey's proposals were ignored by Asquith.

On the 20th Hankey gave an indication in his diary that Churchill may have made some kind of commitment to Fisher and Jackson in terms of waiting for military assistance before launching his naval attack. Hankey wrote: 'had a long talk with [Admiral] Jackson ... and Fisher. Both were very angry with Churchill as they had warned him that troops were necessary to carry the Dardanelles.'[91] On 30 March Asquith shared his appreciation of the situation with his confidante, Venetia Stanley:

> ... had a small enclave here this morning—K[itchener], Winston, myself and Hankey—to go over carefully & quietly the situation, actual and prospective, at the Dardanelles. There are risks, & it will in any event be an expensive operation, but I am sure we are right to go through with it. This is the really critical month of the war; an actual equilibrium, with perhaps a slight turn in favour of the allies. The possible belligerents (Italy, Greece, Bulgaria,

Rumania) all hanging in the balance ... If all (or most) of these doubtful hazards go well for us, the war ought to be over in 3 months.[92]

While Hankey was attempting to instil some sense of reality into Asquith's thinking, Fisher was similarly endeavouring to dissuade Churchill from his Dardanelles obsession. On 27 March Fisher had suggested to Churchill, echoing Hankey, that: '[A]t this critical stage, before the final plunge is taken ... we should be very fully informed by [Sir Ian] Hamilton of his considered opinion of the probabilities of the military operations he has in mind.'[93] The next day Fisher informed Churchill:

> We have, or shall have, sixteen destroyers there [at the Dardanelles] that are very badly wanted indeed at home [plus] three monitors ... three submarines ... mine-sweepers etc etc ... If the Germans decide ...—influenced largely no doubt by our having so large a force away from the decisive theatre—on some big thing at home, there is (you must admit) much cause for anxiety.[94]

Fisher repeated this approach with even greater urgency on the 31st, reminding the First Lord of his own famous dictum (that Jellicoe was the only man on either side who could lose the war in an afternoon), then advising him:

With the departure of the last batch of reinforcements of destroyers, submarines, fleet-sweepers etc for the Dardanelles, we have reached a point when the general situation must be carefully reviewed ... with regard to the margin of superiority over the German Fleets which we retain in Home Waters ... I consider that we have now descended to the bare minimum ... and that to despatch any more fighting ships of any kind to the Dardanelles operations would be to court serious losses at home ... We can recover from an indecisive or even an unsuccessful result of these operations in the Dardanelles; we can recover from an abandonment of the operations if this should be necessary; but we could never recover from a reverse to our Main Fleets in the decisive theatre at home. It would be **Ruin.** Our existence depends on our unchallengeable **Naval Supremacy.**[95]

A note of desperate urgency is apparent in Fisher's plea on 2 April: 'We can't send even another rope-yarn to de Robeck! WE HAVE GONE TO THE VERY LIMIT ... *A failure or check in the Dardanelles would be nothing—a failure in the North Sea would be* RUIN!!'[96] Churchill replied superciliously to Fisher the next day:

> It is clear that the favourable turn to our affairs in S.E. Europe arose from the initial success of our attack on the Dardanelles[19 February to 4 March, and] was checked by the repulse of the 18th [of March] & can only be restored by the general success of the operations. It is thus

necessary to fight a battle (a thing which has often happened before in war) & abide [by] the consequences whatever they are.[97]

By 4 April, Fisher was confiding his 'increasing anxiety over the Dardanelles situation' to Jellicoe, adding:

> No good purpose would be served by my resigning. My opinions are known. But the politicians took the bit between their teeth, and decided it was a Cabinet and not an "expert" question, and Kitchener unwittingly led on by thinking it was going to be a purely naval operation, which Carden undoubtedly said but I never agreed to, and so here we are.[98]

The following day Fisher gave full vent to his frustration and anxiety, writing to Churchill: 'You are just simply eaten up with the Dardanelles and cannot think of anything else! Damn the Dardanelles! They will be our grave!'[99]

A significant finding of the Dardanelles Commission was that: 'After March 19th there was no further meeting of the War Council until May 14th [this erroneous finding has been repeated by historians ever since] and we are unable to ascertain any precise date on which, after the failure of the naval attack, military operations on the Gallipoli Peninsula were definitely decided upon.'[100] Asquith defended this failure on his part by informing the Commissioners that, between 19 March and 14 May, in the absence of War Council meetings: 'there were thirteen meetings of the Cabinet, at eleven of which the operations at the Dardanelles were brought up ... not merely for report, but of long and careful discussion.' Nevertheless, the Commissioners determined that, although the military operations 'were undertaken with the knowledge of the Cabinet ... they should have been fully discussed by the War Council', and found Asquith to have been remiss in this regard.[101]

In fact, on 6 April, a brief, informal War Council meeting *was* held, attended by only Asquith, Churchill, Kitchener and Hankey—and it was at this meeting that the fateful decision to proceed with the military invasion was taken. Hankey had just returned from a battlefield visit to France which lasted from 29 March to 6 April. His diary records: '(After my return from France). The Prime Minister had a meeting of Kitchener, Churchill and myself [which was, nevertheless, accorded the status of a War Council] *to consider questions of the military attack on Dardanelles now being prepared in Egypt.'* [102] Balfour and Lloyd George were conspicuously absent from this meeting. Both men were staunchly opposed to a military invasion of Gallipoli—Balfour, as will be shown and Lloyd George, as was well known. Indeed the Dardanelles Commissioners recorded 'that a different opinion was given by Mr Lloyd George who "strongly urged that the Army should not be required or expected to pull the chestnuts out of the fire for the Navy and that if the Navy failed, we should try somewhere else, in the Balkans, and not necessarily at the Dardanelles."'[103] The Secretary's Notes of this War Council meeting simply state that:

LORD KITCHENER read certain telegraphic correspondence with Sir Ian Hamilton, the Commander-in-Chief of the Dardanelles Expeditionary Force, and stated that no complete plan for the attack of the Straits had as yet been received.

MR. CHURCHILL read the full written report from Admiral de Robeck regarding the attack on the 18th March. *The First Lord urged that the [military] attack should be pressed home vigorously.* LORD KITCHENER *agreed that the attack would have to be made.* LIEUTENANT-COLONEL HANKEY said that the difficulty would be to land the troops at all, owing to the opposition of howitzers in the ravines which intersect the Gallipoli Peninsula.

MR. CHURCHILL did not agree. He anticipated no difficulty in effecting a landing.

After some further discussion the meeting adjourned.[104]

Hankey's diary record of this meeting is more revealing. 'None of them appeared to me in the least to realize the extreme difficulties of the operation', he writes. Hankey, who was a marine, was well versed

228

in the problems associated with amphibious landings. Kitchener's concurrence in the invasion plan may be mitigated to some extent perhaps by the coercive factor of Churchill's press release. In addition, he was reliant on the (sanguine) appraisal of his commander in the field, Hamilton, who would continually offer him the promise of victory with the receipt of more divisions.[105]

'Hamilton's plan', Hankey recorded, 'seems to me fraught with the possibility of an appalling military disaster, if the Turks can fight at all. When I suggested that even the operation of landing would be one of extraordinary difficulty [against well-dug-in Turkish artillery and machine-guns], Churchill merely remarked that he could not see that there was any difficulty at all.'[106] Hankey's impassioned yet professional counter-argument to the invasion proved futile. The following day he attempted, once again, to impress upon Asquith the dire prospects awaiting at Gallipoli. As he recorded in his diary:

> Saw the Prime Minister ... and suggested to him that ... military attack on Dardanelles should be postponed. Urged that success at Dardanelles very doubtful ... The Prime Minister did not take the proposal very kindly at first, and objected that after all our talk [and advance publicity] we must go through with the attack.
>
> I replied that on military grounds this was the best possible reason for abandoning the attack

[with the vital element of surprise forfeited, and the Turks strongly entrenched] ... The Prime Minister promised to think the proposal over.[107]

On 8 April Hankey wrote that he:

Saw Balfour in the afternoon and found him fully agreed on danger of attack on Dardanelles at this juncture. He [Balfour] dictated a letter on subject to Churchill and despatched it. Saw Lord Esher who has just returned from France. He tells me that [the French] are very apprehensive about Dardanelles in view of premature naval attack, and injudicious advertisement.[108]

Balfour's letter to Churchill informed him:

As you know, I cannot help being very anxious about the fate of any military attempt upon the Peninsula. Nobody was so keen as myself upon forcing the Straits as long as there seemed a reasonable prospect of doing it by means of the fleet alone—even though the operation might cost us a few antiquated battleships. But a military attack upon a position so inherently difficult, and so carefully prepared, is a different proposition, and if it fails, we shall not only have to suffer considerably in men and still more in prestige, but we may upset our whole diplomacy in the Near East.[109]

Churchill replied to Balfour immediately, assuring him that:

> No other operation in this part of the world c[oul]d ever cloak the defeat of abandoning the effort at the D[ardane]lles. I think there is nothing for it but to go through with the business, & I do not regret that this sh[oul]d be so. No one can count with certainty upon the issue of a battle. But here we have the chances in our favour, & play for vital gains with non-vital stakes.[110]

If there was any doubt as to who was the driving force behind the military invasion, that question had been answered the previous day. Charles Hobhouse recorded in his diary that, at a Cabinet meeting on 7 April (the day after the informal War Council meeting):

> ... when it [the proposed military attack against Gallipoli] ... for which Ian Hamilton was being given 80,000 troops ... was first mentioned to the Cabinet, McK[enna] asked on whose authority it was undertaken ... McK[enna] observing that the Cabinet had no responsibility for it [to which] Churchill declared that he was willing to take the whole responsibility himself.[111]

The legitimacy of Churchill's proposal is clearly questionable, as only the Prime Minister possessed the requisite authority to sanction such an undertaking.

However, with Asquith reneging on his responsibility, Churchill's will seems to have prevailed. Churchill would subsequently hold this lapse over Asquith. As Lloyd George told Frances Stevenson on 11 October 1915: 'He (Churchill) prevents the Prime Minister from facing the facts, too, by reminding him that he too is implicated in the [military] campaign & tells him that if the thing is acknowledged to be a failure, he (the PM) as well as Churchill will be blamed.'[112] On 8 April Hankey wrote:

Saw Richmond, of the Admiralty War Staff, and arranged with him that he should propose to Fisher, to drop much advertised Dardanelles attack and make, instead, a sudden attack from Haifa and Beirut on the rear of the Turkish Army operating against Egypt, cutting its communications and destroying it. Heard afterwards that Fisher forwarded proposal to Churchill, who was furious with Richmond for suggesting it.[113]

Hankey made one final attempt to persuade Asquith of the foolishness of a Gallipoli invasion. He prepared a lengthy and detailed 'appreciation of the military situation in the Dardanelles' which he sent to Asquith on the 11th:

This was a formidable document [Hankey writes], surveying all aspects of the coming operation. As usual no appreciations had been circulated from either the naval or military staff. I put myself in personal communication with the two staffs and drew up my own appreciation. [Hankey's final conclusions were that]: If the Turkish troops are prepared to fight and if they are well supplied with ammunition and supplies of all kinds, success must be considered extremely doubtful. [And]: The military operation appears, therefore, to be to a certain extent a gamble upon the supposed shortage of supplies and inferior fighting qualities of the Turkish Armies.[114]

Hankey's appreciation was ignored by Churchill and Asquith. On 11 April, following his rejection of the Hankey/Richmond/Fisher proposal, Churchill sent Fisher a mild rebuke:

Seriously, my friend, are you not a little unfair in trying to spite this operation by side winds and small points when you have accepted it in principle? It is hard on me that you should keep on like this—every day something fresh; and it is not worthy of you or the great business we have in hand together. [[115]

By the 20th Fisher had come to an acceptance of the futility of influencing Churchill through any argument he could advance. As he wrote to Jellicoe: 'The Dardanelles will now soon begin. It is a huge gamble, but all the politicians on both sides have shoved us into it, or rather Winston has shoved all of them.'[116]

On 22 April, Admiral of the Fleet Lord Charles Beresford asked in the House of Commons: Who is responsible for the operations in the

Dardanelles; [and] whether it was intended to be in the nature of combined naval and military operations, and whether the ultimate success of the operations will be considerably delayed owing to the naval attack having been delivered before the Army was landed? [Asquith replied that it was a joint operation, but] it was not desirable at the present stage to say anything further.[117]

The exigencies of war had spared Asquith the embarrassment of having to divulge the true, sorry state of affairs at the Dardanelles. That truth was that: due to the unnecessary haste with which he and Churchill had propelled the military into this campaign, there had been no time for any kind of realistic planning or preparations to be conducted.

***

Churchill's Strategy

Essentially, this plan was improvised as he went along. Churchill was primarily concerned with getting his naval operation sanctioned and under way. After that he was faced with the problem of finding the massive army he knew to be essential for success, while at the same time disavowing the very need for large-scale military support and insisting that the fleet would do the job alone. Hence the confusion which descended on War Council proceedings. In the absence of either a massive Balkan or Allied army, Churchill's strategy came to depend entirely on the capitulation of the Turks with the appearance of the fleet, or even of a part thereof, off Constantinople—which was never a realistic possibility. In the event, the Turks fought heroically in defence of their homeland.

General Monash, widely regarded as the outstanding Allied commander of World War I, summarised Churchill's strategic acumen from his position at Anzac in July 1915: 'We have dropped the Churchill way of rushing in before we are ready, and hardly knowing what to do next, in favour of the Kitchener way of making careful and complete preparations on lines which just can't go wrong.'[118]

Responsibility for the Gallipoli Invasion

Admiral Lord Beresford's question to Parliament can now be answered with a certain measure of assurance, courtesy of the foregoing evidence. It was Winston Churchill who assumed responsibility for the military invasion of Gallipoli at a Cabinet meeting on 7 April 1915 following his pressing the matter to an informal War Council meeting the previous day. Churchill's action was unlawful, as only Cabinet, the Cabinet War Council, or the Prime Minister possessed the requisite authority to make such a decision. However, with Asquith failing to exercise his authority in the matter, Churchill's will seems to have prevailed. Responsibility for the escalation to a military invasion of Gallipoli would be assigned subsequently by Churchill to Lord

Kitchener in *The World Crisis.* Following his announcement, 'with grief', to the Cabinet on 23 March of 'the refusal of the Admiral and the Admiralty to continue the naval attack', Churchill described Kitchener's intervention:

> Lord Kitchener was always splendid when things went wrong. Confident, commanding, magnanimous, he made no reproaches. In a few brief sentences he assumed the burden and declared he would carry the operations through by military force. So here again we had no discussion ... No formal decision to make a land attack was even noted in the records of the Cabinet or the War Council.[119]

> Kitchener has carried this burden, unjustly, ever since.

CHAPTER 5

Fisher's Resignation

The circumstances surrounding Lord Fisher's resignation have been the subject of widely varying interpretations over the years, and indeed even in recent times. With the primary sources now available (particularly Fisher's and Hankey's private papers, which can be cited extensively where necessary), it is possible to form an independent evaluation of those events which clears much of the lingering obfuscation.

The Gallipoli Invasion

The Gallipoli campaign was without precedent in military history. To land a massive invasion force on a fortified coastline under the guns of a well-entrenched, waiting enemy; to compel men to carry ashore with them, amidst that storm of shell and machine-gun fire, all their arms, water, food and essential equipment necessary to wage war; and to establish and hold a beachhead, for essential resupply from the sea—where no harbour or docking facilities existed whatsoever—this was a formidable undertaking, never previously attempted. The closest parallel would occur 29 years later. But the Normandy invasion would take not three weeks, but two years of the most careful planning and preparation to organise, and by the best military brains available.[1]

There were no accurate maps of the battleground on which the men would fight. No-one, therefore, had any realistic knowledge of the terrain and of the nature or even existence of roads (these consisted mainly of goat tracks through the formless maze of gullies, ravines and dried-up watercourses, all overlaid with the same hostile, dense undergrowth, that was the Gallipoli battlefield). It was a similar situation in terms of knowledge of the availability of water: there was none. All water had to be supplied from the ships at sea.[2] There was a serious shortage of almost all essential equipment. Only around one-third of the heavy guns needed were available. The supply of high explosive shells was at very low levels. Grenades were non-existent and had to be improvised. There were no materials for building piers and jetties. Small landing craft had to be bought, for cash, from local Egyptians. Everything had to be improvised. The bazaars of Cairo and Alexandria were scoured for skins, oil drums and kerosene tins—anything that would hold water.[3]

Military security, in the meantime, had ceased to exist. Letters addressed c/o The Constantinople Expeditionary Force arrived by ordinary mail. Egyptian newspapers not only announced the arrival of each new unit, but speculated freely on the outcome of the coming campaign.[4] Against such comprehensive ignorance and unpreparedness was arrayed the belief—indeed the certainty—that the Turk was an utterly inferior soldier from a decadent race and with no stomach (unlike Europeans) for a real fight. This conviction was officially promulgated to all personnel just prior to the invasion: 'It is the general opinion that the Turks will offer an energetic resistance to our landing, but once we are firmly established on the Peninsula it is thought possible that this resistance will crumble away, and that they may then turn on their German masters.'[5]

Vast quantities of supplies and equipment would consequently not be required. This was expected to be a short, victorious campaign. A maximum of 5000 casualties was anticipated and allowed for in the medical arrangements. The reality of the situation was that an Allied force of 75,000 troops was about to be launched against a well-prepared, defending Turkish army whose dispositions and strength were unknown, but which reportedly had around 200,000 reinforcements to call on.[6] The immediate defending Turkish force of six divisions was, in fact, 84,000 strong.[7] During the eight-month campaign the Allies would sustain 252,000 casualties, with 50,133 men killed, missing or died of wounds, having made no appreciable advances from any of their landing grounds. Once again, Britain would suffer a humiliating defeat at the hands of a 'third-rate Oriental power'.[8]

The military invasion of Gallipoli began on 25 April 1915, with Hankey's worst fears and warnings entirely vindicated. The anticipated maximum casualties for the entire campaign were sustained on the first day at Gallipoli: 2000 Australians and New Zealanders at Anzac Cove and 3000 British and French troops 12 miles further south at Cape Helles. Within a week 8000 casualties had been sustained at Anzac alone, 2300 of which were fatalities.[9] The Anzacs were landed (by mistake) in the most savage, mountainous and impassible terrain in the entire Gallipoli Peninsula—terrain which would have deterred adventurers in peacetime and which would prove as difficult to overcome as the Turkish defenders. The British and French were burdened by the additional handicap of incompetent leadership, with a commander (Major General Hunter Weston) who insisted on repeatedly battering his troops against the two most heavily defended positions at Helles instead of bypassing and isolating those positions and advancing up the Straits, unopposed, towards the Narrows.[10]

Regardless, as Higgins points out, this was always an exercise in futility. The Turks 'could [always] count upon another twelve to fourteen divisions, taken from nearby Turkish Thrace [and Constantinople] as reinforcements, should the situation ever threaten to become serious', which it never did.[11] The understrength Allied forces were never capable of breaking out of their original landing zones, and were thus doomed to an alternately boring and bloody eight-month stalemate existence.

The Question of a Renewed Naval Attack

On 10 May, Telegram no.490, from Admiral de Robeck, was received at the Admiralty advising that: The help which the Navy has been able to give the Army in its advance has not been as great as anticipated.

From the vigour of the enemy's resistance it is improbable that the passage of the Fleet into the Marmora will be decisive and therefore it is equally probable that the Straits will be closed [by Turkish artillery] behind the Fleet.

The temper of the Turkish Army in the Peninsula indicates that the forcing of the Dardanelles and subsequent appearance of the Fleet off Constantinople will not, of itself, prove decisive. [de Robeck then continued, by posing two essentially rhetorical questions, the answers to which he had already provided, in requesting further orders]:

Can the Navy, by forcing the Dardanelles, ensure success of the operations, [he enquired. And]: If the Navy were to suffer a reverse, which of necessity could only be a severe one, would the position of the Army be so critical [deprived of

At Fisher's request I prepared a Memo for him to give the First Lord, setting forth his objections to separate naval action & declining to be a party to it. At F's request saw PM just before lunch & told him F would resign if such action was taken. PM said it was a very foolish message, but authorized me to say separate naval action would not be taken without F's concurrence.[17] [Fisher's and Hankey's memo reads, in part]:

First Lord,

Yesterday evening you sent me a draft telegram for my concurrence, giving a proposed reply to the telegram received from Vice-Admiral de Robeck earlier in the day. The general tone of this telegram implied that the Board of Admiralty might be prepared to sanction the Fleet undertaking further operations against the Forts irrespective of the Army being unable to advance beyond their present positions ... I have not heard from you whether this telegram, or any, has actually been sent. I presume not, as I have seen no copy. But it is clear in my mind that you yourself would be prepared to sanction such a proceeding. I therefore feel impelled to inform you definitely and formally of my conviction that such an attack by the Fleet on the Dardanelles forts, in repetition of the operations which failed on 18th March, or any attempt by the Fleet to rush by the Narrows, is doomed to failure, and, moreover, is fraught with the possibilities of disaster utterly incommensurate to any advantage that could be obtained therefrom ... The sweeping of the mines in The Narrows is an operation which, in my opinion, experience has shewn not to be possible, even after the batteries have been silenced, until the heights on either side have been occupied by the [Allied] military.

Even after The Narrows are forced we still have to deal with the Nagara group of forts, and there will certainly be further minefields beyond The Narrows and in the Sea of Marmora ... Finally, even if the Fleet or a portion of it is rushed through to the Marmora, it will not be possible to keep it supplied with coal or munitions or to push an Army up to co-operate with it ... I consider that purely Naval action, unsupported by the Army, would merely lead to heavy loss of ships and invaluable men ... I therefore wish it to be clearly understood that I dissociate myself from any such project.[18]

Churchill replied thus:

My dear Fisher,

You will never receive from me any proposition to "rush" the Dardanelles: and I agree with the views you express so forcibly on the subject. It may be that the Admiral will have to engage the forts and sweep the Kephez minefield as an aid to military operations: & we have always agreed in the desirability of forcing them to fire off their scanty stock of ammunition. But in view of Hamilton's last telegram this is clearly not required now ... We are now committed to one of the greatest amphibious enterprises of history. You are absolutely committed. Comradeship, resource, firmness, patience all in the highest degree will be needed to carry the matter through to victory ... A great army hanging on by its eyelids to a rocky beach & confronted with the armed power of the Turkish Empire under German military guidance. The whole *surplus* [Churchill's emphasis] fleet of Britain—every scrap that can be spared—bound to that army & its fortunes ... The measureless advantages—probably decisive on the whole war ... I beg you to lend your whole aid & good will: & ultimately then success is certain.[19]

Hankey noted in his diary on the 12th:

Lord Fisher arrived early at office. Showed me his letter to Churchill, covering Memo, also Churchill's reply, rather a slippery one, which had much dissatisfied him, so that he intended sending Memo to P.M. ... In the afternoon Fisher sent for me to say that he had had it out with Churchill, who had apparently agreed not to attempt naval attack, & had even promised to withdraw the *Queen Elizabeth,* replacing her by two monitors [with] 15 inch guns.[20]

Fisher replied to Churchill on the 12th:

My dear Winston,

Until the Military operations have effectively occupied the shores of the narrows &c no naval attack on the minefield can take place but your letter does not repudiate this and therefore in view of our joint conversation with the Prime Minister prior to March 18 I have sent him a copy of my memorandum to you—With reference to your remark that I am absolutely committed—I have only to say that you must know (and the Prime Minister also) that my unwilling acquiescence did not extend to such a further gamble as any repetition of March 18th until the Army had done their part.[21]

That Churchill had no intention of honouring any promise he may have given to Fisher (concerning a renewed naval attack) is evident from the note he wrote on Fisher's letter for his secretary, Masterton-Smith. This reads: 'Put by Secret. This if acted on w[ould]d prevent V.A. de Robeck from supporting the advance of the Army on Kilid Bahr plateau and w[oul]d therefore rupture the whole plan. But the point can be better dealt with when the moment arrives.'[22]

Fisher wrote to Asquith, apprising him of the situation and enclosing a copy of the memo he had sent to Churchill, asking 'for it to be circulated to the War Council'.[23] Asquith replied to Fisher on the 12th: 'My dear Lord Fisher, since receiving and reading your letter and memoranda of today, I have been given to understand that an arrangement has been come to between the First Lord and yourself. I am very glad.'[24] Fisher wrote to Asquith the following day, advising him of the 'arrangement [he spoke of] ... I regret to have to say:

> Within four hours of the pact being concluded the First Lord said to Kitchener "that in the event of the Army's failure, the Fleet would endeavour to force a passage through", or words to that effect. [Fisher concluded]:
>
> Therefore this purely private and personal letter, intended for your own eye alone and not to be quoted, as there is no use threatening [resignation] without acting, is to mention to the one person who I feel OUGHT to know, *that I feel my time is short!* [25]

On 13 May a telegram was received at the Admiralty from the French Ministry of Marine, stating that they had heard from Admiral Guépratte (French naval commander at the Dardanelles) that 'energetic action on the part of the Allied Fleet was mediated against the Chanak and Kalessi [sic] Forts, a course with which the Ministry did not agree.'[26]Throughout the 13th of May Churchill attempted to persuade Fisher to renew the naval attack. That afternoon Churchill drafted a telegram for de Robeck, encouraging him to once again attempt to sweep the minefields. The draft came to Fisher for his concurrence. Instead, Fisher amended the telegram to read: 'You must on no account take decisive action without our [the Admiralty Board's] permission.'[27] To this Churchill replied:

> At a moment when the Army may be committed to an attack I cannot agree to send a telegram which might have the effect of paralysing necessary naval action as judged necessary by the responsible Admiral on the spot. *The telegram I have drafted is sufficient* but I have made a small amendment in an attempt to meet your wishes. It is dangerous to delay sending the telegram, and I have therefore directed the secretary to send it in this form.[28]

Churchill's telegram, together with Fisher's memo and the amended draft, were shown to the Second, Third and Fourth Sea Lords who, considerably alarmed at this overt usurpation of the First Sea Lord's and Admiralty Board's authority, set down in a memorandum their collective agreement with Lord Fisher's views: 'that the Fleet should not be used to force the Narrows'. They also asked that they might be kept informed of any further developments. The upshot of this incident was that a reply was finally sent to de Robeck which included the following: 'We think the moment for an independent naval attempt to force the Narrows has passed and will not arise again under present conditions.'[29]

Neither of the above incidents is described in *The World Crisis.* Very little mention was made of another incident which took place just before midnight on 13/14 May. The Italian Naval Attaché had arrived at the Admiralty to confirm arrangements for naval cooperation agreed the previous week. Knowing that Fisher was in agreement, Churchill sent the appropriate telegram to the Minister of Marine in Rome, together with the unnecessary additional comment *'First Sea Lord to see after action'.*[30] Admiral Bacon points out that this telegram had nothing to do with Lord Fisher's resignation, despite Churchill's claim that it contributed significantly.[31] Fisher, in fact, had no knowledge of this telegram when he resigned. But later when he saw it:

> ... the unusual and unfortunate marking in a telegram of this nature, *"First Sea Lord to see after action",* hardened his resolve to have no further relations with Mr. Churchill ... [knowing that] the telegram would pass through the hands of several of the Admiralty staff, and the marking could only be read by them as a distinct snub to the First Sea Lord.[32]

The 14 May War Council

On 14 May a War Council was convened, at which the atmosphere was described later by Churchill as 'sulphurous'. Kitchener was particularly incensed, and began by protesting over the way he had been drawn into supporting the Dardanelles operation through the alleged firepower of the *Queen Elizabeth* whose massive guns, according to Churchill, would emulate the giant German howitzers at Antwerp and Liège and virtually demolish all the old Turkish forts on their own. And now this mighty dreadnought was to be withdrawn (due to the threat posed by German submarines).

The 15-inch guns of HMS Queen Elizabeth at Gallipoli (IWM Q_013239).

Kitchener read out a prepared statement, advising the Councillors:

When the Admiralty proposed to force the passage of the Dardanelles by means of the Fleet alone, I doubted whether the attempt would succeed, but was led to believe it possible by the First Lord's statements of the power of the "Queen Elizabeth", and the Admiralty Staff Paper showing how the operations were to be conducted ... I regret that I was led to agree in the enterprise by the statements made, particularly as to the power of the "Queen Elizabeth", of which I had no means of judging.[33]

Churchill subsequently wrote a lengthy refutation of Kitchener's protest in *The World Crisis,* in which no mention was made of his claim to Kitchener that *Queen Elizabeth* 'would revolutionise all previous estimates of naval warfare'.[34]Rather, Churchill rejected (the now-deceased) Kitchener's version of events, in effect holding it up to ridicule, and asserting that:

The naval operations at the Dardanelles did not depend and never had depended upon the *Queen Elizabeth.* They had been planned before it was known she would go. [And] ... It was no good exaggerating the value of the *Queen Elizabeth,* or supposing that a great operation of this kind could turn on a single vessel.[35]

As the Secretary's Notes of the War Council Meeting reveal, however, Churchill offered no such reply or criticism during this meeting, despite his implications to the contrary in *The World Crisis.* [36] Churchill added in *The World Crisis*: 'Lord Fisher at this point interjected that he had been against the Dardanelles operation from the beginning and that the Prime Minister and Lord Kitchener knew this fact well. This remarkable interruption', Churchill continued, 'was received in silence.'[37] Significantly, Fisher's assertion was neither challenged nor refuted by anyone present at the War Council meeting. The Secretary's Notes again differ somewhat from Churchill's interpretation, pointing out that (rather than being a remarkable interruption):

THE PRIME MINISTER [had] asked for Lord Fisher's views.[38]

MR. LLOYD GEORGE [then] asked whether the Turks could not always meet our reinforcements by sending additional men to Gallipoli. He [further] asked if we could *ever* send enough men to drive 150,000 Turks out of their position?

LORD KITCHENER replied in the negative. The situation in Gallipoli was very similar to that in France, and our advance was held up mainly by machine-guns ... He did not see how we were ever to drive the Turks out of Kilid Bahr.[39]

'When [Kitchener] had finished, [Churchill writes in *The World Crisis]*, the Council turned to me—almost on me. [His response was]:

If it had been known three months before that an army of from 80,000 to 100,000 men would be available in May for an attack on the Dardanelles, the attack by the Navy alone would never have been undertaken.[40]

This was a particularly cynical deception by Churchill of his readers. As Sir Edward Grey made abundantly clear, troops were *never* intended to be a part of Churchill's original operation. Grey told the Dardanelles Commission that:

... it was distinctly told to us [at the War Council] that troops would not be asked for; that if the Navy could not carry out the operation by itself, the operation would not be proceeded with ... and I gave my consent on that understanding because I was informed—I believed Lord Kitchener's opinion to be—that no troops were available.[41] And Churchill *had* known, *three months earlier,* when the first of Kitchener's 100,000-strong New

Armies would be ready to take the field—as the Secretary's Notes of the 19 February War Council meeting (at which Churchill was present) reveal. Balfour had asked when the New Armies would be ready—to which Kitchener had replied: 'The 10th April was the present date for the first[100,000-strong New] Army.'[42] Kitchener then told the Council that: 'If you were merely to calculate the force required to render success absolutely certain, and not to continue the operation without such forces, withdrawal would be inevitable... [But] [i]f we abandoned the enterprise, there would be a danger of a rising in the Moslem world.' Lord Crewe (Secretary of State for India) agreed, adding that: 'it was impossible to contemplate the abandonment of the enterprise, owing to its effect in India.' Balfour also concurred, stating that 'it would be a great mistake to abandon the enterprise unless we were absolutely obliged to ... His suggestion was that we should hold the line which we now occupied, and be content with slow progress, avoiding any operations involving heavy losses.'[43] Churchill challenged the prevailing mood by pointing out that:

... we had now 560,000 men in France, and, say 80,000 at the Dardanelles ... Every month new armies were getting nearer completion ... The Dardanelles enterprise was a very small affair compared with our total resources ... He [Churchill] did not share or understand Lord Kitchener's grounds for pessimism ... In his opinion the outlook was by no means gloomy.[44]

The solution, proffered by Churchill in retrospect in *The World Crisis,* was to 'stop these vain offensives on the Western Front [and] concentrate [all] available reinforcements upon the Dardanelles', giving them sufficient munitions 'to reach a decision there at the earliest moment'.[45] The dilemma confronting the War Councillors was eventually summarised by Lord Haldane, who set before them three possible courses of action:

a. To withdraw from the Dardanelles, which was quite out of the question.

b. To push on rapidly and end the business; but this appeared equally impossible.

c. To adopt a policy similar to, but rather better than a state of siege, and this was the one he inclined to.[46]

The War Councillors consequently settled on a compromise and decided 'to send a telegram to Sir Ian Hamilton, asking what force he would require in order to ensure success at the Dardanelles.'[47] Hence, only three weeks after the invasion, the War Councillors had already conceded among themselves (with the conspicuous exception of Churchill) that a victory over the Turkish Army was 'impossible'.

***

Margot Asquith (the Prime Minister's wife) and Lloyd George had already speculated on Churchill's obsessive attitude towards the war, six days earlier:

> MARGOT: ... What a strange being! [referring to Churchill] He really likes war. He would be quite damped if he were told now "The War is over", he has no imagination of the heart.

LLOYD GEORGE: *He has none.* I shall never forget that night ... [on 4 August] when war was declared.

Big Ben struck 11 very slowly came the Boom—Boom—Boom—we sat in complete silence I should say for ten minutes after the last Boom.

Winston dashed into the room radiant, his face bright, his manner keen and he told us, one word pouring out on the other how he was going to send telegrams to the Mediterranean! the North Sea and God knows where!

You could see he was a really happy man. I wondered if this was the state of mind to be in at the opening of such a fearful war as this. You are right, he has no real imagination of the kind that counts.[48]

Margot Asquith related an even more revealing incident she had shared with Churchill on 10 January 1915:

WINSTON [talking about the war]: My God! This, this is living History. Everything we are doing and saying is thrilling—it will be read by a thousand generations, *think of that!!* Why I would not be out of this glorious delicious war for anything the world could give me (eyes glowing but with a slight anxiety lest the word "delicious" should jar on me). I say don't repeat that I said the word "delicious"—you know what I mean.[49]

***

On the afternoon of this same day, following the War Council meeting, Churchill presented Asquith with a virtual *fait accompli,* insofar as his intention to renew the naval attack was concerned. As he wrote to the Prime Minister:

> I must ask you to take note of Fisher's statements today that "he was against the Dardanelles and had been all along", or words to that effect. *The First Sea Lord has agreed in writing to every executive telegram on which operations have been conducted* and had they been immediately successful the credit would have been his. But I make no complaint of that ... My point is that a moment will probably arise in these operations when the Admiral and General on the spot will wish and require to run a risk with the fleet for a great and decisive effort. If I agree with them I will sanction it and I cannot undertake to be paralysed by the veto of a friend who, whatever the result, will certainly say, "I was against the Dardanelles ..." But I wish to make it clear to you that a man who says, "I disclaim all responsibility for failure", cannot be the final arbiter of the measures which may be vital to success.[50]

With breathtaking arrogance Churchill was now formally asserting to the Prime Minister that his (amateur) judgement was superior to that of the nation's most admired and trusted admiral, a man with 60 years' naval experience behind him; together with the collective experience of the Admiralty War Staff Group, Naval Intelligence and Naval Operations. Asquith was not required to respond to Churchill's letter. But in effect, as Admiral Bacon points out, Churchill was serving notice that he intended 'to relieve [Fisher] entirely from all professional control' of the Royal Navy, assuming absolute control himself.[51] Bacon believes that 'the answer the Prime Minister should have given to Mr. Churchill was a sharp injunction to be guided by the views of the First Sea Lord and the Naval Staff.'[52] But, once again, this erstwhile classics scholar did nothing, content to let matters drift.

At around 6.30pm that evening, Churchill went to Lord Fisher's room and, after a long discussion left, saying: 'Well, goodnight Fisher. We have settled everything, and you must go home and have a good night's rest. Things will look brighter in the morning, and we'll pull the thing [the Dardanelles] through together.'[53] Fisher called Commander Crease into his room, telling him, 'You need not pack up just yet.' He then told Crease that he had had a satisfactory interview with the First Lord and had come to a 'definite and final understanding with him concerning the naval reinforcements that could be sent to the Dardanelles.' It was Crease's understanding that six monitors and four Edgar class cruisers had been mentioned. Fisher added, 'But I suppose he'll soon be at me again', then left.[54]

During the course of the night, four minutes came to Fisher's office from Churchill for his attention the next morning (Churchill was in the habit of working well into the night, while Fisher began work at around 5.00am). Commander Crease has provided a detailed account of the events that followed:[55]

> [T]owards midnight Masterton-Smith [Churchill's Private Secretary] came in with the minute [in question] and covering letter ...
>
> Masterton-Smith asked me to read them through, and I did so. He was evidently uneasy about the minute and asked "how I thought the old man [Fisher] would take it". [Churchill had increased the naval reinforcements to include three extra monitors, additional 15-inch howitzers and 9.2-inch guns—but above all, two 'E' class submarines (the newest class), which had not even been discussed the night before—significantly, Churchill makes no mention of these increases in *The World Crisis*].[56]
>
> Knowing well Lord Fisher's frame of mind during the past few days, and his letter to the Prime Minister of the day before, and reading that submarines were now included in the proposed reinforcements [knowing Fisher's strong views that

submarines could not be spared from home waters], I had no hesitation about my reply.

I said at once that I had no doubt whatever Lord Fisher would resign instantly if he received the minute; for these new proposals, coming at that moment, would be the last straw ... After some discussion Masterton-Smith said he would tell the First Lord my opinion before definitely handing me the minute to pass on. After some delay—I believe Masterton-Smith first spoke to [Commodore] de Bartolomé on the subject before going to Mr. Churchill—he came back with the dispatch-box and said it must be sent on, for the First Lord was certain that Lord Fisher would not object to the proposals; but the First Lord had also added *that, in any case, it was necessary that they* [the changes] *should be made* [Crease's emphasis]. I repeated my warning as to the consequences, and then arranged for the dispatch-box to be delivered early in the morning to Lord Fisher.[57]

Churchill was clearly determined to test Fisher's resolve. Had the First Sea Lord acquiesced, he would indeed have been reduced to a mere cypher for Churchill. When Lord Fisher discovered the following morning that Churchill 'had already departed from the agreement of the previous evening; and in his opinion had twice in two days gone beyond his pledges' he knew it would be impossible to work with him any longer. He immediately wrote a letter to the Prime Minister, resigning his office of First Sea Lord, and informing him:

> As I find it increasingly difficult to adjust myself to the increasing policy of the First Lord in regard to the Dardanelles, I have been reluctantly compelled to inform him this day that I am unable to remain as his colleague, and I am leaving at once for Scotland, so as not to be embarrassed, or embarrass you, by any explanations with anyone.[58]

Fisher informed Churchill in a similar fashion: 'After further anxious reflection, I have come to the regretted conclusion I am unable to remain any longer as your colleague … As you truly said yesterday, I am in the position of continually vetoing your proposals. This is not fair to you, besides being extremely distasteful to me.'[59] Churchill's immediate, 'unctuous' reply (in Penn's words), with its appeal to Fisher's sense of honour and loyalty, reads, in part:

The only thing to think of now is what is best for the country and for every brave man who is fighting …

> I do not understand what is the specific cause which leads you to resign. When we parted last night I thought we were in agreement …

> In order to bring you back to the Admiralty I took my political life in my hands—as you well know.

You then promised to stand by me and see me through. If you now go at this bad moment and therefore let loose on me the spite and malice of those who are your enemies more than they are mine, it will be a melancholy ending to our six months of successful war and administration ... and our rupture will be profoundly injurious to every public interest.[60]

Fisher replied:

The Prime Minister put the case in a nutshell when he stated to me yesterday afternoon [at the War Council] the actual fact that I had been dead against the Dardanelles operation from the beginning! How could I be otherwise when previously as First Sea Lord I had been responsible for the Defence Committee Memorandum [of 1906] stating the forcing of the Dardanelles to be impossible? You *must* remember my extreme reluctance in the Prime Minister's room in January to accept his decision in regard to the Dardanelles, and at the War Council held immediately afterwards I stated, in reply to a question by [Lloyd George], that the Prime Minister knew my views, and I left the matter to him, to explain ...

YOU ARE BENT ON FORCING THE DARDANELLES AND NOTHING WILL TURN YOU FROM IT—NOTHING ...

YOU WILL REMAIN AND I SHALL GO—it is better so ... I have told the Prime Minister I will not remain. I have absolutely decided to stick to that decision. Nothing will turn me from it. You say with much feeling that *it will be a very great grief to you to part from me*—I am certain that you know in your heart no one has ever been more faithful to you than I have since I joined you last October. *I have worked my very hardest.* [61]

Soon after receiving Fisher's letter, Asquith telephoned the Admiralty, demanding to see the First Sea Lord. But Fisher was nowhere to be found. Fearing the politicians' persuasive power on his sense of loyalty and patriotism, he had spent the morning 'in Westminster Abbey, where he frequently attended Matins and to where he also repaired when his mind was agitated or disturbed'. 62

Asquith issued the following melodramatic injunction: 'Lord Fisher, In the King's name I order you to remain at your post.' Through the intermediary of Reginald McKenna, however, Asquith had given an assurance to Fisher 'that your resignation is void until [the PM] accepts it.'[63] In the afternoon Fisher met with Asquith, but he maintained a steadfast refusal to return to the Admiralty, though he did agree not to leave London. In fact, all the important Admiralty telegrams, papers, etc, were taken to his house, which was in direct communication with the Admiralty building via a passage. From here Fisher kept a watchful eye on the progress of the war. He sent a cryptic telegram to Jellicoe advising him of the situation. He also sent instructions to the Chief of Staff (Oliver) providing the *Queen Elizabeth* with a safe course home from the Dardanelles so as to avoid German submarines.[64]

Churchill's Downfall

Winston Churchill had been the subject of intense public hostility ever since the disastrous 18 March naval attack, for which he was universally held responsible. The *Morning Post* headline and lead story on 23 April 1915 had been fairly representative of this criticism in stating:

> "The Dardanelles Blunder": British constitutional theory has no place for a civilian Minister who usurps the functions of his Board, takes the wheel out of the sailor's hand, and launches ships upon a naval operation ... We have seen at Antwerp, in the case of Cradock's squadron, and in this disaster at the Dardanelles, how a nation is punished which persists in allowing its politicians to conduct naval operations.[65]

On the 27th, the *Morning Post* had added: 'Mr. Churchill's characteristics make him in his present position, a danger and anxiety to the nation'. And on the 30th: 'Mr. Churchill's instinct for the melodramatic has blossomed into megalomania'.[66]

Commander Crease apprised the junior Sea Lords of the situation early on 16 May. As a consequence they sent a memo to Churchill, on behalf of the Board, expressing '[their] opinion that the present method of directing ... the Fleet, and the conduct of the war, by which the orders for controlling movements and supplies appear to be largely taken out of the hands of the First Sea Lord, is open to very grave objection.' However, disappointingly for Fisher, the junior Sea Lords concluded that 'whatever differences of opinion or defects in procedure' were at fault, these should be resolvable through 'discussion and concession' by the First Lord and First Sea Lord.[67] Lord Esher sent Fisher a letter of support on the 16th, offering him what would turn out to be extremely bad advice:

> My dear Jackie,
>
> You will never *permanently* patch up these quarrels. The only thing to be done is to revive the office of Lord High Admiral and take it yourself. Otherwise we are beaten presently at sea and, unless Lord K takes the war into his own hands, ditto on land.[68]

Churchill wrote a cajoling/accusatory letter to Fisher on the 16th, telling him:

> ... We are now fully agreed that the Fleet is not to attempt to rush the Narrows but is to support

the Army in its gradual advance upon the forts by land.

... The announcement of your resignation at this juncture will be accepted everywhere as proof that the military operations as well as the naval, at the Dardanelles, have failed ... your resignation would be exploited all over the world, [it] might prove the deciding factor in the case of Italy now trembling on the brink [of joining the Allies. Churchill concluded with the thinly veiled threat]:

... Meanwhile, Sir Arthur Wilson could, if you desire it, do your work.[69]

But Fisher was not to be so easily won over. The following day he turned to his old friend and Leader of the Opposition, Bonar Law, answering a letter of support and warning him of the 'national danger' that was Churchill:

Private and Personal. This letter and its contents must not be divulged now or ever to any living soul:

In reply to your letter, after repeated refusals by him I have written to the PM to say that now my *definite decision* is I am absolutely unable to remain with W[inston] C[hurchill] (HE'S A REAL DANGER) *But he is going to be kept* (so I go! *at once,* TODAY ...)

Don't be cajoled *privately* by the PM to keep silence. The danger is imminent and VITAL. I don't want to stay, but WC MUST go at all costs! AT ONCE ...

WC is leading them all straight to ruin *... I feel bound to tell you as leader of the Opposition, because a very great national disaster is very near us in the Dardanelles!* ... against which I have vainly protested and did resign long ago, but Kitchener persuaded me to stop. I was a damned fool to do so. HE ought to have resigned also ...

[Fisher concluded]: This evening Winston sent Lambert, the Civil Lord at the Admiralty, to offer me a seat in the Cabinet if I would return as First Sea Lord with him (Winston) as First Lord! I rejected the 30 pieces of silver to betray my country.[70]

Churchill's offer was, in fact, meaningless as only the Prime Minister had the power to authorise Cabinet appointments. There is no mention of this incident in *The World Crisis.*

Fisher wrote to Jellicoe on the 17th: 'Dear Jellicoe, I have resigned on account of proposed further depletion of our Home resources for the Dardanelles, and also because of absolute incompatibility of view with the First Lord. He is a bigger danger than the Germans! The other Sea Lords agree, but don't resign, and A.K.

Wilson takes my place! Such is life!'[71] On 17 May, Hobhouse recorded that the Cabinet was informed (officially) for the first time that: 'W[inston]. S[pencer]. C[hurchill] had been ordering fleets and ships about without consultation, much less concurrence of L[or]d Fisher'.[72]

On the afternoon of this same day Asquith informed a stunned Churchill that he would no longer be in control at the Admiralty in the forthcoming coalition government agreed to by himself and Bonar Law. Coming on top of a reported shell scandal (there was an alleged shortage of high explosive shells for the British Army in France, with many of those supplied proving to be 'duds'), the resignation of the First Sea Lord brought down the government. The Conservative leader agreed to form a coalition with Asquith's Liberals, but only on the condition that Churchill be removed from the office of First Lord of the Admiralty.[73] To the very end Churchill refused to acknowledge the extent to which he had discredited the Liberals.[74] Even the King wanted him replaced, as he had become 'impossible'.[75]

By 21 May Churchill would be appealing to Asquith for 'any office—the lowest [if it is to be of use] in this time of war'.[76] His request was granted, with the sinecure post of Chancellor of the Duchy of Lancaster, an office with no responsibilities and, as Lloyd George put it, for 'beginners in the Cabinet or for distinguished politicians who had reached the first stages of unmistakable decrepitude.'[77] Churchill would remain a member of the reconstituted and enlarged Dardanelles Committee which replaced the War Council, but with his former influence severely curtailed.

News of Lord Fisher's resignation created a wave of public indignation and support for the admiral, and predictable anger towards the politician. The *Globe's* headline on 18 May announced: 'LORD FISHER MUST NOT GO', followed by, 'Lord Fisher or Mr. Churchill? Expert or amateur?'[78] Similar headlines featured in most of the nation's newspapers. *The Times* sought to explain the situation more fully in its 18 May editorial:

> What long ago passed beyond the stage of mere rumour is the charge which has been repeatedly and categorically made in public, that the First Lord of the Admiralty has been assuming responsibilities and overriding his expert advisers to a degree which might at any time endanger the national safety ... It is no longer possible to keep silence ... When a civilian Minister in charge of a fighting service persistently seeks to grasp power which should not pass into his unguided hands, and attempts to use that power in perilous ways, it is time for his colleagues in the Cabinet to take some definite action.[79]

The Times proposed that Fisher replace Churchill as First Lord, with a seat in the Cabinet, a suggestion which was taken up by the *Daily Telegraph, Daily*

Express, the *Globe* and *The Army and Navy Gazette.* There were a number of precedents to support such a move, with leading admirals Anson, St. Vincent, Keppel and Barham all having successfully occupied this post in wartime.[80]

The prospect of Fisher's departure signalled widespread alarm throughout the Navy. Admiral Sir David Beatty wrote to him: 'I can't believe that it is possible that the Government will accept it [your resignation]. It would be a worse calamity than a defeat at sea. If it is any value to know it, the fleet is numbed with the thought of the possibility ... Please God it is *not* possible.' Beatty confided to his wife: 'The Navy breathes freer now it is rid of the succubus Churchill.'[81]

Jellicoe wrote in similar vein to Fisher, imploring him not to resign. As for the First Lord, the Commander-in-Chief of the Grand Fleet was glad to see him go. He had for long 'thoroughly distrusted Mr. Churchill because he consistently arrogated to himself technical knowledge which, with all his brilliant qualities, I knew he did not possess.' In Jellicoe's assessment Churchill was 'a public danger to the Empire'.[82] On the 17th, the day the coalition was agreed to, and the day Churchill was sacked from office, Asquith wrote to Fisher, advising him: 'Dear Lord Fisher, I feel bound to tell you for your own information only, that a considerable reconstruction of the Government is in contemplation, and in the public interest I trust you will neither say nor do

271

anything for a day or two.'[83] Bonar Law advised Fisher similarly on the 20th, with two letters:

> My dear Fisher,
>
> I wish I could see you but I do not think it right to do so in view of the negotiations in which I am actually engaged with the Gvt.
>
> I do ask you however to keep yourself free until the new Gvt is formed or the attempt to form it has failed.[84]

And on the same day: 'My dear Lord Fisher, I am much obliged by your letter but I can say for the moment that everything is in the melting pot and you ought not to do anything decisive until we see what kind of metal comes out of the crucible.'[85]

The admiration and support at this time from every section of British society towards the nation's most revered admiral was overwhelming. Even Queen Alexandra wrote to Fisher, telling him 'to stick to your post like Nelson! The Nation and we all have confidence in you, and I and they will not suffer you to go. You are the nation's hope, and we trust you.'[86]

In contrast, Churchill was widely reviled and mistrusted as an unprincipled, ego-driven, political adventurer—and a dangerous one at that. On 24 May Frances Stevenson wrote in her diary:

> There is no section in the country, so far as I can see, that wishes him [Churchill] to stay at the Admiralty, [adding] ...
>
> Masterton-Smith, Winston's own private secretary, told the PM that on no account ought Churchill to be allowed to remain at the Admiralty—he was most dangerous there. It seems strange that Churchill should have been in politics all these years & yet not have won the confidence of a single party in the country, or a single colleague in the Cabinet.[87]

There is little doubt that Churchill's conduct had exacted a heavy toll on Fisher's nervous constitution. Churchill had already driven Carden to a nervous collapse by demanding that he perform the impossible.

Churchill would exhibit the same behaviour in the Second World War. As Higgins points out, Churchill's 'strenuous and demanding personality' would again repeatedly infuriate and exhaust his subordinates and even political colleagues, to the point of tears or collapse, in the next war.[88] Fisher's complaints to Hankey and Jellicoe were almost identical to those expressed later by Sir John Dill and Sir Alan Brooke (Chiefs of the Imperial General Staff), who complained that 'managing Churchill took most of the energy they wished to devote to fighting the Germans'. Sir John Dill was driven close to a nervous collapse by

Churchill, before being succeeded by Brooke in December 1941.[89]

Fisher's Preamble

Fisher had repeatedly written to Hankey and Jellicoe advising them of his problems with Churchill. He had even written directly to Asquith in the hope of remedial action against Churchill's usurpation of his authority, but to no avail. '"Surely I can send a private letter to a friend without showing it to you!!!" That's his argument', Fisher had written to Hankey, early on the morning of 14 May, recounting Churchill's self-justification for the 'Secret and Personal from First Lord' telegram instructions he was sending to commanders at sea. Churchill had also told Fisher on the 14th that 'his [Churchill's] conviction [was] that after all, in six weeks time the Fleet would have to do it [force the Dardanelles] *ALONE!*—& would I remain on—quiet for this?' 'What is one to do with such a determined mad gambler?' Fisher had pleaded.[90]

Asquith's and Bonar Law's assurances to Fisher of his retention as First Sea Lord in a re-formed coalition government, together with the adulation he had received from all sections of society, plus the bad advice from Lord Esher and the 'constant prodding' by Churchill may well have combined temporarily to unhinge his judgement—in the opinion of Admiral Bacon.[91] Penn writes that Fisher seems to have believed (mistakenly) that his retention as First Sea Lord was a Conservative condition of the coalition agreement.[92] In the event, on the 19th of May, Fisher presented Asquith with what was virtually an ultimatum, setting down a list of demands. Utterly confident that his position was secure, Fisher dictated his terms for returning. His intention may well have been also to highlight the situation which had, until recently, prevailed at the Admiralty, and to ensure that never again would the authority of the Royal Navy's senior executive officer be usurped as it had been under Churchill. This he spelled out in clauses 4 and 5 of his 'Preamble', which stipulated:

> That I should have complete professional charge of the war at sea, together with the sole disposition of the fleet and appointment of all officers of all ranks whatsoever and absolutely untrammelled sole command of all the sea forces whatsoever.

> That the First Lord of the Admiralty should be absolutely restricted to policy and Parliamentary procedure, and should occupy the same position towards me as Mr. Tennant MP does to Lord Kitchener (and very well he does it).[93]

But Fisher's subsidiary conditions were unreasonable to the point of absurdity. No Prime Minister could allow himself to be dictated to in such a fashion. Fisher also demanded:

That Mr. Winston Churchill is not in the Cabinet to be always circumventing me, nor will I serve under Mr. Balfour [Balfour had been the staunchest supporter of the Dardanelles operation after Churchill, and was mooted to be the next First Lord].

That [Admiral] Sir A.K. Wilson leaves the Admiralty and the Committee of Imperial Defence and the War Council ... [as] his policy is totally opposed to mine, and he accepted the position of First Sea Lord in succession to me, thereby adopting a policy diametrically opposed to my views. That there shall be an entire new Board of Admiralty as regards the [Junior] Sea Lords [who had failed him by giving him poor advice] and the Financial Secretary (who is utterly useless), *New measures demand new men.* [94]

As many historians agree, had Fisher remained silent it is entirely likely that Asquith would have asked him to withdraw his resignation, and considered another First Lord more amenable than Balfour.[95] But Fisher destroyed all chances of reinstatement with this ultimatum. Asquith accepted his resignation on the 21st, and Balfour was appointed First Lord of the Admiralty on the 27th of May, with Admiral Sir Henry Jackson the new First Sea Lord.

The stalemate/attrition tactics of the Western Front soon became the dominant feature of the Gallipoli campaign. Five additional New Army divisions (the 10th, 11th, 13th, 53rd and 54th), sent to Hamilton for his 'big push' in August, altered this situation not one iota.[96] It was simply not possible for Britain to supply the men and armaments needed to wage major campaigns on two fronts simultaneously. By October the proposition of evacuation from Gallipoli was being seriously considered by the Dardanelles Committee. Churchill, needless to say, vehemently rejected any such move.

In October Sir Charles Monro, a distinguished general from the Western Front, replaced Hamilton and visited Gallipoli to assess the situation. After only a few hours' inspection he recommended withdrawal from a position which, with the entry of Bulgaria into the war on Germany's side in October, had become untenable. Lord Kitchener still had reservations however, fearing the losses this could entail, and visited Gallipoli himself in November. He concurred with Monro's findings and plans for the evacuation were drawn up.[97]

A new Cabinet War Committee was formed on 11 November (comprising Asquith, Lloyd George, Balfour, Bonar Law and Reginald McKenna), from which Churchill was excluded altogether.[98] With this final humiliation Churchill resigned his sinecure ministry. He took full advantage of his resignation speech to Parliament to present his version of the events which had led to his demise.

He began by telling the House how this 'brilliant ray of hope' was conceived amid a world of gloom and setbacks on the Western Front. He explained how the idea had occurred to him, and how he had sought the opinion of the Admiral on the spot, and tested Carden's plan with the Admiralty War Staff, who examined it:

> Sir Henry Jackson expressed his full concurrence in it [Churchill told his audience], Lord Fisher, of course, knew everything that was passing and he never expressed any opinion against this specific operation ... We had seen—it was fresh in everybody's mind—great fortresses, reputed the strongest in Europe, collapsing, fort by fort, under five or ten shells from 15-inch howitzers; and here was the Queen Elizabeth ... with eight 15-inch guns on the broadside.[99]

> [Churchill took his audience through the first exciting phase of the naval attack, which was] ... successful beyond all our hopes. The outer forts were destroyed. The Fleet was able to enter the Straits, and attack the forts at the Narrows ... A panic was created in Constantinople. Everyone supposed that the enterprise was going to succeed ... It was not now desired by anyone to go back ... The eyes of the whole world were riveted on the Dardanelles. Every interest, military, naval, political, and economic, urged prosecution of the enterprise ...[100]

I will not have it said [Churchill insisted, indignantly] that this was a civilian plan, foisted by a political amateur upon reluctant officers and experts. ... I have gone through this story in detail in order to show and to convince this House that the naval attack on the Dardanelles was a naval plan, made by the naval authorities on the spot, approved by naval experts in the Admiralty, assented to by the First Sea Lord, and executed on the spot by Admirals who at every stage believed in the operations ...[101]

[Churchill continued] ... Admiralty telegrams were the result of close consultation between the First Sea Lord and myself, and, like every other order of importance which has emanated from the Admiralty during my tenure in peace or war, bear the written authority of the First Sea Lord. I wish to make that point quite clear. I may extend it, and say there is no important act of policy, no scheme of fleet distribution, of movement of ships, or of plans of war which have been acted on during my tenure at the Admiralty in which the First Sea Lord has not concurred in writing. [Churchill ended his peroration by planting the notion of Fisher's culpability, when he told his audience]:

I am not going to embark on any reproaches this afternoon, but I must say I did not receive from the First Sea Lord either the clear guidance before the event or the firm support which I was entitled to expect. [He then laid further responsibility on Fisher by stating]: If the First Sea Lord had not approved the operations, if he thought they were unlikely to take the course that was expected of them, if he thought they would lead to undue losses, it was his duty to refuse consent. No one could have prevailed against such a refusal. The operation would never have begun.[102]

This proved too much even for Asquith, who replied:

... The House is always accustomed, and properly accustomed, to give great latitude to explanations from a Minister of the Crown who has resigned his office, and my Right Hon. friend has taken advantage of that privilege ... I only wish to say two things ... He has said one or two things which I tell him frankly I had rather he had not said, but, on the other hand, he has naturally left unsaid some things which, when the complete estimate of these transactions has to be taken, will have to be said.[103]

Lord Fisher refused to dignify Churchill's accusations with a reply. Instead, in his maiden speech to the House of Lords the following day, he said:

I ask leave of your Lordships to make a statement. Certain references were made to me in the other House yesterday by Mr. Churchill. I have been sixty-one years in the service of my country, and I leave my record in the hands of my countrymen. The Prime Minister said yesterday that Mr. Churchill had said one or two things which he had better not have said, and that necessarily, and naturally, left unsaid some things which will have to be said. I am content to wait. It is unfitting to make personal explanations affecting national interests when my country is in the midst of a great war.[104]

***

Churchill's resignation speech to Parliament signalled the beginning of an alternative account he would construct to explain the circumstances surrounding the Dardanelles campaign. This would be supplemented in his evidence to the Dardanelles Commission in 1916, then perfected in his written apologia *The World Crisis* in 1923.

CHAPTER 6

The Dardanelles Commission

A combination of public criticism and Parliamentary pressure forced the Asquith government to convene a Royal Commission enquiry in 1916 to determine how and why the Dardanelles fiasco had been conceived, and the reason for its failure. More than a thousand pages of evidence were presented to the Commission and it was allegedly on the basis of this evidence that the findings and conclusions of this seriously flawed body were determined—bearing in mind that three of the ten Commissioners recorded strong dissent against the official findings.

Creation

The call for a Royal Commission enquiry into the circumstances surrounding the inception of the Dardanelles campaign was first mooted on 4 May 1915, when Admiral Lord Charles Beresford told Parliament that at some future time an inquiry would have to be made into the campaign's origins, and asked the Prime Minister to 'make a statement on the subject'. Even before the disastrous landing of 25 April, he had already asked in Parliament, 'Who is responsible for the [Dardanelles] operations?'[1]

Liberal MP and newspaper proprietor Sir Henry Dalziel had been denied the right to debate the Dardanelles 'scandals' in the Commons in June 1915.[2] Twelve months later, however, following a similar military fiasco in Mesopotamia (in April 1916), the coalition government yielded unexpectedly to pressure in the Commons demanding that the documents relating to the Dardanelles and the Mesopotamian campaign be laid before the House.[3]

The convening of a large-scale enquiry into a military defeat while the war was still in progress was most unusual, but Asquith's government had attracted frequent and harsh criticism over its handling of the Dardanelles campaign in particular. On 1 June 1916 Bonar Law, who was standing in for Asquith as Leader of the House, rashly acceded to the demands without prior consultation with the War Committee, Cabinet, the War Office, Admiralty or the Foreign Office.[4]Hankey wrote to Asquith two days later, warning him of the likely harm to the government should Bonar Law's commitment be allowed to stand. Asquith agreed, but added that 'Parliamentary pressure was so great that he would have to publish something.'[5] The ten-man Royal Commission appointed was chaired by Lord Cromer and included Field Marshal Lord Nicholson for the Army; Admiral of the Fleet Sir William May for the Navy; Andrew Fisher and Sir Thomas Mackenzie for Australia and New Zealand respectively; Liberal MP and lawyer Walter Roch for the Welsh soldiers at the Dardanelles, Captain

S.L. Gwynne for the Irish and James Clyde for the Scottish; and Liberal MP Sir Frederick Cawley and High Court judge Sir William Pickford. The Secretary was E. Grimwood Mears.[6]

Evidence for the first report, which was published on 8 March 1917, was taken from 34 witnesses over the period 19 September to 4 December 1916. Only this first report, covering the events from 6 August 1914 to 23 March 1915, is germane to this account. The final report covered the military invasion of Gallipoli. The first report is unsatisfactory in many respects, as modern historians have commented.

The exigencies of wartime security required that the answers to a number of the questions in the report be excised, as indeed were some of the questions, leaving only partial answers or questions, or blank spaces in many instances. The complete evidence, comprising 1687 pages, was printed and made available to the public in 1968, but only to researchers willing to travel to The National Archives at Kew.[7]

It was unthinkable that, in time of war, evidence of governmental ineptitude at the highest level in the planning and conduct of the war should be gifted to the enemy. Needless to say, the published findings of the Commission proved equivocal in terms of governmental accountability. Although Churchill and Asquith were deemed to have been remiss in their actions, they escaped with only mild reproofs. Scapegoats naturally had to be found to placate the public conscience and explain away the appalling ineptitude revealed—and these were conveniently to hand, in the persons of the recently deceased Lord Kitchener and the retired Lord Fisher.

Cabinet Secretary Hankey assumed the role of 'Government defender'. Copies of his Secretary's Notes of War Council Meetings, as well as memoranda and minutes connected with the first phase of the campaign, were sent to Asquith, Lloyd George, Balfour and Lord Grey (the only members of the War Committee who had also been members of the War Council). On Asquith's instructions, Hankey denied Churchill access to these documents. Although Churchill was out of office at this time and not eligible to receive secret papers, this act further widened the gulf between the Prime Minister and his former First Lord.[8] Considerable collusion took place between the Admiralty staff and former staff over the presentation of their evidence, with Churchill, Fisher, Oliver and Graham Greene all collaborating and coaching one another in the interests of their own and the Royal Navy's reputations.[9]Hankey initially provided Asquith with 35 papers which could be released without harming the public interest. These would be substantially increased.[10]

However, all diplomatic documents had to be excluded, the Foreign Office assessing that Britain's relations with allied and neutral governments could not be compromised. It had initially been decided to offer the Commission 'any Memoranda prepared for the War

Council', but not the minutes of its meetings (which were, in effect, Cabinet meetings), although this was eventually relaxed, with the Secretary's Notes made available to the Chairman only.[11]

WINSTON (sheathing his Sunday-paper weapon in his best Blenheim manner):
"After all, some say 'The pen is mightier than the sword.'"
—*Punch*, 19th July 1916

Popular satirical appreciation of Churchill as the 'heir to Marlborough' from Punch or The London Charivari, 19 July 1916.

By the beginning of September 1916 Hankey had completed his 'Notes for Evidence' for the Dardanelles

Commissioners. This comprised a masterly 20-page summary of the origins and execution of the naval attack. The final, massive dossier covering all the events, from the pre-war deliberations of the CID to the military invasion of Gallipoli, was compiled and forwarded to Secretary Mears on the 6th of that month.[12] Churchill was delighted at the prospect of an enquiry. Unrealistically, he demanded that all the official documents be presented and published. Only thus, he maintained, would the full facts be known. According to Hankey, what Churchill really wanted was to be 'whitewashed' in the public eye.[13] Churchill would ultimately succeed in his stated aim of having the official documents published (or at least, all those he deemed significant) in *The World Crisis*—with very telling effect.

While many of its findings may have been and remain contentious, the report's final conclusion was beyond question in pronouncing that: 'A surprise amphibious attack on the Gallipoli Peninsula offered such great military and political advantages that it was mistaken and ill-advised to sacrifice this possibility by hastily deciding to undertake a purely naval attack which, from its very nature could not attain completely the objects set out.'[14] Just who was responsible for that 'ill-advised' naval attack would become the major bone of contention. In the final analysis, ultimate responsibility would be ascribed to the service chiefs, Lords Kitchener and Fisher, head of the Army and Navy respectively, for their failure to warn the War

Councillors of the likely outcome of a purely naval attack. As the Commissioners decided: 'If either Lord Kitchener or Lord Fisher had, from the first, expressed on technical grounds, strong objections to the attack on the Dardanelles, the project would have been abandoned.'[15]

Kitchener's Culpability

Lord Kitchener had, in fact, registered the strongest objection to a purely naval operation on technical grounds just prior to the 13 January War Council (as previously described), but he had done so through the proper channels, personally apprising Churchill of his concerns at a private conference with the First Lord. As a consequence, the War Councillors were never made aware of the Secretary of State for War's expert assessment of the operation until it was too late (not until 14 May 1915 in fact). At this private conference, which Kitchener described in the greatest detail to his Private Secretary, Sir George Arthur, Churchill had claimed for *Queen Elizabeth's* 15-inch guns, the same firepower as that of Germany's 'Big Berthas'.[16]

In September 1914 Germany possessed four 'Big Berthas'. These giant 17-inch (42cm) siege howitzers weighed 43 tons and required a 200-man crew to move and operate them. They were capable of lobbing one-ton shells a distance of nine miles and, as the Belgian forts at Liège, Antwerp and Namur demonstrated, no fortification could withstand their firepower.[17] Churchill's specious claims for *Queen Elizabeth's* guns (that they would destroy the old Turkish forts single-handed) was entirely misleading, as artillery fire and naval gunfire are intrinsically dissimilar. Churchill would not only win over the civilian War Councillors with his spurious claims, he would also persist with these in his resignation speech to Parliament in November 1915, when he told that audience similarly: 'We had seen—it was fresh in everybody's mind—great fortresses, reputed the strongest in Europe, collapsing, fort by fort, under five or ten shells from 15-inch howitzers; and here was the *Queen Elizabeth* ... with eight 15-inch guns on the broadside.'[18]

HMS Queen Elizabeth under Turkish fire off Cape Helles (AWM A02647).

Kitchener had remained unmoved and argued strongly against a purely naval attack at the Dardanelles unsupported by a large military force, but was forced eventually to yield to the First Lord's bombast and assertions that he (Lord Kitchener) lacked the expertise (in naval ordnance) to challenge or refute this proposition with regard to *Queen Elizabeth*'s immense firepower. The corroborating evidence of Sir George Arthur concerning this episode was dismissed by the Commissioners as having 'no direct bearing upon the immediate subject of our Inquiry'. Of the similar evidence tendered by Major General von Donop and H.J. Creedy, 'neither added any material information to the facts already in their [the Commissioners'] possession', it was decided. Major General Callwell independently verified Kitchener's quandary in 1920.[19]

Kitchener was further held (by Churchill) to have fatally compromised the Dardanelles operation at the outset by refusing to supply the large-scale military support generally recognised as essential and which was available at that time, thus forcing an inferior, purely naval attack on the War Council. 'I assert', Churchill told the Commission, 'that in February[1915] there was nothing in the situation in France, or on the Russian Front, or in this island [Britain], which would have prevented the War Office [from sending to] the Dardanelles, eight or nine or even ten infantry divisions[180,000 troops].'[20] Churchill would repeat this accusation in *The World Crisis,* naming the divisions available as: 'The 29th Division, two first-line Territorial divisions, the Royal Naval Division, a Yeomanry mounted division ... two Australian divisions, one extra Australian brigade, the Lancashire Territorial Division, one Indian Brigade ... and two French divisions.'[21]

In reality, there was only one spare division available in January/February 1915—the regulars of the 29th, brought back from India and, like the 28th Division, replaced there by a Territorial division. At the time Churchill's numbers were refuted by Hankey in his 'Statement to the Dardanelles Commission' in 1916 (which would not be released for public scrutiny, however, until 1966). This Memorandum stated that:

> At the beginning of January 1915, there were in France 5 British or Indian Cavalry Divisions and 11 Infantry Divisions. [These comprised] 1st, 2nd, 3rd British, 1st and 2nd Indian Cavalry Divisions; and 1st, 2nd, 3rd, 4th, 5th, 6th, 7th & 8th and 27th British, and the Meerut and Lahore [Infantry] Divisions.
>
> In the UK apart from [Territorial] troops allotted for Home defence the only complete divisions were the 28th, which embarked for France between 15 & 28 January & the 1st Canadian [Division] which embarked [for France] on 8 February. The 29th Division had not all arrived in the country, and was earmarked for service in France. The 1st North Midland Territorial Division did not leave for France until end of February[1915], and other Territorial Divisions followed in April and

May[1915], *but none of these were armed or fully trained by the middle of January* [1915].[22]

In 1929, the official military historian, Brigadier Aspinall-Oglander, concurred with Hankey's statistics in his history of the Gallipoli campaign, adding: 'Behind them [the 300,000 British and Indian troops in France in January 1915] stood eleven first-line and thirteen second-line Territorial divisions [in Britain, and] all the divisions of the New Army [but] *none of these divisions were expected to be ready for service for several months.'* [23]

There were, it was true, over a million soldiers of Kitchener's New Armies and 24 Territorial divisions in Britain in January 1915. Unfortunately, however, there were no uniforms, rifles, training personnel or barracks accommodation for such a massive and unexpected influx of volunteers. Britain's required recruitment rate to maintain its small standing army (of 220,000 men in 1896) had been 2500 men per month throughout the previous century.[24] '[T]he machinery and *personnel* intended to deal with 30,000 recruits in a year broke down hopelessly' in the face of such numbers: '30,000 men volunteered on one day alone during the first month of the war'.[25]

It should also be noted that, from September 1914, Lord Kitchener was loath to send out of the country any of those Territorial troops who were armed and were intended for home defence.

Following their setback at the Marne in September, the Germans began spreading false rumours through their embassies in neutral countries of an impending major assault against the British and French on the Western Front. This was to coincide with a military invasion of Britain. The purpose of this deception was to mask the large-scale transfer of German troops to the Eastern Front for a massive assault against the Russians in an attempt to inflict a major defeat on them and drive them out of the war.[26] The likelihood of an invasion thus dominated Kitchener's thinking for the next five months (until March 1915, by which time the hoax was apparent). As Asquith wrote to Venetia Stanley in late October 1914: 'the possibility of a German invasion ... pre-occupies & alarms the mind of Kitchener'.[27] The CID had examined the so-called 'bolt from the blue' theory in 1908 and 1914 and concluded that the only possibility was of 'a limited German landing of some 70,000 men' and recommended 'that two divisions of *regular troops*' be retained at home to deal with the threat.[28]

The need for the Russians to continue tying down large German forces on the Eastern Front, allowing Britain time to create her New Armies (with half a million British soldiers expected to take the field in the spring/summer of 1915), thus became paramount in Kitchener's strategy. He impressed upon Britain's Ambassador to Russia, Sir George Buchanan, in early October 1914, that:

It is important that we should be kept accurately and continuously informed as to the real progress of the fighting on the Eastern [Front] in the next few weeks. Upon this will depend the critical decisions that we shall have to take as regards sending troops abroad or keeping them at home ... [W]e must be prepared for an attempt to land German troops in England and if we are misled as to the real situation that develops between [the] Russians & Germans and denude this country of regular troops in the winter we may suddenly be confronted with a situation at home that would not only be critical but fatal.[29]

Hankey noted that: '[Kitchener] was anxious ... about the position if things went seriously wrong in France', being 'deeply concerned lest the Germans win a major victory in the East and then turn their attention westward.'[30] Kitchener's belief was that Britain could best assist the Russians at this time by tying down the maximum number of German divisions on the Western Front, thus denying reinforcements to their comrades in the East. To this end he would support the French with British (mostly Territorial and Indian) troops in their costly failures at Ypres and Neuve Chapelle in late 1914 and early 1915. Simultaneously, Kitchener would deny Churchill the only regular division available for service at the Dardanelles. The Secretary for War was determined to retain the 29th as a mobile reserve, either for the defence of Britain, or to assist on the Western Front in the event of a German offensive. This was 'War as we must, not as we should have liked', Kitchener later told the Dardanelles Committee.[31]

The Dardanelles Commission erroneously endorsed Churchill's claim concerning the availability of troops in January, stating in its Conclusions that:

> [Lord Kitchener] declared that there were no troops immediately available for operations in the East. This statement [which Hankey, Williams and Aspinall-Oglander demonstrated to be a correct assessment] was accepted by the War Council, who took no steps to satisfy themselves [of its accuracy]. Had this been done we think it would have been ascertained that sufficient troops would have been available for a joint naval and military operation at an earlier date than was supposed.[32]

However, at the risk of repetition, it should be stressed, as Lord Grey did to the Dardanelles Commissioners, that Churchill's entire rationale behind the proposed Dardanelles operation, and the basis on which it was sanctioned by the War Council, was that it was to be a *purely naval attack, not involving the use of troops.* 'On this point all the witnesses whom [the Commission] examined were unanimous.'[33]

Kitchener was taken severely to task (in absentia) by the Dardanelles Commissioners for undermining the effectiveness of the War Cabinet through his reluctance to share sensitive military secrets with his fellow War Councillors and for his dismissive attitude to the General Staff. Hankey verified that 'some difficulties at times arose owing to Lord Kitchener's unwillingness to impart full [secret military] information' to his fellow War Councillors.[34] Hankey, in fact, confronted Kitchener on this issue, 'which was causing discontent among his Cabinet colleagues', on 11 September 1915, to which Kitchener replied: 'I cannot tell them everything because they are so leaky ... If they will only all divorce their wives I will tell them everything.'[35]

Kitchener's concerns were well founded, as the foregoing narrative has demonstrated. Asquith confided all of the War Council's innermost secrets, in the greatest detail, to Venetia Stanley in letters he wrote to her daily, often twice a day. Typically, in a letter dated 9 February 1915 concerned with the Dardanelles operation, he told her: 'This as I said is supposed to be a secret ... But naturally I shall tell you *everything.*' [36] Lloyd George was similarly guilty of this failing, as Frances Stevenson's diary attests, and other Cabinet ministers were equally imprudent in this regard. Churchill, for example, told Violet Asquith that the Naval Division was bound for the Dardanelles and allowed her to 'tell [her brother] Oc and [friend] Rupert [Brooke] ... but *no one else'.*[37] Of a dinner party shortly before 12 March 1915, the day General Sir Ian Hamilton was appointed Commander-in-Chief of the Dardanelles military force, Violet Asquith recorded in her diary: 'I talked to Ian Hamilton after dinner. I knew that he was to be sent in full command and I felt in a difficult position, not knowing how much he knew or guessed as we talked around it the whole time.'[38] Society gossip, at dinner parties in particular, was a real danger to military security in 1915. The notorious gossiping and flouting of official secrecy by the War Councillors themselves, their wives and lady friends, forced Kitchener to protect the Army's most sensitive military secrets in this fashion.

Kitchener was likewise taken to task by the Commission for failing to 'sufficiently avail himself of the services of his General Staff, with the result that more work was undertaken by him than was possible for one man to do, and *confusion and want of efficiency resulted.'* [39] As has been shown, the 'miasma' of confusion which descended on War Council proceedings from mid-February 1915 onwards, derived not so much from Kitchener's overpowering influence as from Churchill's ambivalent insistence that a large army was essential for success at the Dardanelles, while at the same time maintaining that the fleet would do the job alone. Churchill presented the autocratic Field Marshal to the Dardanelles Commissioners thus:

> [Lord Kitchener's] prestige and authority were immense. He was the sole mouthpiece of War Office opinion in the War Council. Everyone had the greatest admiration for his character ... When he gave a decision it was invariably accepted as

final. He was never, to my belief overruled by the War Council or the Cabinet in any military matter, great or small ... All-powerful, imperturbable, reserved, he dominated absolutely our counsels at this time.[40]

Kitchener's career-long practice, as commander-in-chief in his many campaigns, of keeping his battle plans locked up in his head and divulging as few of the details as possible to subordinates, was continued at War Council meetings, much to the chagrin of the other members and leading to inevitable friction. In mitigation of Kitchener's attitude towards the General Staff, the paucity of first-rate officers available to assist him should be noted. At the outbreak of war the General Staff went into abeyance as all of the most capable senior staff officers (Generals Wilson, Robertson, Smith-Dorrien, Plumer, Rawlinson et al.) left for France in the belief that the war would be over by Christmas, leaving only the 'dug-outs' (i.e. recalled retired officers) behind in England.

In addition, and in complete contrast to the dominating presence just described, Lord Kitchener was also portrayed by the Commissioners as vacillating and indecisive, at times to disastrous effect, and never more so than in his delay in sending the 29th Division to the Dardanelles. 'This delay', the Commission determined, 'gravely compromised the probability of success of the original attack.'[41] This erroneous explanation would feature prominently in *The World*

Crisis. However, the facts of Kitchener's 'three-week vacillation' can be simply reiterated.

At a War Council meeting on 9 February, Kitchener had told Churchill 'that if the Navy required the assistance of land forces at a later stage, that assistance would be forthcoming' with the tacit understanding that those troops would be employed in a garrison role. As Admiral Sir Arthur Wilson told the Dardanelles Commission: '[Churchill] kept on saying he could do it without the army; he only wanted the army to come in and reap the fruits [of victory], I think was his expression.'[42] It was at the War Council of 16 February, with a relaxation of German pressure on the Western Front, and following the reading of Sir Henry Jackson's memorandum which stipulated that the naval attack 'was not recommended as a sound military operation, unless a strong military force is ready to assist in the operation', that Kitchener decided to honour his offer of the previous week and send the experienced 29th Division to Lemnos 'at the earliest possible date ... hopefully, within nine or ten days.' It was also decided that '[the Anzacs] be despatched from Egypt, if required', together with the RND, already despatched, 'to be available in case of necessity'. The implicit assumption was still that these men were to be employed as garrison troops.[43]

Churchill wrote in *The World Crisis*: 'When we met in Council again on [February] 19th, it became clear that Lord Kitchener had changed his mind [about supplying the 29th Division] ... He gave as his reason the dangerous weakness of Russia and his fear lest large masses of German troops be brought back from the Russian Front to attack our troops in France.' Kitchener opted to retain the 29th Division in Britain under these circumstances as a mobile reserve, but he was quite prepared to send the 39,000-strong Australian and New Zealand force to the Dardanelles in lieu. The Anzacs were stationed in Egypt and 'would arrive at Lemnos sooner', he advised Churchill. At a subsequent War Council meeting on 24 February, Kitchener relaxed his position on the 29th Division, feeling 'less anxious' about the Russian situation and stating that he was now willing to send the regulars to the Dardanelles. Only two days later, however, at the 26 February War Council, he retracted his promise in the face of disturbing news from Russia. It would not be until 10 March that Kitchener could feel that the Russian situation was 'sufficiently secure' to allow the regulars of the 29th to be sent to the Mediterranean.[44]

Kitchener's priorities at this time were transparently clear. As long as a German invasion threat remained a possibility (following a Russian collapse), the experienced 29th Division was required in Britain. With the lifting of that threat on 10 March, the 29th Division could finally be released for the Dardanelles. There was no vacillation or indecision on Kitchener's part. His decision-making had been entirely consistent with the changing events on the Russian Front, although his decision changes during this period might have appeared puzzling to anyone unacquainted with all the facts. More to the point on this issue, it should be borne in mind that the presence or absence of the 29th Division (or of any other single infantry division for that matter) at the Dardanelles could not have altered the outcome one iota. It is a tribute to Churchill's literary acuity that attention could have been diverted so skilfully from the many flaws inherent in his 'plan' and focussed instead on this *non sequitur.* The Dardanelles Commissioners agreed with Churchill's spurious account of these proceedings, however, which would echo loudly in *The World Crisis*:

> [T]hree weeks of valuable time had been lost, [the Commission decided, and]:It [was] with great reluctance and hesitation that we comment on these proceedings for it is obvious that Lord Kitchener was mainly responsible for the decisions taken during the critical period between February 16th and March 10th. [And]: We think that Mr. Churchill was quite justified in attaching the utmost importance to the delays which occurred in dispatching the XXIXth Division [to the Dardanelles].[45]

The Dardanelles Commission also attributed responsibility to Lord Kitchener for the escalation to a military invasion of Gallipoli. On 19 March Kitchener had telegraphed General Hamilton: 'You know my views that the passage of the Dardanelles must be forced, and that if military operations on the Gallipoli

Peninsula by the Army are necessary to clear the way, those operations must be undertaken after careful consideration of the local defences.' On 23 March Kitchener further informed Hamilton: 'I hear that April 14th is considered by you as about the date for commencement of military operations if the Dardanelles have not been forced by the Fleet before that date. I think that you had better know at once that I regard any such postponement as far too long.' From this the Commissioners determined: 'These telegrams are conclusive proof that Lord Kitchener had by that time wholly abandoned the idea of a purely naval operation, and realised the fact that military operations on a large scale were necessary.'[46] Hamilton telegraphed Kitchener the same day: 'I have now conferred with Admiral [de Robeck], and we are equally convinced that to enable the Fleet to effectively force the passage of the Dardanelles the cooperation of the whole military force will be necessary.'[47]

Kitchener's and Hamilton's communications were conclusive proof only of the fact that Churchill's 'folly' had been finally exposed, and the need for large-scale military support officially acknowledged. The strategic communications between Kitchener and his commander in the field were proof only of their professionalism (in their forward military planning)—*should it be decided to proceed with an invasion.* But that decision was never Kitchener's, Hamilton's, de Robeck's—or Churchill's—to make. As McKenna, Hobhouse and Lloyd

George recognised and pointed out, authority for that decision resided only within the offices of Cabinet, the War Council or the Prime Minister. Kitchener's responsibility for the military invasion and subsequent Gallipoli military disaster would, nevertheless, find expression in the first report, the official press transcripts, *The World Crisis,* and in numerous publications ever since.

Fisher's Culpability

Along with Lord Kitchener, Lord Fisher was held by the Dardanelles Commission to have been ultimately responsible for the Dardanelles disaster through his failure to speak out at War Council meetings and either advise the Councillors himself, or present the expert opinion of the Admiralty naval staff on the technical difficulties associated with a purely naval attack at the Dardanelles.

Fisher explained to the Commissioners that he and Admiral Wilson were not free to voice their opinions spontaneously at War Council meetings. 'We were not members of the War Council', he said. '... We were experts there who were to open our mouths [only] when told to ... nothing else.'[48] Arthur Balfour agreed that the naval experts 'were there [at the War Council] to be what they called loyal to their Chief, and in fact they were not to contradict him.'[49] Fisher added: '[Mr. Churchill] was the head of the department [i.e., the Royal Navy] .... We were not to quarrel there [at the War Council]. We had to wash our dirty clothes at home.'[50] The same constraints applied to Admiral Wilson. Besides, as Fisher told the Commissioners, 'Mr Churchill knew my opinion, [that] I was dead against the Naval operation alone, because I knew it must be a failure.'[51] The Commissioners subsequently presented the following conclusions:

1. It was not the practice to ask the experts attending the [War] Council to express their opinions.

2. The experts themselves did not consider it their duty either to express any opinions unless they were asked to do so, or to intimate dissent.[52]

Lord Fisher's opposition to a purely naval operation at the Dardanelles was well known, the Commissioners found. 'It was common knowledge that naval opinion generally condemned the attack on forts by ships unaided by any military force. The Prime Minister was himself aware of this fact.'[53] Also: 'Lord Fisher, in fact, like all other experts, both naval and military, was in favour of a combined attack, but not of action by the Fleet alone. It is certain that, from the very first, he disliked the purely naval operation.'[54]

Asquith was well acquainted with Fisher's particular objections to the Dardanelles operation. Hankey had warned the Prime Minister 'on the first day [the] proposal was made ... that the fleet could not effect passage [through the Dardanelles] without troops & that *all the naval officers* [at the Admiralty] thought so.'[55] In his evidence Fisher was asked: 'But how was the Prime Minister to know your opinions as a naval expert unless you expressed them [at War Council meetings]?' Fisher replied: 'As a matter of fact, I did not want to bring this in, but I think I told the Prime Minister on the 7th January privately.'[56] Fisher advised Kitchener similarly on this same day, via his Military Secretary, Colonel Fitzgerald, that a naval assault of the Dardanelles was 'damnable'.[57] Asquith conceded the fact to the Commission, stating: 'I knew, of course that he [Fisher] was hostile to it [the naval operation] ... We were very great friends. He was in and out [of my office] constantly [but] I do not like to make a positive statement as to what particular day he first expressed his disapproval.'[58]

Unfortunately, very little of this crucial evidence by Fisher—or the evidence of gunnery experts (Admirals Morgan Singer, Bacon and Tudor) was included in the first report. The Royal Navy's top gunnery expert, Sir Percy Scott, who told Churchill, face to face, that his all-naval scheme at the Dardanelles was 'an impossible task', was not even called before the Commission.[59]

That the War Councillors had no conception that the 'expert opinion' they were being given at War Council meetings consisted of Churchill's own, sanguine viewpoints (which the experts disagreed with vehemently) was evident from their comments to the Commission. Lord Haldane represented the general view when he stated: 'When I heard it said, for instance [by Churchill], "We have considered it and we think the forts can be reduced within a certain time, and with a certain expenditure of ammunition" ... and Lord Fisher and Sir Arthur Wilson sat silent, I thought he [Churchill] was giving the view of the Admiralty War Staff, of which Lord Fisher was the head.'[60] Churchill sought to defend his conduct, insisting:

> When, at the War Council, I spoke in the name of the Admiralty, I was not expressing simply my own views, but I was expressing [expert naval opinion] to the best of my ability ... in the presence of two naval colleagues and friends who had the right, knowledge and power at any moment to correct me or dissent from what I said.[61]

During the course of the Commission enquiry Asquith sought to distance himself from Churchill's duplicity, claiming to have believed (or been misled by) the First Lord in the same fashion as the other War Councillors. Asked how 'he interpreted the view of the experts [as presented by Churchill, to the War Council]', Asquith replied: 'Very favourably. Mr. Churchill told me so and I thought they [the experts] were [in agreement].'[62] Asquith added: 'The First Lord of the Admiralty gave us a very powerful exposition of Naval opinion upon the subject, citing his authorities. He had been in consultation with the Admirals on the spot and with his Naval Advisers here, and we were entitled to assume that was the considered opinion of the Board of Admiralty as a whole.'[63]

The Commissioners found that: 'Mr Churchill appears to have advocated the attack by ships alone, before the War Council, on a certain amount of halfhearted and hesitating expert opinion ... [as] there does not appear to have been [any] direct support or direct opposition from the responsible naval or military advisers.'[64 As their evidence to the Commission leaves no doubt, *opposition* to a purely naval operation at the Dardanelles by *Fisher, Jackson and all of the naval experts,* had been neither halfhearted nor hesitating.

In their summation the Commissioners acknowledged that an obligation had rested with Churchill, Asquith, and the War Councillors 'to see that the views of the Naval Advisers were clearly put before the Council'. Nevertheless, and even though this had manifestly not occurred, the Commissioners were still able to add: 'We also think that the Naval Advisers should have expressed their views to the War Council, whether asked or not.'[65] The most severe censure was reserved for Lord Fisher, with the Commissioners determining that: 'We are unable to concur in the view set forth by Lord Fisher that it was his duty, if he differed from the Chief of his Department, to maintain silence at the Council or resign.'[66]

Ultimately, Churchill's deception of the War Councillors, in presenting his own views as the expert opinion of the Admiralty Staff (at the same time gagging his expert advisers and suppressing their opinions) was deemed to be of less significance than Fisher's refusal to contradict his political head at War Council meetings, and warn the Councillors of the likely outcome of that deception. Fisher was quite philosophical about the whole affair:

> How interesting [he wrote to Admiral Jellicoe, on 14 March 1917], that I'm made the "scapegoat" of the politicians over the Dardanelles! as if every one of them did not know of my determined hostility [towards the naval operation]. Cromer did not put in my [explanatory] statement as he ought to have done. May the Lord have mercy on him ... If only the evidence is published verbatim, it will be just lovely.[67]

But the evidence has never been published to date.

Fisher's and Mackenzie's Dissent

Not all the Commissioners agreed with the censure of Lord Fisher. Andrew Fisher and Sir Thomas Mackenzie, High Commissioners for Australia and New Zealand respectively, disagreed so strongly they insisted on recording a dissenting opinion. Welsh lawyer Walter Roch disagreed with so many of the Commission's findings he refused to sign the first report altogether, and presented his own Minority Report in the form of a Memorandum.

Former Prime Minister of New Zealand Mackenzie wrote to Lord Fisher on 7 June 1920, extending his commiserations for the unjust treatment of the former First Sea Lord:

> ... We [he and Andrew Fisher] felt at the Dardanelles Commission that they wished to entangle you with responsibility, but fortunately the experience of Mr. Fisher and myself as Prime Ministers of our respective countries enabled us to see at a glance how correct was your line of action, and how wrong was the attitude of members of the Commission in endeavouring to place you in a false position. I have greatly admired the manner in which you gave your evidence, and I have on many occasions taken the liberty of referring to it when talking with my friends ...
>
> Ever yours sincerely,
>
> T. Mackenzie.[69]

In his dissenting minute to the Commission, Sir Thomas Mackenzie stated:

> I hold that if the Departmental Adviser of a Minister states his opinion to his Minister, he has discharged what may be reasonably considered his official duty. And in such a case as we have under notice, where the Minister and his adviser were both present at a meeting of the War

Council, I feel that the adviser had fulfilled all that was required of him, seeing that he was not asked to express his views to the meeting. The Minister and not the adviser, must be regarded as responsible for representing the Departmental view, but in such circumstances the Minister should have stated his adviser's opinion fully to the assembly ...[70]

Andrew Fisher's dissenting minute was essentially the same in substance:

I dissent in the strongest terms from any suggestion that the Departmental Advisers of a Minister, in his company at a War Council meeting, should express any views at all other than to the Minister and through him, unless specifically invited to do so. I am of the opinion it would seal the fate of responsible government if servants of the State were to share the responsibility of Ministers to Parliament and to the people on matters of public policy. The Minister has command of the opinions and views of all officers of the Department he administers on matters of public policy. Good stewardship demands from Ministers of the Crown frank, fair, full statements of all opinions of trusted experienced officials to colleagues, when they have direct reference to matters of high policy ...[71]

Walter Roch's Minority Report

Walter Roch attached great importance to the fact that no 'real investigation [of] the strength of the Turkish opposition' was ever conducted, and '[that] the problem of forcing the Dardanelles, even by a purely naval attack, required the consideration of the expert engineer and artilleryman [who were never officially consulted] as much as that of the expert naval officer.'[73]

In contrast with the conclusions of the first report, Roch ascribed to Lord Kitchener no culpability for his three-week delay in supplying the 29th Division; nor for his unwillingness to share sensitive military secrets with his fellow War Councillors; nor his refusal to supply the large army support, purportedly requested by Churchill in January 1915 (and purportedly available at that time).[74]

Neither did Roch ascribe any culpability to Lord Fisher for his failure to contradict his political chief at War Council meetings and warn the War Councillors of the inherently flawed nature of Churchill's naval plan. Responsibility for the disaster belonged elsewhere, Roch determined. 'Mr. Churchill failed to present to the War Council the opinions of his naval advisers', Roch pointed out, 'and this failure was due to his own strong personal opinion in favour of a naval attack.'[75] Roch drew particular attention to the memorandum prepared for Churchill on 5 January

1915 by Sir Henry Jackson—when the plan was first being considered—which:

> ... was not circulated to the members of the War Council, [and which Jackson] insisted in his evidence that he had always stuck to ... "that it would be a very mad thing to try and get into the Sea of Marmora without having the Gallipoli Peninsula held by our own troops or every [enemy] gun on both sides of the Straits destroyed". He had never changed that opinion and had never given any one any reason to think he had.[76]

Roch also stressed the fact that: 'The failure of the naval attack on the 18th March showed the necessity of abandoning the plan ... The [full] War Council should then have met and considered fully the future policy to be pursued.'[77] Roch 'strongly recommend[ed] that operations of a similar character in future be thoroughly considered by a joint naval and military staff before they are undertaken.'[78[Roch placed *repeated* emphasis on the fact that: 'All [of the War Councillors] were agreed in thinking that the proposed operations could not lead to disaster as they could be broken off at any moment.'[79]

Roch returned to this point later in his report: 'One merit of the scheme was that, if satisfactory progress was not made, the attack could be broken off'.[80] He added again that '[t]he attempt to force the Dardanelles as a purely naval operation would not have been disastrous so long as the ships employed could be withdrawn at any moment ... as in the beginning of the operations was the case'.[81] This essential precondition, through which Fisher and Kitchener had been persuaded by Churchill to provide their support, rated only a cursory mention in the first report.[82] In terms of the abandonment of the naval attack, Roch drew special attention to Lloyd George's strong opposition to a military invasion of Gallipoli—a fact omitted completely from the first report's findings.[83]

A Renewed Naval Attack

Winston Churchill told the Dardanelles Commission that 'on the 22nd March ... [he] believed then, as I believe now, that we were separated by very little from complete success ... I proposed that we should direct the Admiral to renew the naval attack.'[84] Churchill's clarion cry—sounded first in his resignation speech to Parliament on 15 November 1915 and restated even more emphatically to the Dardanelles Commission—that he and Britain were denied a spectacular victory at the Dardanelles by the irresolution of the admirals, notably Fisher, Wilson, Jackson and de Robeck, would be taken up by his supporters in later decades. As described in Chapter 4, the Dardanelles Commissioners examined the substance of Churchill's claim as a concluding factor within the 'Results of the Operations'. Their conclusions were expunged from the first report, although they did appear in the *Annual Register 1917,* where they offered the former First Lord no support, stating:

The narrative concludes:

> -Whatever weight may be attached to these opinions and reports it must be remembered that out of sixteen [battle]ships which attacked the Straits on March 18 three were sunk and four were rendered unfit for immediate action. Had the attack been renewed within a day or two there is no reason to suppose that the proportion of casualties would have been less, and if so, even had the second attack succeeded, a very weak force would have been left for subsequent naval operations.[85]

Public Response to the Report

The *Dardanelles Commission First Report* was published on 8 March 1917 by His Majesty's Stationery Office at a cost of sixpence a copy. A slightly abridged, though essentially verbatim account of the first report was published in *The Times,* spread over the 9 and 10 March editions. A special précis of the report was transmitted to Australia, and this was published in the leading newspapers of each state (*The Age, Sydney Morning Herald, West Australian, Brisbane Courier* and Adelaide *Advertiser)* on Saturday 10 March.

The report's findings, as presented by Britain's and the Australian states' news leaders, were circumspect, avoiding overt governmental criticism and couched in the staid, formal language of the Commission. The reading public of both countries was provided with a detailed overview together with official opinion and conclusions purportedly deriving from the evidence. Even without the benefit of that evidence, however (which the *Age* explained would not be published), inconsistencies and contradictions were apparent.[86] Under banner headlines proclaiming: 'Highest Leaders Criticised', 'Fault Found With War Council', 'Unfeasible Project', 'Enterprise Initiated by Winston Churchill', and 'Expedition Badly Planned',[87] readers were presented, via the transcripts, with an equivocal assessment of ministerial conduct, along with that of the service heads:

> Mr. Churchill's views as to the success of a purely naval operation were more optimistic than warranted by expert opinion. Lord Kitchener grasped too eagerly at the proposed use of the fleet alone, but the responsibility rested rather on Mr. Churchill. The latter alleged there were marvellous potentialities in the *Queen Elizabeth,* whose astounding effectiveness would revolutionise naval warfare.[88]

Churchill was further taken to task:

> Referring to Mr. Churchill's presentment of the enterprise to the War Council, the commission says:- Without impugning his good faith, it seems clear he was carried away by his sanguine

temperament and firm belief in the undertaking. The evidence shows that he obtained the support of experts to a lesser degree than he imagined.[89] [Also]: Mr Churchill failed to present fully to the War Council the opinions of his naval advisers.[90]

Readers were additionally informed that:

Admiral Jackson presented Mr. Churchill with a memorandum against the possibility of rushing the Dardanelles, showing the losses which would be involved in even reaching the Straits. Admirals Lord Fisher, Sir Arthur Wilson and Sir Henry Oliver expressed objections to a naval attack ... Admiral Jackson agreed to an attack on the outer forts [only], but considered it was not feasible for a fleet to get through the Dardanelles alone.[91]

Nevertheless, it was Lords Fisher and Kitchener who were deemed most culpable by the Commission, in that: 'Although Admiral Fisher, in evidence, said he was dead against the naval operations alone, he did not at any time express any such decided opinions [officially, to the War Council]'. The fact that Fisher had advised both Churchill and Asquith privately of his serious misgivings (and had testified to the Commission to this effect) went unmentioned. 'The Commission [subsequently determined that] Admirals Fisher and Wilson ... should have expressed their view if they thought the project impracticable from a naval point of view.' Andrew Fisher's and Sir Thomas Mackenzie's dissent on this point was very briefly noted and inadequately explained.[92]

Lord Kitchener was similarly censured for his intransigence in withholding troop support at the outset, thus forcing an ineffectual naval attack on the War Council: 'On 2 January ... Lord Kitchener declared that troops were not available. The acceptance of this declaration was unfortunate, because investigation would have revealed otherwise.'[93] As demonstrated by Hankey and Aspinall-Oglander, this was a false determination by the Commission. Lord Kitchener, who was cast in the role of unyielding advocate for a purely naval attack, was additionally castigated for holding back the 29th Division for three vital weeks, thus 'gravely compromis[ing]' the operation. In the Commission's estimation: 'For three weeks the Government [under Kitchener's influence] vacillated, and the moment for action lapsed ... Mr. Churchill was justified in attaching importance to the delay in despatching the 29th Division.'[94] As has been demonstrated, this was a fallacious determination.

Conversely and conjointly, Kitchener was simultaneously presented as the unyielding advocate for both a purely naval attack and a military invasion. Following his statement to the War Council on 24 February that 'if the Fleet [failed] ... the Army ought to see the business through', the Commission found that: 'The idea of a purely naval operation was gradually dropped, and the prestige argument grew.

We drifted into a big military attack.'[95] No mention was made of Churchill's Press Release on 20 February which precipitated the need for military assistance.

Further, with regard to the disastrous invasion, it was Kitchener who would again prove culpable. 'On 12 March, [when] Sir Ian Hamilton was nominated in command of the Dardanelles force ... no scheme [for a military invasion] was drawn up', the Commission noted. 'There were no water supply arrangements, and there was a great want of staff preparation.'[96] The reality was that on 10 March Churchill was still insisting to the War Council that the fleet would force a passage through the Straits unaided by the Army.[97] Under these circumstances, and at this time, detailed plans for a military invasion of Gallipoli were simply not warranted. Kitchener was additionally chastised for 'not sufficiently avail[ing] himself of the services of his General Staff ... causing confusion and want of efficiency.'[98]

The transcript accounts of these events, as published in *The Times* and in Australia's leading newspapers, were simply a reiteration of the Commission's narrative and findings, delivered verbatim from the first report. *The Times* published a separate leader article in its 9 March edition, however, which was entirely different in tone. In 'The Dardanelles Report', it was stated of Churchill:

> Mr. Churchill remains, as the public have rightly held, the prime mover in the Dardanelles

adventure. He was at least consistent in his purpose when all the rest were vacillating. But it was the consistency of a dangerous enthusiast, who sought expert advice only where he could be sure of moulding it to his own opinion, and unconsciously deceived both himself and his colleagues about the real character of his technical support.[99]

Of Asquith, it was recorded:

It was the Prime Minister and the Prime Minister alone, who had the power to enforce the fullest scrutiny of dangerous experiments, to see that the [Army and Navy] Departments were working in unison and the expert advisers agreed, to ensure that every stage in the operation was thought out with prescience and promptly executed ... As it was, the supreme direction of the war seems to have been left almost to chance. The War Council, as we have seen, would separate "with a very indistinct idea of any decision having been arrived at, at all".

The Commission themselves cannot help being struck with the atmosphere of vagueness and want of precision which seems to have characterized the proceedings of the War Council. It is almost inconceivable that any one, whether military, naval or civilian, could have imagined that

Constantinople would be captured without military help on a somewhat large scale ...

At a later stage, though he knew of the misgivings of the sailors, he [Asquith] neither insisted on eliciting their views nor even encouraged them to speak. Finally, the astonishing suspension of the [full] War Council for two whole critical months must be chiefly attributed, as the Commission did in fact attribute it, to the Prime Minister's personal neglect of an obvious duty. The whole story is a tragic record of drift, disorganization, and ultimate disaster, for which the blame in chief must be placed on want of leadership in the head of the Government.[100]

Fisher was similarly castigated by *The Times,* but for irresolution, it being decided that: 'Lord Fisher's fault was of a different kind ... It cannot be held that he seriously protested and was overruled, and the Commission rightly condemn the feeble excuse that the business of so great an expert was only to answer specific questions ... the verdict on Lord Fisher is that he failed to be resolute in time.'[101] Lord Kitchener was judged as follows:

The truth seems to be that Lord Kitchener, whose influence was overwhelming, heartily supported the Dardanelles Expedition so long as he could leave it wholly to the Admiralty... [however] he was "mainly responsible" for the disastrous delay which followed the decision to attack with troops as well as with ships. Let it rest at that.[102]

The Times' judgement on Churchill and Asquith was echoed even more stridently throughout the popular press. On 9 March, the British *Evening News* called for those responsible for the Dardanelles disaster to be indicted on criminal charges: 'When will they be prosecuted?' it demanded,[103] while the *Daily Mail* told its readers:

Asquith wobbled, Kitchener did not realize the facts and ignored his staff, Churchill misled everybody ... they threw away the lives of 40,000 men and brought on our arms the greatest disaster which those arms ever suffered, through their reckless folly, dereliction of duty, and negligence ... Are politicians whose blunders cost the lives of thousands to escape scot free?

... Mr. Churchill was guilty in the first degree. He misrepresented the experts and interfered in matters of which, as a layman, he knew nothing ... He dazzled everyone concerned with his pictures of the great political and military results which would follow a successful attack on Constantinople, but he never produced, nor ordered his experts to produce, a plan which would make success possible. Lord Fisher was dragged by Mr. Churchill with him in his wild adventure, a reluctant but obedient Sancho Panza

... By a word he could have prevented the campaign, but that word was never spoken ...

During this horrible business, Downing Street was "wining and dining" as usual.[104]

DEFENSIVE DUET BY MESSRS. ASQUITH AND
WINSTON CHURCHILL

Churchill's and Asquith's performances before the Dardanelles Commission, Punch, 28 March 1917.

In Australia the *West Australian* explained to its readers on 12 March how, under Churchill, 'there was a proposal to subdue Turkey, but no scheme ... Like a new Joshua he would sound his trumpet and the walls of Jericho would collapse.'[105] The *Newcastle Morning Herald* similarly deplored the 'lies revealed in [Churchill's] resignation speech [to Parliament] of November 1915',[106] while the *Sydney Morning Herald* observed that '[Churchill] was so possessed by self-confidence that he would be guided by no advice, however expert.' Churchill's failure, it was pointed out, was a rare 'example of the rashness of the amateur in risking great issues on the strength of his opinion on highly technical subjects.'[107[The *Daily Standard* dismissed Churchill simply as: 'always a showman-politician, who liked fame'.[108]

In the immediate aftermath of the first report's publication there was little doubt as to whom the British and Australian public saw as 'the guilty men', in respect of the Dardanelles disaster. However, the exigencies of wartime national security required that governmental ineptitude in war planning be withheld from public knowledge as far as possible. Scapegoats were a necessary alternative and these were conveniently to hand in the persons of (recently deceased) Lord Kitchener and (retired) Lord Fisher. Most of the responsibility for the fiasco would, consequently, be assigned to these two unfortunates. In the process many of Churchill's spurious assertions and claims would be accepted at face value by the

Commissioners, subsequently to be perpetuated in *The World Crisis.*

Within this alternative analysis of the failed Dardanelles operation it may be salutary to note the ignored evidence of Arthur, von Donop and Creedy, explaining how Kitchener was persuaded (reluctantly) to support the Churchill plan through *Queen Elizabeth's* exaggerated firepower;[109] the ignored evidence of Hankey as to the actual number of spare British divisions available in January/February 1915 for service at the Dardanelles; the ignored evidence of Fisher, Jackson, Morgan Singer and all the Admiralty experts on the true naval opinion of the viability of Churchill's purely naval plan; the failure of the Commissioners to mention the impact of Churchill's press release of 20 February; and the excision from the first report of the Commission's evaluation of the likely outcome of a renewed naval attack at the Dardanelles shortly after 19 March 1915.[110]

CHAPTER 7

Official Secrecy and Political Influences

The integrity of Britain's most sensitive official documents has been safeguarded by the *Official Secrets Act* and the Privy Councillor's Oath for almost a century and since around 1250 AD respectively. The means by which Winston Churchill was able to flout that legislation and tradition—to the ire of Parliament—in order to include a wealth of officially secret documents in his 1923 publication *The World Crisis* is deserving of particular note.

Churchill's Recall to the Cabinet

In July 1917 Winston Churchill was restored to the Cabinet in Lloyd George's coalition government as Minister of Munitions, amid a storm of protest from Conservative members of Parliament and newspaper editors alike, which threatened to destroy the coalition. Following shortly after the publication of the Dardanelles Commission's first report, the move prompted over a hundred Conservatives to sign a resolution condemning Churchill's appointment, describing him as 'a national danger' and demanding a debate. The *Sunday Times* had earlier proclaimed that Churchill's return to government constituted 'a grave danger to the Administration and the Empire as a whole'. Nevertheless, Lloyd George stood firm.[1]

In its leading article on 18 July 1917, *The Times* praised the efforts of outgoing Minister of Munitions Dr Addison, stating that he had 'shown capacity, foresight and no little courage in grappling with difficult industrial problems'. In contrast, it was claimed that 'the problem [with Mr Churchill] was to use his gifts where there would be least danger from their qualifying defects of instability and interference.' The article continued: 'But it must be emphatically made clear from the outset that the production of munitions is entirely separate from their allocation and use in the field. The country is in no mood to tolerate even a forlorn attempt at amateur strategy.'[2]

On 20 July, Mr Evelyn Cecil asked the Prime Minister in the Commons 'whether, in view of the feeling which exists in many quarters in this House and in the country, that the inclusion of [Mr Churchill], and particularly at this time, as Minister of Munitions, is a national danger, he will give a day for discussion of the appointment.'[3] It was neither affection nor loyalty which had inspired his return, but rather an awareness of the venomous power of Churchill's brilliant oratory (which he habitually wielded rapier-like, to strip away an opponent's dignity or credibility) which everyone in the House feared—Lloyd George included. As Frances Stevenson had already recorded on 14 September 1915: 'D. [Lloyd George] says that

Churchill is the only man in the Cabinet who has the power to do him harm, and he does not trust him when it comes to personal matters.'[4]

In Rhodes James' estimation, 'no Prime Minister ... could view with equanimity the presence in Opposition, of this formidable personality ... and potential threat'.[5] As Professor Rose observed, '[Churchill] took a positive delight in savaging his political opponents'.[6] Bonar Law, on the other hand, refused to countenance an accommodation with Churchill, replying to a Lloyd George query, 'Is [Churchill] more dangerous if he is FOR you or if he is AGAINST you', with: 'I would rather have [Churchill] against us [the Conservative Party] every time.'[7]

In January 1919 Churchill was appointed Secretary of State for War and Air, a post he held until February 1921 when he became Colonial Secretary where he remained until the fall of the Lloyd George government in October 1922. At the time of writing *The World Crisis,* therefore, between 1919 and 1922, Churchill's connections within the Parliamentary and military hierarchies were considerable. Indeed, during these years Churchill enjoyed Prime Ministerial protection from semi-official criticism. Lloyd George intervened personally to censor the memoirs of Sir Albert Stern (head of a War Office Department appointed to produce the first tanks), in which Churchill had been labelled, among other things, 'a dishonest politician'. At Lloyd George's behest Stern handed over his manuscript to Churchill's Private Secretary,

Masterton-Smith, 'who cut out pages which reflected badly on Churchill'. The reason: Churchill was considered by the Prime Minister to be 'one of the few strong members of his Government [at a time when] the situation of the country was very difficult.'[8]

Official Secrecy and War Publications

The *Official Secrets Act* of 1911 was enacted in the wake of the Agadir Crisis, at a time when the threat of war appeared very real. Section 1 of the Act was directed at the criminal prosecution of enemy spies. Section 2, on the other hand, sought to protect the secrecy of official documents. Under this all-encompassing section it became an offence for anyone holding office under the Crown to communicate any information to any unauthorised person. Section 8 of the Act, however, determined that 'prosecutions under the Act can only be brought with the consent of the Attorney-General', thus restricting prosecutions to serious offences only. Offences under Section 2 carry a maximum of two years' imprisonment but may be punishable by a fine.[9] While the areas of defence and international diplomacy were clearly those of most immediate concern to the framers of this legislation, under a more general consideration it was also an offence for those who had served under the Crown to profit from their 'unauthorised disclosure of information which they had acquired during their period of service under the Crown'.[10]

By 1923, when Churchill was in the process of publishing volumes I and II of *The World Crisis,* several accounts of the First World War by leading military, naval and political figures had already been published. Among these was a defence by Lord Esher of the deceased and maligned (by the Dardanelles Commission) Lord Kitchener entitled *The Tragedy of Lord Kitchener.* In his book Esher provided a brief account of how Churchill became involved in the Antwerp episode. According to Esher:

> One night [Kitchener] was in bed asleep, when Mr. Churchill, then First Lord of the Admiralty, bursting into the room, pleaded for the War Minister's permission to leave at once for Antwerp. In spite of the late hour, Sir Edward Grey arrived in the middle of the discussion, and while he was engaging Lord Kitchener's attention Mr. Churchill slipped away. He was next heard of when a telegram from Antwerp was put into Lord K's hands in which his impetuous colleague asked bravely to be allowed to resign his great office [and be given military command of the force there].[11]

Churchill was incensed by the inaccuracies in this description and also by criticism of his involvement in the Dardanelles campaign by the official naval historian Sir Julian Corbett and the official Australian military historian Charles Bean—criticism Churchill claimed he was powerless to challenge.[12] With soldiers such as

330

French, Hamilton, Callwell and Robertson; sailors such as Jellicoe; official naval and military historians; a Private Secretary (Sir George Arthur); a government adviser (Esher); and *The Times* military correspondent (Repington) already in print, Churchill wrote to then Prime Minister, Bonar Law, in March 1923, requesting his right of redress and permission to quote from the official documents he had retained on leaving office in order to refute the charges against him.[13] 'It would appear unfair and unreasonable', he wrote, 'that a Minister should be the only person debarred from stating his own case in regard to war matters in which he has been held responsible.'[14] Churchill had, in fact, been preparing the ground for the publication of his 'war history' from a much earlier date.

***

When Lloyd George replaced Asquith as Prime Minister in December 1916, his first action was to abolish the archaic procedures then in practice at War Cabinet meetings. On joining Asquith's War Cabinet in May 1915, Bonar Law had remarked that 'he was astonished at the lack of method, [and] the absence of any agenda or minutes.' Asquith had replied 'that everyone who joined the Cabinet made the same observation.'[15]

On 9 December 1916, Lloyd George appointed War Cabinet Secretary Hankey as his agent 'in revolutionizing the mechanism of government in the name of winning the war'.[16] Within a week, under

Hankey's direction, and in accordance with his 'Draft Rules of Procedure', the operative processes of Cabinet were being transformed and invested with the same efficiency they would retain to the present day. On 18 December 1916 four assistant secretaries were appointed to the Cabinet Secretariat whose duties were:

> to record the proceedings of the War Cabinet;

> to transmit relevant extracts from the minutes to departments concerned with implementing them or otherwise interested;

> to prepare the agenda paper, and to arrange the attendance of ministers not in the War Cabinet and others required to be present for discussions of particular items on the agenda;

> to receive papers from departments and circulate them to the War Cabinet and others as necessary.[17]

During the war (from December 1916), in the interests of national security, the 'immemorial custom' whereby Cabinet papers remained the personal property of Cabinet Ministers, to be taken away with them on leaving office, was suspended. In its stead, ministers were required to return all documents to the Cabinet Office for filing as 'The Property of His Britannic Majesty's Government'. Arthur Henderson and Austen

Chamberlain had both complied with this ruling in August 1917 on resigning office.[18] This was yet another Hankey initiative. As he wrote: 'to allow national secrets to pass beyond the control of the Government is seriously to impair the value of these precautions [taken by the Cabinet Office].'[19] Hankey's wartime ruling stipulated that: 'Cabinet Minutes and Papers are not the personal property of members [and were to be surrendered to the Secretariat for filing with] the resignation or death of a minister.'[20] The War Cabinet continued in operation for a further ten months after the end of the war, its efficient practices maintained by the peacetime Cabinet—with one notable exception.

At the first meeting of the peacetime Cabinet on 4 November 1919, the wartime ruling regarding governmental custody of Cabinet documents was 'deliberately waived ... and the old pre-war "immemorial custom", was restored.'[21] Roskill and Naylor ascribed this decision to Lloyd George and Churchill, 'who insisted on this change with an eye on the histories of the period they would one day write, or were already engaged on.'[22] In fairness to those two, Naylor maintains that both had suffered 'concerted military and naval criticism' in published works and, now that military secrecy mattered less, their acquisition of an ample sufficiency of rebuttal evidence seemed perfectly justified.[23] Hankey would subsequently note 'instances ... of Ministers who, on retirement, have required a pantechnicon to remove their papers from their offices [doubtless with Churchill and Lloyd George in mind]'.[24]

At this time Hankey was not concerned with the possibility that official papers might be published, as the 4 November 1919 Draft Instructions stipulated that: 'Secrecy was considered to be safeguarded by the rule that no-one is entitled to make public use of Cabinet documents without the permission of the King',[25] alongside the Privy Councillor's Oath, sworn by all Cabinet Ministers, and the *Official Secrets Act.* Indeed, Cabinet had made these safeguards the basis for its relaxation of wartime controls over the custody of official documents. They would prove to be no barrier to Churchill.

At a meeting of Cabinet on 30 January 1922, with Lloyd George in the chair and Churchill present as Colonial Secretary, Churchill voiced a strong complaint against Lord Esher's portrayal of him in the 1921 publication *The Tragedy of Lord Kitchener,* which Churchill described as 'a travesty of the facts. ... He now had in his possession', he claimed, 'sufficient contemporary telegrams to disprove Esher's account'. Churchill requested that he 'be allowed to publish the secret documents in full', in order to vindicate himself. Martin Gilbert writes that 'The Cabinet decided in Churchill's favour', adding that '[he] and others [were to be allowed] to set out their defence with full documentation'.[26] The actual notes to this meeting read:

In the course of the discussion it was stated that: "There were notorious cases where the policy of [wartime] Ministers had been attacked by partial and misleading quotations from Cabinet papers and *general sympathy was expressed* with the desire of Ministers to be allowed to use official papers to defend themselves in such circumstances."

It was agreed to set up a Committee to examine the question.[27]

This committee failed to materialise and the matter fell into abeyance until 23 February 1923, when it was revived. Gilbert's assertion on Churchill's behalf is a misrepresentation of what was determined at this meeting. General sympathy was only expressed towards the plight of ministers who were then to be permitted the right of limited direct quotation of official documents in order to refute criticism of their wartime actions. Had Churchill been so authorised by the 30 January Cabinet 'to publish secret documents, in full' (as Gilbert claims), there would have been no need for the Curzon Committee.[28]

On 13 June 1922, Lloyd George told the Commons that the massive archive of Cabinet papers which had accumulated since December 1916 would be passed on so that 'the next Administration should know exactly what had happened in respect of certain discussions and decisions [during the war years]'. He added that they would be treated as 'confidential documents [that] could not be published'.[29] On 1 February 1923, *The Times* advised its readers that it:

... had arranged to give in its columns, in advance of the date of publication of [*The World Crisis*], a series of articles based on extracts from the memoirs [of Churchill], relating chiefly to the first months of the war, and more particularly to its naval side. Sixteen articles in all [were to be] published [in daily episodes, from 8 February 1923].[30]

The Times serialisation of *The World Crisis* created a storm of protest. Prime Minister Bonar Law, acknowledging in Parliament that the present First Lord of the Admiralty, Mr Leopold Amery, had granted Churchill the right to publish 'certain Admiralty orders issued to the Fleet during the war', nevertheless criticised what he saw as a flagrant breach of Parliamentary etiquette:

> It is of course an obligation upon Ministers and officials [he told the Commons], not to disclose confidential State or official papers or information without the previous approval of his Majesty's Government for the time being, or in the case of Cabinet information, without the consent of His Majesty.[31]

Four days later, when asked in the House by critics of Churchill challenging his right to publish official documents whether such revelations constituted a breach of the Privy Councillor's Oath, Bonar Law concurred, stating: 'I have taken the oath and personally I think I should consider it a breach.'[32] Criticism of Churchill continued, scathing and unabated. On 22 February Major Cadogan asked the Prime Minister in the House:

[W]hether the indulgence granted to ex-Ministers to publish official documents, the property of His Majesty's Government, or copies thereof, is also extended to private Members, who may have access to such sources of information?

[Mr A.M. Samuel then demanded to know]:

Has not the time arrived when this sort of thing ought to be cleared up once and for all? [To which Major Cadogan added]:

Will the Right Hon. Gentleman inform the House, for the benefit of those who are in possession of Ministerial correspondence ... whether there are two laws on this matter—whether there is a law which applies to ex-Cabinet Ministers, and another which applies to the rest of mankind?[33]

[Captain O'Grady then pointed out to the Prime Minister the fact that]: An ex-Cabinet Minister has divulged wartime secrets in a publication for which money is paid ... will he consider the advisability of instructing the Law Officers of the Crown to institute legal proceedings in future against any persons using State papers that are presumably secret documents? [This prompted Commander Bellairs to ask]:

Is it not possible, on the advice of the Law Officers of the Crown, to apply for an injunction against the publication of the book when it comes out? These are merely newspaper articles.

Bonar Law's reply was that: 'The remed[ies] proposed [did] not appear to be practicable.'[34] But the matter did not end there. A Cabinet committee was appointed to enquire into the substance of these complaints, chaired by Lord Curzon.

The Curzon Committee Report

It was doubtless with some apprehension that Churchill presented his own reply to Bonar Law on 3 March, under the shadow of the impending Cabinet committee enquiry:

> The question of what should be disclosed [Churchill wrote], cannot be decided without reference to what has already been disclosed with the acquiescence of the Government.[35]

> Lord Kitchener's biographer ... has made the freest use of official documents of all kinds, including a

prolonged extract from one of my Cabinet memoranda in 1915.[36]

Lord Jellicoe has written two volumes on the naval war ... in which he attributes to me, in perfect good faith, and courtesy, opinions which I do not accept.[37]

Lord Fisher has published two works full of confidential matter largely related to the period with which I am concerned. He prints various memoranda which he wrote as First Sea Lord.[38]

Sir Ian Hamilton, in his two volumes "Gallipoli Diary", quotes quite freely and where necessary verbatim from the official telegrams which he sent and which he received ... Not the slightest comment has been made in any of these cases, and no complaint or action was evoked from the Cabinet of the day ...[39]

With regard to the *Official Naval History,* anyone who chooses to read the late Sir Julian Corbett's text and compare the lengthy summaries of the telegrams with the actual text, will see how extremely unsatisfactory and unintentionally unfair [to Churchill himself] this method of citation is.[40]

[And] in the "Official History of Australia in the War"... [v]erbatim extracts from telegrams sent by me from the Admiralty are freely quoted when required to build up an argument, which argument I need hardly say is to assign the whole of the blame for the enterprise and its failure to me ...[41]

Sir William Robertson and General Callwell ... have also written books dealing controversially with confidential matters with which they were concerned.[42]

Thus it may be said that practically every important naval and military authority and actor in these events had already told his story to the public, and in doing so has freely used confidential information and quoted from the official documents, both Departmental and Cabinet; and that in no case has the slightest objection been taken by the Government of the day ...

On this basis and in light of these facts I have considered myself entitled to publish the text of the telegrams for which I was responsible or which I wrote myself ... It would appear unfair and unreasonable that a Minister should be the only person debarred from stating his own case in regard to war matters in which he has been held responsible, after every naval or military personage concerned has had the fullest latitude conceded to him. In view of the precedents which have been created ... a former Minister ought, subject to the public interest in regard to any particular topic, to be authorized to exercise a similar freedom.[43]

A more significant precedent had been impressed upon Churchill, however, by Hankey, who had assisted him with this correspondence, which he now stressed:

I may add, that of course I consulted the Prime Minister of the day (Mr. Asquith) in regard to every reference, however general, which I made to Cabinet proceedings, and that I consulted my principal colleagues of those days on every reference to important matters in which they were concerned, and received from them their written assent and even warm approval to what I proposed to say.[44]

On 8 March, Sir Maurice Hankey (as he then was) sent a letter to Bonar Law himself in which he largely agreed with Churchill's comments, subject to 'some exaggeration in his statement that "every important naval and military authority and actor in these events has already told his story, and in doing so has freely used confidential information and quoted from official documents both Departmental and Cabinet":'[45]

[Hankey thought]: the statements in the early part of [Churchill's] letter are justified. A number of persons who have held official positions have undoubtedly used secret information to which they had access, usually in order to defend their own conduct. [And] I do not think there has been any case where it could be shown that these revelations have been detrimental to the public interest.

[However, Hankey added,] I disagree totally with Mr. Churchill's remarks on the Official Naval History. Sir Julian Corbett's work is not, like Mr. Churchill's, an *ex-parte* [from one side only] statement based on such official material as supports his case. On the contrary, it is based on the whole of the information [from] every available source. Moreover, the Official [Naval] Histories were ... sent to the principal actors, including Mr. Churchill himself [for vetting] ... before publication.[46]

[Hankey then drew attention to the key issue as he saw it].

Mr. Churchill's statement that he consulted Mr. Asquith in regard to Cabinet proceedings, and his principal colleagues on every reference to important matters in which they were concerned, is a new factor of great interest, which should certainly be communicated to the Cabinet Committee.

Although the Cabinet Enquiry was brought on by the publication of Mr. Churchill's book, I understand that it is intended as a general enquiry rather than an investigation into Mr. Churchill's book in particular ... Mr. Churchill's letter appears to me to be a real contribution to the subject as setting forth a point of view which ought to be taken into account ...[47]

No doubt it would have been an additional matter of concern for Churchill that the Home Secretary, William Bridgeman, had delivered an address to the undergraduates at Cambridge University on the evening of 2 March 1923, in which he told them:

He hoped that nobody would go into politics with the object of making money by it. It was very unfortunate when they saw, as they sometimes did now, politicians who took to literature in the form of being able to use, for the purpose of making money by their publications, information which they acquired overtly and confidentially.[48]

Churchill had entered into a contract with his literary agent Curtis Brown in 1920 for the publication of his book, for which he was to receive not less than £20,000 or, as he jokingly boasted, 'half a crown a word'.[49]

For a variety of reasons (ill-health and the overseas commitments of its members), the Curzon Committee (chaired by Lord Curzon and including Lord Birkenhead, Balfour, Austen Chamberlain and Sir Gordon Stewart, with Hankey as Secretary) never met.[50] Ultimately, Hankey conducted the entire enquiry himself and presented its conclusions (decided in April but not published until 24 May 1923). He called for evidence from the Home Office, Foreign Office, War Office and the Admiralty. The stated purpose of this enquiry was 'to examine the circumstances in which it is permissible in any publication to use or quote from Cabinet or Departmental documents, however obtained'.[51] Permanent Secretary to the Admiralty Sir William Graham Greene presented the Admiralty position that:

> Ministers and ex-Ministers of the Crown: Are under obligation not to reveal Cabinet proceedings without His Majesty's permission.
>
> [Serving] Naval Officers: Are forbidden by the King's Regulations to publish anything dealing with Service matters without the permission of the Admiralty.
>
> [However, retired Naval Officers] "are under no specific obligation" except in that Section 2 of the Official Secrets Act, 1911, deals with "Wrongful communication etc. & of information".[52]

The position with regard to the War Office, Home Office and Foreign Office was found to be identical, Hankey adding that: 'Every Cabinet Minister is bound by his Cabinet Minister's [Privy Councillor's] Oath to: "Keep secret all matters committed and revealed unto me or that shall be treated of secretly in council".'[53]

In his 'Memorandum by Secretary of CID [and Cabinet]' as part of this report, Hankey noted that:

> The example of Field Marshal Lord French was cited, as having published various confidential documents in his book "1914" [published in 1919]. These included secret Memoranda and telegrams.
>
> The question was discussed by the War Cabinet on June 1919 and it was decided though "publication of certain documents was unauthorized ... had permission been sought, it is probable that it would have been accorded, as publication of none of these documents is in any way detrimental to the public interest".[54]

Similar findings were attached to 'works by Sir George Arthur, Sir Ian Hamilton and Lord Jellicoe'.[55] Hankey stressed the need to safeguard the custody of official documents and the dangers of unlawful access, pointing out how the practice of government control had been 'deliberately over-ruled' at the 4 November 1919 Cabinet meeting.[56] He offered a number of remedial suggestions (which would in fact be enforced a decade later). These included:

(b)   Writers should be requested to obtain the permission of the Head of the Department primarily concerned, who, in cases of doubt, should consult the Prime Minister. [And]:

(c)   A time limit should be fixed within which no Cabinet Papers should be made public, and thereafter only after permission as in (b).[57]

Hankey offered no specific recommendations with regard to Churchill. Lacking legal expertise, he doubtless felt himself unqualified to do so. And, as Churchill had pointed out, there was essentially no difference between his use of official material and that by any of the other military, naval or political figures in print—except in the matter of degree. Churchill, in fact, made 'authenticity', as provided by the liberal inclusion of official documents, the major attraction of his book. As he told his readers in the Preface to *The World Crisis*:

I have made no important statement of fact regarding naval operations or Admiralty business, on which I do not possess unimpeachable documentary proof. I have made or implied no criticism of any decision or action taken or neglected by others, unless I can prove that I expressed the same opinion in writing *before the event* [. And]:

In every case where the interests of the State allow, I have printed the actual memoranda, directions, minutes, telegrams or letters written by me at the time ...[58]

It should be noted that Hankey was not an entirely disinterested party in this matter. He, too, expected to publish his memoirs on retirement, which would of necessity have included a considerable amount of official material. On 16 November 1919 he confided to his diary that, although he would respect all confidences placed in him as Cabinet Secretary 'in or out of office, so long as necessary for the safety of the country, or the stability of the Government, but I do not regard myself or my heirs bound by an oath that I have never been asked to take, and my memoirs will be the more interesting for my not having taken the Privy Councillor's oath.'[59]

Churchill was exonerated, virtually by default, answering Major Cadogan's query in the affirmative—yes, there *was* one law for ex-Cabinet Ministers and another for the rest of mankind, thanks to Hankey. He it was who established the precedent at this time, whereby ex-Cabinet Ministers were allowed the freedom to publish official documents in order to answer criticism of their actions while in office, provided they had obtained the permission of both the Prime Minister at the time those documents were created, and of the Prime Minister in office at the time of the proposed disclosure (this being considered synonymous with permission of the Sovereign, who invariably followed the advice of his Prime Minister).[60]

As for everyone else, as Graham Greene pointed out: '[T]he ex-Minister, the retired Naval Officer and the retired Civil Servant are alike free to publish official information in their possession, subject to there being no infringement of the Official Secrets Act'.[61] Naylor adds, 'The situation remained as it had [been]', with 'officially informed' publications flourishing, notwithstanding the risk 'however dimly perceived, of violating the Official Secrets Act.'[62]

No injunction was taken out against *The World Crisis* on its publication in 1923. Churchill may have received unfortunate assistance at this time through the ill-health of Bonar Law, who was diagnosed with throat cancer and retired from office in May 1923. Law died on 30 October 1923. Following Hankey's lead, Law had declined to make any recommendations against Churchill.[63]

With access to the official documents denied to every other writer on the subject (except the official historians), Churchill's book proved immensely popular with the general public. Churchill had taken away with him from the Admiralty all of his memoranda, letters and minutes, plus official documents, or copies thereof, relating to the Dardanelles operation. It will be remembered that the immemorial custom was in effect throughout 1915. Prior to December 1916, Cabinet papers and related departmental papers were never retained, Cabinet maintaining no archive. After being actioned these documents were either destroyed immediately or taken away by the Cabinet Ministers and Departmental Heads as their personal property.[64] Churchill's vast personal archive (he assured his readers that the documents published represented 'only a fraction of the whole' in his possession) ensured him a captive audience, eager to learn the real cause of the Dardanelles/Gallipoli tragedy from the man at the very heart of those events.[65]

Notwithstanding its imposing credentials, the editor of *The Times Literary Supplement* was somewhat critical of Volume II, dealing with the Dardanelles operation, when it appeared in October 1923, stating in a review: '[*The World Crisis, 1915*] is a plea based upon a partial use of the documents and [is] marred, we think, by undue censure. His [Churchill's] apologia is too much an impatient indictment of colleagues who were antagonized by [his] hastiness of action [notably, Fisher and Kitchener].'[66]

In 1983 Robin Prior provided a more detailed critique, comparing the text of *The World Crisis* with the official documents on which it was purportedly based. His findings were that:

> The Dardanelles chapters of *The World Crisis* [in which Churchill was most concerned to vindicate himself] prove, if proof was needed, that it is quite possible to base a narrative on an enormous number of documents and still produce a misleading account ... Over 40 percent of Churchill's Dardanelles section was taken up with the publication of memoranda and letters. In his Introduction Churchill puts forward the view that

these documents would prove his case. All they prove, however, is that Churchill has adopted an adept process of selection. Also, many of the documents are his own memoranda and the case presented in them is merely stated, rather than argued or critically examined. Finally [it was noted], Churchill is not averse from deleting key sections of the documents.[67]

Historian J.H. Plumb questioned the validity of *The World Crisis* as 'history' from another perspective, maintaining that it was 'really [a] personal account, based on [the] personal papers of a uniquely placed observer ... It is largely storytelling, eschewing analysis in depth [and as such should not] be regarded as a reliable account either of the war or its direction.'[68]

In 1928, Lord Sydenham (first Secretary to the CID) expressed similar criticism, claiming that: '[t]he very attractiveness of Mr. Churchill's writing of itself constitutes a danger, for the layman may well be led to accept facile phrase and seductive argument for hard fact and sober reasoning.'[69]

A professional assessment of Churchill's description of his activities was also offered from yet another source. As Former First Lord of the Admiralty Lord Selborne observed in a review of *The World Crisis* for *National Review* in 1923: '"It was no part of my duty to deal with the routine movements of the Fleet and its squadrons, but only to exercise a general supervision." These are Mr Churchill's own words, and yet his book is one long record of constant interference in routine and consequent failure of supervision.'[70]

Hankey, Churchill and the Official Histories

As Secretary of the CID and the Cabinet (until his retirement in 1938), Hankey took a keen interest in the Historical Department, originally a section within the CID, but absorbed into the Cabinet Office in May 1921. Hankey selected the historians to write the official military and naval histories of the First World War, preferring writers with technical rather than literary expertise. Sir Julian Corbett was the obvious choice for the Naval History, as a former lecturer at the Naval War College and distinguished author of many naval histories.[71]

Section 2 of the *Official Secrets Act* (amended in 1920) denied general historians any access to official documents for the purpose of simply writing 'better books'. There was no way, however, to dam the flood of 'officially informed' war books published during the 1920s and 30s which took the form of personal memoirs, biographies, unit histories and general historical accounts by soldiers, sailors and civilians. Anyone with something to say on the subject, it seemed—from private to general, minister or admiral—went into print. Naturally, the more senior the individual, the greater the authority attached to his publication.[72]

These revelations, whether by soldiers or statesmen, could not be challenged by historians for accuracy and authenticity. With the primary sources unavailable, 'each successive publication quoted extensively from those that had preceded it', and the earlier publications came to be regarded as the bearers of 'the facts' by the general public. This situation persisted right throughout the interwar period. Indeed, even after the official documents became available in the mid-1960s, writers still quoted these 'officially informed' publications as 'primary' sources (prominent among which was Churchill's *The World Crisis).* As Professor Ian Beckett notes, 'In fact, it is instructive to chart the frequency with which certain volumes [of "officially informed" memoirs] ... are cited not only by biographers or memorialists in the 1930s ... but also by popular historians in the 1950s and 1960s.'[73]

It was largely in order to provide a corrective to some of these misleading, misinformed or mischievous accounts that Hankey championed publication of the official military and naval histories—against considerable opposition. Hankey appreciated the arguments for and against publication of the official histories so close to the time of the events described. As he asked in a memorandum to Cabinet: 'Is it fair to publish the narrative when events are so recent that all the principal actors are still on the stage of public life as ... convenient targets, held responsible for all the wartime failures and disasters?'

Hankey's own counter-argument to this was: 'What was required was an authoritative account for the general reader to meet a probable demand, [and] to educate public opinion.'[74] Hankey conceded another [Parliamentary] complaint against official histories, 'that they are costly and never pay their way', but added: 'It is by the standard of their value for professional educational purposes that official histories must be judged. It is doubtful if they will ever pay their way.'[75] He continued:

> A History is essentially a work of reference and education ... It is, however, not only the enlightenment of the public that has to be considered, but what is perhaps even more important, the education of the professional officer. Where is he to go for information if there is no official history? ... Even the personal accounts that have been published of certain naval and military operations are reported to me to be inaccurate. It is only when orders, diaries, logs etc. are considered as a whole, and compared with information from every source, that a true account can be obtained ... Finally, there is the consideration that an antidote is required to the unofficial histories, which habitually attribute all naval and military failures to the ineptitude of the Government, to say nothing of the accounts of individual officers, frequently ill-informed and partisan in character, which are apt to mislead public as well as service opinion. This is one of

the principal reasons which led to the original decision to produce the histories.[76]

Hankey would subsequently point out, echoing Thucydides, that the official histories were written, 'not to win the applause of the moment, but as a possession for all time'.[77]

Churchill's preference was clearly that the Official Naval History not be published at all—unless it was amended considerably—and, as Secretary of State for War and Air between January 1919 and February 1921, he was in a position to insist on the changes he deemed necessary. Corbett's completed manuscript of Volume 1 had been submitted to the Admiralty for vetting on 10 March 1919. A month later, 'after seeing the First Sea Lord, he [Corbett] retained the impression that the book had been approved'.[78]

Such was not the case. The book had, in fact, been rejected by the Admiralty in response to the former First Lord's demands. Among the objections presented by Churchill, in a memorandum circulated on 8 April 1919, was the claim that insufficient 'authentic documents—orders, minutes, telegrams and memoranda—just as they had been written before the event' had been included in the Official History. Churchill maintained that 'there [was] very little of historic value that now needs to be concealed', and that the appropriate official documents should be freely published 'to make the account fully intelligible'.[79]

The Board of Admiralty disagreed, however, and an impasse ensued. Subsequently, on 19 August 1919, at Churchill's behest, the First Lord of the Admiralty, Mr Walter Long, advised the Board that 'certain passages [of the Naval History] had been pointed out to him as open to objection ... [to which] No "disclaimer" would meet the need, and he therefore sought his colleagues' agreement to "suspend publication of the History".'[80] Long took up the matter with CID Secretary Hankey (as head of the Historical Department responsible for the histories), who 'promised that anything to which the Admiralty object shall be taken out'. On 25 August Hankey advised Long that he had gone through the offending passages 'and revised them in accordance with his personal instructions ... On this principle', he added, 'I have revised the whole text as it now stands.'[81] But still the Admiralty was not satisfied:

> Three passages were still unsatisfactory; the sinking of the armoured cruisers *Aboukir*, *Hogue* and *Cressy* by a German submarine on 22nd September 1914; the other two dealt with the loss of *Good Hope* and *Monmouth* in the battle of Coronel on 1st November 1914.
>
> [Churchill] wished to be defended against attacks made on him personally, as the responsible Minister in connection with these two disasters.[82] "These passages", wrote the First Lord, Long, "have been cast in their present form in deference

to the wishes of Mr. Churchill, who ... was prepared to take the matter to the Cabinet [to protect his reputation]."[83]

Countless amendments and alterations to the text were made by the naval historian and months of effort expended by Corbett and Hankey to appease Churchill. But as Naylor points out, 'it is unlikely that he was ever satisfied with Corbett's version.'[84] Hankey's support and persistence proved ultimately decisive, however, to the effect that in a letter (No. M. 04380) dated 25 November 1919, sent 'from Admiralty to Secretary of the Cabinet', Hankey was informed that the Board no longer had any objections 'to the appearance of the history in the form so settled...' One condition of publication, nevertheless, was that 'an Appendix should be added quoting verbatim two minutes written by [Churchill] as First Lord of the Admiralty.'[85] As a consequence, Churchill's minutes of 18 September 1914 and 8 October 1914 (relating to the 'live-bait squadron' and the Coronel disaster) were included in the History as Appendix D.[86] Hankey informed Cabinet the following day that 'the difficulties in regard to the publication of the first volume of the Official Naval History have now been surmounted. Both the Admiralty and Mr. Churchill have now consented to publication.'[87]

Corbett was further threatened, through Cabinet, via Lieutenant Colonel Daniel, Secretary of the Historical Department of the CID, on 12 December 1919. He was told that, while the first volume of the Naval History could be published, 'further volumes of this history should be postponed for further consideration, [and] that the Government do not commit themselves in any way to understanding that the [Naval] Histories will eventually be published.'[88] Corbett responded by informing Daniel on 14 December: '... the terms of my employment [were] to write a history for publication—on no other terms would I have accepted the appointment. Publication was an essential condition of my contract ... I would further point out that should this [threat] be acted on a very serious breach of faith with the Publishers will also be involved.'[89] With Hankey's support, permission was eventually granted for publication of all three of Corbett's volumes.[90]

Captain Stephen Roskill expressed his disgust at the treatment of Corbett for having incurred Churchill's ire in presenting a factual account of the naval events over which Churchill had presided as First Lord of the Admiralty. Roskill insisted that 'this dictatorial attitude of the Admiralty [and Cabinet] was contrary to the constitutional position as [he] understood it, and was permitted to practise, when writing the official history of the Second World War.'[91]

Volume 1 of the Naval History was published in 1920, accompanied by the following prefatory disclaimer, which would appear at the front of all three Corbett volumes: 'The Lords Commissioners of the Admiralty have given the Author access to official documents in the preparation of this work, but they are in no way responsible for his reading or presentation of the facts as stated.'[92]

Hankey's noble aspirations would be thwarted somewhat in their realisation by a combination of lack of public interest (official histories sold notoriously badly, in comparison with the popularity of 'officially informed' war books) and, even more so, by government censorship. Departmental (Army and Navy) scrutiny of proofs assumed daunting proportions. One volume was sent to no fewer than 799 recipients for critical scrutiny.[93] Churchill raised no similar objection to publication of Volume 2 of the Naval History, which dealt with the Dardanelles operation, doubtless in the belief that he could deliver a more effective riposte through his publication of *The World Crisis* with its liberal inclusion of authentic documents.

Following his vetting (and the subsequent exoneration) of Churchill's *The World Crisis* in 1923 on behalf of the Curzon Committee, Hankey continued in this role, vetting both official histories and 'officially informed' accounts by senior politicians, largely for accuracy and content of official material. Given his position as Clerk of the Privy Council (from 1922) and Cabinet and CID Secretary, in time this procedure came to approximate authorisation for these books.[94] Hankey vetted Volume II of *The World Crisis* prior to its publication in October 1923 and Lloyd George's *War Memoirs* during the 1930s. He was quick to point out to these memoirists (Lloyd George in particular) that his involvement in no way constituted official sanction. Lloyd George wrote to Hankey on this point in January 1933, to which Hankey replied:

> I have, of course, no status to give you official permission to publish official documents. I can on my authority, exempt you neither from the Privy Councillor's Oath nor from the Official Secrets Act.
>
> I am no lawyer, but I think that the only way in which you can proceed in absolute security is to ask official permission through the proper channel, viz the Prime Minister.[95]

However Hankey did intercede on Churchill's behalf, advising Lloyd George to temper a particular criticism of Churchill in the third volume of his memoirs, which was 'frightfully damaging ... At the present time he is rather down on his luck', Hankey argued, 'and this passage will hit dreadfully. It will always be quoted against him if he is ever in, or aspires to get into, office again.' The passage in question referred to Churchill's massive unpopularity in 1917 with Parliamentarians, both Conservative and Liberal alike. Hankey continued: 'I ask myself whether it is really to the public advantage that our national heroes should be hauled off their pedestals.'[96]

It is a great irony, therefore, considering the extent of Hankey's efforts on Churchill's behalf, not only in this instance, but also in protecting him from censure in 1923 and defending *The World Crisis* against an injunction that, when Hankey approached Prime Minister Churchill in December 1944 for permission to have his own memoirs (relating to the day-to-day direction of the war at the highest level) published, Churchill refused, replying that 'publication of the book would not be in the public interest', and specifying the need to protect the 'special relationship' between ministers and their chief advisers.[97] Hankey was astounded, confiding to Cabinet Assistant Secretary Tom Jones that:

> It is astonishing that Churchill, who was practically the first to publish all the inner secrets of his rows with Fisher, and so many intimate and confidential letters, should now have the effrontery to turn me down—but I have little doubt that the reason is that the historian who studies my book will sometimes find that Churchill was wrong.[98]

Considering the numerous 'officially informed' memoirs and biographies published by this time, many based on diaries as well as official documents, Hankey insisted that his had been singled out for suppression. In an appeal to his Cabinet Secretary successor, Sir Edward Bridges, in March 1945, Lord Hankey, as he now was, endeavoured to explain the unique value of his contribution:

> My own diary [Hankey explained], aimed at describing the numerous "off the record" decisions, conversations and events bearing on policy, *of which no other record existed.* [Hankey added]

> ... to make a new rule "*ad hoc*" applying to a single individual [himself], whose status differs little from some previous writers, involves a discrimination that is untenable.[99]

Hankey's plea, nevertheless, was in vain. Publication of his memoirs was denied, unless he was prepared to make 'hundreds of excisions' to the text (to meet Churchill's demands). He would be further informed that all extracts from his diary would have to be omitted, and all 'detailed records about your day to day relations with Ministers' deleted, if publication was to be allowed.[100] Hankey decided to bide his time. Such was the reverence accorded to Churchill following the Second World War that his ruling on Hankey's memoirs would be perpetuated by successive Prime Ministers.[101] As a token gesture to Hankey's great service to the nation, on his 80th birthday in 1961, publication of an emasculated version of his memoirs, *The Supreme Command* (shortened from three to two volumes), was permitted.[102] As Professor Beckett observes, however, 'When it did appear, *The Supreme Command* had been purged of many of Hankey's more revealing diary entries and was not the book it might once have been.'[103]

It has only been since the publication of Roskill's three-volume *Hankey, Man of Secrets* (1970–4) and Naylor's *A Man and an Institution* (1984), together with George Cassar's *Asquith as War Leader* (1994) that much of this erstwhile censored Hankey material has been brought into the public domain.[104]

Hankey's Defence of Cabinet Secrecy and its Legacy

From 4 November 1919 onwards, Hankey sought to recover government control over the security of Cabinet (and departmental) documents. For 13 years, Section 2 of the *Official Secrets Act* had proved to be something of a paper tiger. This changed radically under Ramsay MacDonald's prime ministership from 1931 to 1935 when Hankey was given the Cabinet support and authority he needed. Although some 40 leakages of Cabinet secrecy had occurred since 1919, none had been considered 'flagrant' until 1932 when two prosecutions were undertaken.[105] The first of these arose from a somewhat trifling incident in which the *Daily Mail* published details of the wills of three celebrities. This breach of secrecy was traced to a 60-year old clerk who had received a small gratuity from a *Daily Mail* reporter in return for the information. For this 'crime', the unfortunate clerk was dismissed from his £3 a week job, prosecuted under Section 2 of the Act and, though chronically ill, sentenced to six weeks in prison.[106]

The next prosecution under the Act was undertaken against well-known author and former British intelligence agent Compton Mackenzie, again in 1932. Mackenzie approached the whole business with good humour, never for a moment taking seriously the allegation—that he had compromised the Secret Service in a volume of his war memoirs. Nevertheless, by law he had committed an offence, and he was persuaded by his counsel to plead guilty. Mackenzie, who was fined £100, with another £100 in costs, was subsequently advised in several quarters that the government had used his case 'in order to warn Lloyd George and Winston Churchill that they can go too far in using information they could only have acquired in office'.[107]

In 1934 the publication of ex-Cabinet Minister George Lansbury's biography by his son Edgar was deemed 'qualitatively different' to the indiscretions committed over the previous decade, with one document in particular, classified as 'strictly secret and confidential', quoted verbatim. Hankey claimed that Cabinet secrecy had been compromised and turned the matter over to the Attorney-General. In the resulting trial Edgar Lansbury was convicted of two misdemeanour counts under Section 2 of the Act, and fined £20 with 20 guineas court costs on 21 March 1934.[108] No action was taken against George Lansbury. The entire question of ministerial retention of official papers had been exhaustively examined by Cabinet and a ruling made on 9 March.[109] Subsequently, on the day of Edgar Lansbury's conviction, Cabinet acceded to Hankey's request that all living members of post-war Cabinets be instructed to return all official documents in their possession to the Cabinet Office. A similar instruction was sent to the representatives of deceased Cabinet Ministers.[110]

Cabinet further determined that ministers were henceforth to be free to retain documents, but only while in office. On leaving office all such documents were to be returned for filing as 'The Property of His Britannic Majesty's Government'. Further, ministers were advised that Cabinet papers could in no way be regarded as their 'property', to be disposed of as they wished, nor were they free to utilise them in publications (as they had been since January 1922). Only the Cabinet Minister himself had the right of retention of official documents—and only while in office. Any attempt on the part of an executor or an heir to retain Cabinet documents after the minister's death constituted an offence under Section 2 of the Act.[111]

The Cabinet Secretariat sent out 87 requests for the return of official documents, 71 to living ex-ministers and the rest to the representatives of deceased former ministers. There were only eight 'holdouts' who 'declined to cooperate', among whom, unsurprisingly, were Lloyd George and Churchill. Unfortunately, Cabinet did not possess the legal authority to compel the return of these documents, many of which remained (and still do), in private hands. In 1966, however, representatives of the Public Record Office photocopied over 5000 Cabinet papers, circulated between 1880 and 1916, from originals held in private collections.[112]

Ramsay MacDonald played a prominent role in 'beefing up' the *Official Secrets Act.* Under his prime ministership, His Majesty's permission (to publish official documents) came to mean exactly that, with the use of official material in any kind of publication assuming a more hazardous nature than hitherto. Extensive publication of official documents became a thing of the past. Lloyd George was the first ex-Prime Minister to experience the heat of the Cabinet Secretariat's new Draft Instructions. On 21 April 1934, in the course of vetting Volume 3 of his *War Memoirs,* Hankey informed Lloyd George that, henceforth, ministers' access to Cabinet records was to be: 'only to refresh their memory... [and this would not] justify verbatim public quotation of extracts from Cabinet minutes except in particular cases ... deemed necessary in the public interest.' Lloyd George was further advised that 'actual quotation' was to be used as sparingly as possible.[113]

As a consequence, even ministerial memoirs went into a decline over the next decade. As Naylor points out, 'the regulations of 1934 severely handicapped the statesmen of that period', in particular Stanley Baldwin, Neville Chamberlain and MacDonald and their biographers, who were 'given no access to Cabinet [documents]'.[114] Good biographies of these men would not appear until the late 1960s.[115] The restrictions of 1934 effectively placed official documents beyond access to all save official historians and ex-Cabinet Ministers willing to seek the approval of the monarch. The threat of prosecution would serve as an effective (if belated and preferential) deterrent to the publication of official material for the next 30 years, when these documents were released for public scrutiny in the mid-1960s.

***

Between 1923 and the 1960s Churchill's *The World Crisis* held a virtual monopoly as the 'authority' on the circumstances surrounding the Dardanelles campaign. The book proved extremely popular with the British and American reading public in particular, reprinted twice within a month of its publication in October 1923. Between 1933 and 1940 its popularity continued, with cheaper abridged versions, and even a special Sandhurst edition published.[116] Dr Robin Prior adds that:

> ... in 1933-4 an illustrated edition of the whole work was issued in fortnightly parts. A paperback edition of the one-volume abridgement appeared in 1960, following a two-volume edition which remains in print today [i.e. in 1983. Yet another one-volume edition was published in October 2005. Consequently] *The World Crisis* is the only general survey of the war published in the twenties to be currently available.[117] [Further, Prior adds]:
>
> During the period when many of the [official] documents were not generally available to historians *The World Crisis* was used almost as a

primary source. For example, Paul Guinn, writing in the mid-1960s, cites the book no less than 38 times in the course of a chapter on the Dardanelles. Later, when the primary sources became available we still find *The World Crisis* being extensively quoted for Churchill's comments and opinions on various phases of the war.[118]

In addition, the official military historian of the France and Flanders campaigns, Brigadier Sir James Edmonds, drew extensively on Churchill's account of the Antwerp episode in *The World Crisis*. [119]

One reason for the book's popularity may well have been its great readability (even critics of its content such as Prior, Penn, Plumb, Sydenham and others concede this), but perhaps more important was its claim to be telling the inside story of government decision-making at the very highest level with regard to this campaign—a claim which, for 40 years could not be refuted with authority.

Until 1923 Churchill had been shouted down at political meetings with taunts of 'What about Antwerp!', and 'What about the Dardanelles!' From 1923 onwards Churchill gradually began to silence this criticism. A measure of how successful he was in shaping the public perception with regard to the Dardanelles through *The World Crisis* can be gauged by two letters of congratulation which were sent to him following the publication of Volume II, *1915,* on 30 October 1923 from T.E. Lawrence and Leopold Amery.

Celebrated military hero and author Lawrence (of Arabia) wrote to Churchill on 23 December 1923 telling him: 'It's far and away the best war-book I've yet read in any language.'[120] The attitude of Leopold Amery was perhaps even more significant. Then First Lord of the Admiralty, Amery had not been in any of the 1915 War Cabinets and thus had no first-hand knowledge of the events to which Churchill's book alluded (no official minutes were kept at that time). Nevertheless, Amery was an astute judge of military events. As editor of *The Times'* seven-volume history of the Boer War, Amery had been an outspoken critic of Britain's 'sham army' during those years. He wrote to Churchill on 28 December 1923, offering his condolences:

> I have read [*The World Crisis,* Volume II] with the greatest admiration for the skill of the narrative itself, but with even greater sympathy for you in your struggle against the impregnable wall of pedantry or in the appalling morasses of irresolution [which had denied the former First Lord his certain victory at the Dardanelles].[121]

It would surely have been inconceivable to Amery and Lawrence that a senior Minister of the Crown could have misrepresented the facts to the extent Churchill had, just as it would be for the many thousands of Churchill's readers, who would be similarly deceived. By 1927 the influence of *The World Crisis* was unmistakable, with several books echoing Churchill's claims—as exemplified by Carl Roberts, who insisted that:

> The failure at the Dardanelles does not rest on Churchill. The campaign comes within an ace of success; it would end the War in 1915 but for the mismanagement, the irresolution and the infirmity of others. Were Churchill given a free hand the Dardanelles would surely be forced.[122]

The World Crisis, with its extensive reliance on official documents and its aura of government integrity, was pivotal to Churchill's intent in presenting his own version of the events which led to the Dardanelles disaster. Hankey's assistance, in setting the precedent for ex-Cabinet Ministers to draw on official documents in order to defend their actions while in office (in 1923), together with his successful defence of Cabinet secrecy against unauthorised access (in 1934), ensured that, during the interwar years and beyond, *The World Crisis* remained virtually unchallenged as the 'authentic' explanation for what had happened at the Dardanelles.

Winston Churchill also drew on his Cabinet Ministerial privilege to have adverse criticism of his handling of the Royal Navy by the official naval historian censored in 1919. In 1944 Churchill drew on his Prime Ministerial authority to suppress publication of Hankey's day-to-day account of the events relating to the Dardanelles disaster.

CHAPTER 8

Literary Influences: 'the Battle of the Books'

For almost 50 years, between 1923 and 1971, the influence of *The World Crisis* on the Dardanelles/Gallipoli historiography has been profound. Throughout that period it remained the dominant force in shaping the attitude of the world's reading public to that unfortunate episode. This remains very much the case today. It has only been comparatively recently that Churchill's explanation for those events has come under serious challenge, and even then by only a handful of naval and military historians. A final review of that historiography, from the end of the First World War to the present may, consequently, be appropriate, preceded by an evaluation of Churchill's formative publication.

1923. The World Crisis

Significant fallacies: Kitchener and Fisher

Winston Churchill took full advantage of the Dardanelles Commission's erroneous findings in *The*

World Crisis, many of which he had been instrumental in establishing himself. Prominent among these is Churchill's portrayal of Lords Kitchener and Fisher as flawed individuals whose character traits had contributed significantly to the failure of the Dardanelles campaign.

Much is made in *The World Crisis* of the three-week vacillation by Kitchener prior to sending the 29th Division to the Dardanelles which, in Churchill's and the Commission's estimation, 'gravely compromised the probability of success of the original attack'.[1]Churchill attributes his lapse to some kind of Shakespearean character flaw in 'the workings of Kitchener's mind [which] constituted at this period a feature almost as puzzling as the great war problem itself.'[2]

'He [Kitchener] was torn between two perfectly clear cut views of the war', Churchill insists, in directing Britain's war effort towards either full support of the Western Front or to a campaign at the Dardanelles. But Kitchener simply could not make up his mind, vacillating indecisively between both courses. 'As a result his decisions were sometimes contradictory ... now in this direction, now in that' [as exemplified by his indecision over the 29th Division].[3] 'Lord Kitchener did not make up his mind between the two courses', Churchill asserts, 'he drifted into both, and was unable to sustain either.'[4] With the benefit of hindsight, Churchill suggests in *The World Crisis* that:

A well-conceived and elaborated plan ... could have been devised: in January for action in the Near East [at the Dardanelles] in March, April, May or even June[1915] and for a subsequent great concentration and operation on the Western Front in the autumn of 1915, or better still under more favourable conditions in the spring of 1916.[5]

Churchill neglects to remind his readers that it was he who had forced the purely naval operation forward at the 13 and 28 January War Council meetings.

Modern military historians Robin Prior, Keith Neilson and George Cassar refute Churchill's analysis completely, maintaining that Kitchener's decision-making was perfectly consistent throughout. As Prior points out: 'far from failing to make a choice between "east" and "west", Kitchener had made a choice to which he adhered throughout this period. He had chosen, as he was bound to do, the Western Front [because] it was in this theatre [unlike at the Dardanelles] that ... a major defeat would mean the loss of the war.'[6] Neilson similarly maintains that Kitchener's decisions 'were not capricious or vacillating'. Rather, 'they were based on ... a sophisticated understanding of the two front nature of the war and ... of his appreciation of the value of Russia as an ally [together with] his fears for home defence [in the face of an invasion threat], and his belief that the war would be a long one.'[7] Cassar adds that

'Kitchener never doubted for a moment that the war could only be won on the Western Front.'[8]

Churchill's presentation of Kitchener as indecisive and vacillating does the man a grave injustice and, unfortunately, this slander has been accepted uncritically by a great many historians. The public perception of Kitchener has always been equivocal following his inhumane treatment of innocent civilians during the Boer War when 43,000 mostly women and children died of exposure, neglect and disease in the concentration camps he created.[9] Popular folklore even held that, when his ship, the *Hampshire,* struck a German mine and sank in June 1916 taking him to his death, 43,000 souls cried out in jubilation. Kitchener may have been guilty of many failings, but indecision in the battle arena was not one of them. A more fitting epitaph perhaps may have been provided by Field Marshal Sir William Robertson, CIGS from 1915 to 1918, who wrote of him: 'the achievements and foresight of Lord Kitchener place him in a class entirely by himself; and they justify the conclusion that no man in any of the Entente countries accomplished more, if as much, to bring about the final defeat of the enemy.'[10]

Churchill's portrayal of Fisher in *The World Crisis* as weak and irresolute is even more absurd than his corresponding slander of Kitchener. Two months after the failed naval attack of 18 March 1915, the First Sea Lord is presented to Churchill's readers thus:

> I could see ... that Lord Fisher was under considerable strain. His seventy-four years lay heavy upon him. During my absence in Paris upon the negotiations for the Anglo-Italian Naval Convention, he had shown great nervous exhaustion. He had evinced unconcealed distress and anxiety at being left alone in sole charge of the Admiralty.
>
> There is no doubt that the old Admiral was worried almost out of his wits by the immense pressure of the times and by the course events had taken. Admiral de Robeck's letter distressed him extremely. He expected to be confronted with the demand he hated most and dreaded most, the renewal of the naval battle and fighting the matter to a conclusion.[11]

This passage is wholly misleading. Churchill creates the impression that Fisher was, by this time, a tired old man, fearful of the responsibility of high command. The reality was quite the reverse. Fisher was still a dynamic force at the Admiralty (as Churchill would soon himself confirm). The prospect of directing a British fleet in battle against the Germans was Fisher's métier, his *raison d'être,* what he lived for and thrived on.

Fisher most certainly dreaded and hated the idea of a renewed naval attack against land installations at the Dardanelles. But that was another issue altogether,

374

something which, under Churchill's direction, he knew could only end disastrously. Churchill's glib description once again demonstrates how easy it is to present an entirely false picture while approximating to the facts. As for Fisher being fearful, anxious and 'worried almost out of his wits by the immense pressure [of command]', it will be recalled that the First Sea Lord had demonstrated to Churchill the exact meaning of resolve only six months earlier, when he directed the only outstanding British naval victory of the First World War at the Falklands.

Only four months after his resignation from Cabinet on 7 March 1916, during a period of leave from Flanders, Churchill performed a complete and mystifying *volte-face,* demanding Fisher's recall as First Sea Lord by first warning, then astonishing Parliament with the following injunction:

> The times are crucial [he announced]. The issues are momentous. The great War deepens and expands around us. The existence of our country and of our cause depend upon the Fleet. We cannot afford to deprive ourselves or the Navy of the strongest and most vigorous forces that are available. No personal consideration must stand between the country and those who can serve her best.[12]

> I feel that there is in the present Admiralty administration, for all their competence, loyalty and zeal, a lack of driving force and mental

energy which cannot be allowed to continue ... I urge the First Lord of the Admiralty without delay to fortify himself, to vitalise and animate his Board of Admiralty by recalling Lord Fisher to his post as First Sea Lord.[13]

No mention of this curious appeal to Parliament appears in any writing by Churchill. Rather, his slander of Kitchener and Fisher would stand, to be repeated by many writers on the subject following publication of *The World Crisis.* Fisher's reputed fearfulness would justify Churchill's usurping the responsibilities of First Sea Lord (at least in his own mind). Churchill's letter to the Prime Minister on 14 May 1915 (reproduced in full as an official document in *The World Crisis),* immediately after the War Council meeting, built on the timorous picture he had already created of the First Sea Lord to justify his takeover at the Admiralty.[14]This missive concluded with Churchill serving the inert Asquith with clear notice of his intent:

> My point is that a moment will probably arise in these operations when the Admiral and General on the spot will wish and require to run a risk with the Fleet for a great and decisive effort. If I agree with them, I shall sanction it, and I cannot undertake to be paralysed by the veto of a friend who whatever the result will certainly say, "I was always against the Dardanelles".[15]

The pages of this part of Churchill's narrative are filled with minutes, memos and letters between himself, Fisher, Asquith and the Chief of Staff—authenticating Churchill's claim to have been in total control at the Admiralty, issuing detailed, precise instructions on the conduct of the Dardanelles operation—and demonstrating his superior grasp of naval tactics and strategy over that of Fisher and the Naval Staff.[16]

As ludicrous as this proposition now appears, in the absence of any contradictory primary source evidence at the time, 'the facts' and the explanation provided by the former First Lord of the Admiralty, the senior Cabinet Minister at the heart of those very events, virtually had to be taken on trust by the reading public. It would thus be Fisher's weakness and irresolution which brought about his downfall, and caused the naval attack to be ultimately abandoned, rather than Churchill's interference and the inherently flawed nature of the concept itself.

Unfortunately, Churchill's slander of Kitchener and Fisher has misled historians of the calibre of Churchill critic Professor Trevor Wilson, who writes: 'by early 1915, [Fisher] had ceased to be an asset to his country ... He resigned over a fairly trivial matter of naval reinforcements for the Dardanelles.'[17] In fact, the pivotal event which may well have led to Fisher's resignation took place on the evening of 13 May 1915, when Churchill likewise informed Fisher that he intended forcing the Dardanelles again, in six weeks' time, with or without his cooperation. As Fisher wrote to Hankey the following day: 'Last evening ... he [Churchill] re-asserted his conviction that after all, in six weeks time the Fleet would have to do it [force the Dardanelles] *ALONE!*—and would I remain on—quiet for this. What is one to do with such a determined mad gambler?'[18] Churchill's duplicity over the supply of reinforcement *matériel* for the Dardanelles on the night of the 14th merely firmed Fisher's resolve. Resignation became the only means available to him of drawing attention to Churchill's intentions—which Churchill corroborated himself in his letter to Asquith on the afternoon of the same day.

Trevor Wilson additionally cites the Dardanelles Commission's erroneous assessment of Kitchener, maintaining that: 'He [Kitchener] was not an amenable member of the Government. He resisted giving the Cabinet the [secret military] information to which, under the British constitution, it was plainly entitled. Sometimes, when under pressure, he deliberately misinformed it.'[19] Another writer won over or misled by Churchill's prose in *The World Crisis* was Asquith's daughter Violet, who would subsequently describe Fisher as: that 'megalomaniac sailor at the Admiralty [who] ... lived by instincts, hunches, flashes, which he could not sustain in argument [against Churchill].' Of Kitchener she wrote:

> Lord Kitchener was more than a national hero. He was a national institution ... and what he symbolised was strength, decision and above all success ... Who could have suspected that behind

that iron jaw and massive breast there lurked such palsied indecision and infirmity of purpose? Perhaps he too like Fisher, was a hunch-monger whose judgement acted by no rational or calculable process?[20]

Other significant fallacies presented in and perpetuated by *The World Crisis* were: that an army of ten divisions was available in January/February 1915 for service at the Dardanelles; that Kitchener was responsible for the escalation to a military invasion of Gallipoli; that Fisher supported Carden's plan up until 25 January when he suddenly had second thoughts; that all the expert naval staff at the Admiralty endorsed Churchill's purely naval attack at the Dardanelles; and that a renewed naval attack shortly after 18 March would have succeeded.[21]

Churchill's Interpretation of the Primary Sources

One of the major attractions of *The World Crisis* for readers was its claim of authenticity. Churchill certainly provided a wealth of documentary material to support that claim. Official documents, many of which were cited in full, comprise 40% of his text in the chapters on the Dardanelles (rising to 80% in his pivotal chapter, 'The Choice'). Section 2 of the *Official Secrets Act* (which Churchill had been able to flout only by virtue of his high Cabinet office) denied this privilege to any other writer, save for the official naval and military historians who, nevertheless, tended to be far more conservative in their direct citation of the primary sources. It should also be noted that Churchill's interpretation of his sources is in many instances misleading or demonstrably false, and nowhere is this better illustrated than in his account of the naval operation's inception.

The Dardanelles Royal Commission was convened in 1916 essentially to answer one question—who was responsible for the 'purely naval attack [at the Dardanelles] which from its nature could not attain completely the objects set out.'[22] Churchill's minute to the Chief of Staff immediately following the 13 January War Council meeting effectively answers that question. That person was Winston Churchill. Churchill's minute directed Admiral Oliver to begin translating his list of instructions (16 detailed paragraphs) into orders, thus initiating the naval attack at the Dardanelles, which he claimed the Cabinet War Council had just authorised and which the British government regarded 'as of the highest urgency and importance'.[23] Churchill's minute further informed Oliver that he was 'to assume that the principle is settled and all that is necessary is to estimate the force required. ... [and that:] The orders for concentrating the Fleet required cannot be delayed.' Churchill's text leaves his reader in no doubt as to who was in control of this enterprise, albeit that it had been undertaken 'with the steady and written concurrence of Lord Fisher.'[24]

Thus, as far as Churchill's readers would have interpreted the situation, the First Lord was merely carrying out a vital commission entrusted to him by the Cabinet War Council.

However, no such authorisation had ever been given by the War Council. As the Dardanelles Commissioners noted in their findings: 'The decision of the [War] Council, taken on January 13th ... was to "prepare" for a naval expedition, and nothing more. It would naturally be inferred from the wording of the decision that the matter was to be reconsidered by the Council when the preparations were complete, and after the Admiralty plan was matured.'[25] But, as far as Churchill was concerned, his naval operation had been sanctioned, the Commissioners observing that: 'Mr. Churchill apparently considered that the decision of January 13th went further than the approval of *mere preparation.* '[26]

With regard to Churchill's claim of Lord Fisher's participation and 'written concurrence' in these early preparations, Fisher did not even sight (and initial) Churchill's minute until two days after the meeting. While the date of this minute reads 13 January, the heading is marked 15 January and initialled F for Fisher (see Chapter 2). By 15 January Churchill's naval enterprise was well advanced. It should also be remembered that Fisher had no knowledge of the War Council's conclusions on 13 January, having left the meeting before its conclusion along with Admiral Wilson.[27] With no official minutes recorded of War

Council meetings at this time, he was forced to accept Churchill's version of those events.

Churchill's presentation of his own spurious document under the guise of primary source evidence needs to be approached with caution. This same caution should be exercised when considering the many other Churchill documents presented in *The World Crisis* as 'evidence'—too numerous to detail here, but including all Churchill's 'Secret and Personal from First Lord' telegram instructions to naval commanders at sea; his disingenuous letters, minutes and memos to Asquith, Fisher, Jackson, Balfour and the Chief of Staff; his rebuttal of Fisher's memorandum of 25 January; his resignation speech to Parliament, etc. etc.

As Robin Prior points out, Churchill was not averse to omitting key evidence from his account when that evidence conflicted with his version of events. A perfect example can be seen in his approach to the most important factor at the Dardanelles—the role of the minesweepers—which rates only a brief mention in Churchill's narrative of events and a short reference in a later explanatory chapter, indicating that he was aware of the problem.[28] But no mention whatsoever is made by Churchill of Carden's repeated, urgent pleas, via 'Secret and Personal to First Lord' telegrams, for effective minesweepers—which the First Lord persistently ignored—and which eventually resulted in Carden's nervous collapse. Neither is any mention made of the disastrous attempt by Carden to sweep

382

a passage through the minefield on the night of 13 March, leading to the naval attack five days later. Nor is any explanation offered in *The World Crisis* by Churchill for his astonishing decision to launch the naval attack prematurely, before a competent minesweeping force could be assembled.

Prior has offered one explanation. Ever since his boyhood, playing with his thousand toy soldiers, Churchill's interest had been in 'grand strategy' rather than with the more mundane problems associated with warfare. Churchill's fascination with battles, Prior notes, extended to the point of 'writing [his own] operational orders' and 'moving ships' or army formations around 'like chess pieces', while he had 'a tendency to ignore the [difficult] logistical problems [and] practical difficulties' as would have been presented by the minesweepers.[29]

Clement Atlee, a soldier himself at Gallipoli, later British Prime Minister and a colleague of Churchill's in his wartime Cabinet, offered another explanation. 'Winston was always in a hurry', Atlee observed. 'He didn't like to wait for the pot to boil, you know.'[30]Or perhaps Lloyd George came closest to the truth in his character sketch of Churchill—and the chauffeur, apparently perfectly sane and having driven with great skill for months, had indeed taken everyone suddenly over the precipice.

Naval historian Captain Geoffrey Penn wrote the following appreciation of *The World Crisis* as factual history:

> Robin Prior has shown that *The World Crisis* was written as self-justification, not as history. In particular the events of 1914-15 are related with a view to exculpation for the mismanagement of the war and especially the Dardanelles fiasco, by selective quotation, omission of passages detrimental to Churchill, and the clever use of ambiguity to lead the reader to draw conclusions that were not justified by the facts. But Churchill's talent in the use of English and his retention in private hands of official documents give an impression of scholarly impartiality which has caused many historians to use the book as a primary source.
>
> At the time he wrote, much of the documentation was inaccessible to the public and fact could not be disentangled from fiction. In the meantime a huge volume of material has repeated the Gospel according to Churchill and has then been requoted to support his views, so that the incestuous nature of historical writing has led to its acceptance as unimpeachable fact.[31]

I n *The World Crisis* Winston Churchill presented a parallel, false account of the circumstances surrounding the Dardanelles operation, diverting attention from what had actually happened and his part in those proceedings, focussing instead on the alleged negative influence of Lords Kitchener and Fisher, in particular, both of whom continue to carry the lion's share of responsibility for that fiasco. Kitchener, Fisher and the admirals would subsequently be portrayed by Churchill and his supporters as 'nervous Nellies', afraid to take the bold action (of an immediately renewed naval attack) necessary to secure a priceless victory. Churchill's persuasive prose style, together with his complete misrepresentation of the facts (which could not be refuted for some decades) would allow him to persuade his civilian readership to accept his distorted version of events as the truth.

1919 to 1923. Callwell, Scott and Corbett

Prior to the publication of *The World Crisis,* a sizeable body of official and 'officially informed' testimony pertaining to the Dardanelles campaign had already been published by naval and military experts which contradicted many of the suppositions put forward in Churchill's account. In 1919, former Director of Military Operations Major General Sir Charles Callwell drew attention to: 'the presence of a large [Turkish] army in and around Constantinople [which] was well known, and it was apparent that portions of this could be transferred to the immediate vicinity of the [Dardanelles] at short notice.'[32] The Turks had ample troops available close at hand, Callwell pointed out, to counter any reinforcement made by the Allies. As Field Marshal Liman von Sanders stated in 1918, the military forces at his command were always numerically superior to those of his enemy. Throughout the campaign the Turks called on 21 divisions against the 15 committed by the Allies.[33] Callwell further added:

> It has been asserted that the Turks were completely demoralized ... that victory was within grasp of the fleet on 18 March had it persevered, but that they threw it away ... All the portents, on the contrary, indicated that the project of winning a way through the Straits by ship power alone had been a blunder from the very outset, [that] it failed for all practical purposes at the outset owing to faulty strategical and tactical conceptions as to how it ought to be executed.[34]

Admiral Sir Percy Scott was the Admiralty's top gunnery expert in 1915. In his book, *Fifty Years in the Royal Navy,* published in 1919, Scott went to great pains to detail the crucial difference between artillery fire and naval gunfire, and to explain the essential problem at the Dardanelles. In six pages of text, employing a number of diagrams, Scott explained that:

> ... the main difference between sea and land gunnery ... was that in the ships the gunners ...

had to be able to see the object they were firing at, whereas on land this necessity does not exist ... [with howitzers lobbing their shells, often from concealed positions, high into the air to drop onto their targets, assisted by artillery spotters]. This is so important a point that I wish to make it quite clear to my readers.[35]

Scott added that: 'Even if the shore gun is visible from the ship, it is a very small target to aim at, whereas the ship is a very large target.'[36]But at the Dardanelles the Turkish mobile field guns were not even visible to the ships, as they were located below the skyline and out of reach of the naval guns with their very flat trajectory of fire. In addition, the Turkish howitzers were constantly moved from one location to another to further avoid detection. 'With all these advantages on the side of the shore guns', Scott concluded, 'it is obvious that the ships alone could not defeat them, and the authorities should not have made the attempt.'[37] When offered command of the Allied fleet at the Dardanelles on 13 January—immediately after the War Council meeting—Scott told Churchill that he could not accept, as any attempt to force the Dardanelles by ships alone 'was an impossible task'.[38]

Throughout his life Churchill continued to justify his naval operation by insisting that naval gunfire was superior to artillery fire against land installations such as those at the Dardanelles. In *The World Crisis* he presented a six-page 'scientific reply', citing 'the striking force [of] high velocity guns', refuting Scott's analysis, and concluding: 'So precise are the naval guns and so exact is the naval gunnery, granted the proper observation, that it is not only possible to hit *forts* like those at the Dardanelles from ranges at which they could not reply, but to hit in succession every single *gun* in them.'[39] Churchill's claim was quite absurd. He did concede that to gain maximum accuracy the warships needed to be 'at anchor, in calm weather and with perfect observation'.[40] But none of these conditions was attainable at the Dardanelles. Once inside the Straits, the battleships were forced to keep moving to avoid damage from the forts' heavy guns, and no observation was possible with both shores held by the enemy.

Nevertheless, even under ideal conditions the accuracy claimed by Churchill lay in the realms of fantasy. In reality, as Roger Keyes informed his wife (following the bombardment of the outer forts, in near-ideal conditions), 'at a range of 13,000 yards [just outside the range of the forts' guns], this was a "matter of chance" ... Only two shells in a hundred could be expected to hit a [fort] gun.'[41] Admiral de Robeck injected a note of sanity into the situation by informing the Admiralty on 27 March 1915 that:

> The original approved plan for forcing the Dardanelles by ships was drawn up on the assumption that [naval] gunfire alone was capable of destroying forts. This assumption has been

> conclusively proved to be wrong ... to obtain direct hits on each gun has been found impracticable, even at ranges of 700 to 800 yards ... Conclusions drawn from the attack on the cupola forts at Antwerp by heavy[17-inch German] howitzers are quite misleading ... To destroy forts, therefore, it is necessary to land demolition parties.[42]

But of course it was never the forts' guns, but the mobile howitzers and field guns which, in preventing the clearing of a channel through the minefield, and through their threat to unarmoured supply ships, represented the key to the Dardanelles defences. And as Sir Percy Scott pointed out, these guns could not even be located, let alone destroyed. Consequently, the purely naval operation should never have been undertaken.

As previously described, the findings of the official naval historian concerning the Dardanelles operation were at considerable variance with those of Churchill and need only be reiterated briefly. Sir Julian Corbett found that, with the sinking of three Allied battleships on 18 March, and the crippling of four more (out of a total of 16 committed): 'the great attempt to force the Narrows with the fleet had ended in what could only be regarded as a severe defeat'—whereas Churchill's sanguine appraisal of the same situation was that the losses, though a setback, were 'only ... the results of the first day's fighting ... It never occurred to me for a moment that we should not go on.'[43]

Churchill had also promised the War Council that the threat from Turkish artillery would be minimal—'merely an inconvenience'—to the armoured warships.[44] He maintained this stance in *The World Crisis,* in which only *Inflexible* was mentioned as having suffered from this quarter, while omitting the fact (described by Corbett) that *Gaulois, Suffren, Bouvet* and *Agamemnon* had all been seriously damaged by the plunging fire of Turkish howitzers and field guns. Churchill did briefly concede, however, that 'several of the French ships had been a good deal knocked about'.[45]

But doubtless it was the naval historian's final assessment of the situation on 18 March which rankled most with Churchill. Corbett concluded that the damage to the forts 'did little to destroy the general confidence [of the enemy]', with the Turks maintaining that 'so little had the defences of the minefield been touched that the [Turkish] General Staff were confident it could not be cleared, and felt sure that, if the attempt to pass the Straits was repeated, the forts and the Turkish fleet could deal with any ships that might scrape through.'[46] Corbett agreed, writing: 'Their confidence was probably justified', adding that, if further 'disaster [for the Allies] were to be avoided, different methods must be tried'.[47]

The essential error, Corbett pointed out, lay in concentrating on the forts' guns as the main obstacle, whereas it was the minefield which comprised the heart of the Dardanelles defences. Given any immediate renewal of the naval attack, therefore, pursued to a conclusion (as demanded by Churchill) with the same determination and heroism as shown previously, and with the same trawler-minesweepers proving yet again totally ineffective: 'the chances against getting so far through unswept minefields, which in all contained nearly 350 mines, are calculated to have been 15 to 1—that is, out of sixteen ships only one could have hoped to reach the Sea of Marmara [to threaten Constantinople].'[48]

Notwithstanding such an analysis, Churchill could still maintain to the Dardanelles Commissioners, then to his readers in *The World Crisis*: 'I believed then as I believe now that we were separated by very little from complete success' on 18 March 1915 at the Dardanelles.[49]

1926 and 1929. Sir Gerald Ellison and Admiral Bacon

Two significant books published shortly after *The World Crisis* and critical of that work were Ellison's *The Perils of Amateur Strategy* (1926) and Bacon's *Life of Lord Fisher* (1929).

Lieutenant General Sir Gerald Ellison was the military adviser to the government during the implementation of the Esher Army Reforms of 1904. Even without access to the relevant Cabinet and Admiralty documents and the War Council Secretary's Notes, the evidence provided by the Dardanelles Commission, the Mitchell Report, Corbett, Callwell, Scott, Fisher, Grey and others, together with his own sources and contacts, informed Ellison sufficiently to allow him to present an accurate interpretation of the circumstances surrounding the Dardanelles campaign. Only the finer details—which it is now possible to add—were lacking in Ellison's remarkably faithful account of those events. In *The Perils of Amateur Strategy,* General Ellison outlined the manner in which Churchill deceived the War Council into sanctioning his Dardanelles naval operation. Those Councillors, Ellison notes, were entitled to assume:

> ...that he [Churchill, as First Lord] spoke with the authority of the Board of Admiralty behind him, and secondly, that he explained to the War Council fully and fearlessly the arguments against, as well as for [his plan]...

> That neither of these conditions was fulfilled is made evident by the findings of the Dardanelles Commission.[50]

It was also a well-known fact at the time, Ellison adds, that although Lord Fisher favoured a combined operation against the Dardanelles accompanied by massive military support, he was, from the outset, resolutely against a purely naval operation. 'Even ...

the charwomen at the Admiralty' knew Fisher's views in this respect. 'Certainly the First Lord did.'[51] Ellison dismissed Churchill's claim in *The World Crisis* that he had *always* favoured a joint naval and military attack, as did everyone else, but was reluctantly forced to accept the inferior naval option as a result of Kitchener's refusal to supply troops. As Churchill wrote, disingenuously, in *The World Crisis*:

> We had undertaken this operation, not because we thought it was the ideal method of attack, but because we were told that no military force was available, and in response to the appeals for help from Lord Kitchener and the Grand Duke. [And]:

> At the evening meeting of the War Council on January 28 when the final decision was taken, Lord Kitchener repeated: "We have at present no troops to spare". It was on that foundation alone that all our decisions in favour of a purely naval attack had been taken.[52]

Ellison replied by citing Sir Edward Grey's strongly held recollection that 'the attack on the Dardanelles was agreed to on the express condition that it should be a naval operation only. It was under no circumstances to involve the use of troops ... If it did not succeed, it was to be treated as a demonstration and abandoned. It was on this condition only that Kitchener agreed to it.'[53]

Ellison is one of only a handful of observers (Hankey, Lloyd George, Masterton-Smith and Cassar the others), who drew attention to Churchill's press release to *The Times* on 20 February 1915, noting its importance (and how it coerced Kitchener into promising troop support in order to protect Britain's military and imperial reputation). Indeed, Ellison emphasised (in bold print) the fact that: **'Never possibly has an enemy been given fuller warning of when and where to expect attack. Secrecy was ignored.'** [54] Sir Gerald deplored Churchill's practice of corresponding 'directly with the Admirals in command of fleets, [via his 'Secret and Personal' telegrams] regarding their operations ... The First Lord seems to have acted throughout as though the office of Lord High Admiral had been revived in his own person.'[55]

The former military adviser similarly drew attention to Churchill's contempt for expert advice: 'He [Churchill] chose to think that he, a civilian, knew more about naval and military possibilities than the experts.' This hubris reached its apogee on 14 May 1915 when Churchill candidly told Prime Minister Asquith that, should a propitious moment arise for a renewed naval attack at the Dardanelles, 'I shall sanction it', irrespective of the Admiralty standpoint. Not surprisingly, Fisher resigned the following day.[56] Ellison refuted another Churchill fallacy, begun in Parliament in November 1915, that, had sufficient Allied troops been spared from France and sent to

Gallipoli throughout 1915, victory would have been assured:

> On the Gallipoli Peninsula, our Army has stood all summer within a few miles of a decisive victory [Churchill told the House] ... We could reinforce from the sea more quickly than the Turks could reinforce by land ... All through this year I have offered the same counsel to the Government ... take Constantinople; take it by ships if you can; take it by soldiers if you must ... but take it, and take it soon while time remains.[57]

On the contrary, Ellison pointed out (elaborating on Callwell's evidence) that the land attack on 25 April 'never had any chance of success'. Turkish troops were always 'superior in point of numbers ... they knew every inch of a very difficult terrain, they were ably led; and were close to Constantinople, their main base of supply.'[58] The Allied supply line, on the other hand, extended for 3,000 miles, back to England. Even water had to be shipped in for the Allied troops. Every Allied attempt to achieve superiority in troop strength was immediately countered by an increase in Turkish numbers, from "the flower of the [Turkish] Army, some 200,000 strong ... kept in and near Constantinople to serve as the mainstay of the Government."[59]

Admiral Sir Reginald Bacon was a former DNO and gunnery expert. As Lord Fisher's official biographer he was privy to all the minutes, memoranda and letters exchanged between Fisher and Churchill at the Admiralty, many of which he presented verbatim and in full in *The Life of Lord Fisher of Kilverstone,* published in 1929.[60] Bacon was assisted in this endeavour by Fisher's former personal assistant, Captain Thomas Crease, who had retained all of Fisher's correspondence (or copies) between November 1914 and May 1915.[61]

Lord Fisher had no interest in sullying the honour of his beloved Royal Navy in order to defend his reputation against Churchill's aspersions. Rather, as he told the House of Lords in November 1915, he was 'content to wait' for the truth to emerge in the fullness of time.[62] In the interim, Bacon took on this task himself by default. In Volume 2 of his biography, Bacon reproduced a statement prepared by Lord Fisher for the Dardanelles Commission, clarifying his position, but which Chairman Lord Cromer declined to include or mention in the first report, and of which the public were consequently denied any knowledge. In Fisher's statement, presented to the Commission on 7 October 1916, he explained that:

> ...My direct personal knowledge of the Dardanelles problem dates back many years. I had the great advantage of commanding a battleship under Admiral Sir Geoffrey Phipps-Hornby when, during the Russo-Turkish War [of 1877–78], that celebrated flag officer took the Fleet through the Dardanelles.

...[In 1904], in view of the possibility of a war with Russia, I immediately examined the question of the forcing of the Dardanelles, and I satisfied myself at that time, even with military cooperation, the operation was mighty hazardous. Basing myself on the experience gained over so many years, when the project was mooted in the present war [in January 1915] my opinion was that the attempt to force the Dardanelles would not succeed.

...I may be pressed with the question why did I not carry my objections to the point of resignation when the decision was first reached to attack the Dardanelles with naval forces. In my judgement, it is not the business of the chief technical advisers of the Government to resign because their advice is not accepted, unless they are of the opinion that the operation proposed must lead to disastrous results. The attempt to force the Dardanelles, though a failure, would not have been disastrous so long as the ships employed could be withdrawn at any moment ... as in the beginning of the operations was in fact the case...

I may next be asked whether I made any protest at the War Council when the First Lord proposed the Dardanelles enterprise, or at any later date.

Mr. Churchill knew my opinion. I did not think it would tend towards good relations between the

> First Lord and myself, nor to the smooth working of the Board of Admiralty, to raise objections in the War Council's discussions. My opinion being known to Mr. Churchill in what I regarded as the proper constitutional way, I preferred thereafter to remain silent...[63]

This statement merely corroborated the entire corpus of Lord Fisher's evidence to the Dardanelles Commission—which similarly was never published (see Chapter 6). With the passage of time, the testimony of Callwell, Scott, Corbett, Ellison and Bacon tended to be overlooked and dismissed by the reading public as their books went out of print. Churchill's book, on the other hand, remained almost continuously available, through a variety of editions, to serve as the 'authentic' record.

1918 to the 1960s. The Impact of Basil Liddell Hart

Captain (later Sir) Basil Liddell Hart was the most highly regarded military historian in Britain, indeed throughout Europe, during the interwar years. Gassed and invalided from the Western Front in 1916, the intensely patriotic infantry officer subsequently devoted himself to the training of recruits, very soon establishing a reputation for himself as an expert on infantry tactics. His early publications included a 38-page booklet, *New Methods of Infantry Training,* produced in 1918.[64]The author of 56 books on military history, during the 1920s and 30s Liddell Hart's eclectic interest in warfare was reflected in publications such as *Paris, or the Future of War* (1925); *Science of Infantry Tactics Simplified* (1926); *Reputations* (1928); *The Real War 1914-1918* (1930); *Foch: the Man of Orleans* (1931); and *Sherman, the Genius of the Civil War* (1933).[65] But it was in two specific areas of combat that he became best known during the interwar period, with the development of principles which would serve him for the rest of his professional career and lead to his acknowledgement as 'the greatest living thinker and writer on war ... since Clausewitz'. 66 Liddell Hart achieved universal recognition as 'the prophet' of mobile infantry tactics, coordinated with tanks and aircraft in what would become known and developed by the Germans as *Blitzkrieg.* This primacy of rapid movement on the battlefield also gave rise to his strategic doctrine of the 'indirect approach' as exemplified by the Dardanelles campaign, which he would continue to champion throughout his life. But perhaps Liddell Hart's most driving ambition was to write a 'true military history' of the First World War, to assist in the education of young officers through lessons gleaned from the recent conflict.[67]

Liddell Hart's research revealed a shocking disparity between the way he had imagined Britain's commanders had conducted the war and the reality of its conduct. He quickly discovered that his erstwhile heroes and mentors not only had feet of clay 'but wooden skulls' as well.[68] The 'officially informed' war memoirs of former commanders often bore only the most tenuous links to reality. Liddell Hart discovered not only the cover-up of horrendous errors of judgement, but the falsification and fabrication of battlefield accounts in the interests of protecting reputations. 'War diaries were often written up several days after the events they purported to chronicle and by officers who had not been present.'[69] He was particularly dismayed by the indifference or downright hostility he encountered from senior officers he interviewed to the prospect of having the record 'put straight'. The attitude of the official historians of the Western Front and the Gallipoli campaign, Brigadiers Sir James Edmonds and Sir Cecil Aspinall-Oglander, only compounded Liddell Hart's chagrin. Having uncovered much of the truth in terms of the conduct of the war, they refused to publish it. Edmonds admitted frankly that he could not tell the truth in an official history, but hoped it would be evident for those who could 'read between the lines'.[70]

Publication of *The Real War* in 1930 had a massive influence on the historiography of the First World War which persists to this day. Liddell Hart's dominant theme of the paucity of genuine leadership, tactics or strategy on the Western Front would subsequently be developed even further by the author himself between 1932 and 1938.[71] His theme would be echoed by the likes of Leon Wolff in 1959; Alan Clark in 1963;

A.J.P. Taylor in 1963; and John Laffin in 1989,[72] with Haig and his fellow generals emerging as incompetent 'butchers' and, eventually, as self-serving buffoons in the stage play 'Oh, What a Lovely War', for which Liddell Hart acted as military consultant in 1963.[73]

In tandem with his demonisation of the four-year bloody impasse on the Western Front, Liddell Hart advocated his alternative 'indirect approach' against Germany's allies, utilising Britain's traditional naval superiority, accompanied by military force—notably, at the Dardanelles. No matter the inherently flawed nature of this strategy, the idea held great appeal for the general public, sickened by the bloodletting in the main theatre of operations.[74] The unavailability of the primary sources proved no handicap to Liddell Hart, who hardly ever visited the archives and whose preferred mode of research was through voluminous correspondence (and interviews) with official historians and men who had been close to the action.[75] Furthermore, as Hew Strachan points out, Liddell Hart had 'little real interest in, or grasp of naval ... affairs'.[76] As a consequence, he relied almost entirely on *The World Crisis* as his naval authority for the Dardanelles campaign, and it comes as little surprise to find Churchill's sentiments echoed repeatedly throughout *The Real War.* In Liddell Hart's account the reader is reminded that it was 'Kitchener's veil of mystery and authority' that was the cause of confusion at the War Council from 16 February onwards. With 'the 29th Division available' from that time, the Secretary of State for War was simply unable to decide whether, where or when to commit those troops, and 'Prime Minister [Asquith was] loath to question Kitchener's omniscience.'[77]

Conjointly, it was 'the Admirals, at the Admiralty and at the Dardanelles,... as rigid as rock in [their] passive resistance' who effectively shut down this promising operation. 'Carden's caution was disproportionate to the importance of his task', Liddell Hart observed. A desultory bombardment of the forts followed by 'a few rather feeble attempts [by the trawlers] to sweep the first minefield' was all Carden could manage up until 11 March when 'a telegram was sent [by Churchill] to urge him to decisive action, and to free him from any fear of being held responsible if serious loss ensued.'[78] But following the loss of the battleships on 18 March, Liddell Hart discovered 'a far worse loss was that of nerve and of imagination' on the part of de Robeck, Fisher, Wilson and Jackson. Thenceforth, 'the "No" principle—an insurmountable mental barrier' prevailed, and a priceless opportunity to force the Dardanelles, and shorten the war, was forfeited.[79]

In his final analysis Churchill claimed that failure at the Dardanelles had been due, not so much to any human agency, but rather through the intervention of the Fates '[in] at least a dozen situations all beyond the control of the enemy, any one of which, decided differently, would have ensured success [for the Allies].' 80 Liddell Hart arrived at a similar, semi-mystical conclusion in 1934, deciding that '[The Dardanelles/Gallipoli campaign was] a sound and far-sighted conception, marred by a chain of errors in execution almost unrivalled even in British history.'[81] As Edward Spiers points out: 'In several works ... [during the interwar years and beyond] Liddell Hart powerfully endorsed the rehabilitation of the Gallipoli strategy.'[82] Ironically, Liddell Hart's private papers reveal that he was 'a virulent critic of Churchill, and virtually all he stood for.'[83]

1915 to the 1930s. The Romance of Gallipoli—Masefield, Buley, Bartlett, de Loghe and North et al.

John Masefield's hugely popular book *Gallipoli,* written in 1916 a few months after the evacuation, was an extended eulogy to the Allied heroes of that campaign. Masefield (Poet Laureate in 1930) served as a Red Cross volunteer in France during the first year of the war, but spent only three weeks at Gallipoli before being evacuated with dysentery. Nevertheless, he was asked to write the book by the British Foreign Office as a propaganda exercise to help lift the spirits of the English people following that defeat.[84] Given access to military documents and diaries, Masefield presented the campaign 'not as a tragedy, nor as a mistake, but as a great human effort, which came, more than once, very near to triumph'. 85 Masefield invested his tale with a vivid realism within often lyrical descriptions of ordinary men coping with unimaginable conditions. The heroic is never very far away, with each chapter prefaced by a quotation from *The Song of Roland.* [86]

The previous year, writer E.C. Buley had interviewed Anzacs in hospitals throughout England as they recovered from wounds sustained at Gallipoli. From their testimony he created a narrative of the ANZAC experience entitled *Glorious Deeds of Australasians in the Great War* which was published while the fighting was still in progress.[87] Buley rivalled Masefield in his emphasis on the heroic, although his book is written in a more down-to-earth manner. Indeed, the legendary valour of the Australian and New Zealand soldiers had been trumpeted as early as May 1915, following the landing at Anzac. The despatches of British war correspondent Ellis Ashmead-Bartlett described 'a race of athletes' storming the Turkish cliffs and bayoneting everything in its path.[88] Soldier-writers such as Sydney de Loghe, Captain R. Hugh Knyvet, Hector Dinning and a host of others further established the heroic theme within Australian war writing.[89]

The celebration and glorification of war by Australians contrasted starkly with the attitude of European soldier-writers such as Robert Graves, Wilfred Owen, Siegfried Sassoon, Erich Maria Remarque and Henri Barbusse, for whom war held no glory, and who presented the Western Front experience as no more than a ghastly obscenity.[90] The Australian attitude might best be understood and appreciated in the context of nationhood having been bought dearly through this 'baptism of fire'.

The romance of Gallipoli also owed a great deal to the inescapable proximity of legendary battlefields across the Dardanelles. Compounding this classical allusion, British visitors to Anzac such as Compton Mackenzie felt compelled later to draw attention to the Greek-godlike appearance of the ANZAC soldiers, strolling around the cove or swimming off the beach, some almost naked, wearing only shorts and boots, 'their rose-brown flesh burnt by the sun and purged of all grossness', and utterly disdainful of the constant shellfire overhead.[91]

Major John North, in what Edward Spiers praised as 'probably the best of the inter-war commentaries [on Gallipoli]' provided a more restrained evaluation of that campaign in 1936.[92] Nevertheless, North did feel the need to draw a clear distinction between Gallipoli and the Western Front in his observation that: 'Assuredly there is no magic in the soil of France for the men who fought there', while noting of Gallipoli, that: 'If it is anything at all, it is a country of the mind ... no battleground so easily lends itself to retrospective sentimentality' [with its resonance to that earlier, classical encounter on the nearby windy plains of Troy].[93] North's stated aim was to provide an accurate account, 'based on the recorded actions of the protagonists, and, wherever possible, told through their own words.'[94] Together with Masefield,

Buley, Bartlett, Mackenzie and de Loghe et al., North can be credited with investing this campaign with the heroic and classical ambience which defines it to this day. Equally significantly, North provided perhaps the most persuasive defence of Churchill's explanation for the campaign's failure up to that time. 'Mr. Churchill was responsible for the inauguration of the [Dardanelles] campaign', North states, 'and today[1936] it is no longer in doubt that the campaign was brilliantly conceived.'[95]

With *The World Crisis* as his authority, North explained how Churchill was denied any meaningful control at the Admiralty.[96] 'He [Churchill] had no personal responsibility whatsoever for the actual conduct of the operations; he had no direct contact with the fleet, and the Sea Lords through whom he had to work were "at best half-hearted; at the worst, actively antagonistic".' The Sea Lords North is referring to are in fact Admirals Fisher, Wilson and Jackson, as well as Carden and de Robeck—the junior Sea Lords effectively excluded from this campaign by Churchill. Echoing another popular Churchill fallacy, North asserted that: 'The purely naval attack at the Dardanelles was a service plan, made by the naval authorities and fashioned and endorsed by high technical authorities and approved by the First Sea Lord. As such it was ... embarked upon in a general spirit of enthusiasm.'[97] But Lord Fisher's early enthusiasm and support, North observed, rapidly gave way to nervousness and irresolution, when bold action was needed for victory:

> Mr. Churchill's fundamental error as First Lord of the Admiralty [North wrote, was] that [he] failed to remember that he was "a politician" ... His attitude was "too noble to be wise." He was guilty of the amazing indiscretion, at a time of national crisis, of caring primarily and exclusively for "the success of British arms" with a passion that was "pure, self-devoted, and all-devouring".[98]

Repeating the findings of Churchill, the Dardanelles Commission's first report and Liddell Hart, North concluded that: 'Lord Fisher's failure to cooperate', and Lord Kitchener's intransigence and 'delay in the dispatch' of the necessary troops, were the main reasons for the campaign's failure.[99]

The 1930s. The Official Military History, Hamilton, von Sanders and Roger Keyes

The official military history of Gallipoli, published from 1929 to 1932, provided a similar ringing endorsement of the failed campaign (and of its architect, Churchill) to that arrived at by Sir Ian Hamilton in his earlier self-justifying polemic, *Gallipoli Diary.* [100] This was scarcely surprising given that the official military historian was one of Hamilton's staff officers at

Gallipoli. Brigadier Cecil Aspinall-Oglander dramatically summed up the campaign:

> There is little doubt today that the idea of forcing the Straits with a view to helping Russia, eliminating Turkey from the war and rallying the Balkan States to the side of the Entente, was one of the few great strategical conceptions of the World War.
>
> [B]y reason of the grandeur of its theme ... [it] will always rank among the world's classic tragedies ... a record of lost opportunities. [In particular, Aspinall-Oglander noted]:
>
> On the 18th March ... the issue hung in the balance. But the naval attack was abandoned—never to be repeated—at the very moment when the defenders were resigning themselves to defeat.[101]

The memoirs of Hamilton's adversary at Gallipoli, published in 1927, had been equally self-serving, tending to corroborate Aspinall-Oglander's version of the events in many respects.[102] But, as Edward Spiers points out, Field Marshal von Sanders' account contains an element of special pleading to emphasise his resourcefulness in overcoming potentially decisive Allied victories.[103] In fact, he describes only localised battles which could never have influenced the ultimate outcome. Even had the Allies been able to fight their way as far as the Narrows, they had insufficient troops to occupy the shores of the Straits and subsequently threaten Constantinople. The issue was never in doubt. As Kitchener had made transparently clear to the War Councillors as early as 14 May 1915, the outnumbered Allied force never had the remotest chance of victory. In the event, no meaningful advance from their original landing areas was ever made throughout the eight-month campaign.

Roger Keyes concurred with both Churchill and Aspinall-Oglander in that the Straits could have been forced by the Allied Fleet—but with the proviso that this could only have been effected *after 4 April, and the conversion of the Beagle destroyers into heavy minesweepers*—a proviso which Churchill and his admirers tended subsequently to omit.[104]

'[With] Ian Hamilton and Keyes [coming] to his defence, and the British official history—published in 1932–3 [concurring, this] marked the decisive moment in the rehabilitation not only of Churchill but of the Gallipoli campaign.' So wrote Robert Rhodes James in 1970. 'Perhaps this rehabilitation went too far', James added, 'and both the campaign itself and the possibilities of victory have tended to become exaggerated and over-romanticized.'[105] Well before 1940 and his elevation to national-hero status, the albatross of responsibility for the Dardanelles disaster had been removed from around Churchill's neck and consigned elsewhere.

The 1940s. The Churchill Legend

There is some dispute over Churchill's popularity and influence during the Second World War. One body of opinion suggests that the Churchill legend was a retrospective exaggeration, largely self-created by the man himself, assisted subsequently by his supporters, and with a generous contribution from Isaiah Berlin.

As Professor Richard Overy wrote (in 1997): 'Despite the postwar mythology, his popularity [which derived essentially from his speeches and newsreel performances] ... was not as secure as he would have wished.' His appointment as Prime Minister in 1940 was met with only 'a ripple of applause' in the Commons. Overy further states that 'in early 1942 opinion polls showed fewer than half those asked [were] in favour of his premiership. In July 1942 he was subjected to a Parliamentary vote of no confidence [for his handling of the war], though he survived it comfortably.'[106]

Churchill admirer Sir Robert Rhodes James observed that 'many in Britain had hated and distrusted Churchill, even during his war leadership.' Rhodes James remembered 'watching a newsreel in an Oxford cinema in 1954, of [Churchill's] eightieth birthday honours by Parliament in Westminster Hall, when a large element in the audience had booed him.'[107]

As Professor Simon Schama explains, when Churchill was resurrected to high office in 1940, he had not changed one iota. It was the same old Churchill from 1915 (and 1926). All the old failings were still there; the 'belligerence ... the bombast ... the grandstanding egotism ... the pig-headed obstinacy', the theatrical posturing and the interminable perorations—but now, incredibly, these qualities 'were exactly what the country needed'.[108]

Professor Norman Rose (1994), on the other hand, presented an entirely different picture of Churchill's popularity in 1940:

> Everywhere he went, [he] was accompanied by a bevy of press and newsreel photographers ... Churchill, that splendid, irrepressible showman did not disappoint his fans ... On the screen, larger than life ... Marching from one bomb site to another, munching on a cigar ... two fingers extended in his famous V for Victory sign ... he played to his vast gallery [as] newsreels exposed him to a hitherto undreamed of audience ... In June 1940, eighty-eight per cent of the population approved of him as Prime Minister, a figure that remained remarkably stable throughout the war ... Out of it all Churchill emerged as a genuine Superstar.[109]

What is not in dispute is that, at war's end in 1945, Churchill was resoundingly voted out of office. His pugnacity may have been what was needed to combat Hitler, but it was certainly not welcome in peacetime Britain. His vilification of his Labour opponents as

'Socialists' who would employ 'Gestapo methods' once in power[110] did nothing to endear him to the British voters who retained memories of Churchill describing British workers as 'the enemy [who] must be crushed', eager to use troops against them during the General Strike of 1926 when he was Chancellor of the Exchequer.[111]

The Churchill legend seems to owe a great deal to Isaiah Berlin's 1949 essay in *The Atlantic Monthly*, 'Mr. Churchill in 1940'.[112] Written for an American audience and praising Churchill's wartime leadership in fulsome and grandiloquent prose (not that dissimilar to Churchill's own), the essay probably helped lay the foundations for the legend by taking the admiration, already apparent in a number of publications at that time, to a new high. Eminent British philosopher/historian Berlin began by acknowledging the famed Churchill ego thus: 'Mr. Churchill is preoccupied by his own vivid world, and it is doubtful how far he has ever been aware of what actually goes on in the heads of others. He does not react, he acts; he does not mirror, he affects others and alters them to his own powerful measure.'[113] But the overall product was one of pure idolatry, setting the tone for what was to follow from adoring acolytes on both sides of the Atlantic. Churchill's 'commanding position in the history of the world' had been the result, Berlin explained, of a unique gift which elevated him beyond mere mortal status:

Like a great actor—perhaps the last of his kind—upon the stage of history, he speaks his memorable lines with a large, unhurried, and stately utterance in a blaze of light, as is appropriate to a man who knows that his work and his person will remain the object of scrutiny and judgement to many generations. His narrative is a great public performance and has the attribute of formal magnificence. The words, the splendid phrases, the sustained quality of feeling, are a unique medium that convey his vision of himself and of his world...

[This is] a man larger than life, composed of bigger and simpler elements than ordinary men, a gigantically historical figure during his own lifetime, superhumanly bold, strong, and imaginative ... an orator of prodigious powers, the saviour of his country, a mythical hero who belongs to legend as much as to reality, the largest human being of our time.[114]

Thus was the lead set for the 1950s and 60s, and the consequent flood of books which would follow, in praise of the 'Saviour of Britain' and of Western civilisation. Until the early 1960s, *The World Crisis* went largely uncontested as the authentic account of the political circumstances surrounding the Dardanelles campaign. Not everyone agreed with Berlin's analysis, however. Evelyn Waugh, for example, considered Churchill's style during the war to have been 'sham

Augustan ... how we despised his orations.' Herbert Read found Churchill's grandiloquence 'false' and 'artificial', while some later critics simply found it 'florid', and 'overblown'.[115]

The 1950s. Churchillmania—Lewis Broad and Alan Moorehead et al.

A great many books published during the 1950s and thereafter in praise of Britain's saviour reiterated Churchill's fallacies with regard to the Dardanelles, as a matter of course. Lewis Broad's *Winston Churchill* (1956) is fairly representative of the genre. According to this interpretation Fisher was initially keen on Carden's plan, supporting it until 25 January when he had a change of heart, largely because of his perceived 'position of inferiority' *vis-à-vis* Lord Kitchener at the War Council, which was 'intensely galling' to him.[116] Fisher reluctantly agreed to support the naval operation at the 28 January War Council meeting, but 'no one', Broad insists, 'was under any misapprehension about his continued and unabated opposition.'[117]

That opposition manifested itself in the wake of the 18 March naval attack, which 'opened auspiciously' and, even after the loss of six battleships, 'hopes still ran high'. But five days later the Army and Navy commanders at the Dardanelles recommended postponing the operation 'until the Army could cooperate'. Churchill was stunned. 'Why break off when the prize was already partly won?' he asked. Admirals Fisher, Wilson and Jackson refused to budge, however, and 'Winston was not able to move them from their decision ... In Winston's phrase the "No" principle had become established.'[118] With victory virtually in sight the great attempt to force the Straits thus had to be abandoned. Broad drew on the official military history to corroborate his conclusion that: 'So little ammunition had the Turkish gunners left that on March 18, they reckoned defeat to be inevitable.'[119]

Journalist and author Alan Moorehead's *Gallipoli* had a major influence on the Dardanelles/Gallipoli historiography from 1956, setting a new benchmark for modern military history as memorable literature. This work combined brilliant narrative description with a faithful attention to technical detail. In the absence of official documents, Moorehead drew heavily on a vast array of private papers and personal memoirs which included Turkish and German sources. Foremost among his 'officially informed' authorities, however, Moorehead acknowledged Churchill and *The World Crisis,* together with Ian Hamilton and Roger Keyes.

Predictably, Moorehead found that Kitchener's dominating 'prestige [and] the air of almost infallible right and might', together with Fisher's 'deep empirical misgivings of old age', lay at the core of the failure.[120] Moorehead rejected the suggestion that Churchill 'bamboozled the admirals—and no matter how much he proves that he was right and they were wrong there will always be an instinctive feeling among some people that somehow or other he upset the established practices of the Navy at this time.'[121] Moorehead stoutly defended the strategic concept as sound, arguing that the 'ships alone' attack could have succeeded, leading to a Turkish capitulation. Indeed, rather than being:

> ...a blunder or a reckless gamble [Moorehead insisted that the Dardanelles naval attack] was the most imaginative conception of the war, and its potentialities were almost beyond reckoning. It might even have been regarded, as Rupert Brooke had hoped, as a turning point in history.[122] The brilliance of Moorehead's work further cemented the Churchill version of the Dardanelles campaign in the public mind as the valid interpretation.

The 1960s. First Serious Criticism of Churchill since Sir Gerald Ellison, and the Death of a Legend

Lord Hankey's memoirs were finally granted publication in 1961, albeit in an emasculated form, with many of Hankey's more revealing diary entries (as cited throughout this text) censored out.[123] Two years later, in *Winston Churchill and the Dardanelles*, American military historian Professor Trumbull Higgins found it 'astonishing and significant' that the Dardanelles campaign had not as yet 'been considered from presumably its most important facet, that is as a failure in the higher direction of war' by Britain's leaders.[124] Drawing on a vast reference source which included Fisher's papers and an early preview of Admiralty and Cabinet documents, Higgins' brilliant critique went far in redressing that imbalance, with conclusions which Asquith and Churchill in particular would have viewed with considerable disquiet. Unfortunately, both these publications were denied the attention they merited by their proximity to Churchill's demise.

1965. Churchill's 'Beatification'

On Churchill's death, in January 1965, he was given a state funeral on a scale normally reserved for Britain's monarchs, and not equalled for a commoner since that of the Duke of Wellington. In a 'Special Memorial Edition' of *Churchill, His Life and Times* by Malcolm Thomson, published in February 1965, Churchill was proclaimed not only the saviour of his country, but the 'greatest Englishman of all time'—greater than Shakespeare, Newton, Darwin, Drake or Nelson.[125] Violet Bonham Carter's *Winston Churchill as I knew him* captured a similar mood of reverence towards the great man. In this book the Dardanelles campaign was presented as a brilliant strategic opportunity squandered through the lack of foresight, indecision and faint-heartedness on the part of Kitchener and Fisher.[126] In similar fashion, Thomson had found that Churchill's naval operation 'could and should have succeeded [and] that its success would have shortened the war by years.'[127]

Goronwy Rees

> 'When the trumpeter had blown the last reveille, when the gun carriage had discharged its burden on the quay and the journalists had exhausted all their treasuries of social prose...'

> For a week we had been encompassed by so vociferous a cloud of witnesses to Churchill's greatness ... no possible extravagance had been omitted from their praise; the television had luxuriated in funeral tributes, the dead man's literary agent, his valet, his detectives, had scraped the barrel of memory for the last threadbare fragments of reminiscence ... new editions of his works proliferated; the voice of Dimbleby was loud in the land.[128]

In 'Churchill, A Minority View', Goronwy Rees pondered the spectacle he had just witnessed, somewhat akin to Hans Christian Andersen's little boy, having watched the naked emperor's procession go by, asking himself 'what was that all about?' After all, wasn't this the same man, Rees asked himself who, for the first 40 years of his career, through 'overweening ambition, lack of principle, personal disloyalty and irretrievable egotism' had been regarded with the deepest suspicion and dislike by the majority of Parliamentarians and by the British people alike—a mistrust which still persisted in 1945?[129] How, then, could any ceremonial ritual have effected such an utter transformation—nay, a transfiguration?

Rees eventually came to the conclusion that 'it was not Churchill the nation was burying, but part of their own history, not a statesman but an Empire, not a hero but themselves as they once were and never would be again ... It was a nation mourning its past greatness.'[130] Churchill had presided over the last moment in his nation's history when Britain could truly be called 'great'. For this he could be forgiven anything, as he has been.

Robert Rhodes James and Arthur Marder

From the time of its publication in 1965, Robert Rhodes James' *Gallipoli* has been universally acknowledged as the finest single-volume account of the Dardanelles/Gallipoli campaign. Assisted by a preview of the official documents, together with extensive primary and secondary sources, Rhodes James contested the accepted version of events, revealing how Churchill had beguiled Carden and the War Council into approving the naval operation, the hazards involved 'skilfully obscured'. Fisher's, Jackson's and the Naval Staff's opposition to a purely naval attack from the outset was similarly highlighted, along with 'the fog which was enveloping the whole enterprise' from 16 February onwards.[131]

American naval historian Professor Arthur Marder had published much of Lord Fisher's correspondence by 1959, courtesy of the Fisher Papers, Bacon and the Crease Compilation. One fundamental consideration, Marder maintained in his 1965 publication, was the way in which '[Churchill] often initiated orders to the Fleet, and *then* consulted [the First Sea Lord]'.[132] Churchill's 'initial mistake', Marder found, lay in his premature order 'to attack the forts alone, without waiting for the presence of an army that could occupy and hold the Gallipoli Peninsula.'[133] Marder agreed with Jellicoe that 'Churchill's insistent pressure is what prevented the "breaking off" [after the naval attack had failed]. Of that there can be no doubt.'[134]

1970. Robert Rhodes James: Churchill, a Study in Failure, 1901-1939

Having fully accessed the official documents and the evidence presented to the Dardanelles Commission in particular, Rhodes James delivered a scathing indictment of Churchill's role in the Dardanelles fiasco in 1970, finding that:

> Churchill initiated the Dardanelles project, and pushed it forward with vigour, overruling or ignoring the doubts and criticisms of his Service

advisers, [towards a] major operation which most of them regarded with alarm.[135]

Further, James found that:

It cannot be seriously maintained that "the genesis of this plan" was "entirely naval and professional in their character." This was Churchill's plan, which he persuaded the War Council and his Service advisers to accept. The latter did so, but with manifest reluctance.[136]

Also, whereas 'Churchill and ... many distinguished military authorities, including Sir Basil Liddell Hart ... have argued that the gamble was justified, and that it nearly came off', Rhodes James maintained that 'the errors in execution stemmed directly from the fundamental fallacies in the original conception; that this conception was not, in itself, "sound"; and that it was, in short, a wholly illegitimate war gamble.'[137] Rhodes James observed that Churchill 'over-estimated his own knowledge and capacities ... made insufficient use of the professional advice and experience that was available to him, and too often beat down criticism by argument rather than heeding it and utilizing it.'[138]

Churchill's 'criticism of Kitchener' as indecisive yet utterly dominating, and his delay in despatching the 29th Division to the Dardanelles, was dismissed by Rhodes James as 'ill-founded'.[139]

1971. Martin Gilbert: Winston S. Churchill, Vol.3

Martin Gilbert's magisterial official biography of Churchill has probably been the most influential work in the Dardanelles historiography since its publication. Its appearance eclipsed the works of Hankey, Higgins, Rhodes James, Marder, Ellison, Bacon and Liddell Hart et al. As Professor Beckett noted, with the unavailability of the primary sources between 1915 and 1966, *The World Crisis* came to be widely cited in this role as the authority—even after the official sources became available.[140] With its appearance in 1971, Martin Gilbert's Volume 3 (together with its companion volumes) of *Winston S. Churchill* took over from *The World Crisis* in this regard, and continues to do so. Covering the events in Churchill's life from 1914 to 1916, this massive, scholarly, 988-page tome of text, together with two, similarly sized companion volumes of official documents, memoranda, letters, telegrams, etc., has undoubtedly come to represent, for historians and biographers, the complete, authentic account of the Dardanelles episode.[141]

Rightly regarded by historians as the definitive work on Churchill, the sheer scholarship apparent in these volumes demands both respect and admiration. Its exhaustive attention to detail provides the impression of total historical impartiality and, for the most part, Gilbert does provide a comprehensive and well-balanced account of the events. But a closer examination reveals a clear bias in Churchill's favour. Martin Gilbert may possibly be the most significant victim of Churchill's deception, in that many of Churchill's fictions and fallacies have been reproduced by Gilbert for an unsuspecting readership.

The fictitious War Council meeting, which allegedly took place on 5 January, is a case in point. At this meeting Churchill claimed, in *The World Crisis,* that the Councillors 'seemed alive to all [the] advantages' of a naval attack against Turkey, and Carden's telegram, 'which [he] read out, was heard with extreme interest'—the implication that he was thus encouraged to pursue the concept further.[142] In Gilbert's description of the same scene it was Kitchener who initiated the naval attack by pressing 'his colleagues for action at the Dardanelles'. Churchill merely responded 'by reading out [Carden's telegram] to the War Council'. As a consequence, the next day, 'supported by the desire of Kitchener and the War Council to follow this slim opportunity' Churchill telegraphed Carden.[143] But no such War Council meeting ever took place. The naval attack was entirely Churchill's idea, unsupported by anyone. Gilbert's fiction has misled military historians of the calibre of Professor Trevor Wilson, who cites this phantom meeting as evidence that Kitchener and the War Council were aware of Churchill's proposed naval attack as early as 5 January—which was most certainly not the case.[144]

Gilbert similarly reiterates Churchill's disparagement of Kitchener as the intransigent and vacillating opponent of military support at the Dardanelles right up until the naval attack, when he became the intransigent proponent of a military invasion of Gallipoli.[145] Fisher is likewise vilified as weak, anxious and irresolute in his negative response to the naval operation.[146] Another illusory (and ludicrous) scene by Gilbert, validating Churchill's confidence in a renewed naval attack on 19 March with the Turkish forts short of ammunition, may also be noted.[147] Gilbert's fictitious War Council meeting of 5 January appears in publications as recently as 2004 (for example, Jenny Macleod's *Gallipoli. Making History*).[148]

1974. Henry Pelling

Henry Pelling's *Winston Churchill* was described as 'the best one-volume biography of Churchill to date' by Robin Prior and Trevor Wilson in 1994.[149] A brilliantly balanced work, it presents Churchill 'warts and all'. There is particularly good coverage of his early career and the negative influence of his father, a silver-tongued political opportunist, devoid of principles, whom Churchill worshipped and held as his role model. Pelling drew widely on official documents and private papers, as well as from Churchill and Gilbert for his primary sources in the Dardanelles episode. Nonetheless, his sympathies towards the Churchill scenario are unmistakable.

Pelling reiterates Churchill's vilification of Kitchener as the major cause of the naval attack's failure in claiming that the Secretary of State for War was *'not willing* to provide any British military support [in January] ... for an early operation', and describes how this obliged Churchill to devise some other means 'of forcing the Dardanelles with naval forces only'.[150] It soon became apparent that 'if it [Churchill's plan] proved successful there would obviously be a need for military action' to subdue the Turks 'in the Constantinople area'. To this end, 'Kitchener, [on 16] February agreed to provide a regular division, the 29th', although just what any single British division would be expected to achieve against 200,000, Turks Pelling neglects to explain.[151] Nevertheless, it was Kitchener's decision to hold back this division the following week which led Churchill to declare that, 'if a disaster occurred in Turkey owing to an insufficiency of troops, he must disclaim all responsibility.'[152]

Following the naval disaster on 18 March, Pelling finds that 'it would have been possible to call off the whole effort ... But it was Kitchener who now became keen on using troops to follow up the naval attack ... so the military planning went ahead.'[153] In the final analysis Pelling decides that it was Kitchener who was responsible for the Gallipoli invasion and the subsequent disaster, asserting that: 'Kitchener ... had refused military support when it would have been most effective [in January, when none was available] ... then had insisted on undertaking the invasion of

Gallipoli at a time when the enemy was well prepared for resistance.'[154]

1978. Stephen Roskill

The official British naval historian of the Second World War, Captain Stephen Roskill, RN, also examined Churchill's role in the First World War in his 1978 book *Churchill and the Admirals.* Roskill, who drew on the full range of official documents and private papers, was scathing in his criticism of Churchill's role in the Dardanelles campaign as the initiator who had put pressure on the second-rate Carden with his 6 January telegram 'by claiming, not entirely correctly, that "high authorities" in the Admiralty agreed with [Carden's reluctant assessment of the situation].' Further: '[Churchill's] idea was in flat contradiction to the conclusions [arrived at] by the General Staff in 1906 [and] by the CID in 1907.'[155]

Roskill exposed Churchill's misplaced confidence in naval gunfire to silence the forts and mobile field guns unassisted. Against all objections and argument, Roskill notes: 'Churchill's impetuosity, eloquence and doggedness carried the day.' But more tellingly, 'it was inefficient minesweeping rather than ineffective gunfire which kept the Narrows closed to the fleet.'[156] And, in contradiction to Churchill's indictment of Kitchener as responsible both for failing to supply sufficient troops early enough, and then as the initiator of the Gallipoli invasion, Roskill found that

'Churchill, having convinced the War Council that the navy could and would force the Straits alone ... refused to call on the army for help [immediately prior to the 18 March naval attack].'[157]

Captain Roskill drew particular attention to the fact that 'one of the [most decisive] arguments originally used in favour of the purely naval attack was that it could always be broken off if it ran into trouble. It is therefore difficult to understand why it was not called off after the [disaster] of 18 March.'[158] Roskill was clearly unaware of the Hobhouse diary revelation describing Churchill's assumption of responsibility for the invasion at the 7 April Cabinet meeting (the Hobhouse diaries were not published until 1977). Nor does he make mention of Churchill's letter to Arthur Balfour of 8 April, insisting that there was no other realistic course open but invasion (see Chapter 4). Also, in common with almost every other historian to date, Roskill takes insufficient account of Churchill's 20 February press announcement, advertising the Dardanelles operation to the world and forcing Kitchener's reluctant support to protect Britain's military reputation.

The official naval historian does, however, attach importance to Hankey's strenuous warnings of disaster, which Churchill persistently ignored, and similarly to Hankey's belief that 'Churchill wanted to bring off [the] coup by Navy alone to rehabilitate his reputation.'[159] Roskill decided that it 'was the really colossal blunder of starting the naval operations before adequate and properly trained military forces were available, so sacrificing the inestimable advantage of initial surprise' that was the essential cause of failure. And for this Churchill must stand indicted.[160] Roskill assessed that 'Churchill neither consulted the War Staff Group adequately—notably by asking regularly for considered Staff Appreciations ... nor did he represent the top sailors' views adequately to the War Council.'[161] '[I]t is undeniable', he concludes, 'that Churchill was the chief instigator of the campaign and that it was his pressure that prevented the naval attack being broken off.' Roskill also revealed 'a serious [underlying] source of friction [in] Churchill's habit of initiating signals to the fleet, and only consulting the First Sea Lord *after* they had been sent.'[162] 'Taken together', Roskill concludes, 'these faults and failings add up to a formidable indictment—though none of them are admitted in Churchill's historical defence of his actions.'[163]

Commenting on Churchill's historical methodology in *The World Crisis,* Roskill agrees with Plumb and Sydenham's findings that: 'although Churchill developed an extremely readable, even gripping style his historical works cannot be regarded as reliable sources.' He quotes Churchill as having told his research assistant: 'Give me the facts and I will twist them the way I want to suit my argument.'[164] Roskill also cites a telling character study Churchill created (in a volume on Marlborough) of a person described as: 'a military minded civilian fascinated (without any professional knowledge) by the art of war ... He combined the valour of ignorance with a mind fertile in plans of action. His military judgement was almost childishly defective; his energy was overflowing.' Roskill writes that: 'Much of that passage was, in the eyes of the top British service men of both World Wars applicable to Churchill himself.'[165]

Nevertheless, by the 1980s, the romance of the Churchill legend, assisted in large part by Gilbert's official biography and scholarly works by the likes of Liddell Hart, John North, Alan Moorehead, Henry Pelling, Lewis Broad, Isaiah Berlin, Violet Bonham Carter and others, had seemingly prevailed against the facts, which only a small number of military and naval historians seemed interested in disputing.

The 1980s. Robin Prior and Trevor Wilson vis-à-vis William Manchester

Robin Prior's work (in 1983) is the most comprehensive and scholarly critique to date of Churchill's role in the Dardanelles campaign. Relying extensively on the official documents, Prior drew particular attention to the fact that Churchill had deliberately deceived the War Council 'in order to have his [naval] operation accepted.'[166] 'Churchill's knowledge that troops were essential to the Dardanelles operation combine[d] with his need to disguise his real attitude [from the War Council]', Prior observes.[167] 'All he could do [therefore] was to proceed by stealth ... press[ing] for troops, ostensibly to "reap the fruits" of a naval victory'—and creating a miasma of confusion in the process.[168] Prior refuted Churchill's claim that there was 'unanimous agreement in favour of the naval enterprise' at the Admiralty 'up to about January 20', citing Jackson's dissenting memorandum of the 5th, and Fisher's letter to Jellicoe on the 19th complaining that he 'did not agree with a single step taken concerning the operation.'[169] Prior drew particular attention to the futility of Churchill's scheme, pointing out that 'even the [troop] numbers recommended by Churchill (100,000) would not be sufficient to "compel" any Turkish surrender (there being at least 400,000 Turkish troops in the area of the fleet's operations).'[170] The Australian Defence Force Academy lecturer also noted that Carden 'was sent none of the fast fleet sweepers he had requested [urgently, from Churchill, and which would prove to be the decisive factor at the Dardanelles].'[171]

Trevor Wilson's 1986 critique, though much shorter than Prior's, is just as scathing of Churchill's conduct.[172] After deliberating on whether 'any force of battleships ... let alone pre-Dreadnoughts' could have been expected to overcome the Turkish defences and force a passage through the Straits, Wilson found it 'difficult to overlook the profound irresponsibility of [Churchill's] conduct in [this] ... rushed undertaking ... without an exhaustive staff appreciation of the obstacles to be surmounted [or] the resources needed to overcome them.' Or indeed of a potential Allied response should the Turks simply refuse to surrender on cue.[173]

In the same year as Prior's work, William Manchester, renowned historian and biographer of John F. Kennedy and Douglas MacArthur, published a massive tribute to Churchill in his 973-page tome *The Last Lion,* which presents Churchill in the role of victim.[174] Relying exclusively on Churchill and Gilbert as his primary source authorities, Manchester found that Carden's plan, when it arrived at the Admiralty, was regarded by everyone as 'electrifying', and that this was '*the* most important telegram'.[175] Lord Fisher, however, proved to be an immediate stumbling block—as 'a consequence of senility'.[176] Kitchener would prove an even greater liability, critically refusing the 29th Division for service at the Dardanelles on 19 February because of a 'petty quarrel' with Churchill over armoured cars.[177] With the approach of the naval attack, Manchester found that the Allied battleships 'were [not only] invulnerable to the shore batteries in the Narrows [but that Turkish] artillery ... was useless even against trawlers, whose helmsmen could steer beyond their range.'[178] On 11 March, 'shoals of mines, [had been] cut adrift by the trawlers' kites, [and] floated southward with the current.'[179] Then, on 18 March, with Admiral 'de Robeck ... ready to sweep up the last mines and pass his fleet through to the Sea of Marmara ... trouble began', and six battleships were lost, with the fleet only 'a hairbreadth from victory'.[180] Fisher, Wilson and Jackson, in refusing an immediate renewal of the naval attack, denied Churchill what would have been certain victory.

Contrary to Manchester's statements, only a handful of mines were ever swept up by the trawlers which, as has been shown, were incapable of dealing with close-range enemy artillery fire. Almost all of the 350 or so mines in the minefield remained untouched throughout the campaign, while the Turkish artillery proved a significant threat to battleships as well as trawlers.[181] Manchester sympathetically concluded that Churchill had been unjustly held responsible for the fiasco: '[T]he British public believed he had done it all off his own bat', he writes. 'Most of them think so today.'[182] He added: '[The] Dardanelles adventure ... would become a cross he [Churchill] bore for years. Later it was seen as a monument to his genius.'[183]

The 1990s to the Present. Geoffrey Penn vis-à-vis Geoffrey Best, John Keegan and Lord Jenkins

Following in the footsteps of Arthur Marder, Stephen Roskill and Robin Prior, British naval historian Captain Geoffrey Penn presented a scholarly treatise in 1999 on the Churchill/Fisher relationship prior to and throughout the Dardanelles campaign. Drawing on his technical expertise, Penn exposed the many fallacies in Churchill's naval plan, which the First Lord misrepresented, minimised or simply withheld from the War Councillors.[184] Similarly highlighted by Penn is the manner in which Churchill continually deceived Carden with his 'Secret and Personal from First Lord' telegrams, creating the impression that the admiral was receiving expert naval advice from Fisher, Jackson and the Admiralty War Staff Group, when in fact these were Churchill's own instructions.[185] Particularly offensive to Penn was Churchill's fiction to Parliament, the Dardanelles Commission, then to his readers in *The World Crisis,* that the naval operation had been a creation of the Admiralty war staff and: 'At no point did lay or civilian interference mingle with or mar the integrity of a professional conception.' In reality, Penn writes, 'the operation had never been planned; it had taken root from a seed germinated in Churchill's mind.'[186] It was 'Churchill's conduct of the operation [which] doomed it to failure from the beginning', Geoffrey Penn concludes.[187]

Geoffrey Best is one of Britain's foremost historians. He is also a devoted Churchill admirer, as he proudly admits in his biography of the great man. Curiously, Best has not cited and does not appear to have consulted any of the official documents for the facts in his chapter on the Dardanelles campaign. Instead, and in a repetition of the situation described by Professor Beckett with regard to the pre-1960s, Best places all his reliance on Churchill's and Martin Gilbert's interpretation of the primary sources, together with secondary source opinion from other writers like himself. It comes as little surprise, therefore, to find Churchill's fallacies presented yet again as 'evidence'. Indeed Best praises *The World Crisis* as '[Churchill's] excellent book about the First World War'.[188]

In Best's analysis the Dardanelles campaign was a 'bold strategic idea' which could have succeeded had it been given the support it merited by the service heads. But Lord Fisher provided no such assistance. 'To begin with [Fisher] concurred in the Dardanelles plan, but thereafter he wavered ... Now he supported it, now he didn't.'[189] Best ponders 'whether incipient mental illness' may have lain at the door of Fisher's problem, or whether the admiral 'was simply becoming unstable, crotchety and whimsical, as old people often do.' Kitchener remained similarly 'preoccupied and enigmatic' throughout this critical time, his chief contribution that of 'several times, put[ting] the army's contribution on hold.'[190] It thus fell to the 'ardent spirit' of Churchill to assume control of a promising situation. 'The field marshal and the admiral blew hot and cold regarding the Dardanelles', Best notes.[191] In the final analysis, Churchill's ardour would prove of no avail against the irresolution and indecision at the Admiralty and War Office—with the result that a vital strategic opportunity was forfeited.

John Keegan, one of Britain's leading military historians and an unabashed Churchill admirer, solved his dilemma by writing two separate accounts.[192] In Keegan's laudatory biography in praise of the great man, Churchill's role in the Dardanelles fiasco is scarcely mentioned, allowed only half a page in the[192]-page book.[193]In his military history of the campaign, on the other hand, Keegan conceded that, even by 4 March, 'it had become obvious that the enthusiasts' early optimism [for a purely naval attack] had been misplaced.' Then, in the face of the Turkish forces available, Keegan concludes: 'In retrospect, it is possible to see that Hamilton's [invasion] plan [of Gallipoli] could not work, nor could any other have done with the size of the [Allied] force made available.'[194]

Lord Roy Jenkins held many of the same Cabinet offices as Churchill. The former Parliamentarian and biographer clearly shared Best's, North's and Bonham Carter's admiration of the great man—but, as distinct from most Churchill devotees (Rhodes James a fellow exception), Jenkins saw no problem in presenting the flawed conduct of his subject along with the praiseworthy. Jenkins notes that Churchill was:

> ...in full, almost unilateral control of the Admiralty during the first months of the war, [through his] argumentative capacity ... which made him almost impossible to gainsay in any personal encounter ... In particular he persisted in believing that opposition verbally battered down was the same thing as a real meeting of minds.[195]

Churchill also 'assume[d] an excessive responsibility for issuing detailed naval operational orders [to naval commanders at sea].' 196 Jenkins notes the number of naval fiascos during the first months of the war (the escape of the *Goeben* and the Coronel disaster in particular) caused by confusing or garbled telegram instructions, and that 'the responsibility for almost all the unfortunate messages lay directly with Churchill.' He also notes that 'it became the habit, contrary to normal government practice, for [Churchill] himself to draft the minutes or instructions resulting from any meeting [of the Admiralty War Staff Group].'[197] With regard to the Dardanelles fiasco, Jenkins observes that: 'The critical weakness was the failure to plan for an integrated naval and military operation from the outset. Much of the blame for this lies with Churchill ... It was Churchill who argued for a solely naval attack at the War Councils of 13 and 28 January, despite Fisher's obvious misgivings.'[198] Jenkins continues:

> Churchill's later summing up was that the concept was overwhelmingly right, that it was only a singularly unfortunate accumulation of narrowly missed chances that prevented it from working ... Had he been Prime Minister [then] ... he would have won a great victory, substantially shortened the war and saved hundreds of thousands of lives. But [Lord Jenkins concludes], it is difficult to find a serious historian who agrees.[199]

The polarisation of opinion described here with regard to Churchill's responsibility for the Dardanelles fiasco persists to this day. Lord Jenkins' approach (and that of Robert Rhodes James) is a refreshing exception to the rule.[200]

A confluence of serendipitous factors, all acting independently—the demonisation of the Western Front and the romance of the Gallipoli campaign, the impact of Liddell Hart in the 1930s and the self-serving official histories and memoirs of Hamilton, Aspinall-Oglander, von Sanders and Keyes et al., then Churchill's elevation to national hero status from 1945 onwards—served to ensure that his seriously flawed and disingenuous account of the Dardanelles campaign would continue to be accepted within the public mind as the 'authentic' explanation for that tragic episode. Only a small minority of historians continue to challenge that mindset.

CONCLUSION

O what a tangled web we weave,
When first we practise to deceive.
Sir Walter Scott
Marmion vi

The popular understanding of the circumstances surrounding the naval attack against the Dardanelles in 1915 is that it was a 'sound concept' which could and should have succeeded, had it been given the support it merited. That it failed was due to 'a chain of errors in execution almost unrivalled even in British history'.[1] But above all, it was Lords Kitchener and Fisher who are regarded as responsible for the failure through Lord Kitchener's intransigent refusal to supply the troops needed (and which were available from the outset), and Lord Fisher's faint-hearted refusal to order a renewal of the naval attack shortly after 18 March, with victory beckoning.[2]

The reality is that the concept was inherently flawed from the outset, with no realistic possibility of success, and should never have been attempted.[3] That it was undertaken was due entirely to Winston Churchill, who deceived all the main protagonists involved in order to have his naval venture sanctioned. He began by deceiving and coercing Admiral Carden into submitting a 'plan' for the forcing of the Dardanelles by ships alone. Churchill informed Carden that this proposition had the endorsement of 'high authorities' at the Admiralty, which Carden naturally assumed to refer to First Sea Lord Fisher and/or chief planning officer for the Mediterranean, Admiral Sir Henry Jackson. In fact, both Fisher and Jackson were vehemently opposed to any such concept.

Churchill then deceived Lord Kitchener into supporting his plan by claiming, at a private conference just prior to the 13 January War Council meeting, that the *Queen Elizabeth's* eight 15-inch guns would emulate the giant German siege howitzers in Belgium and demolish the mediaeval Turkish forts at the Dardanelles *seriatim.* Nevertheless, the War Minister strongly opposed a naval attack at the Dardanelles unaccompanied by large-scale troop support, and voiced his dissent to Churchill to that effect.[4] Kitchener's fears were allayed at the subsequent War Council meeting when he was assured that 'should any unforeseen difficulties be encountered', or the Turkish opposition prove greater than expected, the naval attack would be broken off and it would revert to merely a naval demonstration as originally requested by Grand Duke Nicholas.[5] Within such a safeguard there was simply no possibility of any kind of disaster occurring, and both Kitchener and Fisher were deceived into pledging their support to a matter of 'high policy' promised by the British government to its Russian ally.

Churchill famously maintained that all the Admiralty experts shared his enthusiasm for the prospects held out by Carden's plan when it arrived on 5 January.[6] Indeed, right up until Fisher's dissenting memorandum of 25 January, Churchill insisted that 'there seemed to be unanimous agreement [at the] War Office, Foreign Office [and] Admiralty ... in favour of the naval enterprise against the Dardanelles. It was not until the end of January', Churchill claimed, 'when [plans] were far advanced ... that Lord Fisher *began* to manifest an increasing dislike and opposition to the scheme.'[7] In fact, as the evidence given by Fisher, Jackson, Asquith and all the Admiralty gunnery experts to the Dardanelles Commission, and the Commission's first report, as well as Hankey's diary testimony reveals, the opposite was the case. Noone at the Admiralty, with the exception of Churchill, ever supported an attempt to force the Dardanelles Straits 'by ships alone'.

The sanctioning of his plan at the 28 January War Council meeting presented Churchill with a quandary. His scheme had been authorised on the implicit understanding that troops were neither needed nor wanted to force the Dardanelles. The Navy would do the job alone, Churchill had insisted to the civilian Councillors (the contrary opinion of his naval experts being suppressed by the First Lord). With no spare troops available at the time, this made Churchill's naval attack a very attractive proposition. The First Lord was well aware, however, that the presence of a large army (to silence the Turkish field artillery) was essential for any chance of success. Consequently, as Prior points out, having deliberately deceived the War Councillors into sanctioning his plan by withholding from them the opposing views of the Admiralty Staff, Churchill was obliged 'to proceed by stealth' to obtain the army he knew was necessary, creating a miasma of confusion in the process.

Churchill's opportunity to press for large-scale troop support arrived on 15 February with a memorandum from Jackson which was read out to the War Council the following day. Jackson's finding, that a naval attack was 'not recommended as a sound military operation, unless a strong military force is ready to assist in the operation', was merely a re-statement of his earlier memoranda to Churchill, which the First Lord had chosen to ignore until now.[8] Notwithstanding the fact that he had been given this selfsame appraisal by all the Admiralty experts, Churchill claimed that it was only with Jackson's 15 February memorandum that he began to question the viability of Carden's 'plan'. Only now did he realise that large-scale army support *was* needed at the Dardanelles after all. Kitchener's offer of troops on the 16th, following on Jackson's memo, thus became, in Churchill's understanding, 'the foundation of the military attack upon the Dardanelles'.[9]

Following the opening bombardment of the outer forts, Churchill's issue of a press release to *The Times* on 20 February describing the forthcoming Dardanelles operation in the most absurd detail transformed the situation utterly, a fact that has largely gone unrecognised. In one stroke the essential precondition which had persuaded Kitchener and Fisher to pledge their support to the naval attack was cynically made redundant. As Lloyd George, Hankey and Masterton-Smith explained at the time, the rationale behind the sanctioning of the naval operation by the War Council had been that 'very little was to be said about it publicly, so that if it failed, or met with unforeseen difficulties, it could be presented as a feint and operations tried elsewhere.' But Churchill's press release effectively destroyed that safeguard, creating a 'prestige' argument in its stead. As Kitchener told the War Council on 24 February: 'The publicity of ... [Churchill's press] announcement had committed us [to a defence of Britain's military and Imperial reputation]'.[10]

Not all the War Councillors agreed with Kitchener, however. Lloyd George insisted that the original plan should still be adhered to, and that Britain should not be committed to a siege situation at the Dardanelles. If things went badly there the operation should be abandoned, as hitherto agreed, and an alternative campaign mounted elsewhere.[11] Over the ensuing weeks the situation would become progressively more confused as Churchill alternately demanded then denied the need for a massive army, and a procession of sanguine reports by the First Lord on the fleet's progress painted a picture pleasing to the civilian War Councillors while the reality at the Dardanelles was proving quite the reverse.[12]

442

Having secured the go-ahead for his naval attack, which he kept securely under his own control at the Admiralty, Churchill had cause to ponder the strategic options available. He assured his fellow War Councillors that, once the Straits were forced, with the battle fleet in the Bosphorus threatening Constantinople, the surrender of the Turks would be a formality. Churchill had promised Fisher that 'the arrival of [even] four or five [battle]ships in the Marmora would decide the issue.'[13] In the absence of a massive Allied or Balkan army to compel a Turkish surrender, this belief came, in fact, to represent Churchill's only strategy (as Sir Edward Grey observed). But how realistic was it? Having arrived off Constantinople, what then was the fleet supposed to do? Bombard the sacred sites of one of the world's oldest and most revered centres of Christian, Moslem and Greek culture to force a surrender? As George Cassar points out, regardless of the moral outrage this would have created throughout Europe, in 1915 the bombardment of an undefended city was against international law.[14] And even had the commander of the fleet boasted the courage necessary to order such an act he would certainly have lacked the means to carry it out. The old battleships' guns were simply incapable of a sustained bombardment. Had they been so employed they could well have proved a greater danger to the British than the Turks. Admiral de Robeck informed the Admiralty of this fact on 27 March: '[W]ear of old guns [on the battleships] is causing me some anxiety, on the 18th [of March] there were several premature bursts of common shell, and the guns were out of action from time to time...'[15]

In truth there was never any reason for the Turks to surrender. The reality is that the Straits could well have been forced by the fleet had Churchill been prepared to wait two to three weeks for a competent minesweeping force of converted Beagle destroyers—but this would have brought the First Lord no closer to the spectacular victory he craved. Churchill and his later supporters seem to have lost sight of the fact that Turkey was Germany's prized ally. Germany had invested a great deal in winning over the Sublime Porte to her cause, and it stretches credibility to suggest that its German military commanders would have permitted the Turkish Army to surrender without offering fierce resistance. In the event, Turkey's soldiers fought magnificently in the defence of their homeland. It also escaped Churchill's attention that, in October 1915, in order to tempt Bulgaria into becoming Germany's newest ally, von Falkenhayn despatched 11 German divisions from the Western Front to the Balkans to help crush the Serbian Army within the space of two months.[16] Had his Turkish ally been under any serious pressure, the German Commander-in-Chief would doubtless have sent the required German divisions to the Balkans six months earlier. But no such assistance was ever required by the Turkish Army. Throughout the Gallipoli campaign Turkey had 15 divisions available on the nearby Thracian border to call on if needed. They were never called.[17]

While Winston Churchill's press release on 20 February may well have severely compromised any remote chance of success of the Dardanelles naval operation, defeat was ensured when Churchill ordered a premature naval attack on 18 March without a competent minesweeping force in attendance.

Following the naval débâcle of 18 March it would have been quite possible to disengage from the Dardanelles, as Lloyd George advocated, in accordance with the original War Council rationale. That this did not happen, and a disastrous military invasion was undertaken instead, was due jointly to Churchill and Prime Minister Asquith. Responsibility for this decision would subsequently be attributed by Churchill to Lord Kitchener,[18] but as the War Council Secretary's Notes and Charles Hobhouse's diary record attest, it was Churchill (and Asquith by default) who instigated this decision at the 6 April War Council meeting, with Churchill offering to shoulder the entire responsibility himself at a Cabinet meeting the following day.[19]

Despite Fisher's and Hankey's desperate pleas throughout April to Churchill and Asquith to have the futile military invasion abandoned, it went ahead, catastrophically fulfilling all of Hankey's worst warnings and predictions. Following Fisher's resignation on 15 May, Churchill was dismissed from his office of First Lord amid revelations that he had usurped the authority of the First Sea Lord to direct his own private naval operation of war. As this text has described, Churchill had been in the habit of bypassing Fisher and the Admiralty Staff and sending his own orders direct to naval commanders at sea since the war's beginning. Indeed, his 'grand deception' began with a 'Secret and Personal from First Lord' telegram to Carden on 6 January (which Fisher was never shown), advising him that 'high authorities' at the Admiralty were in favour of a naval attack at the Dardanelles.[20]Churchill brought his enterprise to an ignominious end through 'Secret and Personal from First Lord' telegrams 101 and 109 to Carden then de Robeck, ordering a premature naval attack before a competent minesweeping force was available.[21] As Lord Roy Jenkins noted, many of the Royal Navy's disasters in the early months of the war (the escape of the *Goeben* and the Coronel tragedy in particular) were the result of confusing or faulty telegram instructions to naval commanders, and that 'responsibility for almost all the unfortunate messages lay directly with Churchill'.[22] The same situation would prevail at the Dardanelles, to even greater effect.

Churchill's resignation speech to Parliament in November 1915 signalled the beginning of his disingenuous account of the Dardanelles campaign.[23]He would be given fortuitous assistance in this undertaking by the Dardanelles Commission enquiry in 1916–17, conducted while the war was still

446

in progress. It would have been unthinkable to gift the enemy evidence of governmental ineptitude at the highest level in the planning and conduct of the war, and the heads of the British Army and Royal Navy, Kitchener and Fisher, were consequently served up as sacrificial offerings to satisfy a public need for accountability.[24]

Churchill subsequently took full advantage of his Cabinet ministerial authority to amass a vast personal archive of official documents in anticipation of the historical apologia he would write and in order to censor criticism of his handling of the Royal Navy during the early months of the war by the official naval historian. He then proceeded to flout the *Official Secrets Act* and his Privy Councillor's Oath, publishing his version of the Dardanelles campaign in 1923. Churchill's *cri de coeur*—that victory was there for the taking on or around 19 March had the admirals only been bold enough to renew the naval attack—was in truth a travesty of the real situation (as the Dardanelles Commissioners concluded but declined to publish).[25]Until the mid-1960s and the release of the official documents, Churchill's account could not be refuted with authority, and eventually came to represent the 'authentic' explanation for what had happened at the Dardanelles. It would surely have been inconceivable to the reading public that a senior Cabinet Minister could have misrepresented the facts to the extent Churchill had. His elevation to national hero status following the Second World War only enhanced his image further, muting criticism by historians. Nevertheless the facts pertaining to this episode are readily accessible in the archives listed in this account. It is now open to others to avail themselves of the full story should they wish.

The evidence now available leaves no doubt that Winston Churchill was responsible for the failed Dardanelles naval operation. As Sir Gerald Ellison pointed out, to have any chance of success, a campaign against the Dardanelles and Constantinople required two elements: complete surprise and a massive accompanying army, as described by Hankey and Fisher in early January 1915. Otherwise, it was 'not a feasible operation of war'.[26] Churchill's press release on 20 February effectively eliminated the primary requirement of surprise, and a massive Allied or Balkan army was never available in January/February 1915. Churchill maintained in the War Councillors a state of confused, unrealistic expectation by withholding from them all contrary expert opinion, and plying them instead with his own sanguine viewpoint. That Cabinet Ministers could have allowed themselves to accept a proposition whereby a large land mass, then a capital city, could be captured by a battle fleet without military assistance, speaks volumes for Churchill's powers of persuasion.

And even if the Straits had been forced, what then? Churchill declined to consider the matter any further. For him, forcing the Straits was synonymous with victory. But how could it have been, with a

German-led Turkish Army of 250–400,000 troops ready to defend their homeland against 75,000 Allied soldiers? Charles Bean's accusation in 1921, rather than being a case of hyperbole, could well be seen as one of the understatements of all time.

Churchill's Motivation

It could be argued that Winston Churchill genuinely believed that he was acting within the purview of his commission as First Lord of the Admiralty, with final and absolute authority to Crown and Parliament for all matters pertaining to the Royal Navy, as Alan Moorehead, John North and many other Churchill supporters maintain. After all, as has been described, Hugh Childers treated the admirals with equal contempt in forcing his government's naval policy on them during Gladstone's reforming government of 1868–74. The essential difference rests in the fact that Churchill, rather than attempting to bulldoze his scheme through the proper channels (in the Childers manner), as he may have attempted had he believed he was acting legitimately, employed deception on a massive scale (particularly of his Cabinet colleagues) to achieve his ends, a deception which was then extended unashamedly to encompass Parliament, the Dardanelles Commission and then an unsuspecting reading public.

It could further be argued that deception on the part of a nation's leading politicians so as to advance a desired military policy is not unique to Churchill. President Lyndon Johnson drew on a fictitious incident in the Gulf of Tonkin in August 1964 (when three North Vietnamese patrol boats allegedly attacked two American destroyers) to massively escalate the war in Vietnam.[27] And President George W. Bush relied on the similarly fictitious weapons of mass destruction to justify his military venture into Iraq in 2003. No other politician in recent times, however, has ever taken it upon himself to personally conduct and direct a major operation of war. In this respect Churchill's conduct is a unique illustration of Clemenceau's famous dictum 'war is too important to be left to the generals', taken to its logical extreme.

Doubtless Churchill's conduct was inspired, and justified in his own mind by the conviction he shared with President Lincoln in the superiority of his strategic judgement over that of his military advisers. Lincoln replaced one ineffectual commanding general after another until he arrived at the ruthlessly efficient Grant. Churchill's admirers would claim that he was motivated by selfless reasons, most notably to bring the war to a speedier conclusion, saving millions of lives in the process. The opinion of those colleagues closest to him, on th[]e other hand, might suggest another explanation. As Hankey observed: 'In my own belief, Churchill wanted to bring off the coup [at the Dardanelles] by Navy alone to rehabilitate his reputation.'[28] Lloyd George was much more scathing,

450

telling Frances Stevenson at the time of Fisher's resignation and Churchill's sacking:

> It is the Nemesis ... of the man who has fought for this war for years. When the war came he saw in it the chance of glory for himself, & has accordingly entered on a risky campaign without caring a straw for the misery and hardship it would bring to thousands, in the hope that he would prove to be the outstanding man in this war.[29]

In the final analysis the truth, in this respect, may never be known.

The reconstruction of events in this book could well have been performed in Britain at any time since 1968. However, for whatever reason, Britain's scholars have shown little enthusiasm for such a task, preferring to leave the question of Churchill's culpability in this matter largely unaddressed and unresolved.

***

If a moment of conjecture on 'what might have been' may be permitted, it is possible to imagine that, had Kitchener and the Admiralty been permitted to plan and prepare for a joint military/naval campaign against the Dardanelles for June/July 1915—as Kitchener had intimated to the War Council on 8 January 1915—and had 150–200,000 Allied troops suddenly descended on the Gallipoli Peninsula as Hankey advocated, with the priceless element of surprise behind them, there is every likelihood that the peninsula would have been captured. The accompanying battleships could then have forced a passage through the Straits, assisted by a force of competent minesweepers, to dominate this waterway. In such a situation both Greece and Bulgaria would in all likelihood have entered the fray out of pure self-interest in order to scavenge on the carcass of Turkey. With armies of 200,000 and 300,000 respectively behind them, together with the Anglo-French military force, Admiral von Tirpitz's fears could well have been realised, and Constantinople forced to surrender.

Any chance of such a scenario being played out, however, was nullified when Churchill assumed control, if not responsibility, for the enterprise.

ENDNOTES

Editor's Preface

[1]   See the website devoted to Churchilliana: http://savrola.co.uk/

[2]   Jenny MacLeod (ed), *Gallipoli. Making History,* Frank Cass, London, 2004. See Gilbert's chapter, pp.21–22.

[3]   Works such as Andrew Suttie's *Rewriting the First Wold War. Lloyd George, Politics and Strategy, 1914–1918,* Palgrave Macmillan, Basingstoke, Hampshire, 2005 (which covers Lloyd George's account of the Dardanelles campaign, pp.54–58) and Andrew Green, *Writing the Great War: Sir James Edmonds and the Official Histories, 1915–1948,* Frank Cass, London, 2003 (see chapters 5 and 6 on Aspinall-Oglander's British official history of the Gallipoli campaign). The Australian official war historian, C.E.W. Bean, is already the subject of a significant body of work.

[4]   David Reynolds, *In Command of History, Churchill Fighting and Writing the Second World War,* Allen Lane, London, 2004, pp.xxi, 126.

[5]   Tom Curran, 'Who was responsible for the Dardanelles Naval Fiasco?', *Australian Journal of*

Politics and History, Vol.57, No.1, March 2011, pp.17–33.

Introduction

[1] C.E.W. Bean, *The Official History of Australia in the War of 1914–1918,* Vol. I, *The Story of Anzac,* Angus & Robertson, Sydney, 1921, p.201.

[2] Winston S. Churchill, *The World Crisis, 1911–1914,* Vol. I, Thornton Butterworth, London, 1923, p.122.

[3] See Bibliography for the details of these works.

[4] See Macleod (ed), *Gallipoli. Making History.*

[5] 'Report by Major-General Callwell' [for Winston Churchill, on the feasibility of a naval attack against the Dardanelles], ADM 137/ 96.735-6 of 3 September 1914; Lieutenant General Sir Gerald Ellison, *The Perils of Amateur Strategy, as Exemplified in the Attack on the Dardanelles Fortress in 1915,* Longmans Green, London, 1926; Admiral Sir Percy Scott, *Fifty Years in the Royal Navy,* J. Murray, London, 1919; Admiral Sir R.H. Bacon, *The Life of Lord Fisher of Kilverstone,* 2 vols, Hodder & Stoughton, London, 1929.

[6] Brigadier General C.F. Aspinall-Oglander, *History of the Great War. Military Operations, Gallipoli,* Vol.2, Heinemann, London, 1932, p.479.

454

[7]   Geoffrey Best, *Churchill, A Study in Greatness,* Penguin Books, London, 2001; Alan Moorehead, *Gallipoli,* Hamish Hamilton, London, 1956; William Manchester, *The Last Lion, Winston Spencer Churchill, Visions of Glory: 1874-1932,* Michael Joseph, London, 1983.

[8]   Macleod, *Gallipoli: Making History* and *Reconsidering Gallipoli,* Manchester University Press, 2004; Nigel Steel and Peter Hart, *Defeat at Gallipoli,* Macmillan, London, 1994; Tim Travers, *Gallipoli 1915,* Tempus, Stroud, Charleston, SC, 2001; Geoffrey Miller, *Straits: British Policy towards the Ottoman Empire and Origins of the Dardanelles Campaign,* University of Hull Press, 1997.

[9]   Brock, Michael and Eleanor (eds), *H.H. Asquith: Letters to Venetia Stanle* y, Clarendon Press, Oxford, 1982; A.J.P. Taylor (ed), *Lloyd George: A Diary by Frances Stevenson,* Hutchinson, London, 1971; Edward David (ed), *Inside Asquith's Cabinet. From the Diaries of Charles Hobhouse,* John Murray, London, 1976; Stephen Roskill, *Hankey, Man of Secrets,* Vols.1 and 2, Collins, London, 1970; John F. Naylor, *A Man and an Institution. Sir Maurice Hankey, the Cabinet Secretariat and the Custody of Cabinet Secrecy,* Cambridge University Press, Cambridge, 1984.

[10]   See Chapter 1.

Chapter 1

[1] Geoffrey Barraclough, *From Agadir to Armageddon: Anatomy of a Crisis,* Weidenfeld & Nicholson, London, 1982, pp.1–15; John A. Moses, *The Politics of Illusion. The Fischer Controversy in German Historiography,* University of Queensland Press, St Lucia, 1975, p.85. See also Fritz Fischer, *War of Illusions: German Policies from 1911-1914* (trans by Marian Jackson), Chatto & Windus, London, 1975; Arthur J. Marder, *From the Dreadnought to Scapa Flow: The Royal Navy in the Fisher Era, 1904-1919,* Vol.1, *The Road to War, 1904-1914,* Oxford University Press, Oxford, 1965, pp.239–46; Geoffrey Penn, *Fisher, Churchill and the Dardanelles,* Leo Cooper, Barnsley, 1999, p.3.

[2] Mansion House speech, as reported in the *Manchester Guardian,* 22 July 1911, Lloyd George Papers, HLD. C/35/1.193 of 21 July 1911.

[3] TNA (PRO), CAB 2/2, Part 2, Minutes of the 114th Meeting of the [CID], August 23, 1911, 'ACTION TO BE TAKEN IN THE EVENT OF INTERVENTION IN A EUROPEAN WAR', pp.1–2. See also Paul Guinn, *British Strategy and Politics, 1914-1918,* Clarendon Press, Oxford, 1965, pp.16–22; H. Temperley and G.P. Gooch (eds), *British Documents on the Origins of the War, 1898-1914,* Vol.7, *The Agadir Crisis,* H.M.

456

Stationery Office, London, 1928–38, nos.364, 640.

[4]   TNA (PRO), CAB 2/2, Pt 2, pp.2, 3.

[5]   Ibid., pp.11, 12.

[6]   Grand Admiral von Tirpitz, *My Memories,* Vol.2, Hurst and Blackett, London, 1919, p.368.

[7]   Penn, *Fisher,\15.*

[8]   Ellison, *Perils of Amateur Strategy,* pp.5–6.

[9]   Basil Liddell Hart, *A History of the World War, 1914-1918,* Faber, London, 1934, p.63; Penn, *Fisher,* p.15.

[10]   Cited by Randolph Churchill in *Winston S. Churchill,* Vol.2, Heinemann, London, 1966–69, p.530.

[11]   Marder, *Road to War,* pp.239–51; Major General Sir C.E. Callwell, *Field Marshal Sir Henry Wilson, his Life and Diaries,* Vol.1, Cassell, London, 1927, pp.99–100.

[12]   TNA (PRO), CAB 2/2, Part 2, pp.12, 13.

[13]   R.B. Haldane, *Autobiography,* Hodder & Stoughton, London, 1929, pp.225–27, 228; Penn, *Fisher,* p.14; Marder, *Road to War,* pp.246–51; Lewis Broad, *Winston Churchill, 1874-1951,* Hutchinson, London, 1956, p.128.

[14]   Churchill, *The World Crisis,* Vol. I, pp.42–69.

[15] Hansard, 4th series, Vol.91, cols 1562–79, 13 May 1901; Broad, *Churchill,* pp.82–5, 89–92; Robert Rhodes James, *Churchill, A Study in Failure 1900-1939,* Weidenfeld & Nicolson, London, 1970, pp.13–16.

[16] Webb and Winterton, cited in James, *Churchill: A Study in Failure,* pp.14, 15, 22; Charles Eade (ed), *Churchill by his Contemporaries,* Hutchinson, London, 1953, pp.86–87.

[17] Martin Gilbert, *Winston S. Churchill,* Vol.3, *1914-1916,* Heinemann, London, 1971, p.329; Brock and Brock (eds), *Asquith Letters,* p.508.

[18] David, *Inside Asquith's Cabinet,* p.73.

[19] Ibid., pp.73, 76, 121.

[20] Michael Lewis, *The Navy of Britain: a Historical Portrait,* G. Allen, London, 1948, pp.335–98, 378–80; Marder, *Road to War,* p.19.

[21] Lewis, *Navy of Britain,* p.376; Penn, *Fisher,* pp.20–21; Churchill, *The World Crisis,* Vol. I, pp.238–42.

[22] Marder, *Road to War,* pp.19–20.

[23] Ibid., p.19; Lewis, *Navy of Britain,* p.380; Churchill, *The World Crisis,* Vol. I, p.70.

[24] Sir John Briggs, *Naval Administrations 1827 to 1892,* Sampson Low, London, 1897, pp.189–90; Penn, *Fisher,* p.20.

458

[25]   Lewis, *Navy of Britain,* pp.379–80.

[26]   *Spectator* and *National Review,* 28 October 1911; Marder, *Road to War,* p.252.

[27]   Churchill, *The World Crisis,* Vol. I, p.77.

[28]   Gilbert, *Winston Churchill,* Vol.3, p.145.

[29]   Marder, *Road to War,* pp.43–46; Penn, *Fisher,* pp.46, 47–48.

[30]   Jellicoe Papers, BLIB, ADD, MSS 49038, autobiographical notes, p.239, circa 1913.

[31]   Bacon, *Life of Lord Fisher,* pp.162–63.

[32]   Marder, *Road to War,* p.255.

[33]   Cited in J.B. Atkins, *Incidents and Reflections,* Christophers, London, 1947, pp.124–26.

[34]   Winston S. Churchill, *Thoughts and Adventures,* Thornton Butterworth, London, 1932, pp.130–31.

[35]   Marder, *Road to War,* p.266; Bacon, *Life of Lord Fisher,* p.161; Penn, *Fisher,* p.24.

[36]   Churchill admitted to this practice in *The World Crisis,* Vol. I, pp.239–41.

[37]   As Fisher testified to the Dardanelles Commission, he was not shown Churchill's telegram instruction to Admiral Carden of 6 January 1915. If he had been he would have

asked for it to be changed, as he did not agree with it: Fisher's *Evidence to Dardanelles Commission,* TNA (PRO), CAB 19/33, Q.3115-7, p.195 (hereafter *Evidence to DC).*

[38]   Penn, *Fisher,* p.24; Marder, *Road to War,* pp.257–58.

[39]   Marder, *Road to War,* p.258.

[40]   Penn, *Fisher,* p.43; Henry Pelling, *Winston Churchill,* Wordsworth Editions, Ware, Hertfordshire, 1999 (first published by Macmillan, London, 1974), p.149.

[41]   The entire Churchill-Bridgeman correspondence covering this unsavoury episode, together with the explanatory—and judiciously edited—paper provided by Churchill to Cabinet, is located at the Imperial War Museum (IWM), within the Bridgeman Papers, Ex 1-44.

[42]   Bridgeman Papers, IWM, Ex 6 of 28 November 1912.

[43]   Ibid.

[44]   Ibid., IWM, Ex 8 of 2 December 1912.

[45]   Ibid., IWM, Ex 9 of 3 December 1912.

[46]   Ibid., IWM, Ex 10 of 4 December 1912.

[47]   *Morning Post,* 14 December 1912; Bridgeman Papers, IWM, Ex 19 of 14 December 1912.

[48]   Bridgeman Papers, IWM, Ex 19 of 14 December 1912.

[49]   Ibid., IWM, Ex 20 of 15 December 1912.

[50]   Ibid., IWM, Ex 15 of 14 December 1912; *The Times,* 14 December 1912.

[51]   Ibid., IWM, Ex 14 of 13 December 1912; the *Standard,* 13 December 1912.

[52]   Ibid., IWM, Ex 17 of 14 December 1912; *The Times,* 14 December 1912. Sir Charles Beresford deplored the fact that 'when Sea Lords differ with [Churchill] on [technical] questions, they are to be suddenly dismissed.' Ibid., IWM, Ex 27 of 16 December 1912.

[53]   Jellicoe Papers, BLIB, ADD, MSS 49007 (ff.45–48), Letter from Commander T.E. Crease, Lord Fisher's Secretary, to Jellicoe, 17 May 1915, expressing Fisher's viewpoint.

[54]   *Dardanelles Commission First Report,* p.10 (hereafter *DCFR).*

[55]   Bacon, *Life of Lord Fisher,* pp.164–67.

[56]   Winston S. Churchill, *The World Crisis,* Vol. II, *1915,* Thornton Butterworth, London, 1923, p.166.

[57]   Bacon, *Life of Lord Fisher,* p.168 (italics added).

[58]   Graham Greene's *Evidence to DC,* Q 3047, p.187.

[59]   TNA (PRO), ADM 137/19. 38, *General Operational Telegrams: The Mediterranean,* Telegram 183 of 30 July 1914.

[60]   Penn, *Fisher,* p.53; Arthur J. Marder, *From the Dreadnought to Scapa Flow; The Royal Navy in the Fisher Era, 1904-1919,* Vol.2, *The War Years: To the Eve of Jutland, 1914-1916,* Oxford University Press, Oxford, 1965 [hereafter, *Dreadnought],* p.22; TNA (PRO) ADM 137/37.38, draft copy of Churchill's telegram instruction to Milne, initialled WSC.

[61]   Sir Julian S. Corbett, *History of the Great War: Naval Operations,* Vol.1, Longmans Green, London, 1921, p.34.

[62]   Ibid., pp.34–36, 54–71; Penn, *Fisher,* p.54.

[63]   Marder, *Dreadnought,* p.40.

[64]   TNA (PRO), ADM 137/19.125b, Telegram 208 of 3 August 1914.

[65]   Corbett, *Naval Operations,* Vol.1, pp.56–57.

[66]   TNA (PRO), ADM 186/605.207, Telegram 222 of 5 August 1914; Corbett, *Naval Operations,* Vol.1, p.58; Marder, *Dreadnought,* p.24. The Austrians had eight battleships and 16 cruisers based at Pola in the Adriatic: TNA(PRO), ADM 137/19.224.

[67]   Corbett, *Naval Operations,* Vol.1, p.60.

[68]   TNA (PRO), ADM 156/76, *Case 662. Escape of German Warships 'Goeben and Breslau'. Court Martial of Rear-Admiral Troubridge, Parts 1 and 2. Held November 5-9 1914, on board H.M.S. Bulwark,* Part 2, p.4. See also Corbett, *Naval Operations,* Vol.1, p.60.

[69]   *Troubridge Court Martial,* Part 2, p.42, attested to by Troubridge's second-in-command, Captain Fawcett Wray.

[70]   TNA (PRO), ADM 186/605.207, Telegram 371 of 12 noon, 8 August 1914; Marder, *Dreadnought,* p.30.

[71]   Marder, *Dreadnought,* p.30; Corbett, *Naval Operations,* Vol.1, p.69.

[72]   TNA (PRO), ADM 186/605.208; ADM 137/19.406, Telegram 239 of 12.50pm, 9 August 1914; Marder, *Dreadnought,* pp.30–31; Corbett, *Naval Operations,* Vol.1, pp.69–70.

[73]   *Troubridge Court Martial,* Part 2, p.2.

[74]   Ibid., Part 1, p.8; Marder, *Dreadnought,* p.33.

[75]   *Troubridge Court Martial,* Milne's evidence, Part 2, pp.16–17.

[76]   Ibid., Part 2, pp.90–91.

[77]   Marder, *Dreadnought,* p.41.

[78]   Churchill, *The World Crisis,* Vol. I, p.240 (italics added).

[79]   Beatty Papers, NMM, BTY/17/30, letter to his wife, 11 October 1914.

[80]   Gilbert, *Winston Churchill,* Vol.3, p.58.

[81]   Richmond Papers, NMM, RIC/1/9 of 20 August 1914. Following a distinguished career at sea, Admiral Sir Herbert Richmond would be appointed Commandant of the Imperial Defence College, 1926–28, then Professor of Naval and Imperial History and Master of Downing College, Cambridge, from 1936 to 1946.

[82]   Churchill, *The World Crisis,* Vol. I, p.237.

[83]   Gilbert, *Winston Churchill,* Vol.3, p.50.

[84]   Richmond Papers, NMM, RIC/1/9.

[85]   Herbert Asquith, *The Earl of Oxford and Asquith: Memories and Reflections, 1852-1927,* Cassell, London, 1928, Vol.2, p.28.

[86]   Hansard, 5th series, Vol.66, cols 176–67, 27 August 1914; Churchill, *The World Crisis,* Vol. I, pp.310–11; Gilbert, *Winston Churchill,* Vol.3, p.56.

[87]   John Keegan, *The First World War,* Vintage, New York, 2000, pp.82–85, 127–28; Liddell Hart, *History of the World War,* pp.49–62.

[88]   Churchill, *The World Crisis,* Vol. I, pp.329–59; Marder, *Dreadnought,* pp.83–85.

[89] Gilbert, *Winston Churchill,* Vol.3, pp.105, 97–133.

[90] Churchill, *The World Crisis,* Vol. I, pp.351, 355.

[91] Henry Stevens, cited in Gilbert, *Winston Churchill,* Vol.3, p.109.

[92] Taylor, *Lloyd George: A Diary,* p.6.

[93] Brock and Brock (eds), *Asquith Letters,* p.263 (Asquith's emphasis).

[94] Penn, *Fisher,* p.64.

[95] Gilbert, *Winston Churchill,* Vol.3, pp.572–607, 608, 611–14, 654–5.

[96] Brock and Brock (eds), *Asquith Letters,* pp.265–66 (italics added).

[97] Ibid., pp.267–68.

[98] Penn, *Fisher,* p.65; Gilbert, *Winston Churchill,* Vol.3, p.125.

[99] Richmond Papers, NMM. RIC/1/10 of 4 October 1914.

[100] Beatty Papers, NMM, BTY/17/30, letter to his wife of 18 October 1914.

[101] *Morning Post,* 13 October 1914.

[102] *The Times,* 14 October 1914.

[103] *Morning Post,* 19 October 1914.

[104]   Taylor, *Lloyd George: A Diary,* p.6.

[105]   Brock and Brock (eds), *Asquith Letters,* p.275 (Asquith's emphasis).

[106]   Gilbert, *Winston Churchill,* Vol.3, p.130.

[107]   Marder, *Dreadnought,* p.84; Penn, *Fisher,* pp.64–66; James, *Churchill: A Study in Failure,* p.62.

[108]   Churchill, *Thoughts and Adventures,* pp.16–17.

[109]   A.G. Gardiner, *Pillars of Society,* Nisbet, London, 1913, p.57.

[110]   Cited in James, *Churchill: A Study in Failure,* p.53.

[111]   Ibid., p.38.

[112]   Marder, *Dreadnought,* p.118.

[113]   TNA (PRO), ADM 137/1022.108A; ADM 186/605.39 of 5 October 1914, 8.20pm. No telegram number given. See also Marder, *Dreadnought,* pp.101–05; Corbett, *Naval Operations,* Vol.1, pp.313–14.

[114]   Bacon, *Life of Lord Fisher,* p.172; Marder, *Dreadnought,* pp.109–10.

[115]   TNA (PRO), ADM 137/1022.109; ADM 186/605.39-40, Telegram 313 of 11 October 1914.

[116]   TNA (PRO), ADM 137/1022.108; ADM 186/605.39, Telegram 312 of 12 October 1914. The confusion in the telegram numbering is symptomatic of this episode. See also Marder, *Dreadnought,* pp.104–05; Corbett, *Naval Operations,* Vol.1, pp.314–15.

[117]   Bacon, *Life of Lord Fisher,* p.175; Churchill, *The World Crisis,* Vol. I, p.414.

[118]   Richmond Papers, NMM RIC/1/10, diary entry of 9 October 1914.

[119]   Corbett, *Naval Operations,* Vol.1, p.315; Bacon, *Life of Lord Fisher,* p.175.

[120]   Ibid.

[121]   TNA (PRO), ADM 137/1022.109; Churchill's Minute (No.8), initialled WSC, of 12 October 1914 (italics added).

[122]   TNA (PRO), ADM 137/1022.109A; ADM 186/605.40, Telegram 100 of 14 October 1914.

[123]   TNA (PRO), ADM 137/1022.109°; ADM 186/605.40, Telegram 316 of 18 October 1914.

[124]   TNA (PRO), ADM 137/1022.110-110A, ADM 186/605.41, Telegram 325 of 27 October 1914.

[125] TNA (PRO), ADM 137/1022.110°, ADM 186/605.41, Telegram 109 of 28 October 1914.

[126] Cited in Marder, *Dreadnought,* p.108; see also pp.112–14.

[127] Ibid., p.111.

[128] Ibid.

[129] Churchill, *The World Crisis,* Vol. I, pp.115, 117; Penn, *Fisher,* p.79.

[130] Asquith letter to the King, TNA (PRO), CAB 41/35/57 of 4 November 1914. See also Asquith Papers, BOD. MSS Asquith 7 (fol.227–28) of 4 November 1914.

[131] Brock and Brock (eds), *Asquith Letters,* p.309.

[132] Beatty Papers, NMM, BTY/17/31, letter to his wife of 11 November 1914.

[133] Taylor, *Lloyd George: A Diary,* pp.10–11.

[134] Gilbert, *Winston Churchill,* Vol.3, p.85; Admiral of the Fleet Sir Roger Keyes, *Naval Memoirs, 1910-1915,* Thornton Butterworth, London, 1934, p.110.

[135] *Morning Post,* 21 October 1914.

[136] Ibid., 22 October 1914.

[137]   TNA (PRO), ADM 186/605.172: Admiralty to CinC, Devonport, of 10 November 1914. Churchill, *The World Crisis,* Vol. I, p.435; Bacon, *Life of Lord Fisher,* p.177; Marder, *Dreadnought,* pp.118–29; Penn, *Fisher,* pp.76–86; Corbett, *Naval Operations,* Vol.1, pp.414–36.

[138]   Churchill, *The World Crisis,* Vol. I, p.435; Bacon, *Life of Lord Fisher,* p.176.

[139]   Geoffrey Bennett, *Naval Battles of the First World War,* Pan Books, London, 1974, p.91.

[140]   TNA (PRO), ADM 186/605.170, Admiralty to I[ntelligence] O[fficer] Monte Video (for forwarding), of 9 November 1914.

[141]   Penn, *Fisher,* p.83; Bacon, *Life of Lord Fisher,* p.177.

[142]   Penn, *Fisher,* pp.83–84; Marder, *Dreadnought,* Vol.2, pp.123–24; Corbett, *Naval Operations,* Vol.1, pp.421–36.

[143]   Marder, *Dreadnought,* p.126; Bacon, *Life of Lord Fisher,* p.179.

[144]   Churchill, *The World Crisis,* Vol. I, p.452.

[145]   Bacon, *Life of Lord Fisher,* pp.178–79.

[146]   Cited in Gilbert, *Winston Churchill,* Vol.3, p.184.

[147]   Cited in Corbett, *Naval Operations,* Vol.1, pp.356–57.

[148]   Spencer C. Tucker, *The Great War 1914-18,* Indiana University Press, Bloomington, 1998, p.48; cited in Gilbert, *Winston Churchill,* Vol.3, p.226.

[149]   Gilbert, ibid., p.302; Gilbert, *Winston S. Churchill, Companion,* Vol.3, part 1, p.530.

[150]   'Suggestions as to the military position', TNA (PRO), CAB 24/1/G.2 of 1 January 1915. See also Lloyd George Papers, HLD, C/16/1.7 of 1 January 1915; Asquith Papers, BOD, MSS Asquith 13 (fol.242–43) of 1 January 1915.

[151]   Lord Hankey, *The Supreme Command, 1914-1918,* Vol.1, Allen & Unwin, London, 1961, pp.250–51.

[152]   Ibid. See also Hankey memorandum, TNA (PRO), CAB 63/4; Penn, *Fisher,* p.114.

[153]   Admiral of the Fleet Lord Fisher, *Fear God and Dread Nought: The Correspondence of Admiral of the Fleet Lord Fisher of Kilverstone,* Arthur J. Marder (ed), Vol.3, Jonathan Cape, London, 1959, pp.117–18 (hereafter *Fisher Correspondence);* Churchill, *The World Crisis,* Vol. II, pp.95–96; Crease Compilation, TNA (PRO), ADM 1/ 28268; Fisher to Hankey, TNA (PRO), CAB 63/4; Hankey, *Supreme*

Command, Vol.1, pp.251–53; Gilbert, *Winston Churchill,* Vol.3, pp.234–36.

Chapter 2

[1]   *DCFR,* p.15, para 49.

[2]   David French, *British Strategy and War Aims 1914-1916,* Allen & Unwin, London, 1986, p.57; A.K. Wildman, *The End of the Russian Imperial Army: The Old Army and the Soldiers' Revolt, March-April 1917,* Princeton University Press, Princeton, 1980, pp.85–88.

[3]   French, *British Strategy,* pp.57, 62.

[4]   L.L. Farrar, *Divide and Conquer: German Efforts to Conclude a Separate Peace 1914-1918,* Columbia University Press, New York, 1978, p.105; G. Ritter, *Sword and Scepter: The Problem of Militarism in Germany,* Vol.3, University of Miami Press, 1972, pp.24–46.

[5]   Norman Stone, *The Eastern Front 1914-1917,* Hodder & Stoughton, London, 1975, pp.33, 67–68, 96.

[6]   *DCFR,* p.15, para 52.

[7]   Crease Compilation, TNA (PRO), ADM 1/ 28268; Hankey's Memorandum, TNA (PRO), CAB 63/18, 51–52; *DCFR,* p.15, para 50.

[8]   Churchill, *The World Crisis,* Vol. II, p.95.

[9]   Hankey Papers, CAM, HNKY 1/1, diary entry, 19 March 1915.

[10]   General Operational Telegrams, The Dardanelles, TNA (PRO), ADM 137/96.715 of 3 January 1915.

[11]   Churchill's *Evidence to DC,* Q. 1261, p.99, 4 October 1916.

[12]   Robin Prior, *Churchill's 'World Crisis' as History,* Croom Helm, London, 1983, p.53.

[13]   TNA (PRO), ADM 137/96. 725 of 5 January 1915.

[14]   Churchill, *The World Crisis,* Vol. II, p.98 (italics added).

[15]   Ibid., p.99.

[16]   Gilbert, *Winston Churchill,* Vol.3, pp.237–38.

[17]   Lynn H. Curtright, *Muddle, Indecision and Setback: British Policy and the Balkan States, August 1914 to the Inception of the Dardanelles Campaign,* Institute for Balkan Studies, Thessaloniki, 1986, p.83. Geoffrey Miller makes a passing reference to this phantom War Council meeting in his 1997 book, *Straits,* p.365.

[18]   TNA (PRO), ADM 137/96.746 of 6 January 1915.

[19]   As Carden wrote to de Robeck, from Malta Hospital on 21 March 1915, three days after the failed naval attack: 'Hope you had satisfactory meeting with [General] Hamilton, and that they will send a proper sized force certainly 150,000 [troops] better if 200,000 I should think, and make a job of it.' De Robeck Papers, CAM, DRBK 4/37.

[20]   Carden's statement to Dardanelles Commission: *DCFR*, p.17, para 56.

[21]   Jackson's *Evidence to DC*, Q. 2051 and Q. 2056, p.142.

[22]   Fisher's *Evidence to DC*, Q. 3115–17, p.195.

[23]   *DCFR*, p.17, para 56.

[24]   TNA (PRO), ADM 137/96.727–8 dated 5 January 1915.

[25]   TNA (PRO), ADM 137/ 96. 738–743 of 5 January 1915.

[26]   *DCFR*, Roch Memorandum, p.50, para 14.

[27]   *DCFR*, p.50, para 16; see also Marder, *Dreadnought*, p.214.

[28]   Commander Crease, Fisher's Naval Assistant and Secretary, described Fisher's response to Churchill's 'Secret and Personal' telegrams to naval commanders at sea as 'sulphurous'. Crease Compilation.

[29] Penn, *Fisher,* p.181; Bacon, *Life of Lord Fisher,* p.260.

[30] *DCFR,* p.50, para 16.

[31] Churchill, *The World Crisis,* Vol. II, p.102; Vice Admiral Carden's Plan, TNA (PRO), ADM 137/96. 777–9 of 11 January 1915.

[32] Prior, *World Crisis as History,* p.56; Marder, *Dreadnought,* p.20.

[33] Churchill, *The World Crisis,* Vol. II, p.102.

[34] Churchill's *Evidence to DC,* Q. 1241, p.98.

[35] Morgan Singer's *Evidence to DC,* Q. 3919 and 3930, pp.229–30.

[36] Tudor's *Evidence to DC,* Q. 2917, p.185.

[37] Jellicoe Papers, BLIB, ADD MSS 49041 (ff.34) of 29 November 1915.

[38] Major General Sir C.E. Callwell, *Experiences of a Dug-out, 1914-1918,* Constable, London, 1920, p.89.

[39] Callwell's *Evidence to DC,* Q. 3665.

[40] Gilbert, *Winston Churchill,* Vol.3, p.203.

[41] Callwell, *Experiences of a Dug-out,* pp.89–91.

[42] Cited by Robert Rhodes James, *Gallipoli,* Batsford, London, 1965, p.4.

[43] 'Secretary's Notes of War Council Meetings', printed for the Committee of Imperial Defence, September 1916, TNA (PRO), CAB 22/1.3rd (henceforth *SNWCM)* of 25 November 1914.

[44] *DCFR,* p.20, para 67.

[45] Balfour Papers, BLIB, ADD MSS, 49703 (ff 166) of 10 February 1915.

[46] General Staff-Admiralty Paper of 19 December 1906, 'The Possibility of a Joint Naval and Military Attack upon the Dardanelles' (endorsed by CID, Paper 92B, February 1907), TNA (PRO), CAB 38/13.12; see also Fisher Papers, CAM. FISR 1/19.1010/103 of 16 May 1915.

[47] *SNWCM,* 7th, of 8 January 1915.

[48] Arthur's *Evidence to DC,* TNA (PRO), CAB 19/28, p.56 of 1 December 1916.

[49] Ibid.

[50] Callwell, *Experiences of a Dug-out,* pp.65–67.

[51] *DCFR,* p.16, para 53. See also George H. Cassar, *Kitchener: Architect of Victory,* William Kimber, London, 1977, p.508.

[52] *SNWCM,* 21st, of 14 May 1915.

[53] TNA (PRO), FO 800/ 377.110 of 6 January 1915.

[54] Fisher's minute to Chief of Staff, Oliver, 12 January 1915, *DCFR,* p.51, para 17, Roch Memorandum.

[55] Admiral of the Fleet Lord Fisher, *Memories,* Hodder and Stoughton, London, 1919, pp.50, 52.

[56] *Public Record Office Handbook, No.11,* Introduction, pp.vii, ix; and Part 1, 'The Cabinet before December 1916', pp.1–2. See also Hankey, *Supreme Command,* Vol.1, pp.238–43.

[57] *DCFR,* pp.5–6, paras 15–16; Penn, *Fisher,* p.111.

[58] Hankey, *Supreme Command,* Vol.1, p.238.

[59] James, *Gallipoli,* p.24.

[60] Sir James Wolfe Murray, *Evidence to DC,* Q. 2648.

[61] *DCFR,* p.47, paras 2–4.

[62] Ibid., p.5, para 15.

[63] Lord Fisher told the Dardanelles Commission that he and Admiral Wilson 'considered themselves to be merely naval advisers, and only entitled to express their opinions when asked for them.' *DCFR,* p.47, para 3.

[64] Lord Crewe's *Evidence to DC,* Q. 5430.

[65] *DCFR,* p.5, para 15.

[66]   Churchill, *The World Crisis,* Vol. II, p.99.

[67]   Hankey, *Supreme Command,* Vol.1, pp.265–66; see also *SNWCM,* 8th, of 13 January 1915.

[68]   *SNWCM,* ibid.

[69]   Prior, *World Crisis as History,* p.57, (italics added). Prior adds: 'The theory that Churchill first gained the War Council's agreement to the naval attack before pointing out the need for followup or occupation troops cannot definitely be proved, but in the light of the available evidence must remain the most likely explanation' (p.80).

[70]   Churchill, *The World Crisis,* Vol. II, pp.183–89; *DCFR,* pp.32–33, paras 101–06.

[71]   Viscount Grey of Falloden. *Twenty Five Years, 1892-1916,* Vol.2, Hodder & Stoughton, London, 1925, pp.297–98.

[72]   Brock and Brock (eds), *Asquith Letters,* p.284.

[73]   *SNWCM,* 8th, 13 January 1915.

[74]   *DCFR,* pp.21–22, paras 70–72.

[75]   Aspinall-Oglander, *Gallipoli,* Vol.1, p.59.

[76]   Churchill, *The World Crisis,* Vol. II, p.113. Martin Gilbert claims, erroneously, that Churchill sent this minute to both Oliver and Fisher on 13 January. Gilbert, *Winston Churchill,* Vol.3, p.253.

[77]   Penn, *Fisher,* p.176.

[78]   Churchill, *The World Crisis,* Vol. II, pp.113–15 (italics added).

[79]   Penn, *Fisher,* p.176. Jackson told the Dardanelles Commission that he 'concurred' on the technical aspects of Carden's proposals because 'it was approved to do it.' He then added, 'Whether the game was worth the candle is another thing.' *DCFR,* p.52, para 20.

[80]   Scott, *Fifty Years in the Royal Navy,* pp.295–96.

[81]   Churchill, *The World Crisis,* Vol. II, p.48 (italics added).

[82]   Sir Julian S. Corbett, *History of the Great War: Naval Operations,* Vol.2, Longmans Green, London, 1921, p.105.

[83]   Hankey, *Supreme Command,* Vol.1, p.269; Asquith, *Memories,* Vol.2, p.37.

[84]   Hankey, *Supreme Command,* Vol.1, p.300.

[85]   Balfour Papers, BLIB, ADD MSS 49703 (ff 152), of 21 January 1915.

[86]   Fisher's *Evidence to DC,* Q. 3089 and 3123, pp.192, 196.

[87]   Ibid., Q. 3129 and 3131, p.196.

[88] Hankey diary entry, CAM, HNKY 1/1 of 12 March 1915.

[89] Ibid. of 19 March 1915 (italics added).

[90] Graham Greene Papers, NMM, GEE/3 of 1 December 1915.

[91] Question to Graham Greene, *Evidence to DC,* Q. 3047, p.187.

[92] Bacon, *Life of Lord Fisher,* p.168 (italics added). See also Crease Compilation.

[93] Penn, *Fisher,* p.76.

[94] Churchill, *The World Crisis,* Vol. I, pp.239–41.

[95] TNA (PRO), ADM 137/ 96. 804 of 15 January 1915.

[96] Churchill, *The World Crisis,* Vol. II, pp.119, 158.

[97] Jellicoe Papers, BLIB, ADD MSS 49006 (ff.119–20) of 19 January 1915 (Fisher's emphasis).

[98] Ibid., (ff.121–24) of 21 January 1915 (italics added).

[99] Fisher's *Evidence to DC,* Q. 3089, p.192.

[100] Churchill, *The World Crisis,* Vol. II, p.120 (italics added).

[101] Ibid., p.121 (italics added).

[102] Ibid., p.122 (italics added).

[103] *DCFR,* p.54, para 28.

[104] Hankey, *Supreme Command,* Vol.1, p.269.

[105] 'Memorandum by the First Sea Lord on the Position of the British Fleet and its Policy of Steady Pressure', TNA (PRO), CAB 63/ 4, 16–20; Hankey, *Supreme Command,* Vol.1, pp.269–70; Balfour Papers, BLIB, ADD MSS 49712 (ff 137–43); Crease Compilation, 25 January 1915.

[106] Fisher Papers, Fisher letter to Churchill, CAM, FISR 1/18, 963 of 31 March 1915 (Fisher's emphasis).

[107] Cited by Marder, *Dreadnought,* p.77.

[108] Bacon, *Life of Lord Fisher,* p224.

[109] *DCFR,* p.7, para 19.

[110] Marder, *Dreadnought,* p.176.

[111] Bacon, *Life of Lord Fisher,* p.205.

[112] Churchill, *The World Crisis,* Vol. II, p.154; Crease Compilation, 25 January 1915.

[113] Churchill, *The World Crisis,* Vol. II, p.157.

[114] Crease Compilation, 26 January, 1915. Higgins writes: 'Most unwisely Fisher consented to this suggestion and much of the War Council

480

thus never became acquainted with the views of the First Sea Lord or of the Admiralty War Staff until it was too late.' See Trumbull Higgins, *Winston Churchill and the Dardanelles,* Heinemann, London, 1963, p.124.

[115]   Churchill, *The World Crisis,* Vol. II, p.159.

[116]   Ibid., pp.159–62. See also Crease Compilation, 28 January 1915, TNA (PRO), CAB 37/137.

[117]   Hankey, *Supreme Command,* Vol.1, p.270.

[118]   Fisher Papers, CAM, FISR 1/18.926; Crease Compilation, 28 January 1915.

[119]   Fisher Papers, CAM, FISR 1/18.927, 28 January 1915.

[120]   Churchill, *The World Crisis,* Vol. II, p.162; Hankey, *Supreme Command,* Vol.1, p.270.

[121]   *SNWCM,* 9th, of 28 January 1915.

[122]   Ibid.

[123]   W.W. Gottlieb, *Studies in Secret Diplomacy during the First World War,* Allen & Unwin, London, 1957, pp.89–90; Higgins, *Dardanelles,* p.95.

[124]   *SNWCM,* 9th, of 28 January 1915.

[125]   Bacon, *Life of Lord Fisher,* p.210.

[126]   Fisher, *Memories,* p.59.

[127]   *SNWCM,* 9th, of 28 January 1915.

[128]   Ibid.

[129]   Howitzers fire individually, at a high angle up into the air, and can thus drop their shells precisely onto their targets. Naval guns, on the other hand, have a very low angle of fire (with a maximum elevation of about 15 degrees), and are designed to fire over long distances (of eight miles or more) in broadside salvoes at distant ships on the horizon. Near misses against land targets from naval guns would, consequently, either drop short or fly harmlessly overhead. This crucial distinction was belatedly clarified at the Dardanelles Commission. See *DCFR,* pp.24–25, paras 78–82; Scott, *Royal Navy,* pp.327–31.

[130]   Churchill, *The World Crisis,* Vol. II, p.165.

[131]   Jellicoe Papers, BLIB, ADD MSS 49006 (ff 129–30) of 29 January 1915 (Fisher's emphasis).

[132]   Asquith's *Evidence to DC,* Q. 5826, p.352.

[133]   Churchill, *The World Crisis,* Vol. II, p.166.

[134]   Ibid., p.165.

[135]   Fisher's *Evidence to DC,* Q. 3087, p.191.

Chapter 3

[1]   Gilbert, *Winston Churchill,* Vol 3, p.277.

[2]   Admiralty Operations Orders for the naval attack against the Dardanelles, TNA (PRO), ADM 137/1089, 83–95, of 5 February, 1915; Prior, *World Crisis as History,* p.85.

[3]   TNA (PRO), ADM 137/ 96.950, of 6 February 1915.

[4]   TNA (PRO), ADM 137/ 96.868, of 25 January 1915.

[5]   TNA (PRO), ADM 137/ 96.972, of 9 February 1915.

[6]   TNA (PRO), ADM 137/ 96.956, of 7 February 1915, re Telegram No.97 from French Marine.

[7]   *SNWCM,* 12th, of 9 February 1915.

[8]   *DCFR,* p.27, para 88.

[9]   Churchill, *The World Crisis,* Vol. II, p.\178 (italics added).

[10]   Richmond Papers, NMM RIC 1/12, of 14 February 1915; Higgins, *Dardanelles,* p.139.

[11]   Lloyd George Papers, HLD LG, C/11/ 5 and 6.

[12]   TNA (PRO), CAB 42/1/33, of 2 February 1915.

[13] Richmond Papers, NMM RIC 1/12, of 14 February 1915 (Fisher's emphasis).

[14] TNA (PRO), CAB 63/17.2 (italics added).

[15] TNA (PRO), ADM 137/1089.108–116, of 15 February 1915.

[16] Churchill, *The World Crisis,* Vol. II, p.179.

[17] Gilbert, *Winston Churchill,* Vol.3, p.287.

[18] Churchill, *The World Crisis,* Vol. I, p.491.

[19] Cited by Marder, *Dreadnought,* p.231.

[20] Cited by James, *Gallipoli,* p.46.

[21] *Conclusions of War Council* (Hankey was not present so notes were not taken), *SNWCM,* 13th, of 16 February 1915.

[22] Churchill, *The World Crisis,* Vol. II, p.181.

[23] Ibid., p.179.

[24] Ibid., p.181.

[25] Gilbert, *Winston Churchill,* Vol.3, pp.296–97.

[26] Churchill, *The World Crisis,* Vol. II, p.182.

[27] *SNWCM,* 14th, of 19 February 1915.

[28] Ibid.

[29] Hankey, *Supreme Command,* Vol.1, p.282; *SNWCM,* 14th, of 19 February 1915.

[30] Heathcote-Smith, TNA (PRO), ADM 137/96.823, of 17 January 1915; *La Guerre Turque dans la Guerre Mondiale,* traduit en français par Major M. Larcher, US Army War College, Washington, 1931, p.73 cites 250,000 Turkish troops (17 divisions) in these areas.

[31] *SNWCM,* 14th, of 19 February 1915.

[32] Ibid.

[33] Ibid.

[34] Higgins, *Dardanelles,* p.141.

[35] Churchill, *The World Crisis,* Vol. II, pp.167–68.

[36] Corbett, *Naval Operations,* Vol.2, pp.145–46.

[37] *The Times,* 22 February 1915.

[38] Taylor, *Lloyd George: A Diary,* p.50.

[39] Lord Riddell, *War Diary, 1914-1918,* Nicholson & Watson, London, 1934, p.204.

[40] Hankey, *Supreme Command,* Vol.1, p.283 (Hankey's italics).

[41] George H. Cassar, *Asquith as War Leader,* Hambledon, London, 1994,68.

[42] Hankey letter to Esher, 15 March 1915, cited by Gilbert, *Winston Churchill,* Vol.3, p.345.

[43] Churchill, *The World Crisis,* Vol. II, pp.183–84.

[44]   Ibid., p.183.

[45]   Ibid., pp.183–84.

[46]   *SNWCM,* 15th, of 24 February 1915.

[47]   Ibid.

[48]   Ibid.

[49]   Ibid.

[50]   Ibid.

[51]   *SNWCM,* 16th, of 26 February 1915.

[52]   Prior, *World Crisis as History,* p.87.

[53]   TNA (PRO), WO 159/ 3 of 24 February 1915; *SNWCM,* 16th, of 26 February 1915.

[54]   *SNWCM,* 16th, of 26 February 1915.

[55]   Prior, *World Crisis as History,* p.82.

[56]   Corbett, *Naval Operations,* Vol.2, pp.157–83; Marder, *Dreadnought,* pp.229–35; James, *Gallipoli,* p.45.

[57]   *The Times,* 27 February 1915; *New York Times,* 27 February 1915.

[58]   *New York Times,* 28 February 1915; *Observer,* 28 February 1915.

[59]   Churchill, *The World Crisis,* Vol. II, p.193.

486

[60] *London Daily Chronicle,* 1 March 1915; *New York Times,* 1 March 1915.

[61] *New York Times,* 2, 3 March 1915.

[62] *The Times,* 3 March 1915.

[63] *SNWCM,* 17th, of 3 March 1915.

[64] Ibid., announced as 'the principal business for which this meeting has been called'.

[65] Ibid.

[66] TNA (PRO), FO 371/2173/46456, British Ambassador to Russia, Buchanan, to Foreign Office, 5 September 1914; French, *British Strategy,* pp.20, 36.

[67] French, *British Strategy,* pp.56–57.

[68] Ibid., p.57.

[69] Grey's *Evidence to DC,* TNA (PRO), CAB 19/33, Q.791.

[70] *SNWCM,* 17th, of 3 March 1915.

[71] TNA (PRO), CAB 37/125.28, of 9 March 1915; David, *Inside Asquith's Cabinet,* p.227.

[72] Cited by William A. Renzi, 'Great Britain, Russia and the Straits, 1914-1915', *Journal of Modern History,* Vol.42, Issue 1, March 1970, pp.1–20. p.20.

[73] General Erich von Falkenhayn, *General Headquarters 1914-1916 and its Critical Decisions,* Hutchinson, London, 1919, p.294.

[74] *SNWCM,* 18th, of 10 March 1915; *Conclusions* of War Council; TNA (PRO), CAB 37/126/3; Grey to Buchanan, of 11 March 1915.

[75] Cited in Marder, *Dreadnought,* p.240.

[76] French, *British Strategy,* p.31; David Thomson, *Europe since Napoleon,* Penguin Books, Harmondsworth, 1966, pp.473–76; A.J.P. Taylor, *The Struggle for Mastery in Europe, 1848-1914,* Oxford University Press, Oxford, 1971, pp.490–500. For Britain, mounting a second front against Austria-Hungary would have meant replacing a 22-mile supply line across the English Channel with a 3000-mile line of communications, either across the Alps along a primitive, single-line railway track, or along the Danube. The idea was quite farcical. Further, as Professor French notes, the Balkan states may have been able to send large peasant armies into the field, but they lacked an industrial infrastructure and were consequently dependent on outsiders for arms and ammunition—of which both Britain and France were acutely short in 1915. French, *British Strategy,* p.31.

[77] Hankey Papers, CAM HNKY 1/1.4, diary entry, 6 March 1915 (as Hankey notes, there was 'a

lag in [this] information reaching London', re the date of his diary entry); Hankey, *Supreme Command,* Vol.1, p.286.

[78] Churchill, *The World Crisis,* Vol. II, pp.201, 202; Hankey, *Supreme Command,* Vol.1, p.286.

[79] Gilbert, *Winston Churchill,* Vol.3, p.328.

[80] TNA (PRO), FO 371/2243, Buchanan to Grey, of 3 March 1915; Prior, *World Crisis as History,* p.89.

[81] TNA (PRO), FO 371/2243, Elliot to Grey, of 3 March 1915; French, *British Strategy,* p.81.

[82] For example, Gilbert, *Winston Churchill,* Vol.3 and Liddell Hart, *A History of the World War* among others.

[83] Cited in Prior, *World Crisis as History,* p.89.

[84] David, *Inside Asquith's Cabinet,* p.208; French, *British Strategy,* p.51.

[85] TNA (PRO), FO 371/2164/37861, British Minister to Roumania, Sir George Barclay to Foreign Office, 10 August 1914.

[86] TNA (PRO), FO 800/377, British Minister at Sofia, Sir Henry Bax-Ironside, to Foreign Office, 12 February 1915; French, *British* Strategy, p.72.

[87] TNA (PRO), FO 371/2243, Elliot to Grey, 4 March 1915; Prior, *World Crisis as History,* p.90.

[88] TNA (PRO), ADM 137/1336, Bax-Ironside to Grey, 10 March 1915.

[89] Cited in Prior, *World Crisis as History,* pp.91–92.

[90] Corbett, *Naval Operations,* Vol.2, pp.186–87; Marder, *Dreadnought,* p.234.

[91] Cited by Prior, *World Crisis as History,* p.86.

[92] TNA (PRO), ADM 137/1089, of 10 March 1915; Prior, *World Crisis as History,* p.92.

[93] TNA (PRO), ADM 137/109.386-8, of 10 March 1915.

[94] Marder, *Dreadnought,* p.231; Penn, *Fisher,* p.122.

[95] TNA (PRO), ADM 137/109.389-90, of 11 March 1915 (italics added).

[96] Churchill, *The World Crisis,* Vol. II, p.217.

[97] TNA (PRO), ADM 137/109.407, of 11 March 1915. Churchill wrote on this telegram: (Note–Not to be filed).

[98] *SNWCM,* 18th, of 10 March 1915.

[99] Ibid.

[100] Ibid.

[101] *SNWCM,* 15th, of 24 February 1915; *SNWCM,* 16th, of 26 February 1915 (italics added).

[102] Falkenhayn, *General Headquarters,* p.77.

[103] Tirpitz, *My Memories,* Vol.2, p.549.

[104] David French, 'Origins of the Dardanelles campaign reconsidered', *History,* Vol.68, No.223 (1983), pp.210–24. The last of 'Victoria's little wars' had been fought at Omdurman in 1898, when Kitchener led a 23,000-strong British army against 50,000 Dervishes. The 'battle' lasted a few hours only. The spear-wielding Dervishes failed even to reach the British line, as they were mown down by artillery and machine-gun fire. They lost 11,000 warriors killed, with a further 13,000 wounded (many of whom subsequently died). The British losses totalled 48 men—killed during a vainglorious cavalry charge into the Dervish ranks, for which three Victoria Crosses were awarded. See Cyril Falls, 'Reconquest of the Sudan, 1896-9' in Brian Bond (ed), *Victorian Military Campaigns,* Hutchinson, London, 1967, pp.294–99. Churchill also took part in the battle of Omdurman as a cavalry lieutenant.

[105] James, *Gallipoli,* p.16.

[106]   Cited in Gilbert, *Winston Churchill,* Vol.3, p.813.

[107]   Marder, *Fisher Correspondence,* Vol.2, p.385.

[108]   David, *Inside Asquith's Cabinet,* p.222.

[109]   Hankey Papers, CAM HNKY 1/1.2, diary entry of 4 March 1915; French, *British Strategy,* p.84.

[110]   David, *Inside Asquith's Cabinet,* p.225.

[111]   Hall's *Evidence to DC,* Q. 4909-11; French, *British Strategy,* pp.84, 218.

[112]   Henry Morgenthau, *Secrets of the Bosporus,* Hutchinson, London, 1918, p.131.

[113]   Prior, *World Crisis as History,* p.101.

[114]   Morgenthau, *Secrets of the Bosporus,* pp.122, 128.

[115]   Ibid., pp.129–30, 134.

[116]   Ibid., pp.134–44.

[117]   Ibid., pp.143–44.

[118]   Corbett, *Naval Operations,* Vol.2, pp.205–11; Marder, *Dreadnought,* pp.230–31; James, *Gallipoli,* p.15.

[119]   Marder, *Dreadnought,* p.265; James, *Gallipoli,* p.49.

492

[120]   Arthur J. Marder, *From the Dardanelles to Oran, Studies of the Royal Navy in Peace and War,* Oxford University Press, Oxford, 1974, pp.24–25; Marder, *Dreadnought,* pp.264–65.

[121]   'Report on minesweeping during March 1915', TNA (PRO), ADM 137/1089.289/1-19; Corbett, *Naval Operations,* Vol.2, pp.206–07.

[122]   TNA (PRO), ADM 137/109. 464, of 13 March 1915.

[123]   TNA (PRO), ADM 137/109. 466, of 13 March 1915.

[124]   Keyes, *Naval Memoirs,* Vol.1, p.212.

[125]   James, *Gallipoli,* p.50; Corbett, *Naval Operations,* Vol.2, pp.206–09; 'Report of minesweeping during March', TNA (PRO), ADM 137/1089.289/1–19; 'Operations of 13 March, re minesweeping', TNA (PRO), ADM 1089/289/20-29; 'Recommendations [for bravery awards]', TNA (PRO), ADM 137/1089/289/75-82; 'Officers and men of *Amethyst,* singled out for particular praise, together with officers and men employed on the trawler-minesweepers', TNA (PRO), ADM 137/1090/289/32-44.

[126]   TNA (PRO), ADM 137/109.503, of 14 March 1915.

[127] TNA (PRO), ADM 137/109.512, of 14 March 1915.

[128] Churchill, *The World Crisis,* Vol. II, p.216.

[129] Jellicoe Papers, BLIB, ADD MSS 49006, Vol. xviii, of 15 March 1915.

[130] Ibid.; Prior, *World Crisis as History,* p.93.

[131] Gilbert, *Winston Churchill,* Vol.3, p.346.

[132] Fisher Papers, CAM, FISR 1/18.951, of 15 March 1915.

[133] TNA (PRO), ADM 137/109.518-519, of 15 March 1915.

[134] TNA (PRO), ADM 137/109, of 15 March 1915. There is no copy of this telegram in the Admiralty files at the National Archives. The only copies are held at the Churchill Archives Centre, Cambridge, and in the Graham Greene Papers, GEE/11, at the National Maritime Museum, Greenwich.

[135] TNA (PRO), ADM 137/109.519, of 15 March 1915.

[136] TNA (PRO), ADM 137/109.569, of 16 March 1915.

[137] TNA (PRO), ADM 137/109.599, of 17 March 1915 (italics added).

[138]   TNA (PRO), ADM 137/110.11, of 18 March 1915.

[139]   Corbett, *Naval Operations,* Vol.2, p.215; James, *Gallipoli,* p.60.

[140]   Marder, *Dreadnought,* pp.246–47; James, *Gallipoli,* p.64.

[141]   Morgenthau, *Secrets of the Bosporus,* p.140.

[142]   'Report and Detailed Narrative of Naval Attack on 18 March 1915', TNA (PRO), ADM 137/39.5-19; Corbett, *Naval Operations,* pp.213–23.

[143]   Corbett, Naval Operations, Vol.2, p.223; Marder, *Dreadnought,* pp.246–49.

[144]   Marder, *Dreadnought,* p.249.

[145]   TNA (PRO), ADM 137/110.26-29, of 19 March 1915; Gilbert, *Winston Churchill* Companion 1 to Vol.3, pp.708–09.

Chapter 4

[1]   Churchill, *The World Crisis,* Vol. II, p.222.

[2]   Corbett, *Naval Operations,* Vol.2, pp.213–24.

[3]   Ibid., pp.223, 217–18.

[4]   Churchill, *The World Crisis,* Vol. II, p.230.

[5]   *SNWCM,* 19th, of 19 March 1915.

[6]   Ibid.

[7]   Gilbert, *Winston Churchill,* Vol.3, pp.357–58.

[8]   Marder, *Oran,* p.15; Admiral W. James, *The Eyes of the Navy: A Biographical Study of Admiral Sir Reginald Hall,* Methuen, London, 1956, pp.62–63 (italics added).

[9]   James, *Eyes of the Navy,* p.62. Admiral G. von Müller was Chief of the German Naval Cabinet. Admiral von Usedom was Inspector-General of (Turkey's) Coastal Fortifications.

[10] Ibid.

[11] TNA (PRO), ADM 137/109.466, of 13 March 1915; Keyes, *Naval Memoirs,* pp.216–17.

[12] TNA (PRO), ADM 137/110.113-4, of 22 March 1915 (italics added).

[13] TNA (PRO), ADM 137/110.52, of 20 March 1915.

[14] Gilbert, *Winston Churchill,* Vol.3, p.359.

[15] Ibid., pp.359–60 (italics added).

[16] James, *Eyes of the Navy,* p.63.

[17] Churchill, *The World Crisis,* Vol. II, pp.256–57.

[18] Cited by Marder, *Dreadnought,* p.230.

[19] Churchill, *The World Crisis,* Vol. II, p.257.

[20]   Ibid.

[21]   'Admiralty Committee appointed to investigate the attacks delivered on, and the enemy defences of the Dardanelles Straits', Commodore F. Mitchell, President, TNA (PRO), ADM 186/600 and 601-2, of 10 October 1919 (henceforth *Mitchell Committee Report*).

[22]   Churchill, *The World Crisis,* Vol. II, pp.257, 262; *Mitchell Committee Report,* pp.71, 436–38; Corbett, *Naval Operations,* Vol.2, pp.223–24; Aspinall-Oglander, *Gallipoli Campaign,* p.105; Prior, *World Crisis as History,* pp.97–101.

[23]   *Morning Post,* 25 March 1915; Penn, *Fisher,* p.156.

[24]   TNA (PRO), ADM 1161/1336, 25 March 1915; Gilbert, *Winston Churchill,* Vol.3, p.372.

[25]   Penn, *Fisher,* p.156.

[26]   Evidence in the German Foreign Ministry Archives, cited in Ulrich Trumpener, 'German Military Aid to Turkey in 1914: An Historical Evaluation', *Journal of Modern History,* Vol.32, Issue 2, 1960, pp.145–49.

[27]   Prior, *World Crisis as History,* p.115.

[28]   TNA (PRO), ADM 137/110.54, of 20 March 1915.

[29] Marder, *Dreadnought,* pp.253, 263–65; Prior, *World Crisis as History,* pp.99–100.

[30] TNA (PRO), ADM 137/110.81, of 21 March 1915 (italics added).

[31] Rear-Admiral de Robeck, Second-in-Command, Eastern Mediterranean Squadron, 'Appreciation of present position in Dardanelles and proposals for future operations', Godfrey Papers, IWM. 69/33/1, of 9 March 1915. De Robeck wrote that 'the forts could be dominated but not destroyed and ... the situation is therefore reduced to a point where strong military co-operation is considered essential in order to clear at least one side of the straits of the enemy and their movable batteries'.

[32] TNA (PRO), ADM 137/110.81, of 21 March 1915 (italics added).

[33] Cited by Marder, *Oran,* pp.23, 25; Marder, *Dreadnought,* pp.253, 263–65.

[34] Marder, *Oran,* p.25. Lieutenant Sandford, volunteer skipper of a trawler-sweeper on the night of 13 March, was responsible for the successful conversion of the Beagle destroyers to heavy minesweepers (correspondence between Captain Boswell and Professor Marder); Marder, *Oran,* pp.24–25.

498

[35]   Admiral Wester Wemyss, *The Navy in the Dardanelles Campaign,* Hodder & Stoughton, London, 1924, pp.41–43.

[36]   TNA (PRO), ADM 137/110.81-2, of 21 March 1915.

[37]   Ibid., p.82.

[38]   Churchill, *The World Crisis,* Vol. II, p.247.

[39]   Marder, *Dreadnought,* pp.241, 251; *DCFR,* p.37, para 114.

[40]   Marder, *Dreadnought,* p.251.

[41]   TNA (PRO), ADM 137/110.129, of 23 March 1915.

[42]   Churchill, *The World Crisis,* Vol. II, p.233.

[43]   Ibid., pp.233–34; TNA (PRO), ADM 116/1348, of 24 March 1915 (italics added).

[44]   Penn, *Fisher,* p.158.

[45]   *DCFR,* p.59, para 51; Marder, *Dreadnought,* p.255.

[46]   Churchill, *The World Crisis,* Vol. II, p.234.

[47]   Ibid., p.235 (italics added).

[48]   Ibid., pp.248–49.

[49]   TNA (PRO), ADM 137/110.116, of 22 March 1915.

[50] TNA (PRO), ADM 137/110.140, of 23 March 1915.

[51] TNA (PRO), ADM 137/110.147, of 23 March 1915.

[52] TNA (PRO), ADM 137/110.168 a-c, of 24 March 1915.

[53] Churchill, *The World Crisis,* Vol. II, p.264.

[54] Ibid.

[55] Ibid., pp.265–66.

[56] Morgenthau, *Secrets of the Bosporus,* pp.148–49.

[57] Churchill, *The World Crisis,* Vol. II, p.265.

[58] Morgenthau, *Secrets of the Bosporus,* p.127.

[59] Churchill, *The World Crisis,* Vol. II, p.261.

[60] Keyes, *Naval Memoirs,* pp.252–53.

[61] Churchill, *The World Crisis,* Vol. II, p.261.

[62] TNA (PRO), ADM 137/96.777-9, of 11 January 1915.

[63] TNA (PRO), ADM 137/96.835, of 19 January 1915.

[64] TNA (PRO), ADM 137/96.868, of 25 January 1915.

[65]   TNA (PRO), ADM 137/96.939, of 4 February 1915.

[66]   TNA (PRO), ADM 137/96.950, of 6 February 1915.

[67]   Marder, *Dreadnought,* pp.71–72.

[68]   Jellicoe, *The Grand Fleet,* pp.121, 210.

[69]   'Report of minesweeping during March', TNA (PRO), ADM 137/1089.289/1-19.

[70]   Carden's telegrams to Churchill: TNA (PRO); ADM 137/109.512, of 14 March 1915 and TNA (PRO), ADM 137/109, of 15 March. There is no page number for this last telegram, as no copy is held in the Admiralty Files at The National Archives, Kew. Copies are only to be found at Churchill College Archives, Cambridge, and at the National Maritime Museum, Greenwich, within the Graham Greene Papers, GEE/ 11.

[71]   TNA (PRO), ADM 137/96.777-9, of 11 January 1915; TNA (PRO), ADM 137/96.835, of 19 January 1915; TNA (PRO), ADM 137/96.938, of 4 February 1915; TNA (PRO), ADM 137/109. 512, of 14 March 1915; TNA (PRO), ADM 137/109, of 15 March 1915, no page number.

[72]   TNA (PRO), ADM 137/109.538, of 15 March 1915.

[73] Churchill's reply to Carden: TNA (PRO), ADM 137/109.519, of 15 March 1915.

[74] Corbett, *Naval Operations,* p.224.

[75] Graham Greene Papers, NMM, GEE/11, of 11 May 1915.

[76] Churchill, *The World Crisis,* Vol. II, p.251.

[77] Prior, *World Crisis as History,* p.96.

[78] Ibid.

[79] *DCFR,* p.40, para 119; *Annual Register, 1917,* p.55.

[80] Churchill, *The World Crisis,* Vol. II, p.169.

[81] Ibid., p.487.

[82] Ibid., p.244.

[83] Marder, *Dreadnought,* pp.256–57.

[84] TNA (PRO), CAB 63/4.16-20.

[85] Limpus Papers, NMM, LIM / 66, of 27 March 1915.

[86] TNA (PRO), ADM 137/110.222-5, of 27 March 1915 (italics added).

[87] TNA (PRO), ADM 137/110.233b, of 27 March 1915.

[88] Hankey letter to Lord Esher, 15 March 1915, cited in Gilbert, *Winston Churchill,* Vol.3, p.345.

[89]   Hankey, *Supreme Command,* Vol.1, pp.291–92.

[90]   Ibid., p.294.

[91]   Hankey Papers, CAM, HNKY 1/1, diary entry of 20 March 1915.

[92]   Brock and Brock (eds), *Asquith Letters,* p.520 (Asquith's emphasis).

[93]   Marder, *Fisher Correspondence,* p.173.

[94]   Ibid., p.176.

[95]   Ibid., pp.180–81 (Fisher's emphasis).

[96]   Fisher Papers, CAM, FISR 1/19.968/22, of 2 April 1915 (Fisher's emphasis).

[97]   Gilbert, *Winston Churchill,* Vol.3, p.765.

[98]   Jellicoe Papers, BLIB, ADD MSS 49007 (ff 5-6), of 4 April 1915.

[99]   Churchill, *The World Crisis,* Vol. II, p.303.

[100]   *DCFR,* p.15.

[101]   Ibid.

[102]   Hankey Papers, CAM, HNKY, diary entry of 6 April 1915 (italics added). Gilbert, *Winston Churchill,* Vol.3, p.386, describes this 'informal War Council' with Churchill and Kitchener 'in agreement'.

[103]   *DCFR,* p.56, para 35.

[104]   *SNWCM,* 20th, of 6 April 1915 (italics added).

[105]   James, *Gallipoli,* pp.202, 319; Higgins, *Winston Churchill and the Dardanelles,* pp.151, 160–61.

[106]   Hankey Papers, CAM, HNKY 1/1, diary entry of 6 April 1915; Hankey, *Supreme Command,* Vol.1, p.300.

[107]   Hankey diary entry, CAM, HNKY 1/1, of 7 April 1915; Hankey, *Supreme Command,* Vol.1, p.301.

[108]   Hankey diary entry, CAM, HNKY 1/1, of 8 April 1915.

[109]   Balfour Papers, BLIB, ADD, MSS 49694, ff 105-6, of 8 April 1915.

[110]   Gilbert, *Winston Churchill,* Vol.3, *Companion,* p.780.

[111]   David, *Inside Asquith's Cabinet,* p.234; TNA (PRO), CAB 37/127, 7 April 1915; TNA (PRO), CAB 41/36/15, of 7 April 1915. Martin Gilbert stresses that Churchill's responsibility for the Gallipoli invasion ended after 27 March when the landings became the responsibility of the War Office and Kitchener: Gilbert, *Winston Churchill,* Vol.3, p.380. Churchill's actions and written statements of 6, 7 and 8 April, as described here, are, however, at odds with that claim.

[112] Taylor, *Lloyd George. A Diary,* p.65.

[113] Hankey Papers, CAM, HNKY 1/1, diary entry of 8 April 1915; Hankey, *Supreme Command,* Vol.1, p.301.

[114] Hankey, diary entry of 11 April 1915; Hankey, *Supreme Command,* Vol.1, pp.301–02.

[115] Gilbert, *Winston Churchill,* Vol.3, p.394.

[116] Jellicoe Papers, BLIB, ADD MSS 49007, Vol. xix of 20 April 1915.

[117] *Hansard,* 5th Series, Vol.71, cols 398–99, of 22 April 1915.

[118] F.M. Cutlack (ed), *War Letters of General Sir John Monash,* Angus & Robertson, Sydney, 1934, pp.69–70. Monash has been lauded by historians as 'a commander of exceptional vision and ability'. See Peter Pederson, 'General Sir John Monash' in D.M. Horner, *The Commanders: Australian Military Leadership in the Twentieth Century,* Allen & Unwin, Sydney, 1984, p.85.

[119] Churchill, *The World Crisis,* Vol. II, pp.248–49.

Chapter 5

[1] Tom Curran, *Across the Bar. The Story of "Simpson", The Man with the Donkey: Australia and Tyneside's Great Military Hero,* Ogmios

Publications, Brisbane, 1994, p.194; Moorehead, *Gallipoli,* p.116; James, *Gallipoli,* p.80.

[2] John Laffin, *Damn The Dardanelles!* Sun Papermac, South Melbourne, 1985, p.31; Moorehead, *Gallipoli,* p.117; Curran, *Across the Bar,* pp.194–95.

[3] James, *Gallipoli,* p.79; Moorehead, *Gallipoli,* pp.117–18.

[4] Moorehead, *Gallipoli,* p.119; James, *Gallipoli,* p.79; Curran, *Across the Bar,* p.196.

[5] James, *Gallipoli,* p.93.

[6] Ibid., pp.93–94; *The Times,* 22 February 1915; Curran, *Across the Bar,* p.195.

[7] James, *Gallipoli,* pp.71–77; Bean, *Official History,* Vol. I, *The Story of Anzac,* pp.236–240.

[8] Australian War Memorial figures, cited in Alan Moorehead, *Gallipoli,* p.300. Turkish casualties numbered 251,000 with 86,692 dead or missing.

[9] Bean, *Official History,* Vol. I, *The Story of Anzac,* pp.565–70, 605.

[10] James, *Gallipoli,* pp.123, 133–34; Laffin, *Damn The Dardanelles,* pp.58–59; Moorehead, *Gallipoli,* pp.145–48; Curran, *Across the Bar,* pp.272–73.

[11] Higgins, *Dardanelles,* pp.132–33.

506

[12]   TNA (PRO), ADM 116/1348, of 10 May 1915; CAM, FISR 1/19.989, of 10 May 1915.

[13]   Churchill, *The World Crisis,* Vol. II, p.338.

[14]   Ibid.

[15]   Gilbert, *Winston Churchill,* Vol 3, p.856.

[16]   TNA (PRO), ADM 137/154, of 11 May 1915; Graham Greene Papers, NMM, GEE/11, of 11 May 1915.

[17]   Hankey Papers, CAM, HNKY 1/1, diary entry of 11 May 1915.

[18]   TNA (PRO), CAB 63/4.30-33; Fisher Papers, CAM, FISR 1/19.990/, of 11 May 1915.

[19]   Fisher Papers, CAM, FISR 1/19.991/, of 11 May 1915; TNA (PRO), CAB 63/4.23-4.

[20]   Hankey Papers, CAM, HNKY 1/1, diary entry of 12 May 1915.

[21]   TNA (PRO), CAB 63/4.22.

[22]   Cited by Gilbert, *Winston Churchill,* Vol.3, p.869.

[23]   Fisher Papers, CAM, FISR 1/19.993/, of 12 May 1915; Crease Compilation.

[24]   Ibid., FISR 1/19.994/, of 12 May 1915; Crease Compilation.

[25] Fisher Papers, CAM, FISR 1/19.996/, of 13 May 1915; Crease Compilation (Fisher's emphasis).

[26] Bacon, *Life of Lord Fisher,* p.245; Crease Compilation, of 13 May 1915 (this should have read Chanak Kalessi and Kilid Bahr forts).

[27] Bacon, *Life of Lord Fisher,* p.246; Crease Compilation, ibid.

[28] Ibid. (Churchill's emphasis).

[29] Ibid.

[30] Ibid.; Fisher Papers, CAM, FISR 1/19/999/, of 14 May 1915 (Bacon's emphasis).

[31] Churchill, *The World Crisis,* Vol. II, p.358.

[32] Bacon, *Life of Lord Fisher,* p.247; Crease Compilation.

[33] *SNWCM,* 21st, of 14 May 1915.

[34] Arthur's *Evidence to DC,* TNA (PRO), CAB 19/28, p.56, of 1 December 1916.

[35] Churchill, *The World Crisis,* Vol. II, pp.351–52.

[36] *SNWCM,* 21st, of 14 May 1915.

[37] Churchill, *The World Crisis,* Vol. II, p.351.

[38] *SNWCM,* 21st, of 14 May 1915.

[39] Ibid. (italics added).

[40] Churchill, *The World Crisis,* Vol. II, pp.351–52.

[41] *DCFR,* p.22, para 71.

[42] *SNWCM,* 14th, of 19 February 1915.

[43] *SNWCM,* 21st, of 14 May 1915.

[44] Ibid.

[45] Churchill, *The World Crisis,* Vol. II, p.352.

[46] *SNWCM,* 21st, of 14 May 1915.

[47] Ibid.

[48] Margot Asquith Papers, BOD, MS. Eng, d.3211 (fol.263-5); diary entry of 8 May 1915 (Lloyd George's emphasis).

[49] Ibid. (fol.138), diary entry of 10 January 1915 (Churchill's emphasis).

[50] Churchill, *The World Crisis,* Vol. II, pp.353–54 (italics added).

[51] Bacon, *Life of Lord Fisher,* p.250.

[52] Ibid.

[53] Ibid., p.251; Crease Compilation.

[54] Ibid.

[55] Crease Compilation of 14 May 1915.

[56] Churchill, *The World Crisis,* Vol. II, p.356.

[57] Crease Compilation of 14 May 1915; Bacon, *Life of Lord Fisher,* p.254.

[58] Fisher Papers, CAM, FISR 1/19.1005/, of 15 May 1915; Bacon, *Life of Lord Fisher,* pp.255–56; Marder, *Dreadnought,* pp.277–78; Penn, *Fisher,* pp.177–79.

[59] Fisher Papers, CAM, FISR 1/19.1004/, of 15 May 1915; Crease Compilation.

[60] Fisher Papers, CAM, FISR 1/19.1006/, of 15 May 1915; Penn, *Fisher,* p.182; Bacon, *Life of Lord Fisher,* p.258.

[61] Fisher Papers, CAM, FISR 1/19.1010, of 16 May 1915 (Fisher's emphasis); Bacon, *Life of Lord Fisher,* p.259; Crease Compilation.

[62] Bacon, *Life of Lord Fisher,* p.259.

[63] Marder, *Fisher Correspondence,* p.232.

[64] Ibid., pp.257–60; Marder, *Dreadnought,* pp.277–79; Penn, *Fisher,* pp.182–83; Crease Compilation.

[65] *Morning Post,* 23 April 1915.

[66] Ibid., 27 and 30 April 1915.

[67] Crease Compilation of 16 May 1915; Fisher papers, CAM, FISR 1/19.1007, of 16 May 1915.

[68] Ibid., FISR 1/19,1008, of 16 May 1915 (Esher's emphasis).

[69] Ibid., FISR 1/19.1011, of 16 May 1915; Crease Compilation of 16 May 1915.

510

[70] Bonar Law Papers, HLD, BL Box 37/2.34, of 17 May 1915 (Fisher's emphasis); Higgins, *Winston Churchill and the Dardanelles,* pp.146–47.

[71] Jellicoe Papers, BLIB, ADD MSS 49007, Vol. XIX, of 17 May 1915.

[72] David, *Inside Asquith's Cabinet,* p.243.

[73] James, *Failure,* p.79. James also stated that 'since the outbreak of the war ... Churchill's eagerness to establish a military reputation, his excitement and ardour for action, and his fascination for bold and dramatic enterprises had made many men regard him with alarm' (p.78).

[74] Higgins, *Winston Churchill and the Dardanelles,* p.147.

[75] Cited in Marder, *Dreadnought,* p.287.

[76] Gilbert, *Winston Churchill,* Vol.3, p.465.

[77] Cited by Marder, *Dreadnought,* p.288.

[78] *Globe,* 18 May 1915.

[79] *The Times,* 18 May 1915.

[80] Marder, *Dreadnought,* p.281.

[81] Fisher Papers, CAM, FISR 1/19.1029, of 20 May 1915; Beatty Papers, NMM, BTY /17/36, letter to his wife of 21 May 1915 (Beatty's

emphasis); Penn, *Fisher,* p.189; Marder, *Dreadnought,* p.288.

[82] Jellicoe Papers, BLIB, ADD MSS 49007, Vol. XIX, of 20 May 1915; Fisher Papers, CAM, FISR 1/19.1028, of 20 May 1915; Marder, *Dreadnought,* p.288; James, *Failure,* p.80.

[83] Fisher Papers, CAM, FISR 1/19.1017, of 17 May 1915.

[84] Fisher Papers, CAM, FISR 1/19.1026, of 20 May 1915; Bonar Law Papers, HLD, BL Box 37/5.25, of 20 May 1915.

[85] Fisher Papers, CAM, FISR 1/19.1027, of 20 May 1915; Bonar Law Papers, ibid.

[86] Cited by Penn, *Fisher,* p.185.

[87] Taylor, *Lloyd George. A Diary,* pp.52–53.

[88] Higgins, *Dardanelles,* p.147.

[89] See Alan Brooke (Lord Alanbrooke), *War Diaries, 1939-1945,* Alex Danchev and Daniel Todman (eds), Weidenfeld & Nicolson, London, 2001 (this edition supersedes the sanitised edition by Arthur Bryant, particularly in respect of Brooke's tribulations in dealing with Churchill); Richard Overy, *Why the Allies Won,* Norton, New York, 1996, p.269.

[90] Hankey Papers, CAM, HNKY 5/2 B, correspondence with Lord Fisher of 14 May 1915 (Fisher's emphasis).

[91] Bacon, *Life of Lord Fisher*, p.270. Bacon wrote: 'The strain of the previous few days, without doubt helped to warp his [Fisher's] judgement.'

[92] Penn, *Fisher*, p.189.

[93] Fisher Papers, CAM, FISR 1/19.1021, of 19 May 1915.

[94] Ibid (Fisher's emphasis).

[95] Penn, *Fisher*, pp.190–91; Bacon, *Life of Lord Fisher*, p.270.

[96] Prior, *World Crisis as History*, p.149; James, *Failure*, p.81.

[97] James, *Gallipoli*, pp.317–32; Higgins, *Winston Churchill and the Dardanelles*, pp.167–77; Churchill, *The World Crisis*, Vol. II, pp.481–99.

[98] Gilbert, *Winston Churchill*, Vol.3, p.563.

[99] Hansard, 5th series, Vol. LXXV, cols.1507–8, of 15 November 1915.

[100] Ibid., col.1511.

[101] Ibid., col.1514.

[102] Ibid., cols.1512, 1514.

[103] Ibid., col.1521, of 15 November 1915.

[104] Hansard, 5th series, Lords, Vol. XX, cols.336–7, of 16 November 1915.

Chapter 6

[1] Hansard, 5th series, Vol.71, col.969, 4 May 1915 and Vol.71, cols.398-9, 22 April 1915.

[2] Ibid., Vol.72, cols 1895–6, 30 June 1915.

[3] Ibid., Vol.82, cols 2976–7, 1 June 1916.

[4] Ibid., John Robertson *Anzac and Empire,* Hamlyn, Melbourne, 1990, pp.227–29; Roskill, *Hankey,* Vol.1, pp.279–80.

[5] Hankey diary entries, CAM. HNKY, 1/1, of 3 and 5 June 1916; Hankey, *The Supreme Command,* Vol.2, p.518.

[6] 'An Act to constitute a Special Commission to inquire into the origin, inception and conduct of Operations of War in the Dardanelles and Mesopotamia', nos 5 and 34, *Public General Acts,* 6 and 7, George 5. The Act received Royal Assent on 17 August 1916.

[7] *DCFR; Evidence presented to the Dardanelles Commission* (Witnesses A-Z), TNA (PRO), CAB 19/28-31; Additional Statements, 19/32; Proceedings, 19/33.

[8] Roskill, *Hankey,* Vol.1, p.292; Gilbert, *Winston Churchill,* Vol.3, p.805.

[9]   Graham Greene Papers, NMM, GEE/11; Oliver Papers, NMM, OLV/ 5; Gilbert, *Winston Churchill,* Vol.3, pp.802–03, 813.

[10]   Hankey to Asquith, TNA (PRO), CAB 17/132, 5 June and 11 July 1916.

[11]   Ibid., 11 July 1916; Roskill, *Hankey,* Vol.1, p.287; Robertson, *Anzac and Empire,* p.227.

[12]   TNA (PRO), CAB 63/17-18; TNA (PRO), CAB19/ 29.

[13]   Hankey to Asquith, TNA (PRO), CAB 17/132, of 11 July 1916.

[14]   *DCFR,* Conclusions, (h), p.42, para 121.

[15]   *DCFR,* p.20, para 66.

[16]   See Chapter 2.

[17]   See http://www.firstworldwar.com/atoz/BigBertha; www.spartacus.schoolnet.co.uk/FWWbertha

[18]   Hansard, 5th series, Vol. LXXV, col.1508, of 15 November 1915.

[19]   *DCFR,* p.16, para 53; Callwell, *Experiences of a Dug-out,* pp.65–67.

[20]   *DCFR,* Q.1195, p.30, para 95.

[21]   Churchill, *The World Crisis,* Vol. II, p.171.

[22]   TNA (PRO), CAB 63/17.43; TNA (PRO), CAB 63/18.99 (italics added).

[23]   Aspinall-Oglander, *Military Operations, Gallipoli,* p.45 (italics added).

[24]   Lieutenant General Sir John Adye, 'Has Our Army Grown with Our Empire?' *Nineteenth Century,* Issue 39, June 1896, pp.1012–24.

[25]   Captain Basil Williams, *Raising and Training the New Armies,* Constable, London, 1918, p.7 (Williams' italics).

[26]   Buchanan to Foreign Office, TNA (PRO), FO 371/ 2095/ 52753, of 24 September 1914; Brock and Brock (eds), *Asquith Letters,* pp.281, 266; David, *Inside Asquith's Cabinet,* p.200; *SNWCM,* 7th, of 8 January 1915; French, *British Strategy,* pp.4, 64.

[27]   Brock and Brock (eds), *Asquith Letters,* p.281.

[28]   Cited by Keith Neilson in 'Kitchener: A Reputation Refurbished?', *Canadian Journal of History,* Vol.15, 1980, p.207 (italics added).

[29]   Kitchener to Buchanan, TNA (PRO), FO 371/ 2095/ 55811, of 4 October 1914.

[30]   Hankey, *Supreme Command,* Vol.1, pp.215–16; Neilson, 'Kitchener Reputation', p.212.

[31]   Minutes of Dardanelles Committee Meeting, TNA (PRO), CAB 42/3, of 20 August 1915; Prime Minister's Report to the King, TNA (PRO), CAB 41/36.40, of 20 August 1915.

[32] *DCFR,* Conclusion (c), p.41, para 121.

[33] *DCFR,* Q. 830, p.22, para 71.

[34] *DCFR,* p.3, para 9.

[35] Hankey, diary entry, CAM, HNKY 1/1, of 11 September 1915. This diary entry was edited out of Hankey's *Supreme Command.* See also Roskill, *Hankey,* Vol.1, p.216.

[36] Brock and Brock (eds), *Asquith Letters,* p.423 (Asquith's emphasis).

[37] Violet Bonham Carter (née Asquith), *Winston Churchill as I Knew Him,* Eyre & Spottiswoode, London, 1965, p.361 (Violet Asquith's emphasis).

[38] Ibid., p.387.

[39] *DCFR,* Conclusions (n), p.43, para 121 (italics added).

[40] *DCFR,* p.4, para 9.

[41] *DCFR,* Conclusions (j), p.42, para 121.

[42] As recounted in Chapter 3.

[43] Ibid.

[44] Ibid.

[45] *DCFR,* p.33, paras 104, 105; p.34, para106.

[46] *DCFR,* pp.37–38, para 114.

[47]   Ibid., p.38, para 114.

[48]   *DCFR,* p.7, para 19.

[49]   Ibid., p.8, para 22.

[50]   Fisher's *Evidence to DC,* Q. 3131, p.196.

[51]   Ibid., Q. 3123, p.196.

[52]   *DCFR,* p.10, para 29.

[53]   Ibid., p.29, para 93.

[54]   Ibid., p.20, para 67.

[55]   Hankey diary entry, CAM, HNKY 1/1, of 19 March 1915 (italics added).

[56]   Fisher's *Evidence to DC,* Q. 3127–8, p.196.

[57]   Ibid., Q. 3087, p.191; Crease Compilation.

[58]   Asquith's *Evidence to DC,* Q. 5850, p.354.

[59]   Rear Admiral Morgan Singer, DNO, asked by the Commissioners: 'Were you consulted about the naval expedition to the Dardanelles...' answered: 'No.' When further asked: 'If you had been asked would you have opposed it?' he replied, 'Certainly!' Morgan Singer's *Evidence to DC,* TNA (PRO), CAB 19/33, Q. 3919 and 3930, pp.229–30. Bacon and Tudor expressed similar opinions. See Scott, *Fifty Years in the Royal Navy,* p.296.

[60]   *DCFR,* p.9, para 23.

[61]   Ibid., p.7, para 20.

[62]   Ibid., p.21, para 68.

[63]   Asquith's *Evidence to DC,* Q. 5766, p.349.

[64]   *DCFR,* Conclusion (e), p.41, para 121.

[65]   *DCFR,* Conclusion (g), p.42, para 121.

[66]   Ibid., Conclusion (o), p.43, para 121.

[67]   Jellicoe Papers, BLIB, ADD, MSS. 49007, Vol. X1X, of 14 March 1917. See Chapter 8.

[68]   *DCFR,* pp.45–46.

[69]   Marder, *Fisher Correspondence,* Vol.3, p.628.

[70]   *DCFR,* 'DISSENT AND SUGGESTION BY THE HONOURABLE SIR THOMAS MACKENZIE, KCMG', p.45.

[71]   *DCFR,* 'MINUTE OF THE RIGHT HONOURABLE ANDREW FISHER', p.44.

[72]   *DCFR,* 'MEMORANDUM BY MR. ROCH', pp.47–60.

[73]   Ibid., Conclusions (1) and (2), p.59, para 53.

[74]   *DCFR,* Conclusions (c), (j) and (n), pp.41–43.

[75]   *DCFR,* Roch Memorandum, Conclusion (3), p.59, para 53.

[76]   Ibid., p.50, para 14.

[77]   Ibid., Conclusion (4), p.60, para 53.

[78] Ibid., Conclusion (6), p.60, para 53.

[79] *DCFR,* Roch Memorandum, p.50, para 16.

[80] Ibid., p.53, para 25.

[81] Ibid., p.54, para 28. Indeed, Kitchener had emphasised this precondition at both the 13 and 28 January War Council meetings; *SNWCM,* 8th and 9th, of 13 and 28 January 1915. Fisher similarly stressed the point: 'At any period we could have called off our ships and cut our loss with no damage to our prestige', he told the Commission: Fisher's *Evidence to DC,* Q. 3140, p.197.

[82] Acknowledged by Asquith thus: 'One of the great reasons put forward in the first instance which appealed to Lord Kitchener and everybody was that if it was merely a naval attack it could have been abandoned at any moment without any serious loss of prestige', *DCFR,* p.23, para 76.

[83] 'Lloyd George ... strongly urged that the Army should not be required or expected to pull the chestnuts out of the fire for the Navy and that if the Navy failed we should try somewhere else, in the Balkans, and not necessarily at the Dardanelles.' Roch Memorandum, *DCFR,* p.56, para 35.

[84] *DCFR,* p.38, para 115.

[85]   *Annual Register 1917,* 'Public Documents', p.55.

[86]   *Age,* 10 March 1917.

[87]   *Sydney Morning Herald, Age* and *Brisbane Courier,* 10 March 1917.

[88]   *Sydney Morning Herald,* 10 March 1917.

[89]   *Brisbane Courier,* 10 March 1917.

[90]   *Advertiser,* 10 March 1917.

[91]   *West Australian,* 10 March 1917.

[92]   *Sydney Morning Herald, Age, Brisbane Courier, West Australian, Advertiser,* 10 March 1917.

[93]   Ibid.

[94]   Ibid.

[95]   Ibid.

[96]   Ibid.

[97]   *SNWCM,* 18th, of 10 March 1915.

[98]   *The Times,* 10 March 1917.

[99]   *The Times,* 'The Dardanelles Report', 9 March 1917, p.12.

[100]   Ibid.

[101]   Ibid.

[102]   Ibid.

[103]   *Evening News,* 9 March 1917.

[104]   *Daily Mail,* 9 March 1917.

[105]   *West Australian,* 12 March 1917.

[106]   *Newcastle Morning Herald,* 17 March 1917.

[107]   *Sydney Morning Herald,* 10 March 1917.

[108]   *Daily Standard,* 12 March 1917.

[109]   Chapter 2.

[110]   *DCFR,* p.40, para 119; *Annual Register 1917,* p.55; Appendices 5, 6; *The Times,* 9 March 1917, p.12.

Chapter 7

[1]   Cited in James, *Churchill: A Study in Failure,* p.70; Hankey to Lloyd George, Lloyd George Papers, HLD, G/212 /4 of 16 April 1934; *Sunday Times,* 3 June 1917.

[2]   *The Times,* 18 July 1917. The following day, in another article headed 'Hostility to Mr. Churchill', *The Times* noted that 'Mr. Churchill's appointment will be critically reviewed' by the House, and 'that a considerable section of the [Conservative] rank and file does not take kindly to the new Minister of Munitions'. *The Times,* 19 July 1917. Such proved to be the case.

522

[3] Hansard, 5th series, Vol.96, col.770, 20 July 1917.

[4] Taylor, *Lloyd George. A Diary,* p.59.

[5] James, *Churchill: A Study in Failure,* p.90.

[6] Norman Rose, *An Unruly Life,* Simon and Schuster, London, 1994, p.344.

[7] David Lloyd George, *War Memoirs,* Vol.1, Nicholson and Watson, London, 1933, p.636.

[8] A.J.P. Taylor et al. (eds), *Churchill Revised. A Critical Assessment,* Dial Press, New York, 1969, p.178; Trevor Wilson, *The Myriad Faces of War,* Polity Press, Cambridge, 1986, pp.340–42.

[9] Jonathan Aitken, *Officially Secret,* Weidenfeld & Nicolson, London, 1971, pp.22–23.

[10] John D. Baxter, *State Security, Privacy and Information,* Harvester, New York, 1990, pp.26–27; *Report of the Departmental Committee on Section 2 of the Official Secrets Act 1911,* September 1972, Cmd.5104 (*Franks Report*).

[11] Viscount Reginald Balliol Brett Esher, *The Tragedy of Lord Kitchener,* John Murray, London, 1921, p.67.

[12] Corbett, *History of the Great War: Naval Operations,* 3 vols; Bean, *Official History of*

Australia in the War of 1914–1918, vols I and II.

[13] Sir John French, *1914,* Constable, London, 1919; Sir Ian Hamilton, *Gallipoli Diary,* Edward Arnold, London, 1920, 2 vols; Callwell, *Experiences of a Dug-out;* idem, *The Dardanelles,* Constable, London, 1919; Sir William Robertson, *From Private to Field Marshal,* Constable, London, 1921; Admiral Viscount Jellicoe of Scapa, *The Grand Fleet 1914-16: Its Creation, Development and Work,* Cassell, London, 1919; Sir George Arthur, *Life of Lord Kitchener,* Macmillan, London, 1920, 2 vols; Esher, *Tragedy of Lord Kitchener;* Charles a Court Repington, *The First World War, 1914-1918,* Constable, London, 1920, 2 vols.

[14] Churchill letter to Bonar Law, Bonar Law Papers, HLD, BL, Box 112/Folder 13/2, of 3 March 1923.

[15] Conversation recorded by Lord Riddell, 4 May 1919, cited in Naylor, *A Man and an Institution,* p.11.

[16] Naylor, *A Man and an Institution,* p.15.

[17] 'Rules of Procedure', *Public Record Office Handbook, No.11, Records of the Cabinet Office to 1922,* HMSO, London, 1966, p.4.

[18] 'Report of Cabinet Committee on the Use of Official Material in Publications', TNA (PRO);

CAB, 27/ 213, C.P. 3966, 24 May 1923 (henceforth the *Curzon Committee Report*), pp.4, 7.

[19]   TNA (PRO), CAB 63/22, 'The Custody of War Cabinet Documents: Note by the Secretary', 14 August 1917; TNA (PRO), CAB 27/213, of 17 August 1917, in which Hankey pointed out the danger of Cabinet papers passing into the hands of executors of deceased former ministers and being taken out of the country beyond the government's control.

[20]   Cited in TNA (PRO), CAB 23/18, of 4 November 1919.

[21]   Hankey, TNA (PRO), CAB 23/18, C.1 (19), of 4 November 1919, p.3. Lloyd George was in the chair for this meeting, and Churchill was present as Secretary of State for War and Air. Para (d) was deleted, which had stated that: 'Cabinet Minutes and Papers are not the personal property of members, and on a Minister leaving office it is the duty of the Secretary to recover from him, or in the event of his death, from his executors, all Cabinet Papers issued to him from the Cabinet Office [for filing].'

[22]   Roskill, *Hankey: Man of Secrets*, Vol.2, p.127; Naylor, *A Man and an Institution*, p.68. On Lloyd George's war memoirs, see Suttie, *Rewriting the First World War*.

[23] Naylor, *A Man and an Institution,* p.68.

[24] *Curzon Committee Report,* p.9.

[25] TNA (PRO), CAB 23/18, C.1 (19), of 4 November 1919, p.3.

[26] Martin Gilbert, *Winston S. Churchill,* Vol.4, p.757.

[27] 'Publication of Cabinet Memoranda', TNA (PRO), CAB 23/29, C.6 (22), of 30 January 1922, pp.81–91 (italics added).

[28] Gilbert, *Winston Churchill,* Vol.4, p.757.

[29] Hansard, 5th series, Vol.155, col.265, of 13 June 1922.

[30] *The Times,* 1 February 1923.

[31] Hansard, 5th series, Vol.160, col.315, of 15 February 1923.

[32] Ibid., col.593, of 19 February 1923.

[33] Ibid., col.1235, of 22 February 1923.

[34] Ibid., cols 1234–5, of 22 February 1923.

[35] Churchill to Bonar Law, Bonar Law Papers, HLD, BL, Vol.3, Box 112, Folder 13/2, of 3 March 1923.

[36] Arthur, *Life of Lord Kitchener.*

[37] Jellicoe, *The Grand Fleet* (one volume only).

526

[38] Fisher, *Memories.*

[39] Hamilton, *Gallipoli Diary.*

[40] Corbett, *Naval Operations.*

[41] Bean, *Official History,* Vol. I, *The Story of Anzac.*

[42] Robertson, *From Private to Field Marshal;* Callwell, *The Dardanelles Campaigns.*

[43] Churchill's letter to Bonar Law, Bonar Law Papers, HLD, BL, Vol.3, Box 112, Folder 13/2, of 3 March 1923.

[44] Ibid.

[45] Hankey to Bonar Law, Bonar Law Papers, HLD, BL Vol.3, Box 112, Folder 13/3, of 8 March 1923.

[46] Ibid.

[47] Ibid.

[48] Cited in Gilbert, *Winston S. Churchill, Companion,* Vol.5, part 1, p.36.

[49] Gilbert, *Winston Churchill,* Vol.4, pp.751–52.

[50] *Curzon Committee Report,* p.13.

[51] Conclusion 4 of Cabinet Meeting, TNA (PRO), CAB 11 (23), of 21 February 1923 (Terms of Reference).

[52]   *Curzon Committee Report,* p.2.

[53]   Ibid., p.5.

[54]   Ibid., p.15.

[55]   Ibid., p.17.

[56]   Ibid., pp.8–9.

[57]   Ibid., pp.12–13.

[58]   Churchill, *The World Crisis,* Vol. I, p.2 (Churchill's italics).

[59]   Hankey Papers, CAM, HNKY 1/ 5, diary, Vol.3, pp.96–98, of 16 November 1919.

[60]   Naylor, *A Man and an Institution,* pp.118, 207; Roskill, *Hankey,* Vol.2, p.341.

[61]   'Memorandum by the Permanent Secretary to the Admiralty', *Curzon Committee Report,* 23 February 1923.

[62]   Naylor, *A Man and an Institution,* pp.69–70.

[63]   Roskill, *Hankey,* Vol.2, p.341; James, *Churchill: A Study in Failure,* p.149.

[64]   Peter Fraser, 'Cabinet Secrecy and War Memoirs', *History,* Vol.70, 1985, pp.397–99; *Curzon Committee Report,* pp.4, 5; *Public Record Office Handbook,* No.11, *The Records of the Cabinet Office to 1922,* pp.vii, 1.

[65]   Churchill, *The World Crisis,* Vol. I, p.2.

[66]   *The Times Literary Supplement,* 8 November 1923.

[67]   Prior, *World Crisis as History,* p.279.

[68]   J.H. Plumb, 'The Historian' in A.J.P. Taylor (ed), *Churchill: Four Faces and the Man,* Allen Lane, London, 1969, pp.144–45.

[69]   Lord Sydenham, Sir Reginald Bacon, Sir Frederick Maurice, Sir W. Bird and Sir Charles Oman, *The World Crisis by Winston Churchill: a criticism,* Hutchinson, London, 1928, p.6.

[70]   *National Review,* August 1923, cited by Sir Peter Gretton, *Winston Churchill and the Royal Navy,* Coward McCann, New York, 1969, p.197.

[71]   'Official Histories, Note [to Cabinet] by the Secretary', TNA (PRO), CAB 24/94, C.P. 202, of 26 November 1919; Roskill, *Hankey,* Vol.1, p.162; Naylor, *A Man and an Institution,* pp.73, 120–22.

[72]   Ian Beckett, 'Frocks and Brasshats' in B. Bond (ed), *The First World War and British Military History,* Clarendon Press, Oxford, 1991, p.92; Naylor, *A Man and an Institution,* pp.70, 125.

[73]   Beckett, 'Frocks and Brasshats' in Bond, *British Military History,* pp.92–93.

[74]   TNA (PRO), CAB 24/ 92, C.P. 9, 'Official Histories, Note by Secretary', of 28 October

1919; Churchill's Memorandum TNA (PRO), Cab 24/77 (G.T. 7087) and CAB 24/94 (C.P. 202).

[75] Ibid; TNA (PRO), CAB 103/68 and 83.

[76] Ibid.

[77] TNA (PRO), CAB 63/ 40. 'Note on Official Histories', 12 June 1928.

[78] TNA (PRO), CAB 24/92, C.P. 9, 28 October 1919.

[79] TNA (PRO), CAB 24/ 77, GT 7087, of 8 April 1919.

[80] TNA (PRO), ADM 116/ 2067, 'Naval Operations, Vol.1'; Corbett Papers, NMM, MS 82/006, Box 7.

[81] Ibid.

[82] Corbett Papers, NMM, MS 82/ 006, Box 7.

[83] Ibid.; TNA (PRO), ADM 167/ 59.

[84] Naylor, *A Man and an Institution,* p.121.

[85] TNA (PRO), CAB 24/ 94, C.P. 202, of 26 November 1919.

[86] TNA (PRO), ADM 167/ 59, Corbett Papers, NMM. MS 82/006, Box 7.

[87] TNA (PRO), CAB 24/ 94, C.P. 202, of 26 November 1919.

[88]   Corbett Papers, NMM, MS 82/006, Box 7.

[89]   Ibid.

[90]   Hankey Memorandum, C.P. 1034 (20), 'Official History of the War', of 8 April 1920.

[91]   Roskill's criticism occurs within the Corbett Papers, NMM. MS 82/ 006, Box 7.

[92]   Corbett, *Naval Operations,* vols 1–3.

[93]   Naylor, *A Man and an Institution,* p.122.

[94]   Ibid., pp.103, 118–20; Roskill, *Man of Secrets,* Vol.2, p.313; Peter Fraser, 'Cabinet Secrecy and War Memoirs', *History,* Vol.70, 1985, pp.397–409, 404.

[95]   Hankey letter to Lloyd George, Lloyd George Papers, HLD, G /212/4, of 8 January 1933; Naylor, *A Man and an Institution,* pp.118–19; Fraser, 'Cabinet Secrecy', p.406.

[96]   Hankey letter to Lloyd George, Lloyd George Papers, HLD, G /212/4, of 16 April 1934.

[97]   Letter to Hankey from Churchill, Hankey Papers, CAM, HNKY 25/1, of 8 December 1944.

[98]   Hankey Letter to Tom Jones, Hankey Papers, CAM, HNKY 25/2, of 25 February 1945; Naylor, *A Man and an Institution,* pp.272–73.

[99]   Hankey letter to Bridges, Hankey Papers, CAM, HNKY 25/1, of 29 March 1945 (italics added).

[100] Letter from Home Secretary Addison to Hankey, Hankey Papers, CAM, HNKY 25/1, of 5 April 1946.

[101] Naylor, *A Man and an Institution,* pp.275–76.

[102] Ibid., p.289.

[103] Beckett, 'Frocks and Brasshats' in Bond, *British Military History,* p.111.

[104] Hankey's complete papers are available for public scrutiny at the Churchill College Archives Centre, Cambridge.

[105] TNA (PRO), CAB 21/457; Roskill, *Man of Secrets,* Vol.2, p.131.

[106] Aitken, *Officially Secret,* p.30.

[107] Ibid., pp.55, 61–62; Naylor, *A Man and an Institution,* p.211; Fraser, 'Cabinet Secrecy', pp.406–07.

[108] Aitken, *Officially Secret,* p.62; Naylor, *A Man and an Institution,* pp.212–14; Fraser, 'Cabinet Secrecy', p.407.

[109] TNA (PRO), CAB 21/ 448, C.P. 69 (34), 'Cabinet Procedure: The Retention by Cabinet Ministers of their Cabinet Papers on Leaving Office', of 9 March 1934.

[110] TNA (PRO), CAB 23/ 78, C 11 (34) 5, of 21 March 1934; Naylor, *A Man and an Institution,* pp.216–18; Fraser, 'Cabinet Secrecy', p.407.

[111]   TNA (PRO), CAB 21/ 448, C.P. 69 (34), of 9 March 1934.

[112]   *Public Record Office Handbook,* No.11, *Records of the Cabinet Office to 1922,* HMSO, London, 1966, p.ix; *Public Record Office Handbook No 17, The Cabinet Office to 1945,* HMSO, London, 1975, pp.12–20; Naylor, *A Man and an Institution,* pp.217–22.

[113]   Hankey letter to Lloyd George, Lloyd George Papers, HLD. G /212/4, of 21 April 1934.

[114]   Naylor, *A Man and an Institution,* pp.234–36.

[115]   Keith Middlemas and John Barnes, *Baldwin: A Biography,* Weidenfeld & Nicholson, London, 1969; David Marquand, *Ramsay Macdonald,* Jonathan Cape, London, 1977; David Dilks, *Neville Chamberlain,* Cambridge University Press, Cambridge, 1984.

[116]   Beckett, 'Frocks and Brasshats' in Bond, *British Military History,* p.95.

[117]   Prior, *World Crisis as History,* Introduction, p.xi; Winston Churchill, *The World Crisis 1911-1918,* Simon and Schuster, New York, 2005.

[118]   Prior, *World Crisis as History,* p.xii; Guinn, *British Strategy, 1914 to 1918,* Chapter 11, pp.48–80.

[119]   Letter from Edmonds to Churchill, in which Edmonds thanks Churchill 'for a copy of the proof of the Antwerp Chapter, that I may bring the "Official History" ... into line with it', cited by Prior in *World Crisis as History*, p.36.

[120]   Gilbert, *Winston Churchill,* Vol.5, pp.14–15.

[121]   Ibid., p.15.

[122]   Carl Roberts, *Winston Churchill: Being an Account of the Life of Winston Leonard Spencer Churchill,* Mills and Boon, London, 1927, p.188.

Chapter 8

[1]   *DCFR,* Conclusions (j), p.42, para 121; Churchill, *The World Crisis,* Vol. II, pp.182–84. The fallacy of this claim is described in Chapter 6.

[2]   Churchill, *The World Crisis,* Vol. II, p.172.

[3]   Ibid., p.174.

[4]   Ibid., p.275.

[5]   Ibid.

[6]   Prior, *World Crisis as History,* p.82.

[7]   Neilson, 'Kitchener Reputation', p.207.

[8]   Cassar, *Kitchener, Architect of Victory,* p.486.

[9]   Ian van der Waag, 'South Africa and the Boer Military System' in Peter Dennis and Jeffrey Grey (eds), *The Boer War: Army, Nation and Empire,* Army History Unit, Canberra, 2000, p.54.

[10]   Robertson, *From Private to Field Marshal,* pp.289–90.

[11]   Churchill, *The World Crisis,* Vol. II, p.340.

[12]   *Hansard,* 5th series, Vol.80, col.1430, 7 March 1916.

[13]   Ibid.

[14]   See Chapter 5 for the full transcript of this letter.

[15]   Churchill, *The World Crisis,* Vol. II, p.354.

[16]   Ibid., pp.353–56.

[17]   Wilson, *Myriad Faces of War,* p.200.

[18]   Fisher's letter to Hankey, Hankey Papers, CAM, HNKY 5/2B, of 14 May 1915 (Fisher's emphasis).

[19]   Wilson, *Myriad Faces,* p.201; Churchill, *The World Crisis,* Vol. II, pp.172–76.

[20]   Violet Bonham-Carter, *Winston Churchill as I knew Him,* pp.21, 333, 375, 379.

[21]   Churchill, *The World Crisis,* Vol. II, pp.102, 121–22, 148, 153–54, 170–72, 189, 249, 262–68.

[22]   *DCFR,* Conclusions (h), p.42, para 121.

[23]   Churchill, *The World Crisis,* Vol. II, pp.113–14.

[24]   Ibid., p.113.

[25]   *DCFR,* pp.21–22, paras 69 and 70.

[26]   Ibid., p.22, para 70 (italics added).

[27]   Aspinall-Oglander, *Military Operations, Gallipoli,* Vol.1, p.59.

[28]   Churchill, *The World Crisis,* Vol. II, pp.205–06, 261.

[29]   Prior, *World Crisis as History,* pp.277–78.

[30]   Cited in Marder, *Dreadnought,* p.261.

[31]   Penn, *Fisher,* p.237.

[32]   Callwell, *The Dardanelles,* p.42.

[33]   Ibid., pp.350–54, 357–59.

[34]   Ibid., pp.3, 25–26.

[35]   Scott, *Fifty Years,* p.329.

[36]   Ibid., p.331.

[37]   Ibid., pp.327–333.

[38]   Ibid., pp.295–96.

536

[39]   Churchill, *The World Crisis,* Vol. II, 'The Choice', p.108 (Churchill's italics).

[40]   Ibid., p.107.

[41]   Keyes, letter to his wife, 20 February 1915, cited by Prior, *World Crisis as History,* p.86.

[42]   TNA (PRO), ADM 137/110.222–5, of 27 March 1915; see also Chapter 4.

[43]   Corbett, *Naval Operations,* Vol.2, p.223; Churchill, *The World Crisis,* Vol. II, p.230.

[44]   *DCFR,* p.51, para 18.

[45]   Churchill, *The World Crisis,* Vol. II, p.226.

[46]   Corbett, *Naval Operations,* Vol.2, pp.223–24.

[47]   Ibid., pp.224–25.

[48]   Ibid.

[49]   *DCFR,* p.38; Churchill, *The World Crisis.* Vol. II, p.268.

[50]   Ellison, *Perils of Amateur Strategy,* p.45.

[51]   Ibid., p.42, *DCFR,* p.20; Fisher, *Memories,* p.70.

[52]   Churchill, *The World Crisis,* Vol. II, pp.167, 170.

[53]   Ellison, citing Sir Edward Grey, in *Perils of Amateur Strategy,* p.39.

[54]   Ellison, *Perils of Amateur Strategy,* p.88.

[55]   Ibid., pp.47, 51.

[56]   Ibid., pp.54, 51.

[57]   Hansard, Vol.75, cols 1517–8, 15 November 1915.

[58]   Ellison, *Perils of Amateur Strategy,* p.xxi.

[59]   Ibid., p.13.

[60]   Bacon, *Life of Lord Fisher,* 2 vols.

[61]   Crease Compilation. This material is now located within an Admiralty file at The National Archives, Kew.

[62]   Hansard, 5th series, Lords, Vol. XX, cols.336–7, of 16 November 1915.

[63]   'Statement by Lord Fisher to the Dardanelles Commission'; Crease Compilation, cited by Bacon in *Life of Lord Fisher,* Vol.2, pp.213–14.

[64]   Brian Bond (ed), *The First World War and British Military History,* Clarendon Press, Oxford, 1991, p.4.

[65]   Basil Liddell Hart, *Paris, or The Future of War,* Kegan Paul, London, 1925; idem, *A Science of Infantry Tactics: Simplified,* W. Clowes, London, 1923; idem, *Reputations,* John Murray, London, 1928; idem, *The Real War 1914-1918,* Little Brown, Boston, 1930; idem, *Foch, the Man of Orleans,* Penguin, London, 1937; idem,

538

Sherman, the Genius of the Civil War, Eyre & Spottiswoode, London, 1933.

[66] Brian Bond, *Liddell Hart: A Study of his Military Thought,* Cassell, London, 1976, p.60.

[67] Ibid., pp.4–7.

[68] Ibid., p.60.

[69] David French, 'Official but not History? Sir James Edmonds and the Official History of the Great War', *Royal United Services Institute* Journal, Vol.131, No.1, March 1986, p.59. '[In 1917, General] Rawlinson's Chief of Staff, A.A. Montgomery-Massingberd, destroyed the War Diary of the Fourth Army chronicling the opening of the battle of the Somme in July 1916 and substituted his own narrative of events'. Ibid., p.60.

[70] Bond, *Liddell Hart,* p.82; idem, *First World War and British Military History,* p.11; French, 'Official but not History', pp.58–63. On the writing of the official histories, see Green, *Writing the Great War.*

[71] Basil Liddell Hart, *The British Way in Warfare,* Faber & Faber, London, 1932; idem, *The Future of Infantry,* Faber & Faber, London, 1933; idem, *A History of the World War 1914-1918;* idem, *Through the Fog of War,* Faber & Faber, London, 1938.

[72] Leon Wolff, *In Flanders Fields,* Longmans Green, London, 1959; Alan Clark, *The Donkeys,* Hutchinson, London, 1963; A.J.P. Taylor, *The First World War: An Illustrated History,* Hamilton, London, 1963; John Laffin, *British Butchers and Bunglers of World War One,* Macmillan Australia, South Melbourne, 1989.

[73] Bond, *British Military History,* p.7.

[74] See Conclusion, pp.xxx, and the need for a massive accompanying army at the outset.

[75] Bond, *Liddell Hart,* p.52.

[76] Hew Strachan, '"The Real War"': Liddell Hart, Cruttwell and Falls' in Bond (ed), *The First World War and British Military History,* p.49.

[77] Liddell Hart, *The Real War,* pp.154, 157.

[78] Ibid., pp.151, 157–58.

[79] Ibid., pp.152, 157.

[80] Churchill, *The World Crisis,* Vol. II, p.515.

[81] Liddell Hart, *History of the World War 1914-1918,* p.188.

[82] Edward Spiers, 'Gallipoli' in Bond (ed), *The First World War and British Military History,* p.172.

[83] Cited in Bond, *Liddell Hart,* p.8.

[84]   Peter Vansittart (ed), *John Masefield's Letters From the Front 1915-1917,* Constable, London, 1984, pp.18–20.

[85]   John Masefield, *Gallipoli,* Heinemann, London, 1916, p.3.

[86]   *The Song of Roland* is an epic French poem based on the Battle of Roncevaux in 778 and written initially in the eleventh century.

[87]   E.C. Buley, *Glorious Deeds of Australasians in the Great War,* Andrew Melrose, London, 1915.

[88]   Cited in Robin Gerster, *BIG-NOTING: The Heroic Theme in Australian War Writing,* Melbourne University Press, 1987, p.13.

[89]   Sydney de Loghe, *The Straits Impregnable,* J. Murray, London, 1917; R. Hugh Knyvett, *'OVER THERE' with the Australians,* Hodder & Stoughton, London, 1918; Hector *Dinning, By Ways on Service–Notes from an Australian Journal,* Constable and Company Ltd, London, 1918.

[90]   Robert Graves, *Goodbye to all That: An autobiography,* Cape, London, 1929; C. Day Lewis (ed), *The Collected Poems of Wilfred Owen,* with an introduction and notes by C. Day Lewis and a memoir by Edmund Blunden, Chatto & Windus, London, 1963; Siegfried Sassoon, *Memoirs of a Foxhunting Man,* Faber & Faber, London, 1928; Erich Maria Remarque,

All Quiet on the Western Front (trans. A.W. Wheen), London, 1968; Henri Barbusse, *Under Fire* (trans. Robin Buss, with an introduction by Jay Winter), Penguin, London, 2003.

[91]   Compton Mackenzie, *Gallipoli Memories,* Cassell, London, 1929, pp.80–81.

[92]   Spiers, 'Gallipoli' in Bond, *British Military History,* p.174.

[93]   John North, *Gallipoli: The Fading Vision,* Faber & Faber, London, 1936, p.15.

[94]   Ibid., p.353.

[95]   Ibid., p.57.

[96]   Churchill, *The World Crisis,* Vol. II, pp.121–22.

[97]   North, *Fading Vision,* p.60.

[98]   Ibid., pp.64–65.

[99]   Ibid., pp.53, 57.

[100]   Sir Ian Hamilton, *Gallipoli Diary,* 2 vols. On Aspinall-Oglander's history, see Green, *Writing the Great War,* chapters 5 and 6.

[101]   Aspinall-Oglander, *Military Operations, Gallipoli,* Vol.2, pp.479–80.

[102]   General Otto Liman von Sanders, *Five Years in Turkey,* US Naval Institute, Annapolis, 1927.

[103]   Spiers, 'Gallipoli' in Bond, *British Military History,* p.170.

[104]   Keyes, *Naval Memoirs,* pp.244, 254–55, 257.

[105]   James, *Churchill: A Study in Failure,* p.86.

[106]   Overy, *Why the Allies Won,* p.268.

[107]   Cited in Robert Blake and Roger Wm. Lewis (eds), *Churchill,* Oxford University Press, Oxford, 1994, p.503.

[108]   Simon Schama, 'A History of Britain', Video Recording, SBS Television, Sydney, 2002.

[109]   Rose, *An Unruly Life,* pp.269–70.

[110]   Roy Jenkins, *Churchill: A Biography,* Farrar, Straus and Giroux, New York, 2001, p.792.

[111]   James, *Churchill: A Study in Failure,* p.173; Taylor, *Churchill Revised,* p.28.

[112]   Isaiah Berlin, *Mr. Churchill in 1940,* Houghton Mifflin, Boston, 1949 (reprinted from an essay published in *The Atlantic Monthly* in 1949).

[113]   Ibid., pp.25–26.

[114]   Ibid., p.39.

[115]   Rose, *An Unruly Life,* pp.214, 269.

[116]   Broad, *Winston Churchill, 1874-1951,* p.103.

[117]   Ibid., p.104.

[118]   Ibid., pp.105–06.

[119]   Ibid., p.106; Virginia Cowles, *Winston Churchill: The Era and the Man,* Hamilton, London, 1953; John Connell, *Winston Churchill,* Longmans, Green & Co., London, 1956; Eade, *Churchill by his Contemporaries.*

[120]   Moorehead, *Gallipoli,* pp.43, 47.

[121]   Ibid., p.46.

[122]   Ibid., p.364.

[123]   Hankey, *The Supreme Command,* 2 volumes. See Chapter 7 re the censorship of Hankey's memoirs by Churchill.

[124]   Higgins, *Winston Churchill and the Dardanelles,* p.ix.

[125]   Malcolm Thomson, *Churchill. His Life and Times,* Odhams, Watford, Herts, February 1965, Special Memorial Edition, p.474.

[126]   Bonham Carter, *Winston Churchill as I knew him,* pp.21, 370, 375, 379.

[127]   Thomson, *Churchill: His Life and Times,* p.159.

[128]   Goronwy Rees, 'Churchill: A Minority View' in Peter Stansky (ed), *Churchill, A Profile,* Macmillan, London, 1973, p.207.

[129]   Ibid., p.212.

544

[130]   Ibid., p.209.

[131]   James, *Gallipoli,* pp.32–41.

[132]   Marder, *Dreadnought,* p.270, citing Graham Greene's *Evidence to Dardanelles Commission* (Marder's italics).

[133]   Ibid., pp.261–62.

[134]   Ibid., p.260.

[135]   James, *Churchill,* pp.67–68.

[136]   Ibid., p.68.

[137]   Ibid., pp.76–77.

[138]   Ibid., p.87.

[139]   Ibid., p.70.

[140]   Beckett, 'Frocks and Brasshats' in Bond, *British Military History,* pp.91–95.

[141]   Gilbert, *Winston S. Churchill,* Vol.3 (plus companion vols 1 and 2).

[142]   Churchill, *The World Crisis,* Vol. II, p.99.

[143]   Gilbert, *Winston Churchill,* Vol.3, pp.237–38.

[144]   Wilson, *Myriad Faces of War,* p.112.

[145]   Gilbert, *Winston Churchill,* Vol.3, pp.233, 291–92, 302–04, 381.

[146]   Ibid., pp.258–60, 268, 326.

[147] Ibid., pp.357–60; see Chapter 4, pp.145–46.

[148] Gilbert, 'Churchill and Gallipoli' in Macleod (ed), *Gallipoli: Making History,* p.22.

[149] Prior and Wilson, 'The Churchill Industry', *Quadrant,* November 1994, p.42.

[150] Pelling, *Churchill,* p.191 (italics added).

[151] Ibid., p.192.

[152] Ibid., p.194.

[153] Ibid.

[154] Ibid., p.197.

[155] Roskill, *Churchill and the Admirals,* p.42.

[156] Ibid., pp.43, 52.

[157] Ibid., p.46.

[158] Ibid., p.48.

[159] Ibid., p.48.

[160] Ibid., p.52.

[161] Ibid.

[162] Ibid., p.51 (Roskill's italics).

[163] Ibid., p.52.

[164] Ibid., p.82.

[165] Ibid., p.26.

[166] Prior, *World Crisis as History,* p.80.

[167] Ibid., p.82.

[168] Ibid. p.67.

[169] Ibid., pp.67, 78.

[170] Ibid., p.87.

[171] Ibid., p.85.

[172] Wilson, *Myriad Faces of War,* pp.108–21.

[173] Ibid., pp.109, 111, 119, 132.

[174] William Manchester, *Death of a President,* Harper and Rowe, New York, 1967; idem, *American Caesar: Douglas MacArthur 1880-1964,* Hutchinson, London, 1979.

[175] Manchester, *The Last Lion,* p.519 (Manchester's italics).

[176] Ibid., p.525.

[177] Ibid., p.530.

[178] Ibid., p.543.

[179] Ibid., p.537.

[180] Ibid., p.540.

[181] 'Report of minesweeping during March', TNA (PRO), ADM 137/ 1089.289/ 1–19.

[182] Manchester, *Last Lion,* p.549.

[183]   Ibid., p.528.

[184]   Penn, *Fisher, Churchill and the Dardanelles,* pp.126–27, 140–43.

[185]   Ibid., pp.174–75, 181.

[186]   Ibid., pp.130, 160.

[187]   Ibid., p.195.

[188]   Best, *Churchill, A Study in Greatness,* p.ix.

[189]   Ibid., pp.63, 67.

[190]   Ibid., pp.60, 63–64.

[191]   Ibid., p.64.

[192]   John Keegan, *Winston Churchill,* Penguin Viking, New York, 2002; idem, *The First World War.*

[193]   Keegan, *Winston Churchill,* p.85.

[194]   Ibid., pp.237–41.

[195]   Jenkins, *Churchill. A Biography,* pp.246, 248.

[196]   Ibid., pp.244–45, 258–61.

[197]   Ibid., p.244.

[198]   Ibid., p.261.

[199]   Ibid.

[200]   For a recent expression of the state of historical opinion that strives for a balanced

assessment, see the entry on Churchill in the *Oxford Dictionary of National Biography in Association with the British Academy,* Vol.11, 2004, pp.659–62.

Conclusion

[1] Liddell Hart, *History of the World War 1914-1918,* p.188.

[2] Masefield, Lawrence, Amery, North, Moorehead, Thomson, Broad, Bonham Carter, Pelling, Manchester, Addison, Best, et al. in Chapter 8.

[3] James, *Churchill: A Study in Failure;* Ellison, *Perils of Amateur Strategy;* Bacon, *Life of Lord Fisher;* Corbett, *Naval Operations;* Callwell, *Dardanelles;* Scott, *Fifty Years;* Roskill, Bond, Prior, Wilson, Penn, Jenkins, et al. in Chapter 8; *DCFR,* Conclusion, p.42, para (h).

[4] *DCFR,* Conclusion, pp.70–72: Sir George Arthur's, Creedy's, von Donop's and Callwell's testimony.

[5] Asquith's *Evidence to Dardanelles Commission,* Q. 5826, p.352.

[6] Gilbert, *Winston Churchill,* Vol.3, p.241; Churchill, *The World Crisis,* Vol. II, pp.99–100.

[7] Churchill, *The World Crisis,* Vol. II, p.148 (italics added).

[8]   TNA (PRO), ADM 137/1089.108–116, of 15 February 1915.

[9]   Churchill, *The World Crisis,* Vol. II, p.181.

[10]   Ibid., pp.110–11; *SNWCM* TNA (PRO), CAB 22/1.15th, of 24 February 1915.

[11]   *SNWCM,* Ibid.; Roch Memorandum, *DCFR,* p.56, para 35.

[12]   *SNWCM,* TNA (PRO), CAB 22/1.18th, of 10 March 1915.

[13]   Churchill, *The World Crisis,* Vol. II, p.251.

[14]   Cassar, *Kitchener, Architect of Victory,* p.321.

[15]   TNA (PRO), ADM 137/110.222-5, of 27 March 1915.

[16]   Prior and Wilson, *The First World War,* pp.62–66.

[17]   Higgins, *Winston Churchill and the Dardanelles,* p.158.

[18]   Churchill, *The World Crisis,* Vol. II, pp.248–49.

[19]   *SNWCM,* TNA (PRO), CAB 22/1.20th, of 6 April 1915.

[20]   Greene's evidence and Churchill's admission that Fisher was often shown telegram orders and initialled them *after* they had been sent.

550

[21]   TNA (PRO), ADM 137/109.599, of 17 March 1915.

[22]   Jenkins, *Churchill,* p.244.

[23]   Hansard, 5th series, Vol. LXXV, cols.1507–14, 15 November 1915.

[24]   Findings of Dardanelles Commission, *DCFR,* p.20, para 66.

[25]   *DCFR,* p.40, paras 118–19; *Annual Register 1917,* 'Public Documents', p.55.

[26]   Ellison, *Perils of Amateur Strategy,* pp.20, 23.

[27]   Joseph C. Goulden, *Truth is the First Casualty: the Gulf of Tonkin Affair: Illusion and Reality,* Rand McNally, Chicago, 1969.

[28]   Hankey Papers, CAM, HNKY 1/1, diary entry, 19 March 1915.

[29]   Taylor, *Lloyd George. A Diary,* p.50.

BIBLIOGRAPHY

Abbreviations for the archives accessed are as follows:

AWM–Australian War Memorial, Canberra

BLIB–British Library, St Pancras

BOD–Bodleian Library, Oxford

CAM–Churchill College Archives Centre, Cambridge

CUL–Cambridge University Library, Cambridge

HLD–House of Lords Records Office, Westminster

IWM–Imperial War Museum, Lambeth

LHRT–Liddell Hart Archives Centre, Kings College, Strand

NLS–National Library of Scotland, Edinburgh

NMM–National Maritime Museum, Greenwich

TNA (PRO)–The National Archives (formerly Public Record Office), Kew Reference expressed as: TNA (PRO), ADM 137/ 96. 771-3, refers to:
Archive location (The National Archives), class of file (Admiralty) and sub-file numbers (137/96), and page number(s) where appropriate (771–73).

ADM, CAB, FO and WO refer to Admiralty, Cabinet, Foreign Office and War Office.

Primary sources: unpublished

Act of Parliament:

'An Act to constitute a Special Commission to inquire into the origin, inception and conduct of Operations of War in the Dardanelles and Mesopotamia', nos 5 and 34, *Public General Acts* 6, 7, George 5. Royal Assent granted on 17 August 1916.

Departmental Records held in The National Archives, Kew Admiralty

Admiralty Operational Telegrams: Mediterranean, South Atlantic and Dardanelles, ADM 137/ 19, 879, 20, 26, 43, 1027, 304, 156, 186, 1022, 96, 1089, 1090, 109, 110, 38, 39 & ADM 156/ 76 & ADM 116/ 1336, 1348, 3486, 3491.

'Admiralty Committee appointed to investigate the attacks delivered on, and the enemy defences of the Dardanelles Straits', Commodore F.

Mitchell, President, ADM 186/ 600 & 601-2, of 10 October 1919 (*Mitchell Committee Report*).

Admiralty Memorandum of Sir Henry Jackson [prepared for Winston Churchill]: 'Note on Forcing the Passage of The Dardanelles and Bosphorus by the Allied

Fleets, in order to Destroy the Turco-German Squadron and threaten Constantinople without Military Co-operation', ADM 116/ 3491, of 5 January 1915.

Admiralty Memorandum by Sir Henry Jackson to Chief of Staff [recommending the use of troops at the Dardanelles], ADM 37/109.389-90, of 11 March 1915.

Admiralty Operations Orders, for the naval attack against the Dardanelles, ADM 137/1089. 83-95, of 5 February, 1915. Admiralty War Staff Memorandum by Sir Henry Jackson, 'Note on Attack of Dardanelles Forts' [warning of the inadvisability of a naval

attack without the support of 'a strong military force'], ADM 137/1089.108-116, of 15 February 1915. *Court Martial of Rear-Admiral Troubridge, Parts 1 and 2. Held 5-9 November 1914, on board*

H.M.S. Bulwark, Case 662, Escape of German Warships *Goeben* and *Breslau,* ADM 156/ 76.

Crease Compilation, TNA (PRO), ADM 1/28268.

Draft copy of Churchill's Telegram Instruction to Vice Admiral Milne, Commander-in-Chief Mediterranean, 30 July 1914, 3.10pm, ADM 137/19.38.

'Officers and men of *Amethyst,* singled out for particular praise, together with officers and men employed on the trawler-minesweepers', ADM 137/1090/ 289/ 32-44.

'Recommendations [for bravery awards]', ADM 137/1089/ 289/ 75–82.

'Report by Major-General Callwell' [for Winston Churchill, on the feasibility of a naval attack against the Dardanelles], ADM 137/ 96.735–6, of 3 September 1914.

'Report of minesweeping during March', ADM 137/ 1089.289/ 1–19.

'Report and Detailed Narrative of Naval Attack on 18 March 1915', ADM 137/ 39.5–19. Cabinet

CAB 2/ 2, 11/ 23, 19/ 28-33, 21/448, 457, 22/1, 23/18, 2987, 24/1, 77, 92, 94, 27/ 213, 37/ 125, 38/13, 41/ 35, 36, 42/1, 2 & 3, 63/ 4, 17, 18, 40.

Cabinet Committee appointed 'to examine the circumstances in which it is permissible in any publication to use or quote from Cabinet or Departmental documents, however obtained', CAB 27/ 213, C.P. 3966, of 24 May 1923 (*Curzon Committee Report).*

Committee of Imperial Defence (CID) Memorandum, 'ACTION TO BE TAKEN IN THE EVENT OF

INTERVENTION IN A EUROPEAN WAR', CAB 2/ 2, Part 2, Minutes of the 114th Meeting of the [CID], August 23, 1911, pp.1–2.

Evidence and Additional Statements presented, and Proceedings of Dardanelles Commission, CAB 63/ 17-18, CAB 19/ 28-32 & CAB 19/ 33.

'Memorandum by the First Sea Lord on the Position of the British Fleet and its Policy of Steady Pressure', CAB 63/ 4.16-20.

'Memorandum by Cabinet Secretary [for Dardanelles Commission]. Based on the Proceedings of the War Council, Dardanelles Committee and War Committee, in connection with the Dardanelles Operations', CAB 63/ 17.

'Cabinet Procedure: The Retention by Cabinet Ministers of their Cabinet Papers on Leaving Office', CAB 21/ 448, C.P. 69 (34), of 9 March 1934.

'Secretary's Notes of War Council Meetings, printed for the Committee of Imperial Defence, September 1916', CAB 22/1; War Council

Minutes, on microfilm (for 1914), CAB 42/1; (for 1915), CAB 42.2; Minutes of Dardanelles Committee Meetings, CAB 42/3; Minutes of CID

Meetings, CAB 2/ 2; Papers and Memoranda delivered to War Council Meetings, on the Dardanelles, CAB 24/ 1.

Statement by Cabinet Secretary for Dardanelles Commissioners: 'Notes for Evidence', CAB 19/ 29, of 6 September 1916.

Statement by Sir George Arthur to the Dardanelles Commission, CAB 19/ 28, 56.

Foreign Office

FO 800/ 57, 63, 80, 88, 102, 375-6, 371/ 2095, 2162–4, 2165, 2166, 2169, 2170, 2173, 2174, 2176, 2243, 2449, 2482, 2504.

War Office

WO 106/ 1538, 158/ 574, 159/ 3.

General Staff-Admiralty Paper, of 19 December 1906, 'The Possibility of a Joint Naval and Military Attack upon the Dardanelles' (endorsed by CID, Paper 92B, February 1907, CAB 38/13.12).

War Office Memorandum, WO. 159/ 3, of 24 February 1915 [on the strength of the Turkish Army in Dardanelles area].

Private Papers

Asquith, Earl Herbert, MSS, Bodleian Library, Oxford.

Asquith, Countess Margot, MSS, Bodleian Library, Oxford.

Balfour, Earl Arthur, MSS, British Library, London.

Battenberg, Admiral of the Fleet, Prince Louis of (later Mountbatten), MSS, National Maritime Museum, Greenwich.

Beatty, Admiral of the Fleet, Earl David, MSS, National Maritime Museum, Greenwich.

Birdwood, Field Marshal Baron William, MSS, Imperial War Museum, London.

Bonar Law, Andrew, MSS, House of Lords Record Office, London.

Bridgeman, Admiral Sir Francis, MSS, Imperial War Museum, London.

Callwell, Major General Sir Charles, MSS, National Archives, Kew.

Carden, Admiral Sir Sackville, MSS, Churchill College Archives Centre, Cambridge.

Churchill, Sir Winston, MSS, Churchill College Archives Centre, Cambridge.

Corbett, Sir Julian, MSS, National Maritime Museum, Greenwich.

Crease, Captain Thomas, MSS, National Archives, Kew.

Crewe, Marquis Robert, MSS, Cambridge University Library.

de Robeck, Admiral of the Fleet, Baron John, MSS, Churchill College Archives Centre, Cambridge.

Esher, Viscount Reginald, MSS, Churchill College Archives Centre, Cambridge.

Fisher, Admiral of the Fleet, Baron John, Churchill College Archives Centre, Cambridge.

Godfrey, Major W., MSS, Imperial War Museum, London.

Greene, Sir William Graham, MSS, National Maritime Museum, Greenwich.

Grey, Viscount Edward, MSS, National Archives, Kew.

Haldane, Viscount Richard, MSS, National Library of Scotland, Edinburgh.

Hamilton, General Sir Ian, MSS, Liddell Hart Archive Centre, Kings College, Strand.

Hankey, Baron Maurice, MSS, Churchill College Archives Centre, Cambridge.

Jackson, Admiral of the Fleet, Sir Henry, MSS, British Library, London.

Jellicoe, Admiral of the Fleet, Earl John, MSS, British Library, London.

Keyes, Admiral of the Fleet, Baron Roger, MSS, British Library, London.

Kitchener, Field Marshal Earl Horatio Herbert, MSS, National Archives, Kew.

Limpus, Admiral Sir Arthur, MSS, National Maritime Museum, Greenwich.

Lloyd George, Earl David, MSS, House of Lords Record Office, London.

MacDonald, James Ramsay, MSS, National Archives, Kew.

Masterton-Smith, Sir James, MSS, National Archives, Kew.

McKenna, Reginald, MSS, Churchill College Archives Centre, Cambridge.

Oliver, Admiral of the Fleet, Sir Henry, National Maritime Museum, Greenwich.

Richmond, Admiral Sir Herbert, MSS, National Maritime Museum, Greenwich.

Robertson, Field Marshal Baronet William, MSS, Liddell Hart Archive Centre, King's College, Strand.

Wilson, Field Marshal Sir Henry, MSS, Imperial War Museum, London.

The Papers of Admiral Sir Arthur Wilson and Commodore (later Rear Admiral) Sir Charles de Bartolomé, could not be located.

Primary sources: published Official publications

Annual Register, Longmans Green, London, 1917.

Aspinall-Oglander, Brigadier General C.F., *History of the Great War. Military Operations, Gallipoli,* vols 1 and 2, Heinemann, London, 1929–32.

Bean, C.E.W., *The Official History of Australia in the War of 1914-1918,* Vol.1, *The Story of Anzac,* Australian War Memorial, Canberra, 1921.

Corbett, Sir Julian S., *History of the Great War: Naval Operations,* vols 1 and 2, Longmans Green, London, 1921.

Dardanelles Commission, First Report, His Majesty's Stationery Office (hereafter HMSO), London, Cd 8490, 1917.

Dardanelles Commission, Final Report, HMSO, London, Cmd 371, 1919.

Hansard Parliamentary Debates, HMSO, Fourth Series, Vol.91, 1901; Fifth Series, vols 66 (1914), 71 and 75 (1915), 155 (1922), 160 (1923), *Lords,* Vol.20 (1915).

La Guerre Turque dans la Guerre Mondiale (traduit en français par Major M. Larcher), US Army War College, Washington, 1931.

Public Record Office Handbook, No.11, 'The Records of the Cabinet Office to 1922', HMSO, London, 1976.

'Report of the Departmental Committee on Section 2 of the Official Secrets Act 1911', September 1972, Cmd.5104 (*Franks Committee Report).*

Turkish General Staff, *Official Historical Account of the Dardanelles,* US Army War College, Washington, 1925.

Wilson, S.S. (ed), *Public Record Office Handbook,* No.17, 'The Cabinet Office to 1945', HMSO, London, 1976.

Memoirs, collections of documents etc.

Asquith, Herbert, *The Earl of Oxford and Asquith: Memories and Reflections, 1852-1927,* Cassell, London, 1928.

Bacon, Admiral Sir R.H., *The Life of Lord Fisher of Kilverstone,* 2 vols, Hodder & Stoughton, London, 1929.

Brock, Michael and Eleanor (eds), *H.H. Asquith: Letters to Venetia Stanle* y, Clarendon Press, Oxford, 1982.

Brooke, Alan (Lord Alanbrooke), *War Diaries, 1939-1945,* Alex Danchev and Daniel Todman (eds), Weidenfeld & Nicolson, London, 2001.

Callwell, Major General Sir C.E., *The Dardanelles,* Constable, London, 1919.

——, *Experiences of a Dug-out, 1914-1918,* Constable, London, 1920.

——, *Field Marshal Sir Henry Wilson, his Life and Diaries,* Vol.1, Cassell, London, 1927.

Churchill, Winston S., *The World Crisis, 1911-1914,* Vol. I, Thornton Butterworth, London, 1923.

——, *The World Crisis, 1915,* Vol. II, Thornton Butterworth, London, 1923.

——, *Thoughts and Adventures,* Thornton Butterworth, London, 1932.

David, Edward (ed), *Inside Asquith's Cabinet. From the Diaries of Charles Hobhouse,* John Murray, London, 1976.

Esher, Reginald Balliol Brett, Viscount, *Journals and Letters,* Viscount Oliver and M.V. Brett (eds), Vol.3, Nicholson & Watson, London, 1936.

——, *The Tragedy of Lord Kitchener,* John Murray, London, 1921.

Falkenhayn, General Erich von, *General Headquarters 1914-1916 and its Critical Decisions,* Hutchinson, London, 1919.

Fisher, Admiral of the Fleet Lord, *Fear God and Dread Nought: The Correspondence of Admiral of the Fleet Lord Fisher of Kilverstone,* vols 1–3, Arthur J. Marder (ed), Jonathan Cape, London, 1952–59.

——, *Memories,* Hodder & Stoughton, London, 1919.

French, Sir John, *1914,* Constable, London, 1919.

Graves, Robert, *Goodbye to all That: An Autobiography,* Cape, London, 1929.

Grey of Falloden, Viscount, *Twenty Five Years, 1892-1916,* Vol.2, Hodder & Stoughton, London, 1925.

Haldane, R.B., *Autobiography,* Hodder & Stoughton, London, 1929.

Hamilton, Sir Ian, *Gallipoli Diary,* 2 vols, Edward Arnold, London, 1920.

Hankey, Lord, *The Supreme Command, 1914-1918,* vols.1 and 2, Allen & Unwin, London, 1961.

Jellicoe of Scapa, Admiral Viscount, *The Grand Fleet 1914-16. Its Creation, Development and Work,* Cassell, London, 1919.

Kannengeisser, Hans, *The Campaign in Gallipoli,* Hutchinson, London, 1928.

Keyes, Admiral of the Fleet Sir Roger, *Naval Memoirs, 1910-1915,* Thornton Butterworth, London, 1934.

Lloyd George, David, *War Memoirs,* Vol.1, Nicholson & Watson, London, 1933.

Morgenthau, Ambassador Henry, *Secrets of the Bosporus,* Hutchinson, London, 1918.

Riddell, Lord, *War Diary, 1914-1918,* Nicholson & Watson, London, 1934.

Robertson, Sir William, *From Private to Field Marshal,* Constable, London, 1921.

Sanders, General Liman von, *Five Years in Turkey,* US Naval Institute, Annapolis, 1927.

Scott, Admiral Sir Percy, *Fifty Years in the Royal Navy,* J. Murray, London, 1919.

Taylor, A.J.P. (ed), *Lloyd George: A Diary by Frances Stevenson,* Hutchinson, London, 1971.

Temperley, H. and Gooch, G.P. (eds), *British Documents on the Origins of the War, 1898-1914,* Vol.7, *The Agadir Crisis,* HMSO, London, 1928–38.

Tirpitz, Grand Admiral von, *My Memories,* Vol.2, Hurst & Blackett, London, 1919.

Wemyss, Lord Wester, *The Navy in the Dardanelles Campaign,* Hodder & Stoughton, London, 1924.

Williams, Captain Basil, *Raising and Training the New Armies,* Constable, London, 1918.

Contemporary Newspapers and Periodicals

Adelaide Advertiser
Age
Brisbane Courier
Daily Mail
Daily Standard
Daily Telegraph
Evening News
Globe
London Daily Chronicle
Manchester Guardian
Morning Post
National Review
Newcastle Morning Herald
New York Times
Nineteenth Century
Observer
Quadrant
Spectator
Standard
Sydney Morning Herald
The Times
The Times Literary Supplement
West Australian

Secondary Sources Books

Aitken, Jonathan, *Officially Secret,* Weidenfeld & Nicolson, London, 1971.

Arthur, Sir George, *Life of Lord Kitchener,* 2 vols, Macmillan, London, 1920.

Atkins, J.B., *Incidents and Reflections,* Christophers, London, 1947.

Barbusse, Henri, *Under Fire* (trans. Robin Buss, with an introduction by Jay Winter), Penguin, London, 2003.

Barraclough, Geoffrey, *From Agadir to Armageddon: Anatomy of a Crisis,* Weidenfeld & Nicolson, London, 1982.

Baxter, John D., *State Security, Privacy and Information,* Harvester, New York, 1990.

Bennett, Geoffrey, *Naval Battles of the First World War,* Pan Books, London, 1974.

Berlin, Isaiah, *Mr Churchill in 1940,* Houghton Mifflin, Boston, 1949. Reprinted from an essay published in *The Atlantic Monthly* in 1949.

Best, Geoffrey, *Churchill, A Study in Greatness,* Penguin Books, London, 2001.

Blake, Robert and Lewis, Roger Wm. (eds), *Churchill,* Oxford University Press, Oxford, 1994.

Bond, Brian (ed), *The First World War and British Military History,* Clarendon Press, Oxford, 1991.

——, *Liddell Hart. A Study of his Military Thought,* Cassell, London, 1976.

——, *Victorian Military Campaigns,* Hutchinson, London, 1967.

Bonham Carter, Violet, *Winston Churchill as I knew him,* Eyre & Spottiswoode, London, 1965.

Briggs, Sir John, *Naval Administrations 1827 to 1892,* Sampson Low, London, 1897.

Broad, Lewis, *Winston Churchill, 1874-1951,* Hutchinson, London, 1956.

——, *Winston Churchill. The Years of Preparation,* Sidgwick & Jackson, London, 1963.

Buley, E.C., *Glorious Deeds of Australasians in the Great War,* Andrew Melrose, London, 1915.

Cassar, George H., *Asquith as War Leader,* Hambledon, London, 1994.

——, *Kitchener: Architect of Victory,* William Kimber, London, 1977.

Churchill, Randolph, *Winston S. Churchill,* Vol.2, Heinemann, London, 1966–69.

Clark, Alan, *The Donkeys,* Hutchinson, London, 1963.

Connell, John, *Winston Churchill,* Longmans, Green & Co., London, 1956.

Cowles, Virginia, *Winston Churchill: The Era and the Man,* Hamilton, London, 1953.

Cutlack, F.M. (ed), *War Letters of General Sir John Monash,* Angus & Robertson, Sydney, 1934.

Curran, Tom, *Across the Bar. The Story of "Simpson", The Man with the Donkey: Australia and Tyneside's Great Military Hero,* Ogmios Publications, Brisbane, 1994.

Curtright, Lynn H., *Muddle, Indecision and Setback. British Policy and the Balkan States, August 1914 to the Inception of the Dardanelles Campaign,* Institute for Balkan Studies, Thessaloniki, 1986.

de Loghe, Sydney, *The Straits Impregnable,* J. Murray, London, 1917.

Dilks, David, *Neville Chamberlain,* Cambridge University Press, Cambridge, 1984.

Dinning, Hector, *ByWays on Service–Notes from an Australian Journal,* Constable and Company Ltd, London, 1918.

Eade, Charles (ed), *Churchill by his Contemporaries,* Hutchinson, London, 1953.

Ellison, Lieutenant General Sir Gerald, *The Perils of Amateur Strategy, as Exemplified in the Attack on the Dardanelles Fortress in 1915,* Longmans Green, London, 1926.

Farrar, L.L., *Divide and Conquer. German Efforts to Conclude a Separate Peace 1914-1918,* Columbia University Press, New York, 1978.

Fischer, Fritz, *War of Illusions: German Policies from 1911-1914* (trans. Marian Jackson), Chatto & Windus, London, 1975.

French, David, *British Strategy and War Aims 1914-1916,* Allen & Unwin, London, 1986.

Gardiner, A.G., *Pillars of Society,* Nisbet, London, 1913.

Gerster, Robin, *BIG-NOTING: The Heroic Theme in Australian War Writing,* Melbourne University Press, Melbourne, 1987.

Gilbert, Martin, *Winston S. Churchill,* Vol.3, *1914-1916,* Heinemann, London, 1971.

——, *Winston S. Churchill,* Vol.4, Heinemann, London, 1975

——, *Winston S. Churchill,* Vol.5, *1922-1939, The Exchequer Years,* Heinemann, London, 1978.

Gottlieb, W.W., *Studies in Secret Diplomacy during the First World War,* Allen & Unwin, London, 1957.

Goulden, Joseph C., *Truth is the First Casualty: the Gulf of Tonkin Affair: Illusion and Reality,* Rand McNally, Chicago, 1969.

Green, Andrew, *Writing the Great War. Sir James Edmonds and the Official Histories, 1915-1948,* Frank Cass, London, 2003.

Gretton, Sir Peter, *Winston Churchill and the Royal Navy,* Coward McCann, New York, 1969.

Guinn, Paul, *British Strategy and Politics, 1914-1918,* Clarendon Press, Oxford, 1965.

Higgins, Trumbull, *Winston Churchill and the Dardanelles,* Heinemann, London, 1963.

Horner, D.M., *The Commanders: Australian Military Leadership in the Twentieth Century,* Allen & Unwin, Sydney, 1984.

James, Robert Rhodes, *Churchill. A Study in Failure 1900-1939,* Weidenfeld & Nicolson, London, 1970.

572

——, *Gallipoli,* Batsford, London, 1965.

James, Admiral W., *The Eyes of the Navy. A Biographical Study of Admiral Sir Reginald Hall,* Methuen, London, 1956.

Jenkins, Roy, *Churchill: A Biography,* Farrar, Straus and Giroux, New York, 2001.

Keegan, John, *The First World War,* Vintage, New York, 2000.

——, *Winston Churchill,* Penguin Viking, New York, 2002.

Kemper, R. Crosby (ed), *Winston Churchill: Resolution, Defiance, Magnanimity, Good Will,* University of Missouri Press, Columbia, 1996.

Knyvett, R. Hugh, *'OVER THERE' with the Australians,* Hodder & Stoughton, London, 1918.

Laffin, John, *Damn The Dardanelles!* Sun Papermac, South Melbourne, 1985.

——, *British Butchers and Bunglers of World War One,* Macmillan Australia, South Melbourne, 1989.

Lewis, C. Day (ed), *The Collected Poems of Wilfred Owen,* with an introduction and notes by C. Day Lewis and a memoir by Edmund Blunden, Chatto & Windus, London, 1963.

Lewis, Michael, *The Navy of Britain: a Historical Portrait,* G. Allen, London, 1948.

Liddell Hart, Basil, *The British Way in Warfare,* Faber & Faber, London, 1932.

——, *Foch, the Man of Orleans,* Penguin, London, 1937.

——, *The Future of Infantry,* Faber & Faber, London, 1933.

——, *A History of the World War, 1914-1918,* Faber, London, 1934.

——, *Paris, or the Future of War,* Kegan Paul, London, 1925.

——, *The Real War, 1914-1918,* Little Brown, Boston, 1930.

——, *Reputations,* John Murray, London, 1928.

——, *A Science of Infantry Tactics: Simplified,* W. Clowes, London, 1923.

——, *Sherman, the Genius of the civil War,* Eyre & Spottiswoode, London, 1933.

——, *Through the Fog of War,* Faber & Faber, London, 1938.

Mackay, Ruddock F., *Fisher of Kilverstone,* Clarendon Press, Oxford, 1973.

Mackenzie, Compton, *Gallipoli Memories,* Cassell, London, 1929.

Macleod, Jenny (ed), *Gallipoli. Making History,* Frank Cass, London, 2004.

——, *Reconsidering Gallipoli,* Manchester University Press, Manchester and New York, 2004.

Manchester, William, *American Caesar: Douglas MacArthur 1880-1964,* Hutchinson, London, 1979.

——, *The Death of a President,* Harper and Row, New York, 1967.

——, *The Last Lion. Winston Spencer Churchill. Visions of Glory: 1874-1932,* Michael Joseph, London, 1983.

Marder, Arthur J., *From the Dardanelles to Oran, Studies of the Royal Navy in Peace and War,* Oxford University Press, Oxford, 1974.

——, *From the Dreadnought to Scapa Flow: The Royal Navy in the Fisher Era, 1904-1919,* Vol.1, *The Road to War, 1904-1914,*

Oxford University Press, Oxford, 1965.

——, *From the Dreadnought to Scapa Flow; The Royal Navy in the Fisher Era, 1904-1919,* Vol.2, *The War Years. To the Eve of Jutland, 1914-1916,* Oxford University Press, Oxford, 1965.

——, *Portrait of an Admiral: The Life and Papers of Admiral Sir Herbert Richmond,* Jonathan Cape, London, 1952.

Marquand, David, *Ramsay Macdonald,* Jonathan Cape, London, 1977.

Martin, Hugh, *Battle: The Life Story of Winston S. Churchill, Prime Minister: Study of a Genius,* Gollancz, London, 1940.

Masefield, John, *Gallipoli,* Heinemann, London, 1916.

Middlemas, Keith and Barns, John, *Baldwin: A Biography,* Weidenfeld & Nicolson, London, 1969.

Miller, Geoffrey, *Straits: British Policy towards the Ottoman Empire and Origins of the Dardanelles Campaign,* University of Hull Press, Hull, 1997.

Moise, Edwin E., *Tonkin Gulf and the Escalation of the Vietnam War,* University of North Carolina Press, North Carolina, 1996.

Moorehead, Alan, *Gallipoli,* Hamish Hamilton, London, 1956.

Moses, John A., *The Politics of Illusion. The Fischer Controversy in German Historiography,* University of Queensland Press, St Lucia, 1975.

Naylor, John F., *A Man and an Institution. Sir Maurice Hankey, the Cabinet Secretariat and the Custody of Cabinet Secrecy,* Cambridge University Press, Cambridge, 1984.

Neilson, Keith, *Strategy and Supply. The Anglo-Russian Alliance 1914-17,* George Allen & Unwin, London, 1984.

North, John, *Gallipoli: The Fading Vision,* Faber and Faber, London, 1936.

Overy, Richard, *Why the Allies Won,* Norton, New York, 1996.

Pelling, Henry, *Winston Churchill,* Wordsworth Editions, Ware, Hertfordshire, 1999 (1974).

Penn, Geoffrey, *Fisher, Churchill and the Dardanelles,* Leo Cooper, Barnsley, 1999.

Prior, Robin, *Churchill's 'World Crisis' as History,* Croom Helm, London, 1983.

——, *Gallipoli: The End of the Myth,* UNSW Press, Sydney, 2009.

Remarque, Erich Maria, *All Quiet on the Western Front* (trans. A.W. Wheen), Putnam, London, 1929.

Repington, Charles a Court, *The First World War, 1914-1918,* 2 vols, Constable, London, 1920.

Reynolds, David, *In Command of History. Churchill Fighting and Writing the Second World War,* Allen Lane, London, 2004.

Ritter, G., *Sword and Scepter. The Problem of Militarism in Germany,* Vol.3, University of Miami Press, Miami, 1972.

Roberts, Carl, *Winston Churchill: Being an Account of the Life of Winston Leonard Spencer Churchill,* Mills and Boon, London, 1927.

Robertson, John, *Anzac and Empire,* Hamlyn, Melbourne, 1990.

Rose, Norman, *An Unruly Life,* Simon & Schuster, London, 1994.

Roskill, Stephen, *Churchill and the Admirals,* William Morrow, New York, 1978.

——, *Hankey, Man of Secrets,* vols 1 and 2, Collins, London, 1970–72.

Rutherford, Ward, *The Russian Army in World War One,* Gordon Cremonesi, London, 1975.

Stansky, Peter (ed), *Churchill. A Profile,* Macmillan, London, 1973.

Steel, Nigel and Hart, Peter, *Defeat at Gallipoli,* Macmillan, London, 1994.

Stone, Norman, *The Eastern Front 1914-1917,* Hodder & Stoughton, London, 1975.

Suttie, Andrew, *Rewriting the First World War. Lloyd George, Politics and Strategy, 1914-1918,* Palgrave Macmillan, Basingstoke, Hampshire, 2005.

Sydenham, Lord, Bacon, Sir Reginald, Maurice, Sir Frederick, Bird, Sir W. and Oman, Sir Charles, *The World Crisis by Winston Churchill: a criticism,* Hutchinson, London, 1928.

Taylor, A.J.P., *The First World War: An Illustrated History,* Hamilton, London, 1963.

——, *The Struggle for Mastery in Europe, 1848-1914,* Oxford University Press, Oxford, 1971.

Taylor, A.J.P. et al. (eds), *Churchill Revised. A Critical Assessment,* Dial Press, New York, 1969.

Thomson, David, *Europe since Napoleon,* Penguin Books, Harmondsworth, 1966.

Thomson, Malcolm, *Churchill. His Life and Times,* Odhams, Watford, Herts, 1965, Special Memorial Edition.

Travers, Tim, *Gallipoli 1915,* Tempus, Stroud, Charleston, S.C., 2001.

Tucker, Spencer C., *The Great War 1914-18,* Indiana University Press, Bloomington, 1998.

Vansittart, Peter (ed), *John Masefield's Letters From the Front 1915-1917,* Constable, London, 1984.

Wemyss, Admiral Wester, *The Navy in the Dardanelles Campaign,* Hodder & Stoughton, London, 1924.

Wildman, A.K., *The End of the Russian Imperial Army: The Old Army and the Soldiers' Revolt, March-April 1917,* Princeton University Press, New Jersey, 1980.

Wilson, Trevor, *The Myriad Faces of War,* Polity Press, Cambridge, 1986.

Wolff, Leon, *In Flanders Fields,* Longmans Green, London, 1959.

Book chapters and journal articles

Adye, Lieutenant General Sir John, 'Has Our Army Grown with Our Empire?' *Nineteenth Century,* Vol.39, June 1896.

Beckett, Ian, 'Frocks and Brasshats' in B. Bond (ed), *The First World War and British Military History,* Clarendon Press, Oxford, 1991.

Curran, Tom, 'Who was responsible for the Dardanelles Naval fiasco?' *Australian Journal of Politics and History,* Vol.57, 1 March 2011. Fraser, Peter, 'Cabinet Secrecy and War Memoirs', *History,* Vol.70, 1985.

French, David, 'The origins of the Dardanelles campaign reconsidered', *History,* Vol.68, No.223, 1983.

——, 'Official but not History? Sir James Edmonds and the Official History of the Great War', *Royal United Services Institute Journal,* Vol.131, No.1, March 1986.

Gilbert, Martin, 'Churchill and Gallipoli' in Jenny Macleod (ed), *Gallipoli. Making History,* Frank Cass, London, 2004.

Hazlehurst, C., 'Asquith as Prime Minister, 1908-1916', *English Historical Review,* Vol.85, No.336, 1970.

Lowe, C.J., 'The Failure of British Diplomacy in the Balkans, 1914-1916', *Canadian Journal of History,* Vol.4, No.1, 1969.

Neilson, Keith, 'Kitchener: A Reputation Refurbished?', *Canadian Journal of History,* Vol.15, 1980.

Paget, Gregory, 'The November 1914 Straits Agreement and the Dardanelles-Gallipoli Campaign',

Australian Journal of Politics and History, Vol.33, 1987.

Plumb, J.H., 'The Historian' in A.J.P. Taylor (ed), *Churchill: Four Faces and the Man,* Allen Lane, London, 1969.

Prior, Robin and Wilson, Trevor, 'The Churchill Industry', *Quadrant,* November 1994.

Rees, Goronwy, 'Churchill: A Minority View' in Peter Stansky (ed), *Churchill, A Profile,* Macmillan, London, 1973.

Renzi, William A., 'Great Britain, Russia and the Straits, 1914-1915', *Journal of Modern History,* Vol.42, No.1, March 1970.

Smith, C. Jay, 'Great Britain and the 1914-1915 Straits Agreement with Russia: The British Promise of November 1914', *American Historical Review,* Vol.70, July 1965.

Spiers, Edward, 'Gallipoli' in B. Bond (ed), *The First World War and British Military History,* Clarendon Press, Oxford, 1991.

Strachan, Hew, '"The Real War": Liddell Hart, Cruttwell and Falls' in B. Bond (ed), *The First World War and British Military History,* Clarendon Press, Oxford, 1991.

Trumpener, Ulrich, 'German Military Aid to Turkey in 1914: An Historical Evaluation', *Journal of Modern History,* Vol.32, No.2, 1960.

van der Waag, Ian, 'South Africa and the Boer Military System' in Peter Dennis and Jeffrey Grey (eds), *The Boer War: Army, Nation and Empire,* Army History Unit, Canberra, 2000.

Documentary

Schama, Simon, 'A History of Britain', Video Recording, SBS Television, Sydney, 2002.

Websites

http://www.firstworldwar.com/atoz/bigbertha.htm

http://www.spartacus.schoolnet.co.uk/FWWbertha.htm —re 'Big Berthas'.

http://savrola.co.uk/—devoted to Churchilliana.

Back Cover Material

The century that has elapsed since the 1915 Dardanelles campgin has done little to quell the debate that rages over its inglorious end . The origins of the campagin are likewise the subject of ongoing scrutiny, particularly the role of First Sea Lord Winston Churchill, with whom the ill-fated campgin has been closely identified. Tom Curran's The Grand Deception: Churchill and the Dardnelles presenta detailed examination of Churchill's landings.

Using unpublished British archival sources and a range of additional materia!, both contemporary and modern, Curran's meticulous research casts new light on the lead-up to a campaign that would profoundly affect Australian military history. Curran portrays Churchill as disingenuous and interfering, a man who disregarded the advice of his commanders to champion a risky military enterprise. 'With the spectre of failure looming large, he attempted to shift ultimate blame for the fiasco to Admiral Jackie Fisher and General Horatio Kitchener in a bid to salvage his political career, obscuring his own role by rewriting the his ton' of the campaign. Curran's hard-hitting account reveals the machinations behind the campaign, his careful research creating a new perspective on an extraordinary period of history, For the first time, the story of Churchills role in the Dardanelles campaign is told in its entirety, adding a crucial chapter to the chronicle of Australia's baptism of fire.

Z

Made in the USA
Middletown, DE
29 July 2024

58216926R00349